American Public Opinion

D1417172

American Public Opinion

Its Origins, Content, and Impact

Seventh Edition

Robert S. Erikson
Columbia University

Kent L. Tedin
University of Houston

PEARSON
Longman

New York   San Francisco   Boston
London   Toronto   Sydney   Tokyo   Singapore   Madrid
Mexico City   Munich   Paris   Cape Town   Hong Kong   Montreal

Vice President and Publisher: Priscilla McGeehon
Executive Editor: Eric Stano
Senior Marketing Manager: Elizabeth Fogarty
Production Manager: Charles Annis
Project Coordination, Text Design, and Electronic Page Makeup: Electronic Publishing
    Services, Inc.
Cover Design Manager: Wendy Ann Fredericks
Cover Designer: Kay Petronio
Cover Photos: From top to bottom: © AP/Wide World Photos; © Kim Kulish/Corbis;
    and © Mike Greenlar/The Image Works
Manufacturing Buyer: Roy Pickering
Printer and Binder: Courier Corporation
Cover Printer: Coral Graphic Services, Inc.

For permission to use copyrighted material, grateful acknowledgment is made to the copyright holders on pp. xiii–xvi, which are hereby made part of this copyright page.

Cataloging-in-Publication data are on file with the Library of Congress

Visit us at http://www.ablongman.com

ISBN 0-321-10753-5

2 3 4 5 6 7 8 9 10—CRS—07 06 05 04

Contents

List of Figures and Tables

Figures

Tables

Credits for
Figures and Tables

Figures
Figure 2.1: Michael R. Kagay, "Why Even Well-Designed Polls Can Disagree," in Thomas Mann and Gary Orren, eds. Media Polls in American Politics (Washington, D.C.: Brookings, 1992); Robert M. Worcester, "A View from Britain: You Can Do Better, " Public Perspective 4 (Nov./Dec. 1992); Public Perspective 8 (Dec./Jan. 1997): 52; Michael Traugott, "Assessing Poll Performance in the 2000 Campaign," AAPOR News (Winter 2001).
Figure 3.1: National Election Studies, 2000.
Figure 3.2: National Election Studies, 2000 election data.
Figure 3.3: National Election Studies, 2000 election data.
Figure 3.4: National Election Studies, 2000 election data.
Figure 4.1: National Election Studies, 1970–2000.
Figure 4.2: National Opinion Research Center; Gallup; General Social Survey.
Figure 4.3: The U.S. Role in the World Poll, 1996: University of Maryland; Gallup; National Opinion Research Center; General Social Survey.
Figure 4.4: Roper; General Social Survey.
Figure 4.5: Gallup; General Social Survey.
Figure 4.6: Richard G. Niemi, John Mueller, and Tom W. Smith, Trends in Public Opinion (New York: Greenwood, 1989); General Social Survey (1989–1998); Harold W. Stanley and Richard G. Niemi, Vital Statistics of American Politics, 2003–2004 (Washington, D.C.: Congressional Quarterly, 2003).
Figure 4.7: James Stimson.
Figure 4.8: Compiled from Gallup Polls.
Figure 4.9: Gallup Poll.
Figure 4.10: Gallup Poll.
Figure 5.1: Institute for Higher Education, University of California, Los Angeles.
Figure 5.2: "America's Views and Mood 1998," Public Perspective (Dec./Jan. 1999): 65.
Figure 6.1: Los Angeles Times; Newsweek; Pew Center.
Figure 6.2: National Election Studies, 1958–2002.

Figure 7.1: National Election Studies, 2000.

Figure 7.2: National Election Studies, 2000 election data.

Figure 7.3: National Election Studies Cumulative File.

Figure 7.4: Gallup Poll, 1952–1976; National Election Studies, 1980–1992; Voter News Service, 1996–2000.

Figure 7.5: National Election Studies.

Figure 7.6: National Election Studies.

Figure 8.1: Daniel Hallin, "Sound Bite News: Television Coverage of Elections," Journal of Communications 43 (Spring 1992), 12; Diana Owen, "Media Mayhem: Performance of the Press in Election 2000." In Overtime, ed. Larry Sabato (New York: Longman, 2002), 130.

Figure 9.1: Compiled by authors.

Figure 9.2: National Election Studies election data.

Figure 9.3: National Election Studies, 2000 election data.

Figure 9.4: Compiled by authors.

Figure 9.5: Michael R. Kagay and Greg A. Caldeira, "A Reformed Electorate? Well at Least a Changed Electorate, 1972–1976." In Paths to Political Reform, ed. William J. Crotty (Lexington, MA: D.C. Heath, 1979); updated for 1980–1992 by Mark Wattier.

Figure 9.6: Hypothetcal Data.

Figure 9.7: National Election Studies data.

Figure 10.1: VNS Exit Polls.

Figure 10.2: Compiled by authors.

Figure 10.3: Compiled by authors.

Figure 10.4: Compiled by authors.

Figure 11.1: Updated from Erikson, MacKuen, and Stimson (2002, Figure 9.1).

Figure 11.2: Robert S. Erikson, Gerald C. Wright, and John P. McIver, Statehouse Democracy (New York: Cambridge University Press, 1994).

Tables

Table 3.1: National Election Studies; Delli Carpini and Keeter 1996; Luntz Research; IRC Survey Research Group; Washington Post; Pew Center for People and the Press; Times-Mirror; CBSNews/New York Times; General Social Survey.

Table 3.2: National Election Studies, 2000.

Table 3.3: National Election Studies, 1989 pilot study data.

Table 3.4: National Election Studies, 1984 election data.

Table 3.6: Adapted from National Election Studies, 1994.

Table 3.7: National Election Studies, 2000.

Table 3.8: National Election Studies, 2000 election data.

Table 3.9: Paul R. Hagner and John C. Pierce, "Correlative Characteristics of Levels of Conceptualization in the American Public, 1956–1976," Journal of Politics 44 (Aug. 1982): 779–809; updates compiled by Paul Hagner and Kathleen Knight.

Table 3.10: National Election Studies, 2000 data.

Table 3.11: National Election Studies data.

Table 3.12: National Election Studies, 2000 data.

Table 4.1: National Election Studies, 2000 (except as noted).

Table 4.2: National Election Studies, 1996, 2003; General Social Survey, 1998; CBS/New York Times, 1997.

Table 4.3: CBS News/New York Times.
Table 5.1: Roberta S. Sigel and Marilyn B. Hoskin, The Political Involvement of Adolescents (New Brunswick, NJ: Rutgers University Press, 1981), 73.
Table 5.2: M. Kent Jennings and Richard G. Niemi, The Political Character of Adolescence (Princeton, NJ: Princeton University Press, 1974), 78. Reprinted by permission of Princeton University Press.
Table 5.3: M. Kent Jennings and Richard G. Niemi, The Political Character of Adolescence (Princeton NJ: Princeton University Press, 1974), 41. Reprinted by permission of Princeton University Press.
Table 5.4: Gallup Opinion Index, Sept. 1975, 19.
Table 5.5: Ernest Boyer and Mary Jean Whitelaw, The Condition of the Professoriate: Attitudes and Trends, 1989 (New York: Harper, 1989); Denise E. Magner, "Faculty Attitudes and Characteristics: Results of a 1998–1999 Survey," Chronicle of Higher Education (Sept. 3, 1999): A20–A21; Dr. Jerry Jacobs, Department of Sociology, University of Pennsylvania.
Table 5.6: Gallup Poll reported in Robert Chandler, Public Opinion (New York: Bowker, 1972), 6–13.
Table 5.7: CBS News/New York Times polls.
Table 6.1: John L. Sullivan, James Piereson, and George E. Marcus, Political Tolerance and American Democracy (Chicago: University of Chicago Press, 1982), 203.
Table 6.2: John Sullivan et al., Political Tolerance and American Democracy (Chicago: University of Chicago Press, 1982); General Social Survey, 1985; Robert Chandler, Public Opinion (New York: Bowker, 1972); Herbert McClosky, 1958; Herbert McClosky, "Consensus and Ideology in American Politics," American Political Science Review 58 (June 1964); Herbert McClosky and Alida Brill, Dimensions of Tolerance (New York: Russell Sage Foundation, 1983); Louis Harris and Alan F. Westin, The Dimensions of Privacy (Stevens Point, WI: Sentry Insurance, 1979); James L. Gibson, Freedom and Tolerance in the United States (NORC: unpublished codebook, 1987); Washington Post 1997; Pew Research Center 1997; Freedom Forum 1997.
Table 6.3: Samuel Stouffer, Communism, Conformity, and Civil Liberties (New York: Wiley, 1954); General Social Survey.
Table 6.4: James Gibson, Freedom and Tolerance in the United States (National Opinion Research Center: unpublished codebook, 1987).
Table 7.1: General Social Survey, 2002; National Election Studies, 2000.
Table 7.2: National Election Studies, 1976, 2000.
Table 7.3: National Election Studies, 2000 election data.
Table 7.4: Princeton Survey Research Associates, 1996; CBS News, 1996; General Social Survey, 1993; Pew Research Center, 2001.
Table 7.5: National Election Studies; Gallup; Washington Post poll.
Table 7.6: National Election Studies; Washington Post poll.
Table 7.7: National Election Studies; General Social Survey; CBS News/New York Times Surveys.
Table 7.8: National Election Studies; General Social Survey; CBS News/New York Times Surveys, 2002.
Table 7.9: National Election Studies, 1992, 1996.

Table 7.10: Howard Schuman, Charlotte Steeh, and Lawrence Bobo, Racial Attitudes in America (Cambridge, MA: Harvard University Press, 1985), 78; General Social Survey.

Table 7.11: Gallup Poll; National Election Studies; General Social Survey; Washington Post poll; Roper.

Table 8.1: Pew Research Center, "Public's News Habits Little Changed by September 11" (June 9, 2002) http://www.people-press.org.

Table 8.2: David H. Weaver and G. Cleveland Wilhoit, The American Journalist in the 1990s (Mahwah, NJ: Erlbaum, 1996), 15–18; William Schneider and I. A. Lewis, "Views on the News," Public Opinion 8 (Aug.–Sept. 1985), 7.

Table 8.3: Adapted from Stephen J. Farnsworth and S. Robert Lichter, The Nightly News Nightmare (New York: Rowan-Littlefield, 2003), 117.

Table 8.4: National Election Studies, 2000 data.

Table 8.5: National Election Studies, 2000 data.

Table 8.6: National Election Studies, 2000 data.

Table 8.7: Stephen J. Farnsworth and S. Robert Lichter, The Nightly News Nightmare (New York: Rowan-Littlefield, 2003), 51.

Table 9.1: National Election Studies, 2000 election data.

Table 9.2: National Election Studies, 2000 election data.

Table 9.3: National Election Studies, 2000 election data.

Table 9.4: National Election Studies, 2000 election data.

Table 9.5: National Election Studies, 2000.

Table 9.6: National Election Studies, 2000 election data.

Table 9.7: Compiled by authors.

Table 10.1: Norman J. Ornstein, Thomas E. Mann, and Michael J. Malaben, eds. Vital Statistics on Congress, 1993–1994 (Washington, DC: Congressional Quarterly Press, 1994); Statistical Abstract of the United States, 1992.

Table 10.2: Kathleen A. Frankovic and Laurily K. Epstein, "Congress and Its Constituency: The New Machine Politics" (paper delivered at American Political Science Association Meeting, Washington DC, Sept. 1979).

Table 10.3: Compiled by authors.

Table 10.4: Harold W. Stanley and Richard G. Niemi, Vital Statistics of American Politics, 2003–2004 (Washington, DC: Congressional Quarterly Press, 2003), 75.

Table 10.5: National Election Studies, 2000 election data.

Table 11.1: Alan D. Monroe, "Consistency Between Public Preferences and National Policy Decisions," American Politics Quarterly 7 (Jan. 1979): 9. Copyright © 1979 by Sage Publications. Reprinted by permission of Sage Publications, Inc.

Preface

In this seventh edition of *American Public Opinion*, we present an accounting of the role of public opinion in the democratic politics of the United States. As previous editions did, this book discusses the contemporary literature on public opinion, supplementing it with our own illustrations and analyses of contemporary public opinion data. It provides an in-depth analysis of public opinion, beginning with its origins in political socialization, the impact of the media, the extent and breadth of democratic values, and the role of public opinion in the electoral process. The book provides the most recent data on such contemporary issues as abortion, gay rights, gun control, race relations, and health care policy.

American Public Opinion is unique in that it goes beyond a simple presentation of data and discussion of the formation of opinion to include a critical analysis of the role of public opinion in American democracy. As previous editions did, the seventh edition examines the relationship between public opinion and policy. This analysis is updated throughout to incorporate the most recent literature. Like previous editions, the seventh edition contains many examples from the National Election Studies that pertain to presidential elections. For this, these are drawn from the 2000 presidential election.

Readers familiar with the sixth edition will notice several changes beyond the normal updates. One change is the disappearance of the "Parties and Interest Groups" chapter (former chapter 11). The discussions of parties and interest groups are now folded into chapter 10 ("The Public and its Elected Leaders"), while the concluding chapter is renumbered as chapter 11 rather than chapter 12. As rewritten for this edition, chapter 10 presents a fresher integration of material on elite responsiveness to public opinion. One of the four models discussed in this chapter has undergone a name change. The model formerly called the "role-playing model" is now referred to as the "delegate" model.

Apart from the folding of chapter 11 into chapter 10, the chapter that has undergone the most change is chapter 8 on the mass media. More so than any other topic explored in this book, the scholarship on the mass media undergoes regular upheavals. Our response is a major overhaul of this chapter.

As this book has evolved through seven editions over thirty years, so too has the list of authors. The first edition (1973) was authored by Robert S. Erikson and Norman L. Luttbeg. With the second edition, Kent L. Tedin joined the team as a third author. That triumvirate held through three editions. By the time of the fifth edition, Luttbeg left the team to pursue other scholarly pursuits. This is the third edition solely authored by Erikson and Tedin. But Luttbeg's contribution to the book remains, most notably in the five linkage models he originated.

The preparation of this volume relies heavily on the survey data of the National Election Studies, conducted by the University of Michigan, supported by grants from the National Science Foundation, and made available by the Interuniversity Consortium for Political and Social Research. We also rely extensively on the General Social Survey (also funded by the National Science Foundation) and the data available online from the Roper Center Data Archive at the University of Connecticut. These organizations bear no responsibility for the analysis or interpretations presented here. We are greatly indebted to them for making their data available to us and to other scholars on whose research we depend. We benefit from the assistance provided by our editor, Eric Stano, and to colleagues, students, and staff at Columbia University and the University of Houston. Special thanks go to Joseph Bafumi for his invaluable research assistance. Finally, we would like to thank the reviewers of the sixth edition who offered helpful comments for preparing this edition: Stephanie Larson, Dickinson College; Fouad Moughrabi, University of Tennessee; Matthew Streb, Loyola Marymount University; and Joel Lieske, Cleveland State University.

Robert S. Erikson
Kent L. Tedin

1 | Public Opinion in Democratic Societies

Few Americans in the twenty-first century can remember a time when public opinion polls—like television, shopping malls, and eight-lane freeways—were not part of the popular landscape. Polls tell us which television shows are the most popular, how frequently people attend church, what person Americans most admire, plus a myriad of opinions on current political topics. We shall see, however, that the study of public opinion is much broader than simply gauging popular reaction to recent events. It is, for example, also concerned with how people learn about government, their trust in existing political institutions, their support for the political rules of the game, the inter-relationships among their opinions, and their beliefs about the effectiveness of political participation. The list could go on. But more than anything else, the study of public opinion is justified by the simple notion that democratic institutions should result in government decisions that reflect the views of everyday people. It is this presumption, and its implications, that guides the systematic analysis of mass opinion.

1-1 PUBLIC OPINION AND GOVERNMENT

Rousseau, in 1744, was among the first to use the term *public opinion* (*l'opinion publique*), meaning the customs and manners of all members of society (as opposed to some elite). By 1780 French writers were using the term interchangeably with *common will*, *public spirit*, and *public conscience* to refer to the political aspects of mass opinion (Price 1992, 8). *Public opinion* soon came into common usage among those writing about government.

However, long before scientific methods were developed to measure attitudes or the term *public opinion* gained currency, political theorists speculated about the "group mind" or the "general will" and how it might influence the political order. Writers beginning with Plato and Aristotle, through Locke and Hobbes as well as Rousseau, did not see public opinion as an aggregation of individual opinions, as is common today. Rather, they saw the whole as greater than the sum of its parts, much in the way a mob with a united purpose behaves in a fashion that would be foreign to any individual member. To these predemocratic theorists, public opinion was a mass entity, which if brought to bear on public affairs had potential for enormous influence. It was like a force of nature, constrained perhaps by certain regularities, but a unified whole that changed continually, like the currents in the ocean (Palmer 1936; Spitz 1984).

It was not until the rise of popular sovereignty that thinking about public opinion began to consider individual or group characteristics. By the eighteenth century, no Western political regime could afford to ignore the views of the masses. This change was brought about by the construction of electoral institutions and parliamentary bodies for regular consultation with the public and the gradual extension of the franchise to the lower classes. Henceforth, governments would find it necessary to take account of public opinion and its distribution throughout the polity. This accounting was not simply a question of government responsiveness to mass policy desires. Government also had to take account of popular support for the ongoing political order. A strong argument can be made that only when the political status quo was threatened did political elites, in an act of self-preservation, grudgingly extend the franchise to portions of the mass public (Ginsberg 1982). But with the granting of the franchise, there soon developed an ethical imperative that governments are morally obligated to heed public opinion in formulating policies.

In the early years of the American republic, to speak of "public opinion" was mostly to speak about the thin layer of the educated, affluent public in a position to communicate their views to government. While the nation's founders agreed on the principle of popular government, they greatly distrusted the wisdom and judgment of the masses on matters political. To Alexander Hamilton,

> The voice of the people has been said to be the voice of God; and however generally this maxim has been quoted and believed, it is not true in fact. The people are turbulent and changing; they seldom judge or determine right (Farrand 1961, 299–300).

While not all took such an uncharitable position, it was generally thought that public opinion was easily swayed and subject to fits of passion. Thus institutions were developed, such as the Electoral College and the indirect election of senators, to distance political leaders from the opinions of everyday citizens.

Nevertheless, by the mid-nineteenth century, many who followed the American political scene voiced concern about an excess of influence on political decision making by public opinion. One reason was the integration of the working class into the electorate via the universal franchise. By the 1850s it became impossible to argue that the public's opinion could be ignored. Writing in 1848, Alexis de Tocqueville, perhaps the most astute observer of nineteenth-century America, thought "there was no country in which . . . there is less independence of mind and true freedom of discussion than in America" (Tocqueville 1966, 254). He felt the numerical majority intimidated the minority so that only a narrow range of opinion could be expressed. In the end, he feared that the views of the majority could result in either social or governmental tyranny (Spitz 1984, 70). History was, of course, to prove him wrong. But those writing later agreed with his assessment of the importance of public opinion. In 1888, the perceptive British journalist and author James Bryce would claim that "in no country is public opinion so powerful as in the United States" (Bryce 1900). He also noted, "the obvious weakness of government by opinion is the difficulty of ascertaining it."

Of those writing before the development of the modern opinion poll, perhaps the most influential critic of public opinion was Walter Lippmann (1922, 1925). Like many of the founders, Lippmann believed mass opinion was subject to passions that could be induced by elite propaganda. He was convinced that the manipulation of public opinion by those opposed to the League of Nations was responsible for the tragedy of America's failure to join after World War I. Famously, Lippmann perceptively observed that the images of politics received by the public are not direct pictures of events, immediate experiences of action, or provable economic and social theories. Rather, they are "pictures in people's heads" generated by political interests to benefit their cause. In a prescient analysis of major findings by modern survey research, Lippmann challenged traditional democratic theory and its notion of an informed and rational public basing opinions on a considered judgment of the facts. He argued that the average person had little time for affairs of state and would rather read the comics than consider the pros and cons of weighty political issues. It should not be expected, therefore, that the mass public be competent in matters of state. Lippmann's prescription for democracy was for the public to choose leaders but for public policy to be developed and implemented by scientifically oriented experts.

The debate over the role of public opinion in democracy was given a new focus by the appearance of scientific polling in 1936. Among the most outspoken proponents of polls as a guide to government decision making was George Gallup, a pioneer of the new technology (Gallup and Rae 1940). Gallup was a prairie populist with a Ph.D. in psychology who believed in the collective wisdom of everyday citizens. He distrusted intellectuals and experts, and he thought elite rule and democratic government were incompatible. The challenge for democracy, as he saw it, was "Shall the common people be free to express their basic needs and purposes, or shall they be dominated by a small ruling clique?" In other words, how does one make those holding high public office responsive to the needs and wishes of the public?

Poll results, Gallup argued, could be considered a "mandate from the people," a concrete expression of the policies the public desires the government to enact. No longer would elected officials have to rely on the ambiguities of elections, self-serving claims by interest groups, or other nonrepresentative channels of public sentiment. Rather, they could turn to the latest opinion poll. In the past, claims that elected officials should heed popular preferences directly when formulating policy could always be countered with arguments like those of sixteenth-century political theorist Michel de Montaigne (1967), who wrote that "public opinion is a powerful, bold, and unmeasurable party."

Gallup saw the modern opinion poll as the high-tech equivalent of the New England town meeting—an opportunity for all citizens (or at least a representative sample) to voice their opinions. The scientific poll gave crispness, clarity, and reliability to mass opinion. Gallup and his supporters argued that through polls the will of the people could accurately be determined. No longer could failure to take seriously popular preferences when enacting public policy be justified by claims that public opinion is unknowable. With the aid of the modern opinion poll, it was the moral responsibility of elected officials to convert the public will into public policy.

Not all were enthusiastic about the new polling technology and George Gallup's prescriptions for it. Sociologist Herbert Blumer and political scientist Lindsay Rogers soon launched frontal assaults on the opinion poll and its implications. Blumer (1948) asserted the "one person, one vote" definition of pubic opinion inherent in polls was precisely what public opinion was not. Public opinion could not be reduced to a nose count of citizens. Rather, it was the interactions and communications among functional groups that percolated through society and came to the attention of government. These interactions and communications were not aggregations of individual opinions but "an organic whole of interacting, interrelated parts." To Blumer, not all opinions counted equally. They merited the label *public opinion* only to the extent opinions surfaced in a public forum and were taken seriously by those in government with power and influence.[1] This view, of course, clashed directly with the populist inclinations of Gallup and other early pollsters.[2]

Lindsay Rogers, on the other hand, was convinced that the public was not intellectually or emotionally fit to play the role Gallup's opinion-poll democracy required of it. In any case, polls were not technically able to ascertain the public's message. Rogers (1949) reformulated the position of the English philosopher Edmund Burke that it is the duty of elected representatives to follow their conscience and best judgment and not be slaves to moments of popular passion.[3] Only in this fashion, argued Rogers, could the true public interest be served. Rogers was also one of the first to raise serious methodological questions about polls—that is, to challenge pollsters on their own turf. He addressed questions of measurement, opinion aggregation, intensity, and framing effects that occupy a great deal of attention among contemporary students of public opinion. In essence, he claimed that polls of public opinion did not really measure "public opinion." Rogers argued that "Dr. Gallup does not make the public more articulate. He only estimates how in replying to certain questions it would say 'yes,' 'no,' or 'don't know.' Instead of feeling the pulse of democracy, Dr. Gallup listens to its baby talk." (Rogers 1949, 17).

A somewhat related argument holds that public opinion changes in a capricious fashion—that over short periods of time policy preferences shift rapidly, frequently, and arbitrarily. This belief was used by the author of Federalist Paper No. 63 to argue for an indirectly elected senate, which would serve as "an anchor against popular fluctuations" and protect the people against their own "temporary errors and delusions." In 1950, this same sentiment was reflected by political scientist Gabriel Almond (1950, 53) when he noted that on matters of foreign policy the public reacts with "formless and plastic moods which undergo frequent alteration in response to changes in events."[4] This view of public opinion was used to buttress arguments about limiting the role of mass opinion in policy decisions, and is still a touchstone of the "realist" school of foreign policy (Russett and Graham 1989). Recently, however, scholars have "rehabilitated" the public on matters of foreign policy. Its opinions are seen as stable and reasonable reactions to international events that often have real influence on foreign policy (Page and Shapiro 1992; Holsti 1996).

The liberal democracy school of thought (Dahl 1989) holds that an essential element of democracy is the creation of institutions and practices that allow for meaningful public input into the governing process. Democratic government works best when elected officeholders and appointed officials respond to the popular will. Citizens are more likely to comply with government decisions when they are backed by the moral force of popular approval. In addition, advocates of liberal democracy argue that decisions based on popular will are most likely to be the correct decisions. This idea traces its heritage to Aristotle's view that the pooled judgments of the many are likely to contain more wisdom than the judgments of the few.[5] The liberal democratic model does not hold that public policy must be driven only by the engine of public opinion. Rather, public opinion must count for something of consequence in government decision making.

The arguments we have just outlined are still occasionally elaborated upon today. However, most current research on public opinion does not address normative issues about the proper role of opinion in the governmental process. Rather, empirical questions dominate the field—that is, questions about "what really is" as opposed to "what ought to be." But empirical questions often have important normative implications. Clearly of consequence are "How much does the public know about public affairs, and how is that knowledge organized?" "How is public opinion articulated?" "Whose voices are heard?" "Are some segments of society (presumably the more affluent) better able to communicate their opinions to political decision makers than those with fewer economic resources?" The answers to these questions are important for theories of how the just polity should be structured.

1-2 PUBLIC OPINION DEFINED

Public opinion is notoriously difficult to define.[6] There are scores, if not hundreds, of variations on a definition (see Childs 1965 for a sampling). A standard definition of *public* is a group that has something in common. Some argue that there is no such thing as a single public; rather, there are many publics (Mac-Dougall 1966). Thus one can refer to the tennis-playing public, the snowmobil-ing public, or the television-watching public. Others, however, take a broader view. For political scientists, what members of the "public" in *public opinion* have in common is a connection to government. At a minimum, all citizens eighteen and older have the right to vote. That binds them together with a common in-terest, even if they choose not to exercise the right.[7] And, of course, everyone is affected in some way by government. That creates a common interest as well. Students of government also regularly speak of several specialized publics. They talk of the "attentive public," those persons who generally pay close attention to politics, and "issue publics," those persons who focus on specific issues while paying less attention to others. It is perhaps helpful to think of these as "sub-publics" of the overall public (i.e., the adult population).

We may first describe an opinion as a verbal expression of an attitude.[8] There are, of course, other ways in which attitudes can be expressed, such as marches, demonstrations, or riots. But we reserve the term *opinion* as the man-ifestation of attitudes in words or writing.[9] Attitudes are latent; they cannot be directly observed. Social psychologists typically define an attitude as an endur-ing predisposition to respond. Normally, attitudes do not change weekly or monthly. Although change is clearly possible, attitudes are mostly stable over extended periods. Opinions are imperfect indicators of the underlying, unob-served attitude. Because opinions are imperfect measures, we sometimes find they are inconsistent or display contradictions. We deal with this problem at length in chapter 3.

Second, opinions are disagreements about matters of preference, which cannot be resolved using the rules of science. Thus, when it comes to music, I may prefer opera. You may prefer hard rock. But there is no systematic way of demonstrating the virtue or goodness of one over the other. The same is true for opinions about welfare policy, foreign aid, or gays in the military. Disagree-ments about questions of fact are not opinions, but beliefs.[10] There was once disagreement about whether the earth circled the sun. Some believed the re-verse—that the sun revolved around the earth. That disagreement has been re-solved by scientific methods. There is still disagreement over whether massive doses of vitamin C will prevent colds and other illness. Some believe this no-tion is nothing more than a hoax; others take large doses of the vitamin daily. But one's position on this issue is a belief, not an opinion, because in principle the question may someday be resolved with finality. Disagreements over classi-cal versus rock music will not be resolved.

No one has yet advanced a definition of *public opinion* that satisfies a sub-stantial number of students in the field. We prefer to keep our definition short and simple. We define *public opinion* as the preferences of the adult population on matters of relevance to government. The first implication is that not all opinions are public opinion. Thus, one's preference for computer operating systems—Windows, Linux, UNIX—is excluded from our definition because it has nothing to do with government. The second implication is that while in the broadest sense we are talking about all adults, that does not exclude the possibility of referencing subgroups, such as the attentive public. A third point is that by the term *preferences* we mean more than simply the affective component of an opinion. *Affect* refers to feelings—like or dislike, approve or disapprove. However, we must also be concerned with the cognitive component of an opinion. *Cognition* refers to the process of knowing, to the intellectual sophistication one brings to the ordering of political opinions. Obviously, the amount of political information one has affects the ability to link one political concept with another and is important for our understanding of public opinion. Finally, while we have defined *opinions* as verbal manifestations of attitudes, events such as riots, demonstrations, and marches are also indicators of public opinion for certain attentive publics.

In the recent era, the meaning of *public opinion* sometimes seems to have evolved into whatever opinion polls show public opinion to be. In many ways, the findings of public opinion polls (or survey research in general) should inspire trust. Counterintuitive though it may seem, mathematical statistics and decades of experience reveal that one *can* generalize from a random sample of one or two thousand individuals to the nation as a whole. And one rarely has reason to believe that survey respondents systematically lie to pollsters.

We must be careful, however, not to reify. Public opinion and the results of public opinion polls are not necessarily the same thing. As shown in later chapters, the results of opinion polls must be interpreted with great care. Findings can vary considerably with different question wordings or different shadings of how issues are presented to respondents. Also, survey respondents sometimes tend to give socially desirable responses. For this reason, surveys often underreport attitudes and behaviors such as nonvoting, racist feelings, and tolerance for pornography because of a tendency for respondents to give socially desirable answers.

1-3 THE EVOLUTION OF THE PUBLIC OPINION POLL

Before the appearance of the modern public opinion poll in 1936, popular sentiment was assessed by newspapers and magazines through a variety of informal and haphazard soundings called *straw polls*.[11] The *Harrisburg Pennsylvanian* is credited with conducting the first of these polls, in the summer of 1824. It showed presidential candidate Andrew Jackson, with 63 percent of the vote, an easy winner over John Quincy Adams and Henry Clay.[12]

But it was not until 1896 that straw polling became a serious business. In that year the *Chicago Record* conducted an elaborate and expensive straw poll to tap voter preferences in the bitterly fought presidential contest between William McKinley and William Jennings Bryan. It sent out postcard ballots to every eighth voter in twelve midwestern states as well as ballots to every registered voter in Chicago.[13] The owner of the *Chicago Record* had clear Republican sympathies, and the Democratic party feared the poll was nothing more than a Republican trick. The party urged Democrats not to return the ballots.

Nevertheless, with the aid of a team of eminent mathematicians, the *Record* predicted in October that McKinley would win Chicago with 57.95 percent of the vote. Amazingly, he received 57.91 percent on election day. Outside of Chicago, however, the *Record's* predictive record was a failure (Jensen 1968).

With the dawn of the twentieth century, straw polls were becoming a regular feature in many magazines and newspapers. Like today, the poll results were "newsworthy." Approximately 84 straw polls were conducted during the 1928 presidential election, of which six were national. The straw polls occupied thousands of column inches in the print media. If anything, they were featured even more prominently than is currently the case.[14] The polls were of major importance to their sponsors as a promotional gimmick. They created interest in the publication. Also, those publishers using mail-out ballots usually included a special subscription offer along with the ballot. By all indications, the scheme worked remarkably well to boost circulation (Robinson 1932).

Like current opinion polls, the straw polls did not limit themselves simply to electoral contests. They polled on the issues as well, most notably the burning issue of the 1920s: Prohibition. The wet-dry controversy was as emotion-laden as any issue to surface in American politics. If popular sentiment on the issue were to be measured by a cutout ballot from a newspaper, one side would sometimes attempt to secure a monopoly on that issue and send in all the ballots. Or one side would urge its people not to participate in a straw poll when the sponsor's sentiments on the issue were known. Thus a poll in Delaware sponsored by Pierre du Pont, a well-known wet, was boycotted by drys. It wound up showing 97 percent of its respondents in favor of repeal. Mr. du Pont wisely decided against publishing the poll results as an indicator of public opinion. Rather, he submitted the returned ballots as a petition to the Delaware legislature urging the repeal of Prohibition (Robinson 1932).

The straw polls were a public relations disaster waiting to happen. By the 1930s, considerable advances had been made by market researchers in the field of applied sampling. However, the magazines and newspapers sponsoring the straw polls were oblivious. Their major concern with straw polls was how they contributed to profitability, not the technical quality of the poll itself. Methodologically, straw polls stayed in the rear guard, learning nothing from the advances in sampling methods, using the same outdated methods year after year.

Straw polls were, in fact, known to be notoriously unreliable. In 1932 Claude Robinson published an analysis of the state-by-state error margins of the major straw polls of the day.[15] The average error of the polls conducted by the Hearst newspapers was 12 percent in 1924. The poll by *The Pathfinder*, a weekly magazine, was off by an average of 14 percent in 1928. The *Farm-Journal* poll of thirty-six states in 1928 had an average error of 17 percent. Even the best-known and most professionally operated of the straw polls—the *Literary Digest* poll—was off the mark by an average of 12 percent in both 1924 and 1928.

It was the 1936 election and the notorious misprediction of its outcome by the *Literary Digest* that brought an end to the era of straw polls. The *Literary Digest* was the largest-circulation general magazine of its time, with over two million subscribers. Much of this success could be traced directly to its straw poll, a regular feature since 1916. While the *Digest* poll experienced more than its share of mispredictions, it had managed each time to get the winner of the presidential election right. And it was not modest. The *Digest* claimed "uncanny accuracy" for its poll, congratulating itself frequently on its amazing record. But in the 1936 presidential election, the *Digest* poll wildly mispredicted the outcome, giving Alf Landon 57 percent of the vote and Franklin Roosevelt 43 percent. Roosevelt won with 62.5 percent of the vote. The *Digest* was off the mark by almost 20 percentage points. Its credibility shattered, the *Literary Digest* went bankrupt a year later.

In that same year, three young pollsters with backgrounds in market research, using "scientific" methods of sampling, did correctly predict the win by Roosevelt. The three were Archibald Crossley, Elmo Roper, and George Gallup, each of whom went on to found his own poll. The best-known of these was, of course, George Gallup, founder of the Gallup Poll.

Gallup was a talented self-promoter. In the 1936 election season he taunted the *Literary Digest*, offering clients a money-back guarantee that his poll would be closer to the actual vote on election day than the *Digest's*.[16] He urged newspapers and magazines to run the two polls side by side (J. Converse 1987, 116–20).

Gallup used in-person interviews as opposed to mail questionnaires, and he employed "quotas" to ensure that his samples looked demographically like the overall population. His poll forecast Roosevelt with 55.7 percent of the vote—6.8 percent off the mark. But he got the winner right, and he used that fact, along with the *Digest's* disaster, to quickly become the nation's preeminent pollster.

But all was not right with the Gallup Poll. While Gallup continued to forecast the correct winner in the 1940 and 1944 presidential contests, his surveys consistently overestimated the Republican vote (Moore 1992b, 66–68). Then, in 1948, the Gallup Poll incorrectly forecast that Republican Thomas Dewey would defeat Democrat Harry Truman by a margin of 49.5 to 44.5 percent. It is important to note that the Crossley Poll and the Roper Poll also predicted a win by Dewey. Roper had the margin at 52.2 percent Dewey and 37.1 percent Truman. Something was clearly wrong with the sampling methodology used by all three of these polls. That something was quota sampling. In a comprehensive study of the failure of the polls in 1948, the Social Science Research Council recommended the abandonment of quota samples and their replacement with probability samples (Bradburn and Sudman 1988). Probability sampling is the method used in today's public opinion polls (see chapter 2).

Gallup, Crossley, and Roper were commercial pollsters. They did polls for clients and by necessity were concerned with costs and profitability. They had little incentive for pure research or for the lengthy surveys necessary to answer complex academic questions.[17] Those topics would be addressed by the major academic survey organizations, most notably the National Opinion Research Center (NORC) at the University of Chicago and the Survey Research Center (SRC)[18] at the University of Michigan. NORC was founded in 1941, and its associates produced several classics in the field of public opinion, including *The American Soldier* (Stouffer 1949) and *Communism, Conformity and Civil Liberties* (Stouffer 1955). The SRC, founded in 1946, has focused on studies of the American electorate. Perhaps the most influential book to date on public opinion and voting, *The American Voter* (A. Campbell et al. 1960), was published by a group associated with the SRC.

Both the NORC and the SRC devote considerable resources to technical issues involving sampling and question wording. The NORC pioneered the split ballot technique, in which different forms of a question are asked of random halves of a sample to investigate the effects of question wording. Researchers associated with the SRC have also devoted extensive time and energy to problems of question wording (Schuman and Presser 1981). But most important are the periodic surveys conducted by each of these institutions.

Every other year since 1948, the SRC and the Center for Political Studies have conducted the National Election Studies (NES).[19] These are large, in-person national surveys of issues relevant to elections. In presidential years, respondents are interviewed in the autumn before the election, then reinterviewed after the election is over. The total interview time is often three to five hours, and hundreds of questions are asked. The NES surveys voters in midterm election years as well, with shorter interviews usually conducted only after the election.

Since 1971, NORC has sponsored the General Social Survey (GSS), conducted on an annual or biennial basis. The GSS has a general set of questions, often repeated from one survey to the next, and a topical module that addresses a specific substantive concern at considerable length. Both the NES and GSS are publicly available, formatted and ready for analysis with common computer statistical packages. Much of the data presented in this book comes from these two sources.

While both the NES and GSS interview people in their homes, this is an expensive undertaking. By the early 1970s, techniques were being developed to scientifically sample telephone numbers using a random-digit-dialing methodology. This greatly reduced the cost of surveys and encouraged the media to conduct their own public opinion polls, much as they did in the days of the straw polls. In 1976, CBS News and the *New York Times* went into partnership to conduct their own polls. They were soon followed by the NBC/*Wall Street Journal* and the ABC/*Washington Post* polls. Other entities, such as CNN, also poll regularly.[20] The principal advantage to the media of in-house polls is that they can decide on the topics and timing of the surveys rather than being confined to the topics and timing of independent pollsters like Gallup. In-house polls also free the media from reliance on leaks from political campaigns about how candidates are faring with the voters. They can find out for themselves on an impartial, firsthand basis. Media polls are occasionally of interest to academic students of public opinion, but their value is limited by their interest in topical issues and by the abbreviated number of questions they ask.

A relatively new innovation is the election day exit poll, developed by CBS News in the late 1960s (Moore 1992b, 255). It did not, however, gain prominence until the 1980 election, when it was first used to forecast the outcome of a presidential election. With an exit poll, one chooses a representative sample of precincts in a state and interviews voters as they leave the polling place.

The networks usually know by 3:00 P.M. who has won the election, although they do not reveal this information for any one state until the polls have closed in that state. Beyond forecasting, exit polls have proved extremely valuable for understanding why people voted for specific candidates. Prior to 1990, each network conducted its own exit polls.

In 1990 the major networks, along with CNN and the Associated Press, formed a consortium, Voter News Service (VNS), to conduct common exit polls and share the information. This worked well until the 2000 presidential election, when VNS prematurely forecast a Gore victory in Florida. Then, in 2002, VNS exit polls were not reported on election night due to concerns over unreliability. As a consequence, VNS was dissolved and replaced by a new consortium called the National Election Pool.[21]

The most recent innovation in polling is measuring public opinion using the Internet. Respondents are selected by random sampling and contacted by telephone. They are then offered an incentive to participate in a fixed number of opinion surveys conducted over the Internet.

A final innovation in polling worth mentioning is the development of a code of standards for those in the field of public opinion. Unlike physicians, lawyers, and morticians, pollsters are not subject to government regulation. On occasion there have been calls by some in Congress for regulation. The first of these came in 1948, with many Democrats charging that the polls were biased in favor of Republicans. Another came in response to using exit polls to call the winner of the presidential election in 1980 before the voting booths had closed on the West Coast. It was argued that many Democrats failed to vote once they learned that President Carter had been defeated. However, most attempts by the government to regulate opinion polls have run afoul of the First Amendment's guarantee of the right of free speech.

In 1986 the American Association for Public Opinion Research (AAPOR) adopted a code of ethics and practices for the profession.[22] Among the major features of this code are full disclosure, confidentiality, and responsibility to those being interviewed. Pollsters must make available full information about who sponsored the survey and give details of relevant methodology, such as how the sample was selected. They must hold as confidential the responses to questions by specific individuals. They must avoid any practice that would harm or mislead a respondent. While the AAPOR has a standards committee, its only power of sanction is the glare of adverse publicity.

1-4 THE MODERN PUBLIC OPINION POLL AND ITS POLITICAL CONSEQUENCES

Prior to 1940, politicians judged public sentiment mainly from newspapers (Herbst 1993; Kernell 1993). For example, William McKinley kept tabs on "public opinion" by compiling a scrapbook, called "Current Comment," of newspaper articles from every section of the country (Hilderbrand 1981). Contemporary political leaders clearly have much better information on the content of public opinion than they did prior to the advent of scientific polling. John Geer (1996) argues that politicians well informed about public opinion use a qualitatively different leadership style than those without reliable opinion information. In particular, he argues certain skills historically associated with leadership are found less frequently in today's political leaders. They include the ability to craft good arguments and a willingness to remain committed to a stand.

According to Geer, before polling, politicians were uncertain if the electorate was on their side, and a premium was placed on the ability to convince both citizens and other politicians of the merits of an argument. Today this skill is less essential because more certainty exists about the electorate's preferences. For example, staff disputes on issues are often resolved by reference to public opinion rather than nuanced argument. Modern politicians are also less likely to remain committed to issue positions if the polls show them to be electoral losers. William Jennings Bryan ran for president in 1896 on the "free silver" platform. Despite being soundly defeated, he showcased the same issue in his 1900 presidential bid. Bryan remained convinced that public opinion was on his side (Anderson 1981). Geer argues that in the absence of reliable opinion data as a reality check, politicians' estimate of public opinion is driven by their personal views and reinforced by those around them, who often think as they do. On the other hand, Ronald Reagan in the 1960s and early 1970s was a strong proponent of a voluntary social security program. Because polls showed a large proportion of public disagreed, it is probably no accident that he dropped the issue when he ran for the presidency. Finally, the modern opinion poll has likely forever changed the standard by which political leadership is judged. Every decision is now evaluated in reference to public opinion. How, for example, would history treat Lincoln's Emancipation Proclamation if a Gallup Poll in June 1862 showed 72 percent of Northerners wanted to abolish slavery (Geer 1996)?

Change is not neutral. Innovations benefit some at the expense of others. The modern public opinion poll is no exception. Benjamin Ginsberg (1986) makes the counterintuitive argument that replacement by the modern opinion poll of traditional methods of expressing public opinion has served to "domesticate" public opinion. In other words, public opinion is a less potent force in American politics now than it was prior to scientific polling.

"Traditional methods of expressing public opinion" refers to letters to newspapers and public officials, personal contact, elections, advocacy group activity, marches, demonstrations, and riots—to list the more obvious. Such methods are still available, but when these indicators of public opinion differ from those reported in polls, it is universally assumed that polls are more representative. If one conceives of public opinion as an aggregation of equally weighted preferences, that assumption is almost certainly correct. However, polling by simply totaling individual opinions has, according to Ginsberg, changed some important aspects of "public opinion" as expressed by methods commonly employed before the advent of the scientific survey.

For example, public opinion was once largely a group phenomenon. At election time, elected officials would consult closely with the leaders of advocacy groups, such as farmers and organized labor, to be informed of membership opinion. Opinion polls have undermined the ability of group leaders to speak for their membership, as the members can now be polled directly. Any difference between the polls and the characterization of group opinion by leaders is usually resolved in favor of the polls. During the Nixon administration, wage and price controls were strongly opposed by organized labor. However, polls showed Nixon was popular with the rank and file, thus undercutting the ability of union leaders to threaten reprisals at the voting booth.

Where it had once been a behavior (letter writing, marches, etc.), public opinion is now mostly a summation of attitudes. In fact, the citizen is relieved of all initiative whatsoever. Pollsters contact respondents, determine worthwhile questions, analyze the results, and publicize them. If a citizen feels strongly about an issue, one mode of expression not available is to call a survey house and demand to be included in the next opinion poll.

Polls weaken the connection between opinion and intensity. It requires little effort to "strongly agree" with a statement proffered by an interviewer. Converse et al. (1965) have demonstrated that public opinion as measured in surveys is much less intense than that offered in voluntary modes of popular expression. Polls, in practice, submerge intense opinions with those held by the much larger, more apathetic population. This characteristic of opinion surveys can be employed by elected officials to promote their policy choices. Both Lyndon Johnson and Richard Nixon used evidence from polls to justify their policies in Vietnam as being in step with majority preferences, despite widespread public protests. Ginsberg claims a good argument could be made that if decision makers had accepted the more intense behavioral indicators of sentiment about the Vietnam War, as opposed to the evidence from polls, the Vietnam War would have ended much sooner.

Finally, modern opinion polls have changed the character of public opinion from an assertion to a response. Before polling, citizens themselves chose the topics on which to express their opinions. Now, as Ginsberg points out, these subjects are chosen mostly by polling technocrats. Most publicly expressed opinion is based less on the concerns of citizens than on the concerns of whomever is paying for the poll. Thus in 1970, a year of both racial strife and antiwar protest, the Gallup Poll devoted 5 percent of its questions to American policy in Vietnam, less than 1 percent to race relations, and had no questions on student protests. On the other hand, 26 percent of its questions (in a nonpresidential year) concerned the electoral horserace.

Whatever the merit of Ginsberg's arguments, they suffer from the same problem as those of Lippmann, Blumer, and Rogers—a rejection of the normative view that all opinions ought to count equally. Whatever its faults, the modern scientific opinion survey best approximates just what democracy is supposed to produce—an equal voice for all citizens (for a dissent, see Berinsky 1999). In the beginning of the twenty-first century, there are few who endorse less democratic input into the political system as opposed to more democratic input, whatever might be the imperfections of the latter. Polls may have shortcomings, but as measures of public opinion they are clearly more representative of all opinion than are the traditional measures. In fact, the traditional measures may be even less representative today than they were in the past. In recent years, paid political consultants have become sophisticated at marshaling local interest groups on issues of importance to their clients, raining letters, faxes, and phone calls on Congress and the White House, as well as newspapers and talk shows (Engelberg 1993; Mitchell 1998). It is often difficult to distinguish between these mobilized outbursts of public sentiment and those that are genuinely spontaneous.

Implicit in Ginsberg's analysis is an assumption that modern opinion polling has discouraged the communication of public opinion by other methods. However, all the means available to express public opinion prior to 1936 are still available, and are often used effectively. One need only witness the controversies over gay marriage or the Iraq war. Explicit in the analysis is a claim that public opinion polls have domesticated public opinion—that it is not as powerful a force in political decision making as it once was. There is, however, no systematic, hard evidence to support this assertion. The simple truth is that poll results are brought forcefully to the attention of government authorities at all levels (P. Converse 1987, 14). The relationship of public opinion to public policy in the modern era is an empirical question, about which we have much to say in this book.

1-5 SOURCES OF INFORMATION ON PUBLIC OPINION

Since the 1930s, tens of thousands of surveys have been conducted, hundreds of thousands of questions have been asked, and millions of respondents have been interviewed (T. Smith 1990a). Much of this data has been housed in several data libraries or archives. In addition, a great deal of public opinion information can be accessed through the Internet. (A list of useful Internet addresses is presented in the section that follows.)

The most comprehensive and up-to-date method for finding particular public opinion items is a computerized database called iPOLL (Public Opinion Location Library), located at the Roper Center in Storrs, Connecticut. Members can access the Roper Center archives through the Internet. By simply entering one or more keywords, such as "gun control," members can obtain question wording, item frequencies, and basic documentation for questions housed at the archive. They can also obtain cross-tabulations on key demographic items. The surveys themselves are available from the Roper Center, but at a cost. The Institute for Research in Social Science at the University of North Carolina houses the surveys conducted by Lou Harris and Associates, plus more than 350 statewide-level polls. An excellent multipurpose site for public opinion data and other social data is Data on the Net, maintained by the University of California at San Diego. It serves as a gateway to almost one hundred data archives throughout the world. Finally, World Associates for Public Opinion Research is a source for public opinion data across a range of subjects. This site tends to focus on market research, but it also archives political surveys. In addition, there are often short feature stories about polling and research methods.

For academic students of public opinion, including undergraduate and graduate students, the most valuable data archive is the Inter-University Consortium for Political and Social Research (ICPSR) at the University of Michigan. Many colleges and universities are members of the Consortium, while membership in other data archives is less frequent. The Consortium publishes annually a complete catalog of its holdings and distributes a newsletter informing members of new acquisitions. This information as well as the frequencies for some of its data sets can be accessed at its Web site. The Consortium also disseminates the National Election Studies, the General Social Survey, and the World Values Survey. These are three of the most important nonproprietary academic surveys available for secondary analysis, and we rely on them extensively in this book. Each of these studies comes with a completely documented codebook. Both the codebooks and the data sets are routinely received by universities that are Consortium members.[23] In addition, a number of journals regularly publish opinion data. Each issue of the *Public Opinion Quarterly* has a section called "The Polls" in which survey data on a specific topic is reviewed.

Current Polling Data

The Internet is now an important resource for monitoring polls. The following sites make available the latest public opinion polling data on a wide range of topics—from public reaction to an event recently in the news to the latest reading on presidential popularity or the current poll data on a high-profile election.

> http://members.bellatlantic.net/~abelson An inventory of several sites for public opinion research, including many of the sites listed below.
>
> www.pollingreport.com A service of The Polling Report, a nonpartisan clearinghouse for public opinion data; provides free reports on current opinion on politics, the economy, and popular culture.
>
> http://nationaljournal.com/ The *National Journal;* provides the most complete up-to-date polling information on electoral contests, but requires a paid subscription to access the information.
>
> www.gallup.com The site for the Gallup Poll.
>
> http://www.pipa.org This site reports original polling and discussion on international issues, conducted by the Program on International Policy Attitudes at the University of Maryland.
>
> www.cbsnews.com The site reporting the latest results from the CBS Television News/*New York Times* polling unit.
>
> www.washingtonpost.com The site for polls conducted by the ABC Television News/*Washington Post* polling unit. See also the column by Richard Moran and Claudia Deane, "The Poll Watchers," for insightful commentary on current polling issues.

www.nyttimes.com The PollWatch site for the *New York Times*; provides a new story about polling every other Thursday; old stories are also archived and available.

www.wsj.com The site for polls conducted by the NBC Television News/*Wall Street Journal* polling unit.

http://www.publicagenda.org A site that presents opinion data and commentary on domestic policy issues.

www.usatoday.com The site for *USA Today* polls.

www.people-press.org The site for the Pew Research Center for the People and the Press, an independent research group that conducts surveys in some depth about current issues, regularly conducts polls on public attentiveness to news stories, and charts trends in fundamental social and political values.

www.vanishingvoter.org A site maintained by the Kennedy School of Government at Harvard. Weekly polls of 1,000 respondents were conducted during the 2000 presidential election, focusing on factors that encourage or discourage public engagement with politics.

www.zogby.com The site for Zogby International, the political polling agency for Reuters; mostly focuses on electoral choice.

Polling Data Archives   Earlier in this chapter we discussed a number of data libraries. The Web sites for these archives are listed below.

www.icpsr.umich.edu The site for the University Consortium for Social and Political Research, home to the National Election Studies (NES). It archives the General Social Survey (GSS), the World Values Survey, and others.

www.norc.uchicago.edu The site for the National Opinion Research Center, home to the General Social Survey and other NORC studies.

www.ropercenter.uconn.edu The site for the Roper Center, which houses the Gallup Poll, media polls, plus others.

http://www2.irss.unc.edu/data_archive/home.asp The Odum Institute archive, associated with the University of North Carolina, home to the Harris Poll and the National Association of State Polls, which houses more than 350 state-level studies.

http://odwin.ucsd.edu/idata/ Data on the Net, maintained by the University of California at San Diego; also provides links to other social databases.

gort.ucsd.edu/calpol The archive for the Field Poll, devoted to political and social issues in California.

Data Archives for Non-American Surveys   Survey research now occurs regularly all over the world. The best of the archives and their Web sites are listed below.

http://www.gesis.org/en/data_service/issp/index.htm The archive for the International Social Survey.

europa.eu.int/en/comm/dg10/infcom/epo/polls.html This site is for
archives for the Eurobarometer and the Central and Eastern
Eurobarometer.

www.mori.com A British-based opinion research firm and archive. MORI
holds mostly British opinion data but also conducts and archives occasional cross-national studies.

Polling Organizations A number of professional polling organizations offer
useful and interesting information on survey research.

www.aapor.org The site for the American Association for Public Opinion
Research, the oldest and most prestigious of the polling organizations;
includes a complete index to articles published in the *Public Opinion
Quarterly*.

www.worldopinion.com The site for the World Association for Public
Opinion Research; often contains useful articles about opinion research.

www.casro.org The site for the Council of American Survey Research
Organizations, the primary organization for those doing commercial
survey research.

www.ncpp.org The site for the National Council of Public Polls; contains
information on national standards and how to conduct and interpret polls.

1-6 LINKAGE MODELS BETWEEN PUBLIC OPINION AND PUBLIC POLICIES

In a democracy, public opinion is supposed to influence the decisions by the
elected leaders. But how effective, in practice, is the public at controlling what
its government does? This book attempts to answer this important question.
The mechanisms of popular control are more complicated than one might
think. (For a sampling of contemporary perspectives, see Manin, Przeworski,
and Stokes 1999; Fearon 1999; Ferejohn 1999; Erikson, MacKuen, and Stimson 2002; Hutchens 2003, and Mansbridge 2003). Here, we sketch five models, drawn from Luttbeg (1968), by which public opinion can get reflected by
public policy.

The Rational-Activist Model

This model is the basis for the widely accepted concept of the ideal citizen's
role in a democracy. Voting on the basis of issues is at the heart of the rational-
activist model. By the standards of this model, individual citizens are expected
to be informed politically, involved, rational, and, above all, active. On the
basis of an informed and carefully reasoned set of personal preferences and an
accurate perception of the various candidates' positions, voters are expected to
cast a ballot for those candidates who best reflect their issue preferences. In this

way, the victorious candidates in elections will be the ones who best represent constituency policy views.

This model places a burden on citizens, who are expected to hold informed and enlightened views about the policy positions of candidates and vote accordingly. As we have noted, politics does not play a salient role in the lives of most Americans. Many people rarely or never vote. Those who do are often inattentive to policy issues, particularly in low-salience elections.

Certainly, issue voting allows for some influence of public opinion on government policy. But in our search for methods by which political leaders can be held accountable, we must look beyond the rational-activist model.

The Political Parties Model

The political parties model greatly reduces the political demands placed on the citizen. The model depends on the desire of political parties to win elections as a mechanism for achieving popular control. According to the model, a party states its positions on the issues of the day in its platform. Because of their interest in winning elections, parties can be counted on to take stands that appeal to large segments of the electorate. Voters then select among platforms, giving support to the candidate of the party whose platform most conforms to their personal preference. Instead of facing multiple decisions for the numerous offices up for election, voters need only make a single decision among the available choice of parties.

A number of questions are raised by a consideration of this model. For example, to what extent do parties take distinct positions, and to what extent do voters recognize them? Does a party's electoral fortunes reflect the degree of public support for its policies, or is a party's vote largely independent of the policies it advocates?

The Interest Groups Model

In the preceding models we emphasized the central importance of communication between elected officials and their constituents. For representatives to respond to public demands, they need to know what these demands are. For the public to achieve accountability from representatives, they need to know what the representatives have done and what alternatives were available. Interest groups can perform this function. They can serve as a link between people and their representatives.

Numerous organized groups in society claim to speak for various segments of the electorate—the Sierra Club, the National Organization for Women, and the National Rifle Association, to mention just three. At one extreme, these groups could be so inclusive of individuals in society and could so accurately represent their members' opinions that representatives could achieve accountability merely by recording the choice of each group, weighing them by the number of voters they represent, and voting with the largest group. This would be in accord with what might be called the interest groups model of popular control.

Under ideal circumstances, interest groups might succeed in communicating public opinion to officials between elections and with greater clarity than can be communicated through election outcomes. Interest groups, like political parties, could simplify the choices for the individual voter, making it possible for an electorate that is largely disinterested in politics to nevertheless achieve accountability.

Several questions arise out of the interest groups model. Does group opinion, the somehow combined opinions of all those persons in all the relevant interest groups, coincide with public opinion? Or do the opinions carried to government by interest groups reflect only the opinions of the wealthy or the business sector of society? Who among everyday citizens belongs to interest groups? Are some segments of society overrepresented and others mostly uninvolved in any type of group activity?

The Delegate Model

When voters are doing their job (via the rational-activist model), elections are decided by policy issues. To win elections under such circumstances, politicians must cater to the views of their prospective voters, and to stay elected, elected officials must anticipate voter preferences in advance of the next election. When politicians take voter preferences seriously in this way, acting as the voters' agent, we say they are behaving as the voters' delegates. This is the delegate model[24] at work. By this model, representation of public opinion can be enhanced simply because elected leaders believe they will be voted out of office if they do not attend to voter opinion—whether or not the voters would actually do so.

Several questions are raised by the delegate model: Can elected officials accurately learn public opinion, or do they receive a distorted view? To what extent do elected officials actually heed public opinion as they perceive it? What do elected leaders view as the consequences of ignoring public opinion? Finally, how often do elected officials see their role as representing constituency preferences, as opposed to their (possibly conflicting) personal views of the constituency's best interests?

The Sharing Model

Because as a society we do not designate leaders early in life and hold them as a class apart from then on, it is unlikely that the personal opinions held by elected officials on the issues of the day differ diametrically from those held by the rest of the electorate. This possibility is the final model of political linkage: the sharing model. This model simply states that because many attitudes are broadly held throughout the public, elected leaders cannot help but satisfy public opinion to some degree, even if the public is totally apathetic. Unilateral disarmament, total government takeover of the economy, a termination of public education, a complete disregard for the preservation of the environment—all are examples of actions so contrary to broadly held American attitudes that they would be rejected by any set of government leaders. Even on issues that provoke substantial disagreement, the distribution of opinion among political leaders may be similar to that among the public. If so, even when leaders act according to personal preference and are ignored by disinterested citizens, their actions would often correspond to citizen preferences. For this model, we need to consider how broadly opinions on national issues are shared and how similar the views of elected officials are to those of the public at large.

1-7 PLAN OF THIS BOOK

We have by necessity ordered facts into chapters that strike us as convenient. Chapter 2 discusses the science of assessing public opinion. Chapter 3 is concerned with the psychology of opinion-holding and focuses on the role of political ideology and party identification. Chapter 4 chronicles trends in public opinion over time. Chapter 5 discusses the formation of political attitudes. Chapter 6 evaluates data on broad public acceptance of certain attitudes that may be necessary for a stable democratic government, and Chapter 7 delves into the group basis of public opinion. Chapter 8 analyzes the effect of the media on those attitudes. Chapter 9 is an analysis of public opinion and elections, and Chapter 10 views the reverse aspect of political linkage—how elected officials respond to the views of their constituents. In the final chapter, we assess the linkage models and draw conclusions about public opinion in the United States based on the data presented throughout the book.

NOTES

1. The Blumer view of public opinion is still held by many in the field. For a more recent statement, see Zukin (1992).
2. The term *pollster* was coined by political scientist and pollster Lindsay Rogers to evoke in the minds of readers the word *huckster* (Hitchens 1992, 46).
3. Or, as Winston Churchill put it, "Nothing is more dangerous than to live in the temperamental atmosphere of a Gallup Poll, always feelings one's pulse and taking one's temperature . . . There is only one duty, only one safe course, and that is to try to be right and not to fear to do or waver in what you believe to be right" (quoted in Bogart 1972, 47.)
4. Almond moderated his opinion on this point in the 1960 reissue of his book.
5. The eighteenth-century French mathematician Marquis de Condorcet, using jury decisions as an example, was able to demonstrate mathematically a greater probability that the majority would come to the right decision than the probability the minority would come to the right decision.
6. For an analysis of the dimensions possible, see Herbst (1993).
7. Choosing not to vote may well be as much of a political statement as casting one's ballot. A nonvote can mean alienation from government or indicate acceptance of the status quo.
8. It also includes the functional equivalent of verbal expressions, such as filling out a written questionnaire.

9. One ambiguity inherent in this conceptualization is that some people may never express orally or in writing some of their opinions. We could possibly conceptualize such opinions as internal, but that has the unhappy consequence of muddying the distinction between attitudes and opinions. Our simple solution for unexpressed opinions is to assert that, if expressed, they would have the same characteristics and qualities of expressed opinion.

10. It should be noted that our distinction between opinions and beliefs is not common to all fields. In a court of law, for example, an expert witness is frequently asked to give an "expert opinion" on a matter of fact. In everyday conversation, it is quite frequently that someone asserts, "It is my opinion that . . . " followed by some assertion of factual truth.

11. The name apparently comes from a practice in rural areas of throwing straw into the air to see which way the wind is blowing. Presumably, a "straw poll" is a method for determining the direction of the political winds. Pioneer pollster Claude Robinson (1932, 6) defined a straw poll as "an unofficial canvass of an electorate to determine the division of popular sentiment on public issues or on candidates for public office." Today the term generally refers to any assessment of public opinion based on nonscientific sampling methods.

12. The sample consisted of 532 respondents from Wilmington, Delaware, selected "without Discrimination of Parties" (Gallup and Rae 1940, 35). Other straw polls were conducted in 1824 as well (see E. Smith 1990a).

13. Straw polls used three methods to gather data. One was the ballot-in-the-paper method, in which the reader filled out the ballot, cut it out of the paper, and mailed it to the sponsoring organization. The second was the personal canvass, in which solicitors took ballots to crowded locations such as theaters, hotels, and trolleys and got willing citizens to complete them. Sometimes ballots were simply left in a crowded area in the morning, and those completed were retrieved in the evening. The third method was to send ballots by mail to a specified list of people and ask that they send them back by return mail.

14. In publications such as the *Chicago Record*, there was a daily front-page feature from September 1896 through election day. Polling updates were also a regular feature of the *Literary Digest*.

15. The sample sizes for the straw polls were so large that they typically made projections on a state-by-state basis.

16. Gallup marketed a column, "America Speaks," which was based on his polls, to newspapers.

17. Although early on, Gallup did do split-ballot question-wording experiments. These were not, however, publicly released.

18. Now a division of the Institute for Social Research.

19. Over the years, these University of Michigan–based surveys have undergone a number of name changes. In the early years, they were dubbed the SRC surveys, after the Survey Research Center. Then they became the CPS surveys, named after the Center for Political Studies, a division of the Institute for Social Research. Currently they are referred to as the National Election Studies (NES).

20. However, only the CBS News/*New York Times* has its own in-house polling operation. ABC, NBC, and CNN contract with outside commercial polling houses for their opinion surveys.

21. The National Election Pool is operated by long-time polling experts Warren Mitofsky of Mitofsky International and Joseph Lenski of Edison Media Research.

22. For a copy of the code of ethics and a discussion, see Cantril (1991, ch. 4).

23. For more information on data archives, see Smith and Weil (1990) or Kiecolt and Nathan (1985).
24. In previous editions we labeled this model the role-playing model, following Luttbeg's original formulation. For the politician, an alternative to the delegate role is the role of the trustee who, rather than following constituency preferences, acts according to the politician's conception of the constituents' best interests. See Wahlke et al. (1962) for various formulations of legislator roles.

2 | Polling: The Scientific Assessment of Public Opinion

The use of scientific polling to gauge and analyze public opinion and elections has now been part of the political landscape for over sixty years. And it continues to grow. This growth is evident in the media's obsession with campaigns as horse races, where journalists' interest lies more in forecasting the outcome than the substance of the campaign. During the presidential election season, the news media is now saturated with polling reports. The 1996 fall campaign saw more than 300 national and 400 state polls monitoring the horse race (Bogart 1998). In 2000, the number of polls increased again (Wlezien and Erikson, 2002). Two-thirds of the election stories that appeared on the networks in 2000 were supported by polling data (Hess 2000).

2-1 THE VALUE OF POLLS

Of course, polling is not confined to election polls and the prediction of the next election outcome. As discussed in chapter 1, academic polls advance our knowledge of public opinion. Commercial pollsters (e.g., Gallup) satisfy the public's (and private clients') curiosity regarding trends in public opinion. Although not as highly publicized as the pollsters' election forecasts, polls routinely ascertain public preferences on a variety of policy issues and monitor the public pulse regarding such indicators as party identification, ideological identification, and the approval rating of the current president. This is the stuff of public opinion analysis and the subject of subsequent chapters.

Politicians and the Polls

Politicians have a particularly strong interest in the polls, as their professional careers may depend on reading public opinion accurately. Like the rest of us, politicians have access to commercial opinion polls such as the Gallup poll. But the politicians often seek further intelligence regarding public opinion by commissioning their own polls. The first president to poll the public was Franklin Roosevelt, who did so in the late 1930s. While his next two successors, Truman and Eisenhower, had little use for private polling, presidential polling picked up in earnest with John Kennedy. Since then, virtually every major presidential decision has been made with the benefit of private polls. Presidents seek updates of public attitudes toward current policies, public reactions to future policy options, and, especially, information on their own standing with the voters (Jacobs 1993).

Politicians below the presidential level also do their own polling, as do the major political parties. Senate and House members spend about 3 percent of their sizable campaign war chests on polling their states or districts (Fritz and Morris 1992). Although the general purpose of this polling is to monitor their electoral standing against current or future opponents, private constituency polls can also register signals regarding shifts in constituency concerns.

A candidate's poor showing in preelection polls makes fund-raising difficult and dampens volunteer enthusiasm. Good poll numbers result in more media attention (Traugott 1992). A strong showing in the polls can legitimize a candidate, ensuring that he or she is taken seriously.

Polls create expectations about who is the likely election winner. Larry Bartels (1988) has demonstrated that in presidential primaries with a number of more or less unknown candidates—such as 1988 for the Democrats—expectations about who will win are a major factor in determining candidate choice on election day. Thomas Patterson (2002) makes a compelling argument that the standing in the polls of a presidential candidate determines the way the candidate's personal qualities are described by the media. When poll numbers are good, news stories are positive; when poll number are bad, stories turn negative (see also Farnsworth and Lichter 2003). In an analysis of *Newsweek*'s reporting of the 1988 presidential campaign, Patterson demonstrates that when polls showed Michael Dukakis doing well in the 1988 presidential race, he was described as "relentless in his attack" and "a credible candidate." As he later dropped in the polls, *Newsweek* described him as "reluctant to attack" and "trying to present himself as a credible candidate." Interestingly, the change in descriptors coincided quite closely with the point he fell behind George Bush in the polls (Patterson 1989, 104–6). Finally, standing in the polls can determine whether or not a candidate is invited to participate in the presidential debates. For example, while Ross Perot's poll numbers justified his appearance in the 1992 debates, his poll support was deemed insufficient for his inclusion in the 1996 presidential debates.

Presidential popularity, now gauged virtually daily, is the public opinion indicator watched with perhaps the most interest by members of Congress, others in the political community, and the media. Arguably, one important aspect of presidential power, including influence over Congress, is the chief executive's personal standing with the public (Canes-Wrone and Demarchi 2002; Bond, Fleischer, and Wood 2002). While it is debatable how much a president can leverage popular approval into public support for his favored projects, there is little doubt that members of Congress and Washington insiders believe that a popular president holds the power to persuade public opinion. It was the high job approval enjoyed by President Clinton (about 70 percent) that in the opinion of many saved his presidency after he was impeached by the House of Representatives. President George W. Bush's surge in popularity following 9/11 smoothed the passage of items from his conservative agenda through Congress.

The Public Looks at the Polls

More and more people say they are paying attention to the polls. In 1944, only 19 percent of the public said that they regularly or occasionally followed poll results; by 1985 it was 41 percent, and in 2000 the figure had risen to 65 percent. Yet few citizens have even a rudimentary understanding of how a public opinion poll works. In a recent study, the Gallup organization asked a national sample whether interviews with 1,500 or 2,000 people (typical sample sizes for national polls) "can accurately reflect the views of the nation's population" or whether "it's not possible with so few people." Only 28 percent said a sample of that size could yield accurate results; 56 percent said it was not possible, and the remaining 15 percent had no opinion. While the public may not understand the technicalities of polling, a sizable majority nevertheless believes polls are important guides for public officials (Traugott and Kang 2000a). In 2001, 66 percent said that "polls are useful for elected officials in Washington to understand how the public feels about important issues."[1]

Polling certainly deserves a critical look. Many surveys are badly conceived, poorly executed, and incorrectly interpreted. Nevertheless, much popular criticism of public opinion polls seems ill informed. Few outside the professional survey community have an appreciation for why candidates who lead in the final preelection poll do not always win, why two surveys taken at the same time report different results, or even why Truman beat Dewey when the Gallup Poll predicted otherwise.

2-2 SAMPLING

Public opinion polls are based on samples. When the Gallup Poll reports that 50 percent of adult Americans approve of the way the president is handling his job, it is obvious that the Gallup organization has not gone out and interviewed 210 million American adults. Instead, it has taken a sample. The reasons for sampling are fairly straightforward. First, to interview everyone would be prohibitively expensive. The Census for the year 2000 is estimated to have cost between $6 billion and $7 billion. Second, to interview the entire population would take a very long time. Months might pass between the first and last interviews. Public opinion might, in that period, undergo real change.

Sampling provides a practical alternative to interviewing the whole population—be it national, state, or local. Furthermore, when done correctly, sampling can provide accurate estimates of the political opinions of a larger population. The theory of sampling is a branch of the mathematics of probability, and the error involved in going from the sample to the population can be known with precision. However, many surveys of public opinion do not meet the demanding requirements of sampling theory. The attendant result, of course, is a loss in accuracy.

Sampling Theory

The *population* is that unit about which we want information. In most political surveys, the population is one of the following: (1) those eighteen and older, (2) registered voters, or (3) those who will (or do) vote in the next election. These are three quite different groups. It is important that the population be clearly specified. When one sees a poll addressing abortion, presidential popularity, or voter intent in an upcoming election, those reporting the poll should provide a clear description of the population about which they speak. It has been shown, for example, that Senator Edward Kennedy is more highly rated among all adults than among registered voters (Roper 1980, 48). Evaluations of Kennedy are, in part, determined by how one defines the population.

The *sample* is that part of the population selected for analysis. Usually, the sample is considerably smaller than the population. National political surveys conducted by reputable firms employ samples of 1,000 to 1,500 respondents, although smaller samples are sometimes used in state and local contests. But as samples get smaller, the probability of error increases. Sample size should always be reported along with the results of a survey. If that information is missing, the alleged findings should be treated with a great deal of caution.

When samples accurately mirror the population, they are said to be *representative*. The term *randomness* refers to the only method by which a representative sample can be scientifically drawn. In a simple random sample, each unit of the population has exactly the same chance of being drawn as any other unit. If the population is American attorneys, each attorney is required to have exactly the same probability of being selected in order for the sample to be random. Attorneys in big cities could not have a greater likelihood of getting into the sample than those from rural areas. This situation obviously requires a detailed knowledge of the population. In the case of attorneys, one could get a list from the American Bar Association and then sample from that list. But suppose the population was unemployed adults. To specify the population in a fashion to be able to draw a random sample would be difficult. As a consequence, obtaining a representative sample of the unemployed is not easy.

A *probability sample* is a variant of the principle of random sampling. Instead of each unit having exactly the same probability of being drawn, some units are more likely to be drawn than would others—but this is a known probability.

For example, if one were sampling voter precincts in a state, it is of consequence that some precincts contain more people than do others. To make the sample of people in those precincts representative, the larger precincts must have a greater likelihood of being selected than smaller ones.

We use simple random sampling (SRS) to illustrate how the principle of probability works in selecting a representative sample. Let us assume our population is a large barrel containing 100,000 marbles, some of which are red and some of which are green. We do not know the percentage of each. Instead of counting them all (a long and tedious job), we will draw a random sample. The question is: How? We could just dip in our hand and take some out, but that would mean that those within our reach would be picked and those close to the bottom would have no chance of being selected. Or we could spin the barrel and take one out after every spin. That would probably work reasonably well, but it still would not be "scientific." Even with a spin, those marbles at the bottom might never get close enough to the surface to get picked. If we are insisting on a pure random sample, we would have to employ a table of random numbers and give each marble a numeral between 1 and 100,000. Random number tables are computer-generated digits that are completely unrelated to one another (i.e., random). They can be found in the appendix of virtually any statistics book. Let us assume we sample 600 marbles. Our first random number might be 33,382. We would then find the marble with that number and note if it is red or green. Our next random number might be 12,343. We would again note its color. The process would continue until we drew 600 marbles and recorded the color of each.

Having completed that task, let us say our sample shows 65 percent red marbles. Given the sampling method, we now know some things about the population. Sampling theory (the central limit theorem) tells us that the most likely percentage of red marbles is 65 percent. Of course, it is very unlikely that the real percentage of red marbles is precisely 65 percent. It might be 65.5 or 64.3, for example. The sample will not get the population value exactly correct for the same reason that flipping a coin 100 times will not likely yield exactly 50 heads and 50 tails—although it should be close if the coin is honestly flipped.

We need at this point to introduce the concepts of *confidence level* and *sampling error*. A sample rarely hits the true population value right on the nose. The confidence level tells us the probability that the population value will fall within a specified range. The sampling error specifies that range. A commonly used confidence level is 95 percent (it is sometimes higher, but almost never lower). For a sample of 600, the sampling error is 4 percent. What all this means is that if we took 100 samples from our population, and each of these samples consisted of 600 marbles randomly drawn, then 95 out of 100 times we would be plus or minus 4 percent of the true population value. Our sample came up 65 percent red. While this figure may not be exactly correct, we at least know that 95 out of 100 times (our 95 percent confidence level) we are going to be within four points—one way or the other—of the true proportion of red marbles in the barrel. This much can be proved mathematically.

Let us turn to a political example. The Gallup Poll reported that President George W. Bush's approval rating shortly before invading Iraq was 57 percent (Gallup Poll, 3–5 March 2003). Since the sample size in this survey was 1,003, we know that if the poll were repeated 100 times, 95 of the 100 repetitions (the 95 percent confidence level) would produce results that are plus or minus 3 percent (the sampling error) of what we would find if we interviewed all American adults.[2] Thus, Bush's popularity on or about March 4, 2002, could have been as high as 60 percent or as low as 54 percent. The best estimate (according to the central limit theorem) is 57 percent. Sampling error decreases as we move away from a 50/50 split, and it increases as the population has more heterogeneous political attitudes. But by far the most important factor is the size of the sample.

The importance of sample size for sampling accuracy can be easily demonstrated by flipping a coin. We know that, in theory, if a coin is flipped honestly a large number of times it should come up about equal proportions of heads and tails. Suppose we flipped a coin ten times. Given a large number of repetitions of ten flips we might frequently get seven heads, eight tails, and so on. But if instead of flipping the coin ten times we flipped it one hundred times, then our large number of repetitions would only occasionally yield 70 heads or 80 tails, and if we flipped it 1,000 times, our repetitions could tend to cluster around 500 heads and 500 tails, with 700 heads or 800 tails being rare events indeed. The larger the size of the sample (i.e., the number of times the coin is flipped), the closer we will come to the theoretical expectation of one-half heads and one-half tails.

Unlike the size of the sample, the size of the population is of little consequence for the accuracy of the survey.[3] That is, it does not make much difference if we are surveying the city of Houston or the entire United States. With a sample size of 600, the sampling error would be identical for both the city and the nation—all other things being equal. Table 2.1 presents the sampling errors associated with specific sample sizes.

Using a large barrel of marbles and a table of random numbers, we drew a "perfect" sample—that is, the sampling method fit perfectly with the mathematics of sampling theory. When we sample humans, we cannot draw a perfect sample. Although a marble cannot refuse to tell us if it is red or green, a person may refuse to be interviewed. Sampling theory does not allow for refusals. Consequently, surveys of public opinion only approximate the underlying theory of sampling. If these deviations from theory are modest, opinion polls can and do work well. But there are many instances in which sampling theory is ignored (or those conducting the polls are ignorant). If the poll simply concerns political opinions (favor/oppose abortion, approve/disapprove of tax reform, favor/oppose the registration of handguns), there is no reality test. The survey may have been done badly and be considerably off the mark, but how would one know?[4] On the other hand, pre-Election Day surveys have a reality test: Election Day. In these surveys, sampling mistakes have, in several dramatic cases, cast opinion pollsters in a highly unfavorable light.

TABLE 2.1 | **Sampling Error and Sample Size Employing Simple Random Sampling★**

Sample Size	Sampling Error (plus or minus)★
2,430	2.0
1,536	2.5
1,067	3.0
784	3.5
600	4.0
474	4.5
384	5.0
267	6.0
196	7.0
150	8.0
119	9.0
96	10.0
42	15.0

★This computation is based on the assumptions of a simple random sampling (SRS) with a dichotomous opinion that splits 50/50 and a 95 percent confidence level.

Bad Sampling: Two Historical Examples

To see how not to sample, it is worth reviewing two classic polling mistakes from the past. One, discussed in chapter 1, was the *Literary Digest* fiasco of 1936. The other was when the seemingly scientific polls all failed in the presidential election of 1948.

The previous chapter discussed the prescientific straw polls that were used to gauge candidate fortunes prior to 1936. The best known of the commercial publications conducting straw polls was the *Literary Digest*. The *Digest* accurately forecast the winner (if not the exact percentage points) of each presidential election between 1920 and 1932. In 1936, as in previous years, it sent out some 10 million postcard ballots "drawn from every telephone book in the United States, from the rosters of clubs and associations, from city directories, lists of registered voters, [and] classified mail order and occupational data" (*Literary Digest*, August 1936, 3). About 2.2 million returned their postal ballots. The result was 1,293,699 (57 percent) for Republican Alf Landon and 972,867 (43 percent) for President Franklin Roosevelt. On Election Day, Roosevelt not only won but won by a landslide, receiving 62.5 percent of the vote and carrying every state except Maine and Vermont. The *Literary Digest* was not only wrong; it was wrong by 19.5 percent. On November 14, 1936, the *Literary Digest* published the following commentary:

WHAT WENT WRONG WITH THE POLLS?

None of Straw Votes Got Exactly the Right Answer—Why?

In 1920, 1924, 1928 and 1932, the *Literary Digest* Polls were right. Not only right in the sense they showed the winner; they forecast the actual popular vote and with such a small percentage of error (less than 1 percent in 1932) that newspapers and individuals everywhere heaped such phrases as "uncannily accurate" and "amazingly right" upon us. . . . Well this year we used precisely the same method that had scored four bull's eyes in four previous tries. And we were far from correct. Why? We ask that question in all sincerity, because *we want to know.*

Why *did* the poll fare so badly? One reason that can be discounted is sample size. The *Digest* claims to have polled 10 million people (and received 2.2 million responses). Thus, a large sample is no guarantee for accuracy. Rather, their sampling procedure had four fundamental defects. First, the sample was drawn in a biased fashion. The *Digest* clearly did not use random selection or anything approaching it. Even though questionnaires were sent out to 10 million people, a large part of the sample was drawn from telephone directories and lists of automobile owners—during the Depression, a decidedly upper-middle-class group, predominantly Republican in its political sentiments. In other words, the *Digest* did not correctly specify the population. A second factor contributing to the *Digest's* mistake was time. The questionnaires were sent out in early September, making impossible the detection of any late trend favoring one candidate or the other. Third, 1936 was the year that marked the emergence of the New Deal Coalition. The *Digest* had picked the winner correctly since 1920 using the same methods as in 1936, but in 1936 voting became polarized along class lines. The working class and the poor voted overwhelmingly Democratic, while the more affluent classes voted predominantly Republican. Since the *Literary Digest's* sample was heavily biased in the direction of the more affluent, it is not surprising that their sample tended to favor Landon.

Finally, there was the problem of self-selection. The *Digest* sent out its questionnaires by mail. Of the 10 million they mailed, only a little over 2 million were returned—about 22 percent. Those people who self-select to respond to mail surveys are often quite different in their political outlook from those who do not respond. They tend to be better educated, to have higher incomes, and to feel more strongly about the topics dealt with in the questionnaire (Dillman 1978). So even if the sample of 10 million had been drawn in an unbiased fashion, the poll probably still would have been in error due to the self-selection factor (Squire 1988). A fundamental principle of survey sampling is that one cannot allow the respondents to select themselves into the sample.

Despite the failure of the *Literary Digest*, several public opinion analysts did pick Franklin Roosevelt as the winner. Among them was George Gallup, who built his reputation on a correct forecast in 1936. In terms of percentage, Gallup did not get particularly close. He missed by almost 7 percent. But he got the winner right, and that is what most people remember.

Following Gallup's success at predicting the 1936 election, "scientific" polling surged in popularity and became perceived within the political class as almost infallible. Gallup and other pollsters predicted the winners of the presidential elections of 1940 and 1944. Then, in 1948 the pollsters all predicted that the Republican presidential candidate, Tom Dewey, would defeat Truman. The pollsters were so confident of Dewey's victory that they did not even poll during the last few weeks of the campaign, seeing it as a waste of time. Virtually all politically knowledgeable observers saw the outcome as certain. Famously, Dewey began to name his cabinet.

The 1948 presidential election jarred the pollsters from their complacency. President Truman defeated Dewey in an upset. Gallup's prediction of Truman's vote was off by 5 percentage points. While this error was actually smaller than that in 1936, the crucial fact was that Gallup got the winner wrong.[5]

Why were Gallup and the other pollsters wrong in 1948? The technique used by Gallup in 1936 and up until the Dewey-Truman disaster is called *quota sampling*. This technique employs the Census to determine the percentage of certain relevant groups in the population. For example, what percentage is male, Catholic, white, and college-educated? Within these groups, interviewers are then assigned quotas. They must interview a certain percentage of women, a certain percentage with less than high school education, a certain percentage of blacks, and so on. But there are few, if any, constraints as to which individuals in these groups are to be interviewed. Once the interviews are completed, the sample is weighted so it will be representative of the population on those variables. If 15 percent of the population is male, high school-educated, and making over $25,000 a year, the sample is weighted to reflect those proportions.

The principal problem with quota sampling is a variation on the problem of self-selection. The interviewer has too much opportunity to determine who is selected for the sample. An interviewer who must get a specified number of "female blacks" may avoid certain areas of town or may get the entire quota from a single block. There is a natural tendency to avoid shabby residences, long flights of stairs, and homes where there are dogs. Experience with quota samples demonstrates that they systematically tend to underrepresent the poor, the less educated, and racial minorities.

Research on Gallup's misprediction in 1948 reveals he had too many middle- and high-income voters.[6] A second factor contributing to Gallup's mistake was that he quit polling two weeks before the election (Bradburn and Sudman 1988, 29). When significant movement takes place, it often occurs just before the election. For example, in 1980 Jimmy Carter and Ronald Reagan were virtually tied the weekend before the vote. A strong move toward Reagan over the weekend allowed him to pile up a substantial victory. To capture these changes, Gallup and other survey organizations now poll right up to the day of the election.

Contemporary Sampling Methods

We used simple random sampling (SRS) to illustrate the principles involved in drawing a scientific sample. However, SRS is seldom used in actual public opinion surveys. There is no master list of all Americans that could be sampled. Even if there were, the persons selected would be widely scattered throughout the country, making in-person interviews prohibitively expensive. For example, an interviewer might have to travel to Kerrville, Texas, just to talk to one respondent. Rather, polls where respondents are personally interviewed use *multistage cluster samples.*

The first step in drawing a multistage cluster sample of the American electorate is to divide the country into four geographic regions. Within each region, a set of counties and standard metropolitan statistical areas (SMSAs) is randomly selected. To ensure a representative selection of the national population, each county or SMSA is given a chance to be selected proportional to its population (probability sampling). National surveys typically include about 80 primary sampling units (PSUs). Once selected, the PSUs are often used several years before they are replaced. The reason is economic: Compact geographic areas save time and money. Interviewers are expensive to train, but once trained they can be used over and over.

About twenty respondents are chosen within each PSU. First, four or five city blocks (or their rural equivalents) are randomly selected. Then, four or five households are sampled within each block.[7] It is at the household level that the continued use of probability methods becomes most difficult. Ideally, the interviewer obtains a list of all persons living in the household and samples from the list. And indeed, some academic polls (such as the General Social Survey and the National Election Studies) attempt to meet this ideal. Most survey organizations, however, abandon probability methods at the block level and rely on some type of systematic method for respondent selection. The problem is that specific individuals are hard to locate. Interviewers are given a randomly drawn starting point and then instructed to stop at every *n*th household. The interviewer first asks to speak to the youngest man of voting age; if no man is at home the interviewer asks to speak to the youngest woman.[8] If both refuse, or if no one is home, the interviewer goes to the next adjacent dwelling. Each interviewer has a male/female quota and an age quota, but this is not a quota sample because the interviewer cannot choose who gets into the sample.

Multistage cluster samples work well and are an efficient compromise, given the expense involved in a simple random sample approach. The drawback is that cluster samples have a greater sampling error than SRS, as would be expected because the respondents are clustered into 75 to 100 small geographic areas. A simple random sample of 1,000 has a 3 percent sampling error. Gallup reports that its national samples (cluster samples) of 1,000 have a 4 percent sampling error.

Today, most surveys are conducted by telephone rather than in person. The principal advantage of the telephone is its low cost. It also frees one from having to use clusters, as the physical location of a respondent is irrelevant in a phone survey. However, there are disadvantages as well. Nationwide, it is estimated that 37 percent of all phone numbers are unlisted. In some areas, like Los Angeles, unlisted numbers are estimated as high as 62 percent. Those most likely to have unlisted numbers are younger, lower income, renters, and non-white households with children.[9]

The solution to this problem is random digit dialing. A ten-digit phone number is composed of an area code (the first three numbers), an exchange (the next three), a cluster (the next two), and the two final digits. If one knows the geographic assignment of area codes, exchanges, and clusters, one can define and sample a population. In large cities (for example, Houston, Texas), there are approximately 10,000 of these eight-digit codes. The following is an example:

713-496-78__ __

The first eight digits are randomly sampled from the population of 10,000. Then the last two digits are chosen from a table of random numbers or by a computer program that generates random digits. These methods bring persons with unlisted numbers into the sample. On the negative side, many calls are made to nonworking numbers. But the sample of households is representative. Once the household is selected, it is then necessary to sample residents within it. Sophisticated methods to ensure random selection have been developed by statisticians, but they require an enumeration of all household members by age and sex—information many respondents are unwilling to provide over the phone. One simple alternative is the last birthday method. Interviewers ask to speak to the person in the household who had the last—that is, the most recent—birthday. This technique gives a good approximation of random sampling within the household (Lavrakas 1993).

A significant problem with telephone surveys, although it applies to in-person surveys as well, is refusal. The telephone, however, particularly lends itself to abuse, as persons selling aluminum siding, upholstery, or can't-miss real estate deals sometimes attempt to gain a respondent's confidence by posing as a pollster. The sales pitch comes later. A study by the Roper Organization showed that 27 percent of a national sample had experienced these sales tactics (Turner and Martin 1984, 73). People, especially those in large cities, are becoming wary of callers claiming to be taking polls.

However, nonresponse involves more than refusals. It includes any reason why the designated respondent is not interviewed, such as ring–no answer or contacting an answering machine. The response rate is computed as a percentage. In simple terms, it is the number of people successfully interviewed divided by the total number of people called.[10] In the 1970s and earlier, it was common to find response rates in the 70 percent range.

Most pollsters believe that survey nonresponse has become a serious problem and seems to be getting worse (Groves and Couper 1998; Harris-Kojetin and Tucker 1999). Still, response rates for high-quality surveys have declined only modestly. One example is the University of Michigan's Survey of Consumer Attitudes, a telephone poll that has been conducted every month since 1977. It has been able to maintain an approximately constant response rate (70 percent) over the past 25 years—but at a cost. The cost is more time in the field, more interviewer training, more calls to ring—no answer numbers, and sophisticated attempts to convert refusals into a successful interviews by calling respondents a second time.[11] For surveys where resources are not abundant and time windows are short (as is often the case in media surveys), response rates have declined (Steeh, Kirgis, Cannon, and DeWitt 2001). For three typical media surveys, the *Washington Post* reports their response rates were 40 percent (AIDS Poll, June 13–23, 2002), 23 percent (9/11 anniversary, September 3–6, 2002), and 35 percent (terrorism study, February 13–16, 2003) (Deane 2003). Nonresponse is of consequence only if those sampled but not interviewed differ on questions of interest from those sampled *and* interviewed.

In an analysis of the NES and GSS, Brehm (1993) found nonresponse led to an overrepresentation of the elderly, blacks, women, the poor, and the less educated. For simple frequencies, this bias in response can be corrected by weighting the sample. For example, we know from the 2000 Census that African Americans are 12 percent of the U.S. adult population. If our sample contained only 9 percent blacks, we could easily use weights to raise the percentage. But weights are not an entirely satisfactory solution, as those reluctant to participate may not share the same opinions as the more willing. A study by the Pew Research Center (Keeter, Miller, Kohut, Groves, and Presser 2000) showed few opinion differences between those readily willing to be interviewed versus those who were reluctant (who initially refused but were recalled one or more times and convinced to participate). The two groups did, however, differ significantly on race-related questions. The reluctant respondents held views a good deal less sympathetic to the political and economic aspirations of African Americans than did the willing respondents.[12]

The exact percentage of Americans with access to telephones is a question open to debate, given that not everyone lives in a conventional household. It is certainly high, but how high? The 2000 Census reports that 97.6 percent of all households have phone service. Broken down by state, the lowest percentage is found in Mississippi, where 94.6 percent of households have telephone access.[13] The Census reports that 43 percent of homes without telephones are found in tracts where the median income is less than $20,000.[14] Thus, those without phones are among the least affluent segments of society. This *Lumpenproletariat* is one population subgroup that rarely finds its way into any survey, regardless of methodology.

Given the rising cost of high-quality telephone surveys, polling via the Internet has become a tempting alternative. Of course, one cannot simply send out a survey on the Internet and expect to get meaningful results. Even assuming a population is clearly defined, this approach suffers from the same self-selection bias as the *Literary Digest* poll. Rather, the usual approach is to recruit a large representative panel—say 100,000 people—by random digit dialing and pay people an incentive to participate in a fixed number of Internet surveys. The sample for each individual survey is then drawn from this large panel. The sample is weighted to reflect demographics reported in the Census. Still, not everyone has access to the Internet. Those who do are younger, whiter, better educated, and more affluent than the general population. On the other hand, response rates for professional Internet surveys are quite high—often about 95 percent. Another alternative also involves sampling from a large, representative panel. Respondents are offered free WebTV access in exchange for participating in opinion surveys. This approach allows for sophisticated polling, as complex questions can be combined with visuals. The principle drawback is that once people agree to participate, they sometimes change their behavior (for example, pay more attention to politics), so they may not be entirely comparable to a similar group not recruited (Dillman 2000; Harwood and Crossen 2000). Also, respondents participate in many surveys, and this experience may affect responses.[15]

2-3 QUESTION WORDING

It should surprise no one that in survey research, as in everyday life, the answers received are often dependent on the questions asked. This reality has both an upside and a downside for opinion polling. The upside is that people are sensitive to the way survey questions are phrased. That means they are paying reasonably close attention to what they are being asked, and their answers can be taken seriously. If changes in question wording had no impact, the opinion poll would likely be too blunt an instrument to be of much use. The downside is that because the distribution of public opinion can be a function of question wording, incorrect or inappropriate inferences about its true nature are easily possible. Not all variations in question phrasing affect the distribution of responses, but in some cases they clearly do. In this section we review some of the aspects of question wording that can affect the distribution of opinion.

Multiple Stimuli   Many questions have more than one stimulus to which respondents may react. Such questions are not faulty but rather are often a necessary requirement for measuring opinions on complex topics. Examples of commonly used single-stimulus questions are: "Generally speaking, do you consider yourself a Democrat, an Independent, a Republican, or what?" or "Do you approve or disapprove of the way the president is handling his job?" But suppose we were interested in public support for the First Amendment right of free speech. We could ask people to agree or disagree with the statement "I believe in free speech for all, no matter what their views might be." In 1978, 89 percent of opinion-holders agreed (Sullivan et al. 1982). But that tells us little other than in the abstract there is near consensus on a fundamental principle of the American creed. However, real controversies over free speech do not occur in the abstract but in concrete circumstances. Thus we might ask, "Suppose an admitted Communist wanted to make a speech in your community. Should he be allowed to speak or not?" In 1991, only 68 percent of opinion-holders said the person should be allowed to speak. If the admitted Communist was teaching in a college, 43 percent said he should be fired. It is quite clear that in specific circumstances, people are responding to both the free speech stimulus and Communist stimulus. As we shall see, the level of support for free speech is a matter of considerable controversy (see chapter 6).

Many less obvious instances of multiple stimuli can affect the distribution of opinion. One way is to preface the question with the name of an authoritative or admired person or institution. Consider the responses of white Americans to different phrasings of a question about the controversial policy of minority set-asides (Sniderman and Piazza 1993, 113).

Form A	Form B
Sometimes you hear it said there should be a law to ensure that a certain number of federal contracts go to minority contractors. Do you favor or oppose such a law?	The Congress of the United States—both the House of Representatives and the Senate—has passed a law to ensure that a certain number of federal contracts go to minority contractors. Do you favor or oppose such a law?

Form A		Form B	
Favor law	43%	Favor law	57%
Oppose law	57	Oppose law	43
	100%		100%

Invoking the symbol of the law in this question transforms the policy of set-asides from one backed by a minority of white respondents to one backed by a clear majority—a change that may not be trivial in the politics of affirmative action. The use of authoritative symbols also provides a cue for the uncertain, decreases the don't-knows, and raises the percentage of those favorable and unfavorable among those who know little or nothing about the issue in question (Smith and Squire 1990).

Question Order Effects   By *order effects* we mean the effect the previous content of the interview might have on a specific question. For example, respondents usually desire to be consistent in their answers. When asked in 1980 if "the United States should let Communist newspaper reporters from other countries come here and send back to their papers the news as they see it," 55 percent said yes. But if the question is preceded by one that asks whether "a Communist country like Russia should allow American newspaper reporters to come in and send back the news as they see it," then 75 percent favor letting Communist reporters into the United States (Schuman and Presser 1996, 27). Since most answered yes to allowing American reporters into (Communist) Russia, it is obviously inconsistent to bar Communist reporters from the United States. With respect to the abortion issue, general support for abortion will increase if a specific item with a high level of support is asked first. Thus, if respondents are asked if abortion should be permitted "if there is a strong chance of serious defect in the baby" (84 percent say yes), general support for abortion is 13 percent greater than if the specific abortion item is not asked first (Schuman and Presser 1996, 37).

Other examples of order effects include the questionnaire placement of presidential popularity or presidential vote items. Incumbent presidents do worse on both if the question comes late in a survey as opposed to early. The reason is that content of the interview reminds respondents of troublesome aspects of the incumbent's presidency (Sigelman 1981). Pocketbook voting (voting on the basis of changes in one's personal finances) can be induced by asking questions about finances immediately before ascertaining vote choice (Sears and Lau 1983). Finally, pollsters sometimes provide information on somewhat obscure topics before asking opinions about the topic. Suffice it to say that the content of the information provided in the stem of the question can easily affect the answer given.

Balanced Arguments   If a question mentions only one side of a controversy, that side will often get a disproportionate number of responses. An example is "Do you favor the death penalty?" Because only one option ("favor") is given, we might expect that option would be more frequently chosen than if the question is balanced, as in "Do you favor or oppose the death penalty?" The same is true for questions that use an agree/disagree format (called *Likert scales*). The common practice is to inform the respondent of both the agree and disagree options in the stem of the question.[16]

At best, however, agree/disagree questions present only one side of the issue. Respondents must construct the other side of the issue themselves. In the example below, providing balanced alternatives on a question about unemployment yields quite different results compared to an agree/disagree alternative (Cantril 1991, 126).

Form A	Form B	
Do you agree or disagree with this statement: Any able-bodied person can find a job and make ends meet?	Some people feel that any able-bodied person can find a job and make ends meet. Others feel there are times when it is hard to get along and some able-bodied people may not be able to find work. Whom do you agree with most?	
Agree	65%	Can make ends meet	43%
No opinion	10	No opinion	18
Disagree	25	Sometimes hard to get along	39
	100%		100%

If one wishes to describe the level of opinion, questions that present two polar alternatives are clearly superior to Likert-type questions (see the Appendix for examples used in the 2000 NES). Likert items are most useful for building scales or perhaps comparing subgroup differences. A scale made of several agree/disagree items can score respondents according their level of support for some policy, such as gradations of the circumstances under which they would permit abortions (see Chapter 4).

The Middle Position   The public seldom splits into polar camps on any issue, and even when a middle position is not offered, many will volunteer an intermediate alternative. When the question-wording explicitly includes a middle position, many respondents seize this middle response as the safe alternative. In one study, Schuman and Presser (1996, 166) found that when respondents are asked on political issues if they "are on the liberal side or the conservative side," 16 percent volunteer that they are "middle of the road." But if the "middle of the road" option is offered, it is taken by 54 percent. While there is little doubt about the consequence of offering a middle position (or an "unsure" or "undecided" option for issue questions), there is no consensus about the desirability of doing so. Some argue that most respondents do have a preference, albeit in some cases a weak one. Offering the middle alternative encourages certain respondents not to express their opinion.

Response Acquiescence   Often when people are asked whether they agree or disagree with an abstract statement, or one about which they know little, they tend to agree rather than disagree. This tendency is called *response acquiescence*. It arises mostly because the public is ill-informed and may not have genuine opinions on many issues (see chapter 3). We can illustrate this with a 1986 study of attitudes about pornography. Respondents were asked whether they agreed or disagreed that "people should have the right to purchase a sexually explicit book, magazine, or movie, if that's what they want to do." Evidently, people saw this statement as a referendum on individual rights, since an overwhelming 80 percent agreed with the statement. However, in the same poll respondents were also asked whether they agreed or disagreed with the opposite statement, that "community authorities should be able to prohibit the selling of magazines or movies they consider to be pornographic." Sixty-five percent agreed with this opposite view as well.[17] Overall, a large number of respondents agreed that the public had a right to purchase pornographic materials *and* also agreed that the community has the right to stop people from purchasing the same material. The most likely explanation of this contradiction is response acquiescence. These examples indicate the danger of using single Likert-type items to measure the level of public opinion. The best strategy for dealing with response acquiescence is to use two or more items where half are worded positively and half negatively—that is, to support free speech the respondent must agree with one statement and disagree with one another.

Filter Questions   Most people believe that good citizens should have opinions on current political topics. Thus, when interviewed by polling organizations, they tend to offer opinions on subjects about which they know little or nothing. In an otherwise conventional survey of the Cincinnati area, Bishop et al. (1980) included a question asking respondents whether the nonexistent "Public

Affairs Act" should be kept or repealed. Eighteen percent thought it should be kept; 16 percent favored its repeal. Given these findings on a fictitious issue, it should not be surprising that on real but somewhat obscure issues many will offer opinions on matters about which they have no true attitude.

One way to reduce this problem is by using filter questions. Respondents are read a question and response alternatives and then asked, "Where would you place yourself on this scale, or haven't you thought much about this?" Using the 1996 NES question that asks people to indicate on a 1–7 scale if they feel more or less money should be spent on defense, 13 percent of the sample indicated they had not thought enough about the issue to have an opinion. But that does not mean that all the remaining 87 percent have a true attitude. Another 29 percent took the middle position on the scale. It seems likely some taking this position have either no attitude or one that is poorly developed.

One danger in using screening questions is that some people with real attitudes, but hesitant to express them, may be filtered out of surveys (Berinsky 1999). An alternative is to use branching questions, where those who say they are undecided or unsure are encouraged in follow-up probes to make a choice (T. Smith 1984; Krosnick and Kerent 1993). But, of course, this strategy runs the risk of eliciting opinions where no true underlying attitude exists.

Conclusion: The Pitfalls of Question Wording

Variations in question wording can clearly influence the distribution of public opinion. That fact should be recognized and considered when using opinion data. Some questions are obviously biased (see next section). Read the questions carefully. What are the stimuli? Are authorities being invoked? Are inferences being made about the level of opinion from single Likert items? Are "no opinion" screens used on obscure issues? Are balanced questions truly presenting both options in a fair manner? All of these possibilities are cause for concern. Some types of inferences are more reliable than others. Multiple questions on the same issue can give insight into the range of opinion. But the most reliable strategy is to compare responses to the same question. Thus, subgroup differences on the same question are usually quite meaningful. Even better is to compare change over time in response to the same question. Because the stimulus is identical, variation is likely due to a change in the public's view.

2-4 THE MISUSE OF SURVEYS

One might think that the advent of modern survey methodology would have marked the end to unscientific polls that report the opinions of unrepresentative samples. Similarly, one might think we would see the end of purported "surveys" reporting "opinions" based on blatantly biased question wording. Not so. Unscientific surveys continue to abound. Let us look at a sampling of the worst offenders.

Politicians' Mail

Politicians know not to trust the content of their mail as a true gauge of public opinion. Still, they sometimes report the direction of mailed opinion as if it were a natural poll. For instance, when a national crisis occurs that is generally perceived as presenting the president in a poor light, the White House will frequently report that "the mail" is running 10 to 1, 5 to 1, etc., in favor of the president. When Special Prosecutor Archibald Cox was fired during the Watergate scandal of the 1970s, the Nixon White House reported that the mail was running more than 2 to 1 in favor of the president's actions. Many in the Senate and House of Representatives, on the other hand, reported that their mail was running overwhelmingly in opposition to the president's action.

A lesser crisis early in the Clinton administration provides a somewhat different example. In response to the revelation that President Clinton's first nominee for attorney general, Zoe Baird, had employed illegal aliens for child care, mail to U.S. senators was running more than 400 to 1 in opposition. On the other hand, an ABC/*Washington Post* poll done at the same time showed a more modest 58 percent opposed to her confirmation (Clymer 1993).

Letters to politicians are basically meaningless as an indication of public sentiment. We know that people who self-select to write to public officials overwhelmingly tend to write to those whom they feel are sympathetic. Moreover, one-sided barrages of mail to politicians typically are the result of organized interest group activity rather than spontaneous public sentiment.

Biased Samples, Biased Questions

While politicians are known to obtain political intelligence from scientific surveys, they often justify their positions by releasing results of pseudosurveys based on biased samples, biased questions, or both. These are sometimes published by the media, heralded in bold headlines as if they constituted a reasonable assessment of public opinion. For example, in 1978 a story in the *Houston Chronicle* carried the following headline: "Survey Here Shows Opposition to President's Energy Program." The "survey" turned out to be responses to 200,000 questionnaires mailed out by Houston area Republican congressman Bill Archer. There was a total of 43,010 responses to this mailout, or about 22 percent (about the same response to the *Literary Digest* poll). The poll also reported that respondents favored production of the B-1 bomber and retention of "right-to-work laws."[18] Suffice it to say that a survey of this sort measures virtually nothing. It is severely contaminated by self-selection. There is no way to compute sampling error, given the bias in the way respondents got into the sample. While the information might be valuable to Congressman Archer as an indication of what his attentive constituents think, it has little or no value as a measure of public opinion.

A variety of partisan organizations sometimes claim they are assessing public opinion by using mail surveys, often in combination with highly biased questions. For example, a questionnaire from the Democratic National Committee with a return date of October 16, 1995 (in time for the presidential campaign), included the following items:

- Do you favor or oppose Republican proposals to dismantle Head Start and programs that provide health care and nutrition to young mothers in poverty?
- Republican leaders are advocating a welfare reform plan that would end welfare benefits to single parents who cannot find work and spend the money on orphanages to house their children. Do you support or oppose this approach?

Even more biased is a question in a newsletter poll sent by then-Democratic congressman John Dowdy of Texas, which asked the following question (Morin 1997):

A drive has recently been announced to destroy the independence of Congress by purging Congressmen who refuse to be rubber stamps for the executive arm of government. Would you want your representative in Congress to surrender to the purge threat and become a rubber-stamped Congressman?

In April 1993, Ross Perot paid $190,000 to *TV Guide* to have a seventeen-question survey inserted in the magazine (Kolbert 1993). The questions were clearly slanted in a fashion to reflect his personal views on American politics. For example:

- Should we eliminate foreign lobbyists completely—no loopholes—and make it a criminal offense?
- Should laws be passed to eliminate all possibilities of special interests giving huge sums of money to candidates?

Given the highly loaded questions, it should come as no surprise that Perot supporters would be more likely to detect the "correct" answer and then return the questionnaire than those who preferred other candidates.[19] These polls have many of the same defects as the mail surveys periodically conducted by *Playboy* and *Penthouse* about sexual habits.[20] There is a great likelihood that those willing to divulge information about their sex lives differ in important ways from those who are unwilling. Mail surveys are not always meaningless, but they must be conducted with great care by people with specialized training. Most that are done correctly are published in academic journals, and their findings rarely show up in the popular media.

"Modern" Straw Polls

Regrettably, television, including highly regarded network news programs, has gotten into the straw poll business. Television journalism is a combination of news and entertainment, and often in the competition for ratings, entertainment takes precedence over hard news. That was certainly the case in 1992, when CBS News ran a program, called "America On Line," immediately following the first President Bush's State of the Union address. The idea was to provide program viewers with a toll-free number via which they could respond to a short survey (mostly about the state of the economy). More than 24 million citizens attempted to call, of whom about 315,000 got through.[21] However, the anchors frequently referred to the call-in poll as though it were a representative survey. The poll was introduced by Dan Rather as "taking the public pulse." Based on call-in results, Connie Chung reported that "53 percent were worse off [financially] than four years ago. It's important here to note that this is quite dramatic." She explained to Dan Rather that only a month ago a periodic CBS News poll had found only 30 percent claiming to be "worse off." According to Chung, "This does not bode well for President Bush on his night of the State of the Union." Of course, the 53 percent to which Chung referred was meaningless as a measure of public opinion. Although not mentioned on the show, it was later revealed that the companion "scientific" survey showed only 32 percent "worse off" than four years ago (Tierney 1992).

Call-in polls continue to be a regular feature on television news programs. The program host usually introduces these polls with a disclaimer that "we don't pretend the results are scientific, but here's what we found." Viewers should treat that statement as the equivalent of "certain bored people with strong feelings on some subjects are willing to pay a long-distance charge to register their views in a poll that means nothing. Here are the results."

With the advent of the Internet, straw polls are a booming business. The home page for many Web sites include a straw poll. For example, on many days one can respond to a straw poll on the MSN Web site and get instant feedback. As soon as you indicate your opinion, the results for all respondents are displayed. One hopes that everyone understands this is entertainment and indicates nothing meaningful about public opinion.

2-5 POLLS AND PREDICTING ELECTIONS

When it comes to predicting elections, how accurate are the pollsters? Even polls that are correctly executed do not always predict the actual Election Day winner. Polls taken at the same time sometimes show conflicting numbers. Occasionally the numbers swing wildly over a short period. These characteristics do not necessarily mean the polls are defective, but they do require explanation.

National Preelection Polls

The media tend to attribute more accuracy to preelection polls than even the best-designed polls can possibly deliver. First, an obvious point. Preelection polls refer to sentiment at the time they are conducted, not on Election Day. The horse race analogy commonly used to discuss elections is, in this case, appropriate. The horse that is ahead going into the stretch is not always the horse (or the candidate) that wins. But even given the overall trend, there are still "house effects"[22]—variations in survey results due to idiosyncratic ways in which survey organizations conduct their polling. For example, there is surprisingly great variation in the way the candidate choice question is asked in presidential elections.[23] Thus, we frequently find the polls at some variance with one another during the campaign due to question wording effects. In fact, in an analysis of preelection polls in 1996, Erikson and Wlezien (1999) show most of the movement in that election, a subject of much interpretation by the popular media, is nothing more than survey error—due to house effects and routine sampling error.

Figure 2.1 displays the final vote predictions (as percentage point lead for the winner) for the six presidential elections, 1980–2000, along with the actual vote margins. Over these six elections, the average range between the most pro-Republican error and the most pro-Democratic error in the final readings is seven points. Happily for the pollsters, the actual margin is typically near the center of the observed range in the polls. In some instances, most of the polls systemically miss the target, evidently because their final polls are not swift enough to fully capture last-minute swings. In 2000, all polls accurately detected the late surge to Gore, even though not all foresaw Gore's capture of the popular vote plurality after trailing in the polls for much of the campaign.

Nevertheless, the reason why the polls can differ so much over the course of the campaign, up to and including the weekend before the election, merits explanation. Typically, 15 percent or more of the electorate is undecided during a presidential campaign (the figure is much higher for lower-level races), winding down to 5 to 8 percent a few days before the balloting. Survey houses differ in the way they handle these undecideds.[24] While common sense might dictate a simple reporting of candidate preferences plus undecideds, most media polls do not follow that strategy. If voters claim to be unsure, they are pressed in a follow-up question to indicate which candidate they "lean to." Voters who maintain they are really undecided must be quite firm in their conviction in the face of pressure to make a choice. The inevitable result of this strategy is a sizable swing in candidate preferences, mostly accounted for by those forced to make a choice when their initial reaction was undecided (Crespi 1988; Moore 1992b).

Another practice common to media polls is allocating the undecideds to one candidate or the other. If the undecideds are not split, there is an implicit assumption that either they will not vote or will vote in proportion to those who have decided. As one approaches the election, there is often a momentum that favors one of the candidates—the undecideds do not split 50/50. This flow of the undecideds was one reason Truman beat Dewey (the last Gallup Poll showed that 19 percent of the electorate was undecided). It is also the reason that Richard Nixon barely squeaked out a win of less than 1 percent over Hubert Humphrey in 1968, when the polls had shown Nixon with a 15-point lead in the final weeks of the campaign. And it is the reason Ronald Reagan soundly defeated Jimmy Carter in 1980, when polls showed the contest to be very close, and why Ross Perot performed better in 1992 and 1996 than almost all preelection polls indicated.

If undecideds in preelection polls do not split evenly on election day, how, then, is one to allocate them before the election? There is no one correct answer for all circumstances. Sometimes the undecideds are reported as just that—"undecided." However, the poll will then underestimate the percentage of the

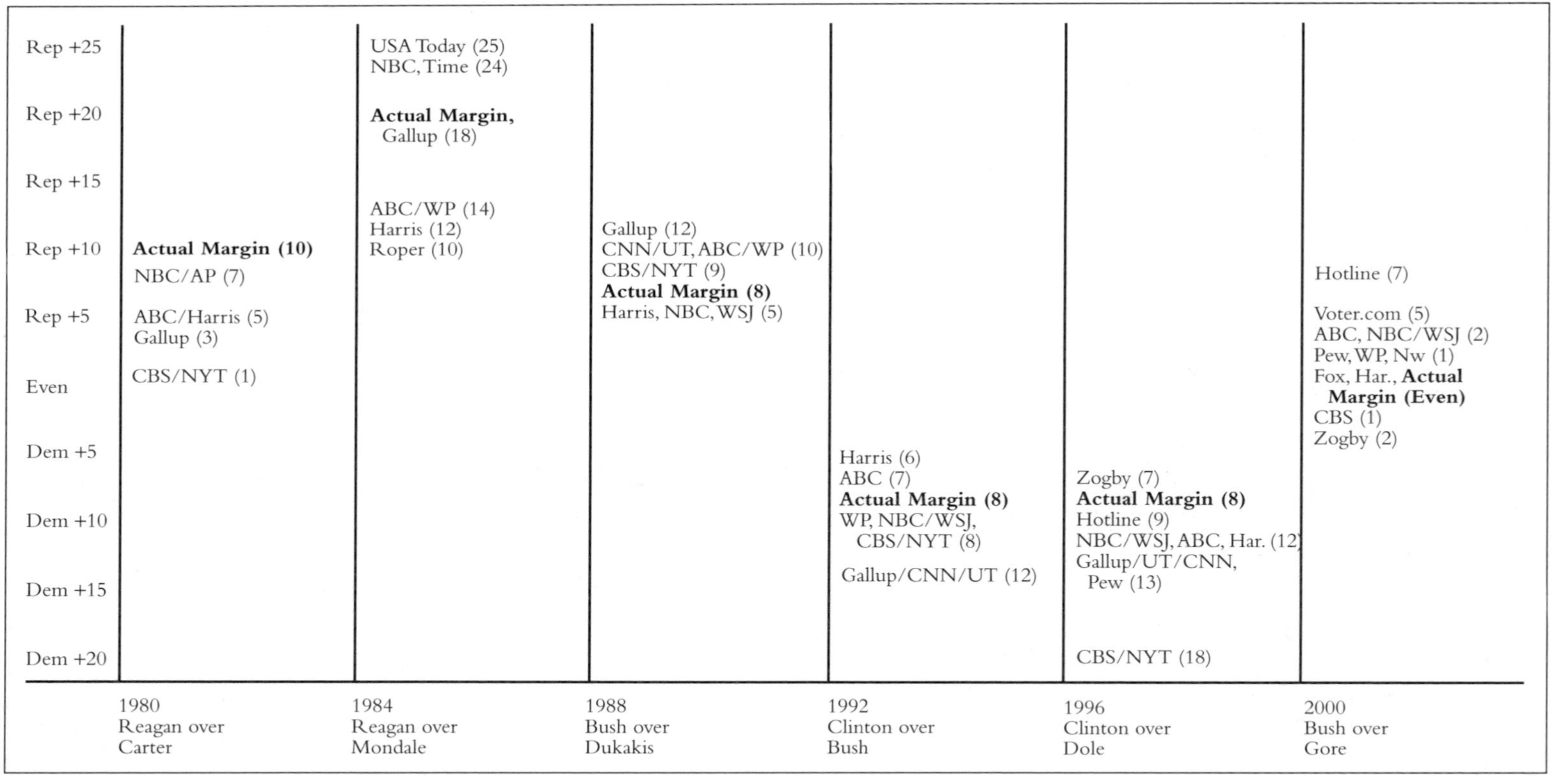

Figure 2.1 Candidate margins in final preelection polls by survey house. *Sources:* Michael R. Kagay, "Why Even Well-Designed Polls Can Disagree," in Thomas Mann and Gary Orren, eds. Media Polls in American Politics (Washington, D.C.: Brookings, 1992); Robert M. Worcester, "A View from Britain: You Can Do Better," *Public Perspective* 4 (Nov./Dec. 1992); *Public Perspective* 8 (Dec./Jan. 1997): 52 (corrected table); Michael Traugott, "Assessing Poll Performance in the 2000 Campaign," *AAPOR News* (Winter 2001).

Har = Harris, NW = *Newsweek*, NYT = *New York Times*, UT = *USA Today*, WP = *Washington Post*, WSJ = *Wall Street Journal*.

Margin	1980 Reagan over Carter	1984 Reagan over Mondale	1988 Bush over Dukakis	1992 Clinton over Bush	1996 Clinton over Dole	2000 Bush over Gore
Rep +25		USA Today (25) NBC, Time (24)				
Rep +20		**Actual Margin,** Gallup (18)				
Rep +15						
Rep +10	**Actual Margin (10)** NBC/AP (7)	ABC/WP (14) Harris (12) Roper (10)	Gallup (12) CNN/UT, ABC/WP (10) CBS/NYT (9)			Hotline (7)
Rep +5	ABC/Harris (5) Gallup (3)		**Actual Margin (8)** Harris, NBC, WSJ (5)			
Even	CBS/NYT (1)					Voter.com (5) ABC, NBC/WSJ (2) Pew, WP, Nw (1) Fox, Har, **Actual Margin (Even)** CBS (1) Zogby (2)
Dem +5				Harris (6) ABC (7) **Actual Margin (8)** WP, NBC/WSJ, CBS/NYT (8)	Zogby (7) **Actual Margin (8)** Hotline (9) NBC/WSJ, ABC, Har. (12)	
Dem +10				Gallup/CNN/UT (12)	Gallup/UT/CNN, Pew (13)	
Dem +15					CBS/NYT (18)	
Dem +20						

vote going to a candidate who has momentum. Sometimes undecided respondents are asked to rate candidates on a 0–10 scale. The undecideds are then allocated to the candidate they like best. If there is a tie on that question, party identification is used to assign the undecideds to a candidate.[25] Other polls exclude the undecideds altogether and base their preelection forecasts only on those voters willing to make a choice.[26] In 1992 the Gallup Poll, in particular, engaged in questionable practices in assigning the undecideds. On the weekend before the election, it assigned all the undecideds in its tracking poll to Clinton, causing Clinton's lead to grow from 2 points on Friday to 12 points on Monday. Gallup made this decision based on electoral history, which suggested that most undecideds in a presidential election vote for the challenger. But in 1992, rather than moving to Clinton, the undecideds moved to another challenger, Ross Perot (Morin 1992).

Allocating undecideds in a contest that pits a black candidate against a white candidate causes particular problems, and polls in a number of races have greatly overestimated the proportion of the vote going to the black candidate. Studies of a number of such races now suggest the best strategy is simply to assign all the undecided voters (who normally are almost entirely white) to the white candidate. What seems to be operating is a cross-pressure in which some white Democrats are reluctant to vote for a black candidate and declare to pollsters that they are undecided. On Election Day, however, they vote Republican (Morin 1991; Davis 1997).

Perhaps the most fundamental problem with pre-Election Day polls as predictors is an inability to define the population properly. Recall that a random sample must be drawn from a finite population. However, it is impossible to precisely define the Election Day population. Only about one-half of adult Americans vote in presidential elections. No one has yet determined a method that predicts with great accuracy who will vote (Daves 2000). Yet it is those Election Day voters who constitute the population, not adult Americans or even registered voters. In a preelection survey in 1996, the Pew Research Center asked a national sample of those over eighteen if they were "absolutely certain," "fairly certain," or "not certain" to vote in the upcoming election for president.[27] Here are the results:

Absolutely certain	69%
Fairly certain	18
Not certain/unsure	13
	100%

Actual turnout in 1996 was about 49 percent.

Screens are of consequence for poll results, in part because among the eligible electorate, Republicans are more likely to vote than Democrats. The tougher the screen in terms of weeding out potential nonvoters, the greater the support for Republican candidates. For example, in surveys taken in 1992 between August 26 and August 31, a *Washington Post*/ABC News poll had Bill Clinton leading the first President Bush by 19 percent, while a Harris poll had

Clinton ahead by only two percentage points. The *Washington Post* poll used an easy "registered voter" screen—that is, the interviewer simply asked the respondent if he or she was registered. The Harris poll used a battery of "tough" screens to identify "likely voters" and weed out nonvoters. While the lesson may seem to be that tough screens are always better, consider the difficulty of predicting who will vote and who will not if the survey is conducted, say, two months before the election. As the election approaches, the accuracy of pollsters' voting screens increases.

To adjust their preelection samples for nonvoting, pollsters first ask respondents whether they are registered and then ignore the choices of the unregistered. Registered respondents are asked a set of questions designed to measure their likelihood of voting. Pollsters use one of two methods at this stage. By the cutoff method, they divide registered respondents into those more and less likely to vote (above or below the cutoff value of voting likelihood) and then count the preferences only of the most likely. (For instance, if they anticipate a 60 percent turnout, they count the preferences of the 60 percent most likely to vote.) By the probable electorate method, the pollster weights registered respondents by their likelihood of voting. For instance, the preferences of a voter estimated at 30 percent likely to vote would be weighted only 0.30 as much as a certain voter. Which method is better is a matter of debate (Hugick and Molyneux 1993; Erikson 1993; Ferree 1993; Dawes 2000). The important point is that the type of screen and its application can have an important consequence for a poll result.[28]

It is, by the way, the use of screens to define likely voters (plus weighting factors) that allows a pollster working for Democratic candidate Smith to say his client is ahead while the pollster working for Republican candidate Jones says her client is ahead. Neither has "faked" the numbers; rather, they disagree on the probable composition of Election Day voters. The Republican pollster sees a big turnout among affluent whites; the Democratic pollster sees an atypically high minority turnout. As one prominent pollster observes:

> I think there is a little bit of Julia Child in every pollster. There is an impulse to cook things in a way most favorable to [your] candidate. People do not want to carry bad news. So there is a tendency, if you're a Democratic pollster, to weight black respondents at their proportion of registered voters even though there is a lot of historic data that the black turnout is disproportionately lower.[29]

State-Level Preelection Polls

National polls are only the tip of the polling iceberg. For every national poll predicting a presidential election there is at least one poll predicting the presidential vote in some particular state. And pollsters actively survey state electorates for important races such as for governor and U.S. senator. Election polls are found for important local races as well.

Although perhaps not always conducted up the standards of the best national polls, the track record of state polls is quite good. Consider their performance in the 2002 midterm election. Of 159 state polls for governor or U.S. senator conducted in the final two weeks of the campaign, the average margin of error was a mere 2.4 percentage points. Moreover, the final poll of the campaign accurately predicted the winner in fifty of the fifty-seven contests where state polls were conducted in the final two weeks.[30] Only in one state (Georgia) did polling fail badly, presumably due to an undetected last-minute Republican surge. Like national polls, state polls are far from perfect, and the occasional misprediction captures our attention. But in general, the pollsters who sample opinion at the state level perform their job well.

Election–Day Exit Polls

An important innovation in opinion polling is the *exit poll*. Representative precincts are selected, and voters are interviewed immediately after leaving the voting booth. Exit polls are commissioned by the news media so they can project the winner soon after the polls close on Election Day and report on the demographic and issue correlates of the vote choice.

From 1976 to 1988, the three major broadcast networks each conducted their own national exit polls. There was often a lively competition among them to see which would first to call the winner. The expense of this operation led the networks, along with CNN and the Associated Press, to pool resources and create a single polling unit, Voter News Service (VNS), which conducted exit polling from 1992 through the 2002 midterm election. (For a discussion of exit poll methodology, see Merkle and Edelman 2000.)

In 2000, calamity struck when VNS overestimated the Gore vote in Florida, contributing to an early call by the networks that Al Gore had carried the state (and seemingly the nation).[31] Although VNS interviewed 1,818 respondents in the Florida exit poll, the sampling error was not less than 2.5 percent, as one might conclude from Table 2.1. The reason is those 1,818 respondents did not constitute a simple random sample; rather, they were a sample randomly selected from only forty-five precincts. The true sampling error was, therefore, a good deal larger (Frankovic 2003; Biemer et al. 2003).

The 2002 election was the final blow to the Voter News Service. VNS was unable to reliably process exit poll data due to flaws in its analysis software, and exit polls were not reported on election night. The owners of VNS then dissolved the consortium and contracted with a new service for election night exit polls, the National Election Pool, operated by two polling industry veterans.[32] However, there is still only one exit poll on election night. With all networks relying on the same data, it remains a distinct possibility that the consensus winners they project may turn up as losers the following day.

Exit polls are usually able project the winner of a statewide election by 3:00 P.M., even though the polls do not normally close until 7:00 P.M. The media have, however, agreed not to release the results of exit polling in a specific state until the polls in that state have closed. But when the winner is forecast in the East Coast and Midwestern states in a presidential election, the polls are still open for several hours on the West Coast due to different time zones.

The polls were still open in eleven states when CBS News first projected that Vice President Bush had won the 1988 presidential election (*New York Times*, Nov. 10 1989, 17). In 1980, Jimmy Carter actually conceded the election to Ronald Reagan based on network projections while voting was still in progress in the West. In 2000, the networks called Florida for Al Gore while the polls were still open in the northern Florida panhandle—an area of strong Bush support. It is claimed by some that this mistaken early call based on exit poll data may have discouraged some Bush voters from going to the polls in Florida— perhaps crucial in an election decided by 537 votes.

The effect on West Coast voters of learning Reagan had won the presidency before their polls closed has been the subject of lively controversy. As in Florida, the claim is that certain voters in the West, having heard the election winner projected by the networks, were less likely to go to the polls. While it is true these West Coast voters could not affect the outcome of the presidential contest, many other contests on the ballot could be affected by a drop-off in voter participation. Research on this question is mixed. Based on a study of the 1980 election, John Jackson concluded that the exit polls and Carter's early concession resulted in a turnout decline of 6 to 12 percent—to the detriment of down-the-ticket Democrats—in those states where the polls were still open.[33] The data show conclusively that those who had heard the early projections were more likely to abstain from voting than were those who had not heard these projections. However, this simple relationship raises the question of cause and effect. Was the turnout differential due to those hearing the projection not voting? Or is the fact that those who did not hear the projection voted in greater numbers than those did hear explained by their being occupied at the voting booth when the projections were made?

There have been many calls for the media to voluntarily restrain from projecting the winner until voting is finished in all states. Congress has held hearings on the subject, and there are numerous calls for legislation requiring the polls to stay open for the same hours in the contiguous forty-eight states. Some states have tried to make it difficult for exit pollsters to do their work by restricting how close they can get to the voting booth. Such laws have been invalidated by federal courts. The networks argue that any government-imposed limitations on exit polls would constitute censorship and violate the First Amendment.

2-6 CONCLUSION

For more than sixty years, public opinion polls have been part of the political landscape, and there is every sign that their influence is growing. While the scientific pollsters have an admirable track record, it must be recognized that polls are imperfect predictors. Even the best preelection poll is based on a probability model that on rare occasions can go wrong due to an unlucky dose of sampling error. Preelection polls can also go wrong when the behavior they are sampling changes underneath their feet. The electorate's choice is often volatile in the days before an election, and the pollsters race to catch up by means of polling until the last minute. Polls can go wrong because people are increasingly likely to refuse requests to be interviewed. And polls can go wrong when they miscalculate which eligible voters will actually show up to vote. Under the circumstances, contemporary polls do a surprisingly good job at predicting elections. One reason may be that pollsters know they must do a good job because they lose credibility and their jobs if they do not.

In this book, our central interest is in polls regarding public opinion, not election outcomes. A challenge is that unlike with election polls, we do not know for sure how close opinion polls are to the correct result. Unless the target opinion is the outcome of an initiative or referendum election, opinion polls lack direct validation. And opinion polls are sensitive to matters of question framing and question wording. The key to understanding polls is a realization that the numbers do not speak for themselves; they require interpretation. Among the keys to that interpretation are how the sample was selected, how the questions were phrased, an appreciation for the context in which the survey was conducted, and a comparison to other surveys taken at the same time or an analysis of trends over time.

NOTES

1. Survey by Princeton University Research Associates, January 3–March 26, 2001.
2. Strictly speaking, in terms of statistical theory, if the poll were repeated an infinite number of times, in 95 percent of the trials the result would be between 54 and 60 percentage points. We are assuming simple random sampling, which is a useful simplification of Gallup's sampling procedure.
3. The exception is when the population itself is quite small (say, less than 10,000). With a small population, a correction can be made to properly lower the sampling error. Table 2.1 shows that a sample of 384 drawn from a very large population has a sampling error of 5 percent. However, if our barrel contained only 1,000 marbles and we randomly drew 384, then, instead of a sampling error of 5 percent, the true sampling error would be 0.785×5.0 percent or 3.9 percent. The sampling error correction for small populations is the square root of N-n/N-1 where N is the population size and n is the sample size (Wallis and Roberts 1956, 369).
4. One's suspicions are aroused, however, if polls on the same topic at about the same time with similarly worded questions show quite different results.
5. In 1948, Gallup had Dewey at 49.5 percent and Truman at 44.5 percent (with 6 percent going to minor-party candidates). The vote, in fact, was Truman 49.5 percent and Dewey 45.1 percent, with others getting 5.4 percent. The Roper poll in 1948 was further off the mark than Gallup. Roper had Dewey at 52.2 percent and Truman at 37.1 percent (with 10.7 percent going to minor-party candidates).
6. In *The Superpollsters*, David Moore (1992a) reports on interviews with a number of those who worked as field staff for Gallup during the days he used quota samples and provides an interesting firsthand account of the hazards and biases of allowing the interviewers leeway in selecting respondents.
7. For a more detailed discussion of sampling by the NES or GSS, see the sampling appendix usually included with each codebook.

8. Interviewers usually ask for the youngest male or female because they are the least likely to be home. However, if a sufficient number meeting specified age and sex distributions are met, interviewers will then ask for the oldest male or the oldest female.

9. Among some groups, the proportion of unlisted phone numbers is quite high. For those under thirty-four years of age, it is 51 percent; for blacks, it is 55 percent; for Hispanics, it is 58 percent; and for renters, it is 54 percent. These estimates are from *Genesys News* (spring 1996), published by Genesys Sampling Systems of Fort Washington, Pennsylvania, and *The Frame* (March 1993), published by Survey Sampling of Westport, Connecticut. Both are commercial sampling firms.

10. Actual formulas, however, are a good deal more complex. Not every unanswered call is included in the denominator, depending on the survey. A detailed discussion of response rates can be found at the Web site for the American Association for Public Opinion Research http://www.aapor.org.

11. While the overall response rate for the Survey of Consumer Attitudes between 1977 and 1999 was 70 percent, it dropped to 66 percent in the period between 1995 and 1999.

12. The Pew Research Center conducted two surveys of 1,000 adults, one rigorous and the other less rigorous. The rigorous survey spanned an eight-week period. In addition, respondents were sent advance letters announcing the survey and offered a small monetary gift for participating; those refusing were recontacted to persuade them to participate. The response rate was 79 percent. The less rigorous survey was conducted over five days and had a response rate of 65 percent. The response rate of 65 percent for the less rigorous survey is still, however, a good deal higher than many critics contend is currently the case for atypical media surveys. Almost all major polling organizations refuse to disclose their response rates, so the exact response rates are difficult to know.

13. Reported in Survey Sampling International, *The Frame*, March 2003.

14. *The Frame*, March 1993. The other states falling below 90 percent are New Mexico, Arkansas, West Virginia, and Kentucky.

15. Another recent innovation is to replace with autodialers using recorded questions. The allure of automatic polls is the ability to obtain many interviews at low cost. One flaw is that they offer no control over the person in the household (a child? a visitor?) who actually answers the telephone and punches a set of replies. And it is not in everybody's nature to respond to automated surveys. Needless to say, the results of automated polls cannot be taken as accurate representation of public sentiment.

16. The evidence indicates that using only "agree" or "favor" in the stem of a question often makes no difference—for example, "Do you favor the death penalty?" as contrasted to "Do you favor or oppose the death penalty?" Nevertheless, good survey practice dictates that questions be formally balanced, as in the second example (Schuman and Presser 1996, 181).

17. A 1986 *Time*/Yankelovich Survey, cited in "Opinion Roundup," *Public Opinion* (Sept./Oct. 1986): 32.

18. Reported in the *Houston Chronicle*, Oct. 8, 1977, 3.

19. In the case of the Perot poll, CNN conducted a poll in which half the sample was asked the Perot version of the question (80 percent said "yes") and the other half was asked a more neutral version, which read "Should laws be passed to prohibit interest groups from contributing to campaigns, or do groups have the

right to contribute to candidates they support?" In this latter version, only 40 percent said laws preventing contributions should be passed (Kolbert 1993).

20. Another example of this type of survey is those done by pop psychologist Shere Hite. Hite has published a number of books on the sexual and romantic relationships of men and women. For *Women and Love: A Cultural Revolution in Progress* (Hite 1987), she mailed out 100,000 questionnaires to women selected from the mailing lists of a variety of women's organizations. She received 4,500 responses (4.5 percent). Given the self-selection problem (women most likely to respond were those who had unsatisfactory romantic relationships), some of the "findings" were quite surprising. For example, Hite reported that 75 percent of the women in her study married more than five years had extramarital affairs. A survey by ABC News/ *Washington Post*, using conventional sampling methods, found 7 percent of women reported extramarital affairs. The ABC poll was reported in the *Houston Chronicle* (Oct. 27, 1987, sec. 1, p. 2).

21. Simultaneously with the publicized straw poll, CBS also conducted another "scientific" poll intended for use on the program. This poll was a panel called back from a survey of 2,800 respondents that CBS/ *New York Times* had conducted two weeks previously. These respondents were also provided with a (different) toll-free number and asked to call back immediately after the State of the Union address. The response rate from the original panel was only 43 percent, casting considerable doubt on the validity of the "scientific" survey used in the program (Frankovic 1992).

22. For a good analysis of house effects in preelection polling, see Crespi (1988).

23. For a list of the way the major polling firms ask this question, see Crespi (1988, ch. 5).

24. The option of "unsure" is usually not offered to respondents. Rather, they are asked to choose between or among the candidates (Moore 1992b).

25. This practice of pushing undecideds to make a choice is defended by Frank Newport, editor-in-chief of the Gallup Poll, in the following words: "[I]f pollsters allow voters the explicit option to call themselves 'unsure' about their vote, the number of reported undecideds would jump. All major polling organizations, however, eschew this structure because it would make polling less valuable and less interesting. Most voters, when asked in which direction they lean, have a preference and are willing to express it. It would not be very instructive . . . to allow large numbers of voters to claim they are undecided through the election season. We would miss the dynamics of change, we would be unable to tell how well the candidates were doing in response to events, and publicly released polls would be out of synchronization with private, campaign polls" (Letter to the editor, *New York Times*, Nov. 6, 1992, sec. A).

26. Irving Crespi, "Letter to the Editor," *New York Times* (Sept. 7, 1988, sec. A).

27. The Pew Research Center for the People and the Public. News Release (Aug. 2, 1996).

28. The same is true for the number of callbacks. If a respondent cannot be located on the first call, it is standard practice to make another two or three attempts to contact the person before replacement. Research by Gallup has shown that the more callbacks used by a survey house, the more Republican the sample. In other words, substitution of the appropriate respondent by a new respondent biases the sample in a Democratic direction. This finding means that "overnight" surveys, in which only one call is made to a specific person, may have some serious biases (Cantril 1992, 102).

29. The quote is from Harrison Hickman, of Hickman and McWheter, a polling firm that works predominantly for Democrats. See Edward Walsh, "Polls Are Telling Us More, But Are They Telling It Like It Is?"(*Washington Post*, Apr. 13, 1987, nat'l. ed., 37).
30. Press release, "Polling Review Board Analysis of the 2002 Election Polls," National Council on Public Polls, December 19, 2002.
31. For a detailed report on what went wrong with the vote projection in Florida in 2000, see the report of the hearing before the House Committee on Energy and Commerce at:
    http://energycommerence.house.gov/107/hearings/02142001Hearing216/print.htm.
32. Warren Mitofsky of Mitofsky International and Joseph Lenski of Edison Media Research.
33. For arguments that exit polls do affect turnout, see Jackson (1983) and Delli Carpini (1984). For a study arguing there is no effect on early projections, see Epstein and Strom (1984).

3 | Microlevel Opinion: The Psychology of Opinion-Holding

$\mathbf{I}$n theory, democracy works best when the people actively attend to public affairs—ideally, when they direct policymakers toward the problems most deserving of attention and actively monitor their deliberations. In this best of all worlds, people might disagree with one another, but their opinions are soundly reasoned and logically consistent. Their preferences transcend conflict among self-interested parties to reflect a concern for the general welfare.

In actuality, public opinion falls considerably short of this ideal. As early survey researchers explored the nature of public opinion, they found several reasons for pessimism. For instance, respondents often express preferences so thoughtless as to be arguably too shallow for consideration as meaningful opinions. The opinions that people do hold sometimes seem like unconnected preferences in no logical relationship to one another. Where predictability exists, opinions often flow from disturbing prejudices rather than thoughtful consideration. Often it appears that political leaders find it all too easy to manipulate political symbols so as to fool a politically gullible mass public.

Although recent discussions of the capabilities of mass opinion vary in theoretical perspectives, they find some significant reason for optimism (compare Popkin 1991; Page and Shapiro 1992; Zaller 1992; Miller and Shanks 1996; Delli Carpini and Keeter 1996; Fishkin 1996; and Kuklinski, Quirk, Jerit, and Rich 2001). Many ordinary people stay politically informed and can be considered politically sophisticated. Actually, it may seem remarkable that people hold political opinions at all. Why, we might ask, do people bother to develop and maintain political opinions when the time spent on politics might be better devoted to dealing with matters that affect their private lives? As most of our political involvement is as passive spectators watching helplessly on the sidelines, why do we not only pay attention but invest time and effort developing opinions? Indeed, a strong argument can be made that if the main purpose of following politics is to affect policy outcomes, staying informed and thinking about politics is, from a cost-benefit perspective, an irrational investment (Downs 1958).

Because many people are sufficiently political to have ignored such advice, political opinions must be of some benefit to the people who hold them. It has long been recognized that holding political opinions serves several positive psychological functions (Smith et al. 1956). Opinions can serve a social function—for instance, when people learn to agree with the prevailing views within their preferred social groups. Opinions can serve a direct psychological function—when political opinions follow as an extension of personality. A frequently cited example is the person who seeks an ordered and disciplined personal environment being more susceptible to authoritarian political ideologies (Altmeyer 1997). Opinions can also promote economic self-interest—when people develop political opinions consistent with their economic standing. Sometimes people develop elaborate ideologies to rationalize their economic status, as when rich people adopt a conservative economic ideology to justify the wealth they have accumulated.

As one would expect, opinions often reflect self-interest—for example, when the rich adopt more conservative economic positions than the poor (see chapter 7). But the pull of self-interest is far from universal. People often derive opinions from values that have little if anything to do with obvious self-interest (Sears and Funk 1990). One example of an attitude that does not reflect self-interest is concern for the plight of others; others include nationalism and racial resentment (Kinder and Winter 2001). Even economic interests are not always subject to obvious self-interest calculations. In a study of school districts affected differently by court-ordered financial equalization, property-rich districts had to pay more school taxes and property-poor districts had to pay less. While attitudes toward this decision generally reflected how one's district was affected, many liberals who had to pay more taxes favored the equalization and many conservatives who had to pay less opposed the measure—contrary to their economic self-interest (Tedin 1994b).

While sometimes it seems that people arbitrarily generate opinions, those opinions usually have reasons behind them. Consider opinions about the issue of whether the government should spend more on welfare for the disadvantaged. People who favor less spending argue the principles of limited government and self-reliance, or they voice concern about people falling into a welfare "trap." People who favor more spending cite egalitarian arguments and express sympathy for the immediate needs of the poor (Feldman and Zaller 1992).[1] Abstract values such as egalitarianism and liberal/conservative ideology are important to politics because they cause people to have opinions when they have no direct stake in a particular issue (Bawn 1999). For example, many Americans living in small, homogeneous Midwestern farming communities have opinions about bilingual education. These opinions have political consequences, even though the lives of the opinion-holders are almost certainly not touched by the issue.

This chapter examines public opinion at the microlevel of the individual citizen, usually when observed as a survey respondent. We first examine the extent of political knowledge and the depth of opinion-holding. We then explore the core values and beliefs that sometimes hold opinions together. For politically sophisticated respondents, it is possible to summarize core political values in terms of position on the liberal-conservative ideological spectrum. Finally, we explore a source of political orientation adhered to by sophisticates and nonsophisticates alike—that is, the respondent's party identification or relative allegiance to the Democratic or Republican party.

3-1 POLITICAL ATTENTION AND OPINION-HOLDING

When public opinion is reported on some issue, underlying the division of opinion is considerable diversity in terms of attention and caring about the matter at hand. At one extreme we find highly attentive citizens who follow public affairs closely and hold informed (if diverse) opinions regarding even complicated questions of public policy. These citizens vote regularly, and their votes are based on issue preferences that have been well thought out. Moreover, they make their views known to elected leaders, even during the time intervals between political campaigns.

At the other extreme we find citizens who can be best described as "apolitical." Virtually disengaged from politics, they ordinarily pay no attention to the political happenings reported in newspapers and on television, and they do not vote. Their interests in politics is perked up only by unusual events, such as the threat of war or a political sex scandal. But by being passive, they collectively forfeit their influence on policy outcomes.

Most people fall between these two extremes, and their attention to the world of government and politics varies considerably. Cognitive ability or general intelligence is certainly an important factor for understanding politics and holding political opinions (Delli Carpini and Keeter 1996; Joslyn 2003). But we should not assume that when people are politically inattentive they lack the mental capacity to follow public affairs, or that politics is too complicated for ordinary folks to figure out. Whether one follows politics closely is largely a matter of personal taste, similar to the choice of whether to follow certain sports, like football and baseball. And just as sporting events are more fascinating and comprehensible to regular followers, so too is following politics easier for those who have invested time and effort learning about the political world. For those who choose not to invest in an understanding of politics, following political events and holding informed opinions is a considerably more difficult task (Zaller 1992).

Just as it is misleading to describe public opinion by focusing on the typical citizen, it can be misleading to assume that a citizen's attention level regarding one aspect of politics extends to all others. People vary not only in their taste for public affairs but also in the aspects of public affairs that engage their interest most. For instance, some people focus on national politics but ignore their local political environment, while others do the reverse. Some people are issue serialists who become members of the attentive public only when issues dear to their interests enter the public agenda. On some issues, they hold strong opinions and make their views known; on others, they react with indifference.

Political Knowledge

In March 1999, armed forces of the North Atlantic Treaty Organization (NATO) conducted an intensive bombing raid on the nation of Serbia in an attempt to halt "ethnic cleansing" by Serbs in the predominantly Albanian province of Kosovo. Prior to the bombing, it is safe to say, most Americans had never heard of Kosovo. However, within a few days of the bombing, a Pew Research Center poll (29 Mar. 1999) found that 43 percent of Americans were able to identify Kosovo as a province of Yugoslavia located in central Europe. This was a remarkable amount of learning for a nation often scolded for its lack of geographical knowledge. But of course this event was unusual. Other political events can attract near universal attention, but only if they contain the necessary elements of drama—the United States going to war, a hostage drama, or a sex scandal. Complicated political matters are often ignored by much of the general public. For example, when a controversial presidential appointment consumes the attention of Washingtonians "inside the Beltway," polls suggest that most Americans tune out. With rare exceptions, even the best-known Cabinet members, Supreme Court justices, senators, and congressional representatives are anonymous to most Americans.[2]

A common assumption in American political discourse is that democracy functions best when its citizens are politically informed. Since the 1930s, more than 2,000 factual pop quiz political knowledge questions were asked of the American public (Delli Carpini and Keeter 1996). Table 3.1 presents a sampling of factual questions across a variety of issue domains from a variety of polling sources. The table suggests a level of public ignorance that is shocking when observed for the first time.

Although the items presented in Table 3.1 are taken from a variety of years, there has been little change over time in the level of political knowledge. Americans are no better informed about political matters than they were fifty years ago. For example, the table shows that 50 percent could recall the name of their congressional representative in 1942 compared to 40 percent in 1997. Given the rise in levels of education and the greater availability of political media, many find this lack of improvement puzzling. Perhaps there are countertrends that cancel out improvements in education and technology, or there may be inherent limits to how much political information the public can absorb.

Public knowledge *does* improve when an issue is consistently in the news. U.S. involvement in Nicaragua's civil war in the 1980s provides a case in point. In 1983, only 29 percent of American adults knew that the United States backed the rebels and not the government in Nicaragua. By mid-1986, after years of headlines about the controversial funding of the Contra rebels, this figure had increased to 46 percent. Following the publicity of the Iran-Contra

TABLE 3.1	Level of Information Among the Adult U.S. Population		
Percentage		**Year**	**Source**
96	Know United States is a member of the United Nations	1985	D&K
96	Know president's term is four years	1989	D&K
89	Know Republicans have a House majority	1996	NES
88	Know Cuba is communist	1988	D&K
74	Know governor of home state	1989	D&K
72	Know states cannot prohibit abortion	1989	D&K
70	Know there are 50 stars on the American flag	1998	Marist
63	Know party of congressional representative	1995	IRC
58	Know Roe v. Wade is about abortion rights	1989	D&K
57	Know how congressional representative voted on Gulf War	1991	D&K
54	Can identify Newt Gingrich as Speaker of the House	1995	IRC
50	Can name president of Russia (Yeltsin)	1994	T-M
48	Can name Secretary of State (Powell)	2002	Pew
47	Know congressman's vote on Clinton impeachment	1999	WP
40	Know name of congressional representative	1997	Luntz
37	Know job of Yasser Arafat	1988	NES
36	Know how many senators needed to convict president	1999	Gallup
34	Can name the secretary of state (Baker)	1990	GSS
33	Can name the secretary of state (Albright)	2000	Gallup
32	Can locate Vietnam on a map	1988	D&K
31	Know what affirmative action is	1985	D&K
29	Can name Secretary of Defense (Rumsfeld)	2002	Pew
27	Know that more is spent on Medicare than foreign aid	1995	IRC
22	Know Senate passed Balanced Budget Act	1995	IRC
12	Know who presided over Clinton impeachment trial	1999	Pew
08	Can name chief justice of U.S. Supreme Court	1987	CBS/NYT

Sources: NES (National Election Studies), D&K (Delli Carpini and Keeter 1996), Luntz (Luntz Research), IRC (IRC Survey Research Group), WP (*Washington Post*), Pew (Pew Center for People and the Press), T-M (*Times-Mirror*), CBS/NYT (CBSNews/*New York Times*), GSS (General Social Survey).

scandal, the figure "soared" all the way to 54 percent in mid-1987 and 66 percent in early 1989 (Sobel 1989). After many years of publicity, a majority of Americans had finally absorbed the most rudimentary facts about American involvement in Nicaragua. On the other hand, years of controversy about whether the United States should support the Contras evidently went over the heads of almost half of all Americans.

The most shocking aspect of the public's ignorance may be people's inability to recall the names of leading political officeholders. Some examples are included in Table 3.1. Over two-thirds of the public can name their state's governor, but few can immediately name key Washington leaders. When the Republicans gained control of the House of Representatives in 1995, Speaker Newt Gingrich became a rival to the president for the center of the political stage—but he became no household name. At the height of his political power in 1995, only 54 percent could identify him as House speaker.

Less than a year after 9/11 made foreign affairs salient in a way they had not been before, less than half of American adults could name Colin Powell as secretary of state, and less than a third could name Donald Rumsfeld as secretary of defense. The problem must be selective inattention to the details of politics. Fewer people identified Rumsfeld than in a 1998 Pew survey could name all four main characters on the TV show *Seinfeld*. Fewer identified Powell than in 1998 knew that Seinfeld's first name is Jerry.

People have an easier time recognizing celebrities than identifying them by job titles. For example, after 9/11 vast majorities could offer opinions about Powell or Rumsfeld even though some needed to be reminded who they were by an identifying prompt. But recognition is not always widespread. When people are asked their opinion about specific Supreme Court justices, the majority of survey respondents are likely to admit to not knowing enough to offer an opinion. Even the chief justice generally escapes widespread public evaluation. In January 2001, shortly after ruling that Bush won the 2000 election and two years after presiding over Clinton's impeachment hearings, Chief Justice Rehnquist was the subject of an NBC/*Wall Street Journal* poll. The division was 24 percent favorable and 15 percent negative, with the rest claiming to be neutral or not knowing who Rehnquist was.

One concern about the public's low attention to politics is that policy preferences of the informed public may differ substantially from the uninformed majority. There are two ways of looking at this problem. On one hand, those who believe that informed opinion should carry greater weight can argue that poll results are contaminated by the counting of passive, uninformed opinions. On the other hand, those who believe that people should have equal influence can argue that disproportionate weight should not be given to the perhaps one-sided views of the assertive minority who make their views known (Berinsky 2002). The differences between informed and uninformed opinion that are known to exist are generally attributed to the greater education and income of those who are more knowledgeable.

We present below examples from the 2000 National Election Studies (NES) survey. For this task, we introduce a summary index of political information. We score respondents on the basis of their knowledge of candidate policy differences, which studies show to be a good measure of relevant political information (Luskin 1987; Zaller 1992). Details of this index are presented in the Appendix to this book. When we use this index, we compare voters at two information extremes. High-information respondents are the 20 percent (25 percent of voters) who correctly saw Bush to the right of Gore on five issues. Low-information respondents are the bottom 41 percent (33 percent of voters) whose knowledge of candidate differences on issues appears to be so impoverished that their evaluation of candidate positions approached the "guess" range.

Table 3.2 shows differences in opinion-holding by knowledge level in the NES survey. Generally we would expect the largest differences to be on issues where opinions are in flux. The more knowledgeable will be quicker to learn the new conventional wisdom and adjust their opinions accordingly. Thus, back in 1992 high-information respondents were more likely to favor increased aid to Russia, and in both 1992 and 1996 they were more likely to favor a reduction in defense spending than were low-information respondents. Evidently, the more knowledgeable were the first to learn that the cold war had ended and Russia was now more friend than foe. Some other issues showed modest tendencies for liberal opinion to increase with knowledge, perhaps an indication of greater acceptance of liberal social policies among the most politically sophisticated. High-information respondents tend to be more liberal on social issues such as abortion, minority rights, and the status of women. But there are exceptions. Low-information respondents are more likely to favor gun control, and they are decidedly more liberal on issues like national health insurance and increased government services.

Converting Information into Opinions

Information is the basis for (most) opinions about politics. But what is the process by which information becomes converted into opinions? One interpretation

TABLE 3.2	Opinion by Level of Political Information, 2000		
Opinion	High Information (%)	Low Information (%)	Difference (%)
Increase U.S. aid to Russia★	46	19	+27
Legalize abortions	68	55	+13
More government aid to blacks	31	21	+13
Oppose death penalty	31	25	+06
Support equal role for women	93	87	+06
Reduce defense spending	28	26	+02
Favor gun control	55	63	-08
Favor tougher environmental regulations	65	77	-12
Support national health insurance	42	63	-21
Increase domestic spending	46	78	-22
Favor isolationism in foreign affairs	12	40	-28
Liberal (of ideological identifiers)	44	41	+03
Democratic (of party identifiers)	52	70	-18

Source: National Election Studies, 2000. Coefficients represent percentages among opinion-holders. For measure of high- and low-income respondents, see the Appendix.

★NES, 1992.

popularized by Anthony Downs (1958) in *An Economic Theory of Democracy* holds that citizens translate information into opinions using the rules of *instrumental rationality*—that is, for the issue at hand, citizens form opinions based on the personal costs and benefits that accrue to them. For example, farmers favor free trade because it opens more markets for their products.

Another approach is based on psychology, and it stresses the consequences for opinions in the way information is processed. There are two popular variations on this approach. The *online perspective* starts with the messages sent out by candidates, interest groups, the media, and others. Some of these messages are noted by citizens and, based on the information conveyed, opinions are formed or existing opinions are updated immediately online. The process is seen as a running tally, with opinions constantly being updated in response to new information. Updated opinions are then stored in long-term memory and recalled when needed (Lodge et al. 1995). The second approach is *memory based* (Zaller and Feldman 1992; Zaller 1992). Rather than a formed opinion, what is retrieved from memory is a series of considerations that favor one side of an issue or the other. A weighted average is mentally computed of the considerations that come to mind, and based on that weighted average an opinion is expressed (a more detailed explanation of this approach is presented below). Both approaches cannot be correct, at least as stated in their pure form. Online processing is particularly applicable to political campaigns, where information is relatively abundant and attitudes are accessed with some frequency. The memory-based approach helps us understand opinions where information is less plentiful, and it may be more appropriate for attitudes not accessed as regularly.

Depth of Opinion-Holding

Chapter 2 presented examples of how seemingly minor variations in the framing and wording of survey questions can provoke major variations in survey results. Such phenomena could not occur if people were not often ambivalent about their political convictions. On a given political issue, some survey respondents can call from memory long-term convictions that they have held on the particular subject. Many, however, can offer no more than the top-of-the-head casual opinions of the kind sometimes known as *doorstep opinions*. One consequence is a disturbing degree of response instability when people are interviewed more than once, in what is called a *panel survey*. Many panelists who offer opinions in successive interviews change their position from one side to the other—which is seemingly inconsistent with the traditional notion of an attitude as an enduring predisposition. The implications are important for understanding public opinion.

Table 3.3 shows examples of response turnover from a special (pilot) NES survey in 1989. The issues varied from the hotly debated (abortion, death penalty) to the technical and obscure (funding the Stealth bomber, building a new Alaska pipeline). Respondent views were measured in the summer and again in the fall of 1989. The questions were part of framing experiments in which subjects were randomly assigned different ways in which the questions

TABLE 3.3 | **Turnover of Opinion Response on Selected Issues, 1989 NES Pilot Study**

Death penalty			
		Summer 1989	
		Oppose	Favor
Fall 1989	Oppose	19%	5%
	Favor	5%	73%

Stealth bomber			
		Summer 1989	
		Oppose	Favor
Fall 1989	Oppose	41%	8%
	Favor	9%	42%

Abortion			
		Summer 1989	
		Legal	Restricted
Fall 1989	Legal	34%	5%
	Restricted	6%	53%

More welfare spending			
		Summer 1989	
		Favor	Opposed
Fall 1989	Favor	35%	11%
	Opposed	11%	43%

Affirmative action			
		Summer 1989	
		Favor	Oppose
Fall 1989	Favor	13%	8%
	Oppose	5%	74%

New Alaska oil pipeline			
		Summer 1989	
		Oppose	Favor
Fall 1989	Oppose	36%	10%
	Favor	12%	42%

More gun control			
		Summer 1989	
		Favor	Oppose
Fall 1989	Favor	59%	7%
	Oppose	13%	21%

More cooperation with Russia			
		Summer 1989	
		Favor	Oppose
Fall 1989	Favor	38%	10%
	Oppose	13%	39%

More spending to fight AIDS			
		Summer 1989	
		Favor	Oppose
Fall 1989	Favor	48%	8%
	Oppose	15%	29%

More aid to Nicaraguan Contras			
		Summer 1989	
		Oppose	Favor
Fall 1989	Oppose	49%	11%
	Favor	10%	30%

Source: National Election Studies, 1989 pilot study data. In some instances, framing of question varied with respondent and with wave.

were framed. Different subjects received different framing conditions, which sometimes also varied for the same respondent over time. Still, the exact question asking for an opinion was the same for all respondents for all issues. Respondents received no filter to encourage nonresponses, and over 90 percent offered opinions to each question.[3]

The table shows from 13 to 22 percent switching sides between interviews just a few months apart. As discussed below, analysts agree that almost all of such switching represents not true opinion change but rather some sort of response error. As one would expect, more response error appears for obscure issues such as Alaska pipelines and Stealth bombers, about which people typically do not think much, than for salient moral issues like abortion and the death penalty.

The setup of Table 3.3 enhances the observed stability because multiple respondent choices are collapsed into two alternatives. Responses appear less stable when a middle ground is included. Table 3.4 presents the abortion example again, this time with three alternatives.

Whereas in Table 3.3 the choices for restrictions on abortion were combined as one, for Table 3.4 we separate out the extreme "right-to-life" position that abortions should never be permitted or permitted only under exceptional circumstances from the more moderate or middle position that abortions "should be permitted . . . but only after the need has been clearly established." The turnover table now shows 25 percent changing their position from one survey to the next, with many respondents finding the middle position attractive. Notably, however, virtually no respondent switched from pro-choice to pro-life or vice versa.[4]

If the amount of turnover of responses to the abortion question seems high, consider that abortion positions are probably the most stable of political attitude responses, rivaled perhaps only by party identification (Converse and Markus 1979; Wetstein 1993; Green, Palmquist, and Schickler 2003). Less morally charged issues show considerably less response stability. Typical is the turnover of responses to the NES's "guaranteed living standard" question between the preelection and postelection surveys in 1984, shown in Table 3.5.

Only a minority of the respondents (40 percent) had a sufficiently firm attitude to take the same side consistently (pro/pro or con/con) in both interviews. A few (10 percent) changed sides completely from one interview to the

---

TABLE 3.4 | **Opinion Consistency on Abortion, 1989**

	Summer 1989		
Fall 1989	Never permitted, or only if rape, incest, or woman's life in danger	Other than if rape, incest, or woman's life in danger, after need established	Always permitted as a matter of personal choice
Never permitted, or only if rape, incest, or woman's life in danger	31%	6%	1%
Other than if rape, incest, or woman's life in danger, after need established	6%	12%	4%
Always permitted as a matter of personal choice	2%	5%	34%

Source: National Election Studies, 1989 pilot study.

next, and others (14 percent) took no position in either interview. The remainder (35 percent) took sides in one interview but not in the other.

The most studied patterns of response instability are from several four-year, three-wave panels as part of the NES (Converse 1964; Converse and Markus 1979). In a 1950s panel, the same respondents were interviewed at two-year intervals—in 1956, 1958, and 1960. The NES 1970s panel interviewed the same respondents in 1972, 1974, and 1976. In the 1990s, NES conducted a small panel with the same respondents interviewed in 1992, 1994, and again in 1996.

One important fact learned from the NES panel studies is that the time interval between panel waves has little bearing on the observed amount of response stability. For instance, the degrees of response turnover to questions on abortion and guaranteed living standards asked four years apart in the NES 1970s and 1990s panels are only slightly larger than the amount of response turnover shown in Tables 3.3 and 3.4 for the same issues when the same question was asked only a few months apart.

This evidence suggests that most response change does not represent true change in underlying attitudes. If people were really changing their minds frequently, long time intervals would produce greater decay of initial positions. While scholars agree that response instability generally does not indicate true attitude conversion, they disagree in what the unstable responses mean. One position, developed by Philip E. Converse, holds that people who change positions usually have no position but instead respond randomly. This "nonattitude" explanation has been challenged by other scholars, who prefer a

TABLE 3.5	Opinion Consistency on Government Guarantee of a Job and Good Standard of Living*		
	Preelection Response, 1984		
	Government should guarantee job and good standard of living	In between, no opinion	Government should let each person get ahead on own
Postelection Response, 1984			
Government should guarantee job and good standard of living	14%	9%	4%
In between, no opinion	8%	14%	7%
Government should let each person get ahead on own	6%	12%	26%

Source: National Election Studies, 1984 election data.

*Cell entries represent percentage of the entire sample.

"measurement error" explanation. While the details of the opposing interpretations are too complicated to receive full treatment here, we can present brief sketches of the competing points of view.

The "Nonattitudes" Explanation

After analyzing turnover patterns from the 1950s panel, Converse (1964) proposed that virtually all respondents who change their position over time hold no true convictions but instead express random responses or "nonattitudes." The strong evidence for infrequent true change is that response instability varies little with the time between surveys. Surveys four months and four years apart yield about the same amount of response turnover. If people were actually changing their minds, observed opinions would be more stable over the briefer time interval.

If the nonattitude thesis is correct, most observed response change is random error, as if changers are simply flipping coins. Just as coins can be flipped heads one time and tails the next, they can also be flipped consistently heads or tails both times. Thus a further implication of the nonattitudes thesis is that many consistent responses are random responses that appear stable only by chance. On one notorious issue from the 1950s panel, the abstract "power and housing" question (whether "the government should leave things like electric power and housing for private businessmen to handle"), Converse reached a startling conclusion (1964, 293). He estimated that less than 20 percent of the adult public held meaningful attitudes on this issue even though about two-thirds ventured a viewpoint on the matter when asked in a survey.

Many have found the implications of the nonattitudes explanation quite disturbing. In a democracy, public officials presumably respond to the policy preferences of the public, enacting these preferences into law. But if large segments of the public do not really have coherent preferences or preferences at all, why should elected officials heed their views? How, in fact, could they?

The "Measurement Error" Explanation

If the nonattitudes explanation is correct, the reason why many people give unstable responses to opinion questions is that they lack the political sophistication necessary to form crystallized opinions. But contrary to this prediction, response instability varies little if at all with measures of political sophistication or political knowledge (Achen 1975; Erikson 1979; Feldman 1989). The disturbing level of instability found for surveys of the general public is also found for subsamples representing the sophisticated and informed. If even politically sophisticated individuals respond with a seeming random component, what is to blame? It probably is not a lack of capability on the part of those being interviewed.

For this reason, a measurement error explanation has been proposed to account for response error (Achen 1975; Erikson 1979). This explanation does not challenge the evidence that most response instability represents error rather than true change. However, by the measurement error explanation, the "blame" for the response instability is placed not so much on the capabilities of the respondents as on the survey questions themselves. Even the best survey questions produce some instability from respondents who hold weak or ambivalent attitudes about policy issues. Some inherent limitations in the survey enterprise make measuring attitudes an imprecise task. These include ambiguities in question wording, the problem of investigator-defined responses to close-ended questions that may not be congruent with the way respondents think about issues, and the problem of respondents having to give immediate answers to perhaps 100 or more questions with virtually no opportunity for reflection or considered judgment. Thus it is the inherent limitations of the survey method that mostly explain response instability, not the inherent limitations of the respondent.

An Explanation Based on Response Probability

In 1992, John Zaller and Stanley Feldman offered a "theory of the survey response" that provides a more general explanation for response instability and incorporates the findings of both the nonattitudes and measurement approaches (see also Zaller 1992). From this perspective, respondents do not have fixed, stable attitudes on many issues, but they *do* have propensities to respond one way or another. The answer they give, however, depends on the considerations that come to mind when a question is asked. A consideration is simply anything that affects how someone decides on a political issue, one way or another. For example, when one is asked for an opinion on universal health insurance, considerations may include higher taxes, sick people unable to get medical care, and big government. The actual survey response depends on the considerations that are accessible when the question is asked. Assuming the considerations listed were of equal importance, the respondent would oppose universal health insurance as two considerations point in that direction versus one that points to support.

But the considerations that come to mind at one point in time may not be the same as at another. Usually, for our hypothetical respondent, the considerations that come to mind induce opposition to universal health care. But perhaps she recently saw a TV news story about a hardworking man paid poverty-level wages who could not afford medical treatment for his bedridden wife. When asked the universal health care question, that consideration may be at the top of the head and induce support for universal health care. But the news story will eventually be forgotten, and considerations that induce opposition will again predominate. Thus, for many issues, responses are probabilistic. There is a propensity to come down on one side of an issue, but the probability is something less than 1.0.

The measurement approach can also be treated in terms of response probabilities. Considerations relevant to the survey response can be brought to mind by the way a question is phrased or where it is placed in the questionnaire. For example, question location may affect the probability of a response. As we noted in chapter 2, a respondent is more likely to "disapprove" of presidential job performance when the item is asked late in the questionnaire than when it is asked early. The content of the questionnaire brings to mind considerations (mostly negative), which increases the probability of a "disapprove" response. If the question is asked early in the questionnaire, the probability of a "disapprove" response is reduced because negative considerations brought to mind by the content of the questionnaire come after the "approve/disapprove" item is answered. Like the TV news program discussed above, the survey instrument itself can be a source of considerations that affect responses to questions.

Even though the opinions expressed on an issue may vary, the underlying attitudes that give rise to them may be quite stable. Suppose our hypothetical individual has a 70 percent probability of choosing the conservative response on national health insurance, and further assume that this places her at the 80th percentile of conservatism on the issue (the respondent is more conservative than 80 percent of citizens). Within a period of two to four years, our respondent should still be near the same eightieth percentile. Stimuli in the environment might cause minor variations in probabilistic responses—for example, a liberal national mood swing might lower everybody's probability of a conservative response. But our hypothetical respondent would still be more conservative than 80 percent of citizens.

If people's attitudes are as stable as just described at the microlevel, should we expect opinion trends at the macrolevel? We show in the next chapter that net public opinion on an issue is often very stable over time. We observe interesting exceptions, however, that occur when the electorate responds in a uniform way to one-sided environmental stimuli.

3-2 LIBERAL-CONSERVATIVE IDEOLOGY AND THE ORGANIZATION OF OPINIONS

When a person expresses viewpoints on a number of political subjects, we might expect that these opinions are connected to each other in some pattern. One expectation is that opinions are connected by logical consistency with core political values. For instance, a person who believes strongly in individual responsibility would be inclined to respond negatively toward government help for the inner cities or toward the government guaranteeing a job and a good standard of living. A person with strong egalitarian values would be expected to respond in an opposite fashion. To take another example, a person committed to traditional social values probably would oppose abortion rights and oppose people who are gay serving in the military. A person with a strong belief in individual choice would take the opposite view.

We could try to account for opinions in terms of how people weight political values such as individual responsibility, equality, tradition, and individual freedom. When we describe a person's core political values in this way, we begin to describe his or her political ideology. In the broadest sense, a person's ideology is any set of beliefs about the proper order of society and how it can be achieved. People with strong ideologies use their personal ideology as a guide for understanding the political world.

As a convenient shorthand, observers often prefer to reduce ideology to the single dimension of the left-right ideological continuum, classifying political values simply according to their relative liberalism versus conservatism. The left-right ideological distinction between liberals and conservatives has considerable meaning when describing the opinions of political elites, or politically active people. For instance, delegates to national political conventions clearly understand ideological labels and tend to polarize as consistent liberals or conservatives (Herrera 1992; Jennings 1992). Because the ideological liberal-conservative continuum holds less meaning to those near the bottom of the sophistication ladder, the importance of liberal-conservative ideology within the mass public is a matter of uncertainty and controversy.[5]

A standard poll question is to ask respondents their ideological identification, usually with the three choices of liberal, moderate, or conservative. As discussed in chapter 2, one-fourth or more decline to classify themselves ideologically given the choice of "not interested." Of those who choose, almost half choose the "moderate" or "middle-of-the-road" alternative when it is offered.

Ideally, ideological classification is a convenient way to measure individuals' core political values and to summarize their political views on a variety of issues. In practice, the result is mixed. The most politically sophisticated segment of the public approximates the ideal. For them, ideological identification goes a long way toward describing their political convictions. But when less sophisticated people respond to the ideological identification question with a response of liberal, moderate, or conservative, we can be less sure of what the response means. At worst, the response represents some idiosyncratic meaning known only to the respondent, or perhaps a doorstep opinion made up on the spot.

Liberal and Conservative Terminology

What do the terms *liberal* and *conservative* actually mean? At the philosophical level, political thinkers with reputations as liberals and conservatives differ in several ways. Conservatives view society as a control for humanity's worst impulses; liberals view the human condition as relative to the quality of society. Conservatives consider people inherently unequal and due unequal rewards; liberals are egalitarian. Conservatives venerate tradition, order, and authority; liberals believe planned change brings the possibility of improvement.[6]

Of course, people who are liberal or conservative in their practical politics need not strictly adhere to the philosophy associated with their ideological label. Nevertheless, we can see the implications of these philosophic distinctions at work in the common applications of the ideological labels to political points of view. Conservatives are more afraid than liberals of "big government," except on matters of law and order and national security. In foreign policy preferences, conservatives are more aggressive; liberals are more cooperative or yielding. Conservatives are more likely to see harmful consequences of government help for the disadvantaged, while liberals see the benefits. Conservatives tend to be moralistic; liberals are more permissive.

These kinds of relative distinctions are familiar to people who follow politics closely. But the language of ideology holds less meaning for the public as a whole. One test is whether the individual can both identify the Republican as the more conservative party and offer a plausible definition of the term *conservative*. Roughly half the public passes this test of understanding of ideological labels (Converse 1964; Luttbeg and Gant 1985).

What do people think of when they hear the terms *liberal* and *conservative*? Table 3.6 summarizes the responses from a 1994 NES study of how people describe liberals and conservatives. Respondents were asked, "What sorts of

TABLE 3.6	Perceived Meaning of Ideological Labels, 1994	
Question:	*What sorts of things do you have in mind when you say someone's political views are liberal?*	
	What sorts of things do you have in mind when you say someone's political views are conservative?	
Type of Mention	**Example**	**Percentage Mentioning**
Change	L's accept change/new ideas/innovative. C's resist change/protect status quo/rigid.	23
Fiscal	L's for socialism/welfare state/give-away programs. C's for free enterprise/capitalism/oppose social programs.	24
Personality	L's are open-minded/not concerned with consequences. C's are moralists/concerned with consequences.	14
Morality	L's not interested in setting moral standards/not religious. C's have definite moral standards/religious.	13
Spend/save	L's free spenders/favor government spending. C's thrifty/economize on government spending.	24
Civil liberties	L's support upholding of Bill of Rights/human rights. C's want to limit Bill of Rights/human rights.	5
Class	L's for little people/working people/unions. C's for big business/the rich.	12
Abortion	L's are pro-choice. C's are pro-life.	15
Gay rights	L's favor gay rights. C's oppose gay rights.	9
Defense	L's weak on defense/national security. C's strong on defense/national security.	4
People	L's identify label with prominent national figures. C's identify label with prominent national figures.	5

n = 595

Source: Adapted from National Election Studies, 1994. The questions allow for multiple responses.

things do you have in mind when you say that someone's political views are liberal?" and similarly, "What sorts of things do you have in mind when you say that someone's political views are conservative?" They were allowed up to three responses to each question, six overall. Seventy-eight percent of the sample gave at least one response.

As in other years, economic distinctions were used most often to explain the difference between liberals and conservatives. Liberals spend; conservatives save. Liberals are seen as favoring the welfare state and giving away programs; conservatives are seen as favoring free enterprise and opposing big spending social programs. Liberals were also seen as being more change-oriented and innovative, while conservatives were viewed as more status quo–oriented and rigid. All these are reasonably broad distinctions. But the public also sees differences between liberals and conservatives on narrower issues. Conservatives are seen as moralistic and religious, while liberals are seen as having more flexible moral standards and not as religious. The contemporary issues of abortion and gay rights show up in the expected fashion. However, with the end of the cold war, fewer respondents mention defense and national security issues than in the past. In addition, a number of responses deal with peripheral matters such as liberal and conservative positions on narrow policy issues.

When survey respondents are asked to classify themselves on the liberal-conservative spectrum, their answers tend to correspond to their policy positions. Examples of the relationships and positions on specific issues are shown in Table 3.7. Self-declared liberals, in fact, take positions considerably more liberal than do self-declared conservatives.

This tendency is even clearer when issue positions are summed over several issues. Table 3.8 shows that, as measured by their composite stands over ten issues, people who are very liberal identify as liberals and people who are very conservative overwhelmingly identify themselves as conservatives. It may also be noted that people who cannot identify themselves as liberal, moderate, or conservative tend to cluster in the center of the political spectrum as measured by their stands on specific issues.

Use of Ideological Language

Although the ideological terms are within the vocabularies of a large share of the American public, few actually employ them to defend their choices of party or candidate. For each National Election Study, respondents are asked what they like and dislike about each major party and presidential candidate. The profile of responses to these questions in 1956 is reported in the classic study of American voting behavior, *The American Voter* (Campbell et al. 1960, 216–49). The researchers were interested not only in the individuals' image of the parties and candidates but also in the conceptual sophistication of the responses. Respondents who spontaneously and knowledgeably evaluated the parties and candidates in terms of their placement on the liberal-conservative spectrum were labeled as "ideologues."

Thus began a search for ideologues within the electorate that continues to hold a central place on the research agenda of public opinion analysts. In some

Table 3.7	Ideological Preferences and Opinions on Selected Policy Issues, 2000*		
Belief		Support Among Self-Declared Liberals	Support Among Self-Declared Conservatives
The government should provide "more services even if it means an increase in spending"		86	38
The government should guarantee "that every person has a job and good standard of living"		41	15
Favor "government insurance plan which would cover all medical and hospital expenses for everyone"		70	33
The government "should make every effort to improve the social and economic position of blacks"		34	12
Permit abortion "always" or "if needed"		80	44
"Tougher regulations are needed to protect the environment"		90	61
"Government should make it more difficult to buy a gun"		76	47
Favor laws to "protect homosexuals from job discrimination"		82	52
Oppose "death penalty for persons convicted of murder"		42	19
The United States "should spend less on defense"		39	9

Source: National Election Studies, 2000.

*Reported figures are percentage of opinion-holders only.

respects, *The American Voter*'s label *ideologue* was unfortunate, because in popular usage it holds a negative connotation: the ideologue as ideology-driven fanatic. As the term is used in *The American Voter*, however, the ideologue is a political sophisticate whose central view of political actors is in terms of their place on the ideological spectrum. The ideologue's own political perspective could be moderate, extremist, or anywhere in between.

Even with a generous definition of what the ideologue response would demand (to include what *The American Voter* calls "near ideologues"), only 12 percent of the 1956 respondents fit the ideologue category. A typical ideologue response was that of an Ohio woman who, when asked what she liked about the Democratic party, answered, "Nothing, except it being a more liberal party, and I think [of] the Republicans as being more conservative and interested in big business." A weaker ideologue response was given by a Texas man: "I think the Democrats are more concerned with all the people . . . they put out more liberal legislation" (Campbell et al. 1960, 232).

An added 42 percent of the 1956 sample expressed their likes and dislikes about the candidates (Eisenhower and Stevenson) and parties in terms of the groups they represented. Farmers often expressed their political likes and dislikes

| TABLE 3.8 | Correspondence of Ideological Self-Ratings and Summary of Positions on Ten Issues, 2000 |

Summary Position on Ten Issues*

Ideological Self-Rating	Very liberal	Liberal	Center	Conservative	Very Conservative
Liberal	56%	29%	15%	13%	4%
Moderate	27	29	28	23	21
Conservative	6	18	29	43	65
Don't know	10	24	28	20	10
	100%	100%	100%	100%	100%
(Percentage of total sample)	(13)	(23)	(29)	(21)	(15)

Source: National Election Studies, 2000 election data.

*See the Appendix for construction of ten-item summary scores. The full distribution of scores is shown in Figure 3.1. The categories here are as follows: Very liberal -10 to -5, Liberal -4 to -2, Center, -1 to +1, Conservative +2 to +4, and Very Conservative +5 to +10.

in terms of "group-benefits"—for example, "I think [the Democrats] have always helped the farmers (Campbell et al. 1960, 236). Most group-benefit responses were class-related, evoking the notion that Republicans favor big business while the Democrats favor the "little person."

Still another 24 percent of the 1956 respondents referred to the "nature of the times" the different parties are associated with when in power. Nature-of-the-times voters were guided by perceptions of past performance, such as which party brought economic prosperity or which party kept their promises. Finally, 23 percent were found to offer no issue content whatsoever when asked to describe their partisan likes and dislikes. Typical was the North Carolina man who answered as follows (with interviewer questions abbreviated):

(Like about the Democrats?) "No, Ma'am, not that I know of."
            (Dislike?) "No, Ma'am, but I've always been a Democrat, just like my daddy."
(Like about the Republicans?) "No."
            (Dislike?) "No."(Campbell et al. 1960, 246)

This distribution of how people conceptualize partisan politics may be interpreted to mean that Americans are not very ideological, and in one sense this is correct. The authors of *The American Voter* account for the scarcity of ideologues in terms of the public's "cognitive limitations," particularly a lack of intellectual ability to think in terms of ideological abstractions (Campbell et al. 1960, 253). But our knowledge that many citizens use the liberal-conservative terms and can apply them to issues positions suggests the alternative interpretation—that the

American public does not always find the ideological terms useful to describe their partisan likes and dislikes. Now many political scientists see *The American Voter* judgment as overly harsh. Although the authors did not realize it at the time, the 1956 presidential election was probably the least ideological of all modern campaigns, conducted essentially as a referendum on President Eisenhower's first term. Because the 1956 campaign was not conducted at an ideological level, respondents in that year were not apt to explain their likes and dislikes about parties and candidates in terms of ideological nuances. They chose the easier criteria of group representation and the nature of the times.

In later elections, ideology and policy issues played greater roles. The 1964 (Johnson vs. Goldwater) and 1972 (McGovern vs. Nixon) campaigns were particularly ideological. As ideological cues became more visible, the proportion of the public who could be labeled *ideologue* increased considerably.[7]

Table 3.9 enumerates the electorate by "level of conceptualization" based on NES surveys for each presidential year from 1956 to 1988, the last year for which measurement is available. The table depicts an electorate divided roughly equally into the four levels of conceptualization. To summarize: At the top level, "ideologues" view parties and candidates in terms of their ideological and policy differences. At the second level, "group-benefits" people see party and candidate differences in terms of the differences in the groups they represent rather than the policies they offer. At the third level, "nature-of-the-times" people evaluate parties and candidates only by past judgments of party and candidate performance. At the bottom, "no-issue-content" types seem unresponsive to political cues.

As we have seen, a greater proportion of the electorate can utilize the ideological language than are classifiable as ideologues. One explanation is that many individuals can use ideological labels without pursuing much ideology. For instance, many at the "group-interest" level identify with liberals or conservatives as a group with which they share a common interest, much as some may feel about teachers or labor unions (Tedin 1987).

TABLE 3.9 | **Levels of Political Conceptualization, 1956–1988**

	1956	1960	1964	1968	1972	1976	1980	1984	1988
Ideologues	12%	19%	27%	26%	22%	21%	21%	19%	18%
Group benefits	42	31	27	24	27	26	31	26	36
Nature of the times	24	26	20	29	34	30	30	35	25
No issue content	22	23	26	21	17	24	19	19	21
	100%	99%	100%	100%	100%	101%	101%	99%	99%
Number of cases	1,749	1,701	1,431	1,319	1,372	2,870	1,612	2,257	2,040

Source: Paul R. Hagner and John C. Pierce, "Correlative Characteristics of Levels of Conceptualization in the American Public, 1956–1976," *Journal of Politics* 44 (Aug. 1982): 779–809; updates compiled by Paul Hagner and Kathleen Knight.

Some people learn to associate terms like *liberal* and *conservative* with groups and symbols rather than specific policies (Conover and Feldman 1981). A person might associate the term *liberal* with *black* or *feminist* or the term *conservative* with *the middle class* or *business* (Miller et al. 1991). These cues may serve to simplify politics and provide an informational shortcut (much like party identification), even if in most instances they are unaccompanied by a high degree of ideological sophistication. If one knows a candidate for public office is a liberal, or a policy is characterized as liberal, one need seek no further information to make a judgment. The labels can be used to minimize the costs of gathering information.

Ideology as Liberal-Conservative Consistency

One might suspect that many people are actually quite liberal or quite conservative in the views they express, even when they do not choose these terms to describe their political orientation. Figure 3.1 shows one distribution of the American public's liberal-conservative "scores" as measured by their cumulative responses to ten opinion questions in the 2000 NES survey. A person with all liberal opinions would score at −10, whereas a person who expresses conservative outlooks on all ten issues would score at +10. Most respondents were near the midpoint of the scale (0), indicating that their liberal and conservative viewpoints balanced each other out.

Because over a series of issues most people give some liberal and some conservative positions, there is a temptation to label the public as political

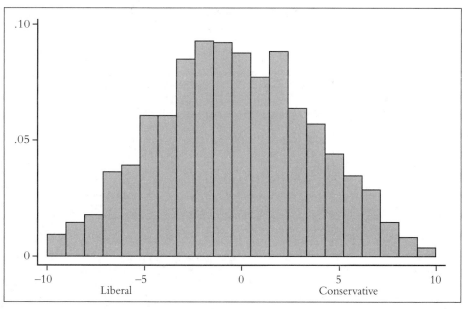

Figure 3.1   Distribution of ten-item composite opinion scores, 2000. *Source:* National Election Studies, 2000 election data.

moderates. But these voters in the center cannot be grouped as sharing the same moderate ideology because they differ greatly in their pattern of responses on individual issues. For instance, one voter with balanced liberal and conservative views may be liberal on social welfare issues and civil rights but conservative on foreign policy and law and order, while another with equally balanced views professes exactly the opposite opinions. Still a third person may have an overall score that is neither very conservative nor very liberal for the reason that he or she expresses few opinions at all.

If ideology influences people's opinions, opinions on two separate issues should be predictable from one another because both are "constrained" by the opinion-holder's ideological perspective. If a conservative ideology binds some to oppose spending programs for example, their conservatism should compel them to support of the death penalty or perhaps to oppose abortion rights. Table 3.10 shows examples of the search for ideological constraint.

For a pair of issues, an individual is more likely to offer consistently liberal or conservative positions if the issues are logically related or share content. The top row of Table 3.10 presents several examples. In Table 3.10(a), people's opinions regarding government involvement in health care are predictable from their general views on domestic government spending. In Table 3.10(b), people's opinions regarding government help in providing jobs and a good standard of living show consistency with their views on government aid for minorities. In Table 3.10(c), people's opinions on abortion appear consistent with their views on

TABLE 3.10 | Correlations Between Opinions on Selected Issues, 2000

		(a) Increase domestic spending				(b) Guaranteed job, living standard				(c) Legalize abortions	
		Pro	*Con*			*Pro*	*Con*			*Pro*	*Con*
National health insurance	*Pro*	48%	8%	Federal aid to minor	*Pro*	15%	9%	Equal role for women	*Pro*	59%	31%
	Con	17	23		*Con*	12	64		*Con*	4	6
Gamma = .81				Gamma = .79				Gamma = .48			

		(d) Legal abortions				(e) Need laws to protect gays				(f) More domestic spending	
		Pro	*Con*			*Pro*	*Con*			*Pro*	*Con*
National health insurance	*Pro*	34%	20%	Guar. living stand.	*Pro*	22%	7%	Cut military spending	*Pro*	19%	6%
	Con	25%	20%		*Con*	41%	29%		*Con*	43	33
Gamma = .15				Gamma = .41				Gamma = .42			

Source: National Election Studies, 2000 data. See the Appendix for the full text of opinion questions.

whether women deserve an equal role with men in business and government. Each example shows many exceptions, however, of individuals holding a liberal position on one issue but a conservative position on the other.

When issues are not closely related in content, liberal-conservative consistency tends to fade. Table 3.10(d) shows that one cannot predict an individual's position on abortion from his or her position on national health insurance. Table 3.10(e) shows a similar lack of predictability for the issue pair of a guaranteed living standard and gays in the military. Of course, for neither of these pairs is there a requirement of logical consistency. But consider also the relationship between domestic spending and less military spending, shown in Table 3.10(f). Seemingly people should gravitate to ideologically consistent choices of either more domestic spending and less military spending (liberal) or less domestic spending and more military spending (conservative). Table 3.10(f) shows only a modest correlation. Many people favor either more spending for both domestic and military purposes or less spending for both.[8]

The low levels of ideological constraint within the general public reflect real variations in ideological sophistication. Liberal-conservative opinion consistency is quite high among those most knowledgeable about politics, such as people identified as "ideologues" (Stimson 1975; Knight 1985). We can illustrate this point by comparing the respondents classified as least knowledgeable and most knowledgeable in the 1996 NES survey. Among the select "high information" group, opinions on different issues are highly correlated, while for the "low information" group there is essentially no correlation at all. Our illustration is for the relationship between opinion on a national health insurance program and opinion on abortion.

		Low Information Legal Abortions		High Information Legal Abortions	
		Pro	Con	Pro	Con
National Health	Pro	31%	30%	34%	8%
Insurance	Con	25%	14%	30%	27%
		Gamma = -.23		Gamma = .60	

We see that with the accumulation of a high level of political information, people tend toward consistently liberal or consistently conservative positions, while we see no relationship at all for those with low levels of information. A broader illustration compares the high-information group and the low-information group in terms of their distributions on the composite ten-item liberal-conservative scale. Figure 3.2 shows the results. The informed show some gravitation toward the liberal and conservative poles. The uninformed are highly clustered in the center of the spectrum.

Despite the fact that the most knowledgeable are the most responsive to liberal versus conservative distinctions, we should not insist that use of the liberal-conservative dimension is a requirement for political thinking. Liberal-conservative consistency is not the only possible ordering principle for political

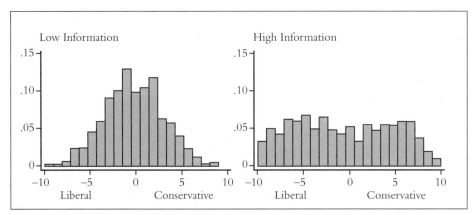

Figure 3.2   Composite opinion by information level. *Source:* National Election Studies, 2000 election data.

opinions. On foreign policy, for example, core values regarding the morality of warfare and ethnocentrism appear to be important (Hurwitz and Peffley 1987). More generally, people can make their opinions consistent with their own personal ideologies and need not apply the notion of liberal versus conservative ways of thinking. Consider abortion attitudes, which until recently did not correlate much with conventional liberal-conservative orderings as measured by other policy opinions. According to Kristen Luker, attitudes concerning abortion result from "beliefs and attitudes about motherhood; about sexuality; about men and women; about the role of children; and more broadly, about such global things as morality and the role of rational planning in human affairs" (Luker 1984, 31).

Ideological Thinking: A Summary

The public is mixed in its understanding and usage of ideological language and thinking. Most citizens do not engage in the ideological thinking of the sort found among political elites. But ordinary citizens often use ideological labels in at least a limited way as part of their political vocabulary. Many, however, do not do even this. For perhaps as much as half the electorate, the liberal versus conservative component of political discourse is nothing more than a confusion of background noise. The fact that there is little ideological consistency to people's issue positions demonstrates that few people use their ideological position as a cuing device to arrange their responses to the political world. The kind of attitudinal constraint that motivates people toward consistently liberal, conservative, or moderate political viewpoints is reserved for a relatively small, politically active segment of the public.

In our effort to understand public opinion, we should not ignore this politically sophisticated segment of the American public, which does follow government and politics in terms of the liberal-conservative continuum. Thinking about politics in liberal versus conservative terms is sophisticated not because it is preferable to hold ideologically extreme convictions or to view the political world through a distorted lens. Rather, to have the liberal-conservative spectrum as a political frame of reference is necessary to understand the language of politics as it is practiced by political elites. Many ordinary Americans do follow this ideological discussion.

3-3 PARTY IDENTIFICATION AND THE ORGANIZATION OF POLITICAL OPINIONS

So far, we have ignored partisanship as a way of organizing political opinions. More than on the basis of ideology, Americans divide on the basis of party identification. Whereas ideological identification may be of particular relevance only for a select segment of the public, people at all levels of sophistication appear to hold meaningful party identifications. Whereas the pollster's ideological identification question is intended to summarize the person's political values, party identification represents the person's net evaluation of the Republican and Democratic parties. It is relatively easy to prefer one party over the other without considering nuances of ideological placement.

For most people, party identification is a central aspect of political identity. Compared to ordinary political opinions, people's party identifications are quite stable over time, both before and after adjustment for measurement error (Green, Palmquist, and Schickler 2002). For instance, when interviewed during two successive presidential campaigns four years apart, most respondents persist with their original basic identification as a Democrat, Independent, or Republican. Only a small percentage of respondents switch party identification from Democratic to Republican or vice versa. Those who switch generally move in and out of the Independent category rather than "convert" from one side to the other.

As discussed in chapter 5, the source of one's party identification is often the political values that were transmitted in the family during childhood. At the other end of the causal chain, party identification is the best predictor of how people vote. Following the sequence through, we find that people vote for the party with which their parents identified.

Survey researchers normally ascertain party identification by asking respondents whether they consider themselves Democrats, Independents, or Republicans. Partisans may then be asked whether they consider themselves "strong" or "not so strong" (often translated as "weak") Republicans or Democrats. Classifying on strength plus partisan direction makes four categories of partisans. Meanwhile, Independents are sometimes asked whether they "lean" toward one of the parties. The Independents can be classified as Republican leaners, Democratic leaners, and pure Independents. Pure Independents typically make up no more than about 10 percent of a national sample, suggesting that few citizens are purely neutral when it comes to partisanship. Altogether, there are seven potential categories of party identification, on a scale from "strong Democrat" to "strong Republican." Usually, however, the three-category classification is sufficient. Except where otherwise indicated, this book employs the simple three-category division of party identification as Republicans (strong plus weak), Democrats (strong plus weak), and Independents (pure plus partisan leaners).

Party identification can be a handy cue by which to orient the remainder of one's political beliefs. An alert Republican, for example, learns that a good Republican is supposed to subscribe to conservative positions on certain issues and responds accordingly. At the same time, we might expect that the rare event of a partisan conversion results when the convert becomes aware that his or her ideological views are out of alignment with his or her partisan heritage. These causal processes could not occur, however, unless people were aware of the Democratic versus Republican differences on the issues of the day.

Perceptions of Party Differences

As we show in chapter 10, Democratic and Republican leaders are ideologically different, with the Republicans generally conservative and Democrats generally liberal. In other words, at the leadership level the usual party stereotypes are true. Here we can ask: To what extent does the public perceive these party differences?

The National Election Studies regularly ask their respondents to place the major parties' positions on selected issues of the day. Respondents can rate the Democrats to the left of the Republicans (correct), the Republicans to the left of the Democrats, rate them tied at the identical position, or declare no interest in the issue. Table 3.11 presents the perceptions of the parties' relative positions in recent NES surveys. Typically, about half rate the Democrats as the more liberal (left) party. Few guess incorrectly and identify the Republican party with the liberal position.

TABLE 3.11 | Public Perceptions of Party Differences on Issues, 1988–2000

Perceptions of Which Party Is More in Favor of . . .	Democrats	Republicans	No Difference, Don't Know, No Interest
More domestic spending (2000)	66%	10%	24%
National health insurance (1988)	43	8	50
Guaranteed living standard (2000)	54	13	33
Aid to blacks (2000)	43	7	50
Abortion rights (1996)	57	9	34
Regulating the environment (1996)	48	9	44
Reducing defense spending (2000)	44	19	34

Source: National Election Studies data.

Interestingly, the public's perceptions of party differences on issues have been growing over the years. As recently as the early 1960s, the public saw party differences only in terms of social welfare issues. The public image of the parties as distinct on social welfare issues goes back to the New Deal era of the 1930s, when the parties began to develop opposite philosophies toward the role of the federal government in the economy. Until about 1964, party differences on issues outside the social welfare sphere were not sharply focused at the leadership level, such as congressional and presidential politics. It is no surprise, therefore, that before the 1960s people generally did not see either party as liberal or conservative on civil rights or foreign policy issues.

Nowadays, Americans generally perceive the Democrats as the more liberal party not only on social welfare issues but on civil rights, foreign policy, and even social issues like gay rights. This happened largely because the parties became more polarized at the elite level. Public perceptions simply followed the behavior and the rhetoric of party leaders. The biggest change occurred with the ideological Goldwater election of 1964 (Carmines and Stimson 1989). Senator Goldwater, the 1964 Republican candidate, campaigned as a forthright conservative. By opposing the Civil Rights Act of 1964, he altered the Republican image on civil rights. By his tough posturing about the Soviet Union, he made the Republicans appear to be the most belligerent on foreign policy. His Democratic opponent, President Lyndon Johnson, was able to exploit Goldwater's image as an extreme conservative. Goldwater lost the election in a landslide, but he and his supporters moved the Republican party sharply to the right in a manner that has lasted into the twenty-first century.

Events after 1964 added to the growing perceptions of party differences, as growing polarization of Democratic and Republican elites fueled a further division between Republican and Democratic identifiers in the mass public (Hetherington 2001). By the 1980s, public perceptions of the parties began to seriously diverge on "social issues" such as abortion, "toughness" on crime, and gay rights, with Republicans seen as moralistic and Democrats as permissive. Today, on virtually all national issues that divide Americans, the two major parties are seen as taking quite different sides. While there was once a time when critics complained that the parties did not offer meaningful policy choices, the more typical complaint today is that the chasm has become too wide. As discussed in chapter 10, a sharpening of divisions between congressional Democrats and Republicans maintains the liberal-conservative party polarization that began in 1964.

Party Identification and Policy Preferences

On most issues, the views of Democratic and Republican identifiers diverge in predictable liberal versus conservative ways. Examples from 2000 NES data are shown in Table 3.12. Although the differences among "weak Democrats," "Independents," and "weak Republicans" are slight, the policy differences between "strong Democrats" and "strong Republicans" generally are rather sharp. Following historical tradition, party differences are greatest on social welfare issues. On

TABLE 3.12 | Party Identification and Policy Opinions, 2000

| | Percent Liberal Among | | | | | |
Issue	Strong Dem.	Weak Dem.	Ind.	Weak Repub.	Strong Repub.	Gamma
More domestic spending	94	84	61	38	25	.70
Job guarantee	52	32	28	20	04	.46
Less defense spending	30	29	25	18	02	.32
Aid to blacks	33	21	17	12	04	.40
National health insurance	78	65	59	35	22	.44
More environmental laws	84	87	76	64	50	.39
Laws protecting gays	76	74	69	65	47	.26
Oppose death penalty	42	30	26	22	12	.31
Favor gun control	73	76	60	51	40	.35
Favor abortion rights	66	64	60	51	43	.22
Mean	*63*	*56*	*48*	*37*	*27*	
Liberal identifiers★	77	73	45	9	5	.78

Source: National Election Studies, 2000 data.

★Percent liberal among liberal and conservative identifiers.

one issue, aid to Russia, Republicans are slightly more liberal, perhaps because friendship with Russia was an idea associated with Republican presidents.

Figure 3.3 displays the difference between Democratic and Republican identifiers in terms of scores on the composite ten-item index of liberalism-conservatism. In terms of their net ideological direction, most Democrats are left of center and most Republicans are right of center, but there are many exceptions. In fact, the reader might be surprised by the proportions of the public who appear as conservative Democrats and liberal Republicans. Clearly, ideology and partisanship are not the same thing.

The correlation between partisanship and ideological direction sharpens if we isolate informed citizens. Figure 3.4 repeats the ideological comparison of Democrats and Republicans, this time separately, for voters at the low and high ends of the information scale.

Among low-information voters there exists almost no correlation between partisanship and ideology; in this set, Democrats are only barely to the left of Republicans on average, with considerable overlap. But among high-information voters, virtually all Democrats are to the left of center, and virtually all Republicans to the right. In other words, find an informed voter and partisanship follows ideology, or perhaps it is the other way around.

Issue differences between Republican and Democratic identifiers have grown in response to the perception of widening party differences. While Democratic identifiers have been somewhat more liberal than Republicans on social welfare

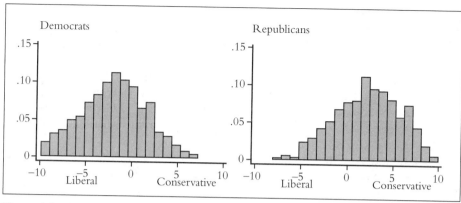

Figure 3.3 Composite opinion by party identification. *Source:* National Election Studies, 2000 election data.

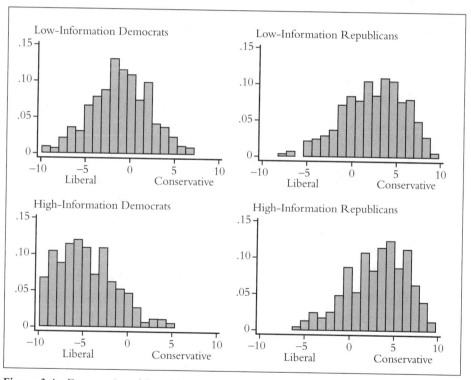

Figure 3.4 Democratic and Republican composite opinion, by information level. *Source:* National Election Studies, 2000 election data.

issues since the 1930s, only recently have Democratic identifiers become more liberal than Republican identifiers on other issues. As with perceptions, differences in Democratic and Republican views showed their greatest increase around the time of the ideological 1964 election. Before that time, Democrats in the electorate were not identifiably more liberal on civil rights, foreign policy, or social issues. Of course, they had no reason to be, as people saw the two parties as differing only on the social welfare dimension.

What causes the consistency between political opinions and party identification? Do people learn their political opinions from their party identifications, or do political opinions shape party identifications? Undoubtedly both causal processes are at work, but their relative contributions can be only roughly estimated.

Because party identification can be such a strong and stable attitude, some have argued that partisanship drives policy opinions more than the reverse (Campbell et al. 1960, ch. 6; Luttbeg 1981). Often, when parties realign their positions on an issue, their supporters follow. A classic example occurred among partisans after Republican President Nixon initiated the thaw in U.S. relations with the People's Republic of China in the early 1970s. Republicans abandoned their hostility to "Red China" faster than Democrats did.[9] Similarly, when President Reagan initiated a new friendship with the Soviet Union, Republicans were quicker to think the cold war was over.[10] When in early 1991 many congressional Democrats balked at supporting President Bush's intervention in the Persian Gulf, the Democratic rank and file became more dovish and the Republican rank and file became more hawkish (Zaller 1992, 104–5). Finally, just the reverse occurred in the spring of 1999 when congressional Republicans balked at supporting President Clinton's policy of halting ethnic cleansing in Kosovo by bombing Serbia.[11]

While partisanship influences people's perceptions of the world and shapes their opinions, often it is party identification that changes when initial partisanship and issue positions get out of alignment (Markus and Converse 1979; Page and Jones 1979; Franklin and Jackson 1983; Jacoby 1989). Some people who become ideologically disaffected by their home party become Independents (Luskin et al. 1989). Those who go all the way and shift from one party to the other often display the ideological zeal of true converts.

Party Identification: Psychological Identification or Running Tally?

Political scientists still do not fully understand party identification. *The American Voter* (Campbell et al. 1960, ch. 6) presented one influential interpretation—that one's party identification is essentially a psychological attachment or "affective orientation" to one's favorite party. By this view, party identification can approach blind loyalty, as when people find reason to support their party's position and vote for its candidates long after they have rational reasons for doing so.

Some scholars, however, emphasize the more rational aspects of party identification. By this view, people learn a party identification based on what Morris Fiorina (1977) calls a "running tally" of their partisan decisions. For example, voters who find repeated reason to vote Republican begin to call themselves Republican—not so much out of psychological attachment as by way of learning a convenient shorthand rule for deciding how to vote. If reasons develop for such voters to vote Democratic instead, they do not blindly continue down the Republican path in the face of contrary evidence. Instead, they vote Democratic or even change partisanship in response to the new running tally.

Both interpretations of partisanship carry some validity. For example, many partisans persist in voting loyally for their party even when it no longer represents their views on issues. But many partisans casually change allegiance when circumstances seem to warrant it. Perhaps our question should be whether by forming a standing decision to vote Democratic or Republican, people enhance or detract from their ability to vote rationally. We address this question in later chapters.

NOTES

1. Analysts must be sensitive to the accuracy of the reasons people give for their opinions. For instance, people can recall their position on some matters but not the original reasons for it, and then rationalize their choice with new reasons that may not have had any bearing on their choice. A lengthy literature now exists on how people store and retrieve political information when making or remembering political judgments. For recent examples, see Lodge and Stroh (1993) and Wyer and Ottati (1993).

2. Increasingly, scholars are investigating the consequences of information on political opinions to see what happens when people gain information, both general and specific, and what guides their searches. See for instance Gilens (2001) and Kuklinski (2002). See also the discussion in chapter 11 regarding the consequences of political awakening.

3. Sample sizes represent 500+ respondents. The fact that the responses shown in Table 3.3 are part of a framing experiment is not a source of serious distortion. In some instances, different framing in the two waves enhances response turnover. Yet this contamination appears slight. For issues in which some respondents were given variable framings and others the same framing, the effect of this difference in stimulus appears to have been but a few percentage points. Where some respondents repeatedly received an elaborate framing of the underlying arguments for the two points of view while a control group got none, responses were more stable when respondents received framing.

4. The abortion question was actually asked three times in the 1989 NES pilot study. The pilot respondents were first asked their abortion views in late 1988 as part of the regular NES 1988 election survey. Over three waves, only 26 percent took a consistent pro-life position and only 27 percent took a consistent pro-choice position. An even smaller 5 percent were consistently in the middle, but 42 percent took a middle position in at least one wave.

5. As a practical matter, the single dimension of liberal-conservative ideology is a better measure of underlying political values than specific values measured individually. Zaller (1992, 26) states the case nicely: "There is . . . a tendency for people to be fairly consistently 'left,' 'right,' or 'centrist' on such disparate value dimensions as economic individualism, opinions toward Communists, tolerance of nonconformists, racial issues, sexual freedom, and religious authority. The correlations among these different value dimensions are never so strong as to

suggest that there is one and only one basic value dimension, but they are always at least moderately strong, and among highly aware persons, the correlations are sometimes quite strong. And, of course, there are also moderately strong correlations between people's self-descriptions as liberal or conservative and their scores on the various value measures."

6. For discussions of the origins of liberal-conservative terminology, see Kerlinger (1984) and Rotunda (1986).

7. On the increase in ideologues in 1964, see Nie et al. (1976) and T. Smith (1990). Some studies (Nie et al., Smith) define ideologues far more inclusively than we do here, to include any mention of the liberal-conservative language.

8. Correlations between opinions have increased since the early readings in the 1950s. The greatest jump occurred at the time of the ideological 1964 election (Nie and Anderson 1974; Nie et al. 1976). Some scholars believe this increase is largely illusory, the result of better questions asked by survey researchers (Sullivan et al. 1978; Bishop et al. 1978).

9. For instance, between 1966 and 1971, the percentage of Democratic opinion-holders who told Gallup they favored U.N. admission for China rose from one-third to nearly half. Meanwhile, Republican support rose from 1 in 4 to a clear plurality in favor of admission.

10. For instance, in 1984 (pre-Gorbachev) and 1988, "strong Democrats" (with opinions) increased their support for cooperation with Russia by four percentage points. "Strong Republicans" (with opinions) increased their support by 24 points (1984 and 1988 NES data).

11. Pew Research Center poll, June 9–13, 1999.

4 | Macrolevel Opinion: The Flow of Political Sentiment

Public opinion specialists begin their investigations of survey data by analyzing the *frequencies*, or the percentaged divisions, of opinion for the sample. The frequency distributions reflect the content of public opinion at the moment of the poll. When a particular survey question has been repeatedly asked in the past, the latest frequencies also provide information about opinion trends.

Frequency distributions must be interpreted with caution because, as we saw in chapter 2, responses are often influenced by question wording. When the polls show a certain percentage favoring a particular response to a question, we need some anchor, a reference point, by which to measure the significance of the finding. One way is to compare the frequencies for one question with those for slightly different but related questions. This comparison allows us to see what distinctions the mass public makes in the kinds of policies it is willing to support. A particularly useful anchor is to compare answers to the same question over time. If the public displays a different level of support for some policy today than one year ago or five years ago, then we may have located a potentially important change in public opinion.

Unfortunately, the data that would allow for the accurate assessment of trends in public opinion are often not as available as one might expect. Commercial pollsters naturally ask questions of current interest to their media clients. As popular interest fades, those questions are often not repeated. Academic polling units are more concerned with the continuity and comparability of questions over time, but even they are not immune to the wax and wane of topical issues. Thus questions dealing with civil liberties were frequently asked in the McCarthy era of the early 1950s, when many people thought their basic personal liberties were threatened. Such questions were not asked again until the early 1970s. Before the 1960s, questions about race relations were seldom asked; the aspirations of the black minority were given little thought by white politicians, press, and public. Even when the polls monitor opinions on the same issue over time, they often vary question wording, making it difficult to separate real change from question-wording effects.

In the following sections we present an overview of macrolevel public opinion, or what polls tell us about the content of public opinion both today and in the past. Poll trends are often described in ideological or partisan terms, as if the public's frame of reference is shifting on the liberal-conservative or Democratic-Republican continuum. We begin by examining opinion on specific policy issues that have been polled over the years, searching for liberal or conservative trends that might be specific to the issue at hand. Second, we consider the possibility of general ideological movement. Third, we examine changes in the distribution of party identification over the years. And fourth, we consider one important partisan question well known for its volatility: the president's approval rating.

4-1 TRENDS IN POLICY OPINIONS

For convenience, most policy questions can be divided into four general domains: (1) social welfare, (2) civil rights, (3) foreign policy, and (4) social issues. Social welfare controversies pertain to the distribution of wealth and government efforts to help the disadvantaged; civil rights refer to the quest for equality under the law; foreign policy, obviously, refers to views about the U.S. role abroad, and social issues usually involve differences over lifestyles or "moral values" such as abortion, prayer in the public schools, and capital punishment.

Social Welfare Issues

From the New Deal to the present, the American public has been receptive to government programs to accomplish economic welfare objectives. In fact, on social welfare legislation, mass opinion has often been well ahead of congressional action. For example, the earliest polls revealed an overwhelming majority (89 percent) in favor of "old age pensions" prior to the adoption of the Social Security Act in 1936 (Cantril 1951, 521). A majority also supported the right of workers to organize and bargain collectively before the 1941 Wagner Act transformed these principles into law (Page and Shapiro 1992, 136). Majority approval has continually been found prior to each increase in the federal minimum wage (Erskine 1962b, 26; Gallup Poll Index, Sept. 1985, 17).

It has long been noted that the American public is ideologically conservative but operationally liberal (Free and Cantril 1968; Cantril and Cantril 1999). Polls persistently show self-identified conservatives outnumbering self-identified liberals. When it comes to specific social welfare programs, however, most people generally are supportive of liberal spending. For example, when NES asked in 2000 if the government should "provide fewer services, even in areas such as health and education, in order to reduce spending" or instead "provide more services and spending," 41 percent chose more services and spending, 18 percent chose fewer services and less spending, with the remainder taking the middle position.[1]

Table 4.1 shows levels of support for federal spending on a variety of social programs. Program by program, few Americans want reductions in federal spending. The most frequent preference, in fact, is not to reduce spending or even to keep spending the same but rather to increase spending across a wide variety of programs such as social security, medical research, grants to college students, and protecting the environment. Despite occasional rhetoric to the contrary, the services provided by government to its citizens are popular.

Of course, there are limits to the public's enthusiasm for social welfare programs. Most notably, Americans clearly make the classic distinction between the "deserving poor" (those who have fallen on hard times through no fault of their own) and the "shiftless poor," who would rather receive a government handout than hold a job.[2] Thus, in the mid-1980s one poll showed that 88 percent of people with opinions agreed that the government ought to help those "who are unable to support themselves," while at the same time 91 percent agreed that "too many people on welfare could be working" and 94 percent said "too many people on welfare get money to which they are not entitled" (Page and Shapiro 1992, 125).

This distinction can be seen most graphically by large changes in poll numbers when slight changes are made in the way questions are phrased. For example, in a question-wording experiment, one-half of the 1998 GSS sample

---

TABLE 4.1 | **Opinions on Selected Federal Social Welfare Programs, 2000**

Should spending increase, decrease, or stay the same for:	Increase	Stay the Same	Decrease
Social Security	63%	32%	4%
Improving and protecting health†	69	25	6
Public schools	76	18	5
Welfare programs	17	38	45
Poor people	62	39	9
Protecting the environment	51	39	9
Food stamps*	16	51	33
Aid to college students*	55	38	8
Aid to homeless*	57	31	12
Research on AIDS	51	39	10
Child care	63	29	8

Source: National Election Studies, 2000 (except as noted).

†General Social Survey, 1998.

*National Election Studies, 1996.

was asked their view on spending "for assistance to the poor." Sixty-three percent said the government should increase spending.[3] The other half of the sample was asked for their views on spending "for welfare." Only 16 percent said the government should increase spending. (Table 4.1 shows similar figures when these options were offered to the 2000 NES sample.)

More than a mere illustration of question-wording effects, this experiment reflects a belief among Americans that the government should help those who cannot help themselves—the deserving poor. But Americans see people on welfare as able but unwilling to work, and thus meriting little sympathy. There is a widespread belief among the American public that people who receive financial assistance ought to work for their money, even if the work they do is of little use.

But this may not be all to the story about Americans' hostility toward people on welfare. Martin Gilens (2002) argues that race, regrettably, is an important part of the explanation. Many whites harbor the belief that blacks are lazy; they tend to exaggerate the extent to which blacks populate the welfare rolls. The effect of this on support for welfare can be seen in the fact that those whites who believe (mistakenly) that most welfare recipients are black are also those who are most opposed to welfare.

Health Care   As we noted earlier, the public has frequently been out in front of elected officials on many innovations in social welfare policy. This has certainly been the case with regard to health care. Since the 1930s, opinion polls have consistently shown the public favors some form of government intervention. In 1937, a Gallup poll showed that over 70 percent favored the notion that "the federal government should provide free medical and dental care for those who cannot pay." During the 1950s and 1960s, 60 to 65 percent supported the principle of the government paying the medical bills of the elderly, which was enacted into law in 1965 with Medicare (Erskine 1975). In 1975 and 1985 Roper polls, 76 percent and 73 percent respectively thought adequate medical care was a "right" to which citizens were entitled. But these sentiments do not necessarily mean the public wants socialized medicine or the government directly running health care. Most Americans seem to prefer a mixed system wherein private insurance is available, perhaps subsidized by the government or employers, with the state acting only as the provider of last resort (Page and Shapiro 1992, 131).

Using the NES seven-point Medicare question—where point 1 represents a "government health insurance plan which would cover all medical and hospital expenses," and point 7 indicates that expenses would be "paid to individuals through private insurance"—we can see that preferences for the two approaches are about equal as shown in Figure 4.1. The only exception occurred in 1992, when Clinton's reform package—the Health Security Act—was a prominent campaign theme.[4] Preference for a government plan rose to an all-time high of 45 percent, and preference for a private plan dropped to 24 percent. As Congress was poised to act on the Clinton plan, the health care industry mounted a major counterattack; two years later, in 1994, only 37 percent preferred a government

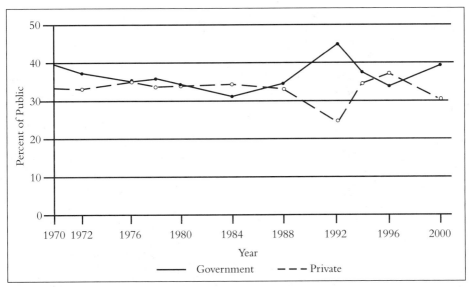

Figure 4.1   Private versus government health insurance. *Source:* National Election Studies, 1970–2000.

plan, and 35 percent favored a private plan. By 1996, fortunes had reversed and a slightly larger percentage of the public (38 percent) preferred a private health plan over a government health plan, only to reverse again in 2000.[5] The failure of the Clinton health care initiative demonstrates the difficulty of achieving fundamental change on a complex issue. It is easy to point out certain negative aspects of a proposal, even if taken in whole the proposal has considerable merit. There seems little doubt that the reversal in public opinion was a major factor leading to the defeat of Clinton's proposed Health Security Act (Koch 1998, Jacobs and Shapiro 2000).

Taxes   Regardless of how the question is phrased, a majority of the public invariably respond that taxes are too high. When asked in 1998 how to spend the projected federal budget surplus, 66 percent said a tax cut should be the top or a high priority. When asked in 1997 if federal taxes were too high, about right, or too low, 65 percent responded "too high." Only 1 percent said "too low." In 1991, 77 percent said taxes in this country were "unreasonable," and 66 percent claimed that high taxes had pushed their family to the breaking point.

Antitax sentiment has fluctuated over time. Gallup has asked its sample question about "too high" federal income taxes regularly since 1947. For this question, the least antitax sentiment was in March 1949, when only 49 percent said taxes were too high. With new taxes to pay for the Korean War, the number quickly shot up to 73 percent in March 1952. It then declined gradually, dropping to 49 percent in 1961. The costs of the Vietnam War helped push the figure upward again, to 73 percent in 1969. After the war, antitax sentiment declined through the mid-1970s, only to rise again in the late 1970s as part of an overall antigovernment right turn. With the Reagan tax cuts of 1981, sentiment that taxes were too high declined to 55 percent in 1988 (Page and Shapiro 1992, 162–163). But with the Democrats recapturing the White House and memories of the Reagan tax cuts fading, sentiment that taxes are too high rose to 68 percent by 1999. However, by 2003, with the tax cuts enacted under the George W. Bush administration, belief that taxes are too high fell to 51 percent.

Some cynical observers point to the seemingly inconsistent poll data on spending and taxes as demonstrating that the public irrationally expects to have its cake and eat it too. Citizens want a plethora of public services (as shown in Table 4.1), but they do not want to pay for them (Free and Cantril 1967; Sears and Citrin 1985). But when the views of the public are assessed with realistic questions designed to measure the trade-offs between taxes and services, the public appears quite rational on the subject. An example of a question assessing trade-offs is "Do you favor cuts in national defense spending in order to cut the taxes paid by ordinary Americans?" Using this strategy, Hansen (1998) probed trade-offs among domestic spending, military spending, taxes, and deficits. Majorities in 1994 rejected all trade-offs that would cut services to reduce taxes but accepted every trade-off that would cut military spending. The public mostly endorsed the status quo, but in a fashion that lends strong evidence to the "rational public" argument. That is, the respondents clearly recognized they cannot have it both ways—more spending and lower taxes.[6]

Civil Rights

Discerning the true attitudes held by white Americans on civil rights issues has proved a difficult and controversial task. Taking easy issues first, polls clearly show at a minimum that Americans have rejected the prevalent white supremacist ideology that pervaded mass attitudes as recently as a few decades ago. Poll data from the 1930s and 1940s suggest that perhaps a majority of white Americans once believed blacks to be intellectually inferior and undeserving of equal status with whites. In 1939, a Roper poll found 76 percent of white respondents agreeing that "Negroes" had generally "lower" intelligence than white people (Page and Shapiro 1992). As late as 1944, just 44 percent believed that "Negroes are as intelligent as white people" (Erskine 1962a). By 1994, according to a Harris survey, only 12 percent of whites agreed with the stereotype that blacks have less native intelligence than other races.

In the analysis of public opinion on racial issues, it is common to distinguish between questions concerning the goals or ideals of the civil rights movement and government action to actually implement those goals into public policy. The public is more supportive of the abstract goals of the civil rights movement than their implementation. For example, when asked in 1995 if black and white children should go to the same or separate schools, 96 percent of whites preferred the ideal of both races "going to the same schools" (Schuman, Steeh, and Bobo 1997). But when asked if the government in Washington "should see to it" that black and white children attend the same schools or if this is "not the government's business," just 47 percent of whites supported implementation of the ideal by federal government action (NES 2000).

We see a somewhat similar pattern in the trends over time. Whites have become much more liberal on questions concerning the ideals of the civil rights movement but not on the implementation of these ideals. In terms of ideals, endorsement of fair employment practices for blacks rose from 42 percent in 1944 to 96 percent by 1972 (Smith and Sheatsley 1984, 15–16). In 1958, only 37 percent of white respondents indicated they would vote for a well-qualified black presidential candidate, but by 1996, 93 percent would do so (Niemi et al. 1989; GSS 1996). In 1944, 45 percent said Negroes should have as good a chance as whites to get a job; by 1972, a near consensus of 97 percent shared that belief (Page and Shapiro 1992, 69).

Figure 4.2 presents trends in white support for integrated schools, both in terms of principle and implementation. First, consider the question of whether white and black children should attend the same or separate schools. In 1942, just 30 percent said "same school" and 66 percent said "separate schools." Figure 4.2 picks up the series in 1956, when the trend had moved 19 points in a liberal direction to 49 percent for "same school." By 1985, 93 percent of the white public favored the ideal of black and white children attending the same school (rising to 96 percent in 1995, the last year the question was asked). From 1942 to 1985, there was a 62 percent increase in white support for integrated schools, perhaps the largest change in public opinion for which we have data.

Figure 4.2 shows a different trend, however, on the question of whether the "government in Washington should see to it" that black and white children go to the same schools. When framed in terms of possible federal action, there is

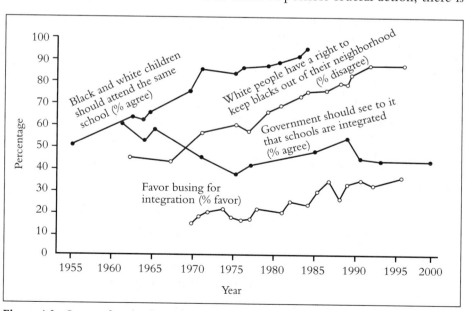

Figure 4.2 Support for school integration, open housing, and busing to integrate public schools.
Source: National Opinion Research Center, Gallup, and General Social Survey.

less support for the integration positions, with white Americans more in favor of government action in the 1960s than in the 1970s and later. While opposition to racial discrimination is almost universal, attitudes about government intervention are anything but consensual.

Still, not all implementation trends are conservative. Figure 4.2 shows that in the case of busing children to achieve racial balance in schools, whites have become more supportive. While busing remained generally unpopular into the 1990s, there was nevertheless a net increase of about 20 percentage points in support over a quarter-century of polling. Perhaps busing is not as threatening now as it was in the past. Few white children are actually bused out of their neighborhoods, and the magnet school approach, which often requires busing, has generally met with approval.

Finally, Figure 4.2 shows that whites have increasingly rejected the right to keep blacks from their neighborhoods. Note, however, that it was not until 1972 that a majority of whites settled on that view. By 1996, the number disagreeing that white people "had a right" to keep blacks out of their neighborhood had grown to 87 percent. This change in attitude is mirrored by a change in behavior. In 1966, only 20 percent of whites said there were blacks living in their neighborhood. In 2000, 68 percent said blacks lived there (GSS).

Affirmative Action   The most contentious civil rights issue of contemporary politics is "affirmative action" to help blacks (plus other racial minorities and women) advance in the education system and the workplace. While surveys show considerable white opposition to affirmative action programs, the extent of this opposition depends heavily on how the question is framed. If the survey question emphasizes helping the advancement of the disadvantaged, one can obtain majority support for affirmative action in principle. For instance, a 2003 Pew survey asked: "In order to overcome past discrimination, do you favor or oppose affirmative action programs designed to help blacks, women, and other minorities to get better jobs and education?" Fifty-seven percent of whites supported affirmative action, while only 29 percent opposed. But when the question emphasizes "preferences" for minorities without mentioning a rationale, support for affirmative action plunges. A 2002 *Washington Post* poll asked respondents simply whether they "support or oppose affirmative action programs that give preferences to blacks and other minorities." The responses (including all races) was 38 percent support and 55 percent oppose. When the argument for preferences is balanced by a counterargument of discrimination against whites, support for affirmative action declines further, as with this 1996 NES survey question (white responses only):

> Some people say that because of past discrimination, blacks should be given preference in hiring and promotion. Others say that such preference in hiring and promotion is wrong because it discriminates against whites. What about your opinion—are you for or against preferential hiring for blacks?

For	Against	Unsure
17%	78%	5%

Public reaction to existing affirmative action policies can be interpreted as mixed. When offered the choice of whether "affirmative action programs that provide advantages or preferences for blacks, Hispanics, and other minorities in hiring, promoting, and college admissions" should be continued or abolished, respondents (all races) in a 2003 Associated Press poll voted 53–35 for continuation. When asked about the pace of affirmative action, 36 percent in a 2003 *Los Angeles Times* poll (all races) said affirmative action programs had "gone too far," while 18 percent said they "had not gone far enough." Thirty-six percent saw these programs as "just about adequate now."[7]

Although the degree of support for affirmative action varies markedly with the exact question asked, we should not conclude that people generally lack fixed attitudes on the issue. After an extensive investigation, including attempts to change respondents' minds with counterarguments, Sniderman and Piazza (1993, 145) argue quite the contrary. They assert, "The positions white Americans take on affirmative action are remarkably firmer, less malleable, than the positions they take on more traditional forms of government assistance for the disadvantaged."

How does one explain the tepid support among whites for specific remedies to solve the problem of racial discrimination in the face of their overwhelming support for the ideals of racial integration? Two explanations are commonly debated: race per se and the politics of race. The first of these, the "symbolic racism" argument (Sears and Kinder 1971; Kinder and Sanders 1996), holds there has been little change in whites' attitudes about African Americans, which remain mostly hostile. When asked opinions about policy questions with racial implications, whites are more likely to respond to the racial symbol (e.g., "black") rather than the policy content of the question. However, over the years public expression of racist sentiment became increasingly unfashionable. Outright racial discrimination also became illegal. Consequently, people learned it was socially unacceptable to express overtly racist opinions. Instead, racial hostility is expressed indirectly by a glorification of traditional values such as "the work ethic" and "individualism," in which blacks and some other minorities are seen as deficient (Sears et al. 1997). Thus some of the apparent liberal trend in racial attitudes is not real change but rather reflects the need to express "socially desirable" opinions. Opposition to implementation, usually on grounds other than race, is simply disingenuous.[8]

A rival explanation is simple, straightforward politics. Sniderman and Piazza (1993, 107) argue that "the central problem of racial politics is *not* the problem of prejudice" (italics original). The agenda of the civil rights movement has changed from one of equal opportunity to equal outcomes. No fair-minded person could find consistency between the American Creed and denial of voting rights; segregated universities, workplaces, and lunch counters; and confinement to the back of the bus. But in the eyes of many, the new civil rights agenda of affirmative action very much clashes with the principle of equal treatment for all. Its implementation also requires an activist, expansionist government. Antistatism, manifested as hostility to federal power, is a long-standing tradition in American politics. The political explanation holds that inconsistencies with the American Creed, and concerns about the power and trustworthiness of the federal government, prevent many whites (particularly conservative whites) from translating an abstract commitment to racial equality into support for specific federal policies (Sniderman and Carmines, 1997).[9]

Foreign Policy

Scholars often depict public opinion on questions of foreign policy as being particularly shallow and without meaningful content. Typical is the observation by Light and Lake (1985, 94) that "public opinion polls show that people do not follow foreign affairs closely and often do not know enough about the specifics of a particular issue to form opinions." As applied to most citizens on most foreign policy issues, one cannot easily object to this statement. However, an important foreign policy matter can easily grab the public's attention and profoundly affect the popularity of the president or the outcome of the next election.

Foreign policy opinions are subject to more abrupt changes than are domestic policy opinions. If *abrupt change* is defined as ten or more percentage points over a single year, abrupt changes are twice as likely on foreign policy as on domestic issues (Page and Shapiro 1989). The explanation is straightforward: There are more dramatic events on the international scene than on the domestic scene. Few domestic occurrences have the impact of the Cuban missile crisis, the Iran hostage crisis, 9/11 and subsequent U.S. involvement in Afghanistan, and the two wars involving Iraq.

Internationalism Versus Isolationism   One volatile indicator of foreign policy sentiment is mass preference for an internationalist versus an isolationist posture in foreign policy. Prior to World War II, American opinion was strongly isolationist. In 1937, 70 percent of opinion-holders said U.S. entry into World War I had been a mistake (Free and Cantril 1968, 62). That same year, 94 percent of opinion-holders said the United States should "do everything possible to keep out of foreign wars" rather than "do everything possible to prevent war. . . . " Between 1939 and late 1941, the percentage who said they would vote in favor of entering the war against Germany rose only from 13 to 32 percent. Support for war with Japan a month before Pearl Harbor was even lower, with just 19 percent endorsing the view that "the United States should take steps to keep Japan from becoming too powerful, even if this means risking a war with Japan" (Hero n.d.).

But once the United States was involved in World War II, internationalist sentiment increased sharply. By June 1943, 83 percent said the United States would have to play a larger part in world affairs than before the war (Page and Shapiro 1992, 176). Figure 4.3 tracks post–World War II internationalist versus isolationist sentiment as monitored by the question of whether the United States should "take an active part" or "stay out" of world affairs.

One high point of internationalist sentiment occurred in the mid-1960s, just before full American involvement in the Vietnam conflict. Poll results such

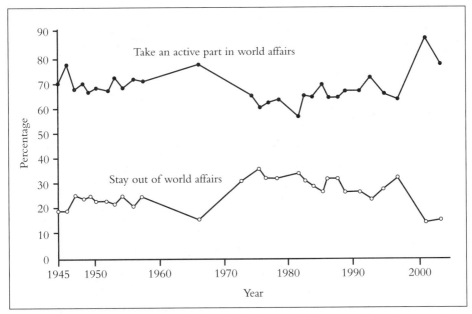

Figure 4.3 "Do you think it would be best for the future of this country if we take an active part in world affairs, or if we stayed out of world affairs?" *Sources:* The U.S. Role in the World Poll, 1996: University of Maryland, Gallup, National Opinion Research Center, and General Social Survey.

as these helped convince the makers of American foreign policy that the American public would put up with a long and protracted war in Vietnam. Of course, they were tragically mistaken. The public turned against the war, and internationalist sentiment took a sharp decline. In August 1965, 24 percent thought it was a mistake sending troops to Vietnam; by December 1967 this number had risen to 45 percent, and as American involvement faded, it increased to 61 percent in May 1971 (Niemi et al. 1989, 71).

By 1975, the proportion who wanted the United States to "stay out of world affairs" surged to 36 percent. Then, for the next twenty-five years, internationalists led isolationists by only about a 2–1 ratio (see Figure 4.3). This changed in polls shortly after the 9/11 terrorist attack, with 81 percent saying we need to take "active part" in world affairs and only 14 percent saying it would be best for the country to "stay out of world affairs." In the following years, internationalist sentiment dipped only slightly from this post–9/11 peak.

Just as Figure 4.3 shows most Americans have favored an internationalist position in foreign affairs, most Americans have historically also favored U.S. participation in the United Nations—despite a minority of vocal critics. In 1997, only 9 percent of the population said we "should give up" our membership in the U.N. (versus 88 percent who said we should not), and 70 percent had a "mostly favorable" view of the United Nations (21 percent said "mostly unfavorable"). With the advent of the war in Iraq and friction between the United States and the United Nations, by June 2003 the "mostly unfavorable" view of the United Nations had risen to 32 percent, although 66 percent still had a "mostly favorable" view.[10]

Defense Spending   One source of frequently shifting opinion is public perception of the adequacy of defense spending. Figure 4.4 shows a roller coaster of changing beliefs regarding whether the United States is spending "too little on the military, armaments, and defense."

Beginning in 1978, large segments of the public began to believe that U.S. defenses were underfunded. This conservative trend resulted in part from the Soviet Union's invasion of Afghanistan in 1979, which President Carter denounced as "the worst threat to world peace since World War II." In protest, he withdrew American participation in the 1980 Moscow Olympics. Also in 1979, American hostages were held in Iran, and the United States seemed powerless to get them back. Both the Democratic and Republican party leadership became convinced the United States was spending too little on defense. Without a credible alternative elite counterargument, public opinion quickly fell into line.

Following the renewed military buildup under both Carter and Reagan, the citizenry became reassured that America's defenses were again strong. As the 1980s progressed, support for increased defense spending retreated to the level of the early 1970s. With the collapse of the Soviet Union in the early 1990s, support for increases in defense spending fell to record lows. Then, support for more military spending showed a new upturn as result of 9/11 and hostilities in the Middle East.

Statistical analysis of trends in public attitudes toward defense spending shows that it follows a rational course. It is not just that spending attitudes responds to the severity of the perceived threat (or the threat people are told to

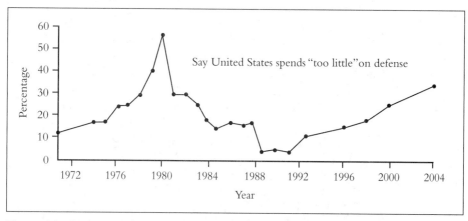

Figure 4.4   Percentage who say the United States is spending "too little" on the military, armaments, and defense. *Source:* Roper and General Social Survey.

believe). In addition, support for defense spending responds to the waxing and waning of the actual defense buildup. When spending goes up, demand for further spending goes down, and vice versa (Wlezien 1995a).

Russia and China   Between the end of World War II and the end of the cold war, the most relevant foreign policy question has been how the United States conducts its foreign policy in relationship to the former Soviet Union and to China. Mass attitudes toward these nations generally followed the lead of American foreign policy. During World War II, when the Soviet Union and the United States were allies, favorable attitudes toward the Soviet Union grew until, at war's end, 55 percent said, "Russia can be counted on to cooperate with us once the war is over." This trust, born of wartime camaraderie, soon evaporated, and by October 1946 the percentage who thought Russia could "be trusted to cooperate with us during the next few years" dropped to 28 percent. By the late 1940s, most Americans thought it was more important "to stop Soviet expansion in Europe and Asia than avoid a major war." During the Korean War and in the early 1950s, a majority said they expected war with Russia during their lifetime (Hero n.d.).

The chill of the cold war reached its nadir in the early 1950s. As can be seen from Figure 4.5, in 1953 and 1954 only 2 percent of the public claimed to "like" the Soviet Union.[11]

But beginning in the 1950s, Americans gradually began to warm to the world's other superpower. By 1973, with the Vietnam War winding down, liking of Russia surged to 45 percent. Following the 1979 Soviet invasion of Afghanistan and, later, President Reagan's rhetoric about the Soviet Union as

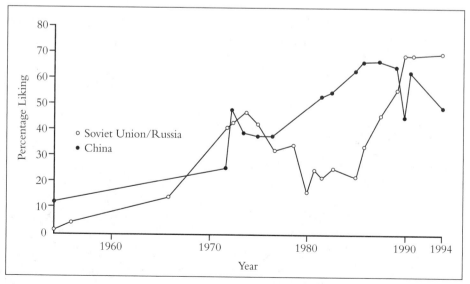

Figure 4.5   Percentage who "like" Russia/Soviet Union and China. *Source:* Gallup and General Social Survey.

the "evil empire," a new chill in attitudes set in. Then a major warming of attitudes toward Russia occurred after the demise of the Soviet Union in 1991, the implementation of democratic elections, and the end of the cold war.

Americans' attitudes toward China have also responded to events. In the 1960s and earlier, the United States did not even recognize the Chinese government and vigorously opposed the membership of "Red China" in the United Nations. As late as 1964, only 14 percent of the public favored U.N. membership for China. (Even in 1971, the year China was admitted, a majority of Americans still opposed membership.) Public sentiment toward China gradually warmed (see Figure 4.5), except for a temporary plunge in 1990 following the crackdown on student protesters in Tiananmen Square. By 1993, favorable sentiment toward China, while on the increase, lagged for the first time behind favorable sentiment toward Russia. By that index, Russia forged slightly into the lead.

Social Issues

In the first half of the twentieth century, the only types of policy issues that drew strong national attention, including from pollsters, were social welfare matters involving spending and taxing and foreign affairs. Starting in the 1950s, civil rights pushed toward center stage. Soon after, a new set of concerns called *social issues* arrived and never left. In their broadest context, these issues involve conflicts between forces of social change and forces committed to maintaining "traditional moral values." Examples of social issues include prayer in public schools, decriminalization of marijuana use, government restrictions on pornography, and tolerance for gay lifestyles. Recent opinion on these issues is shown in Table 4.2.

TABLE 4.2	Opinion Distributions on Social Issues (Percentage of Opinion-Holders)	Liberal	Conservative
Marijuana	Do you think marijuana should be made legal or not?†	34 (yes)	64 (no)
Gay rights	Should there be laws to protect homosexuals against job discrimination?★	64 (yes)	36 (no)
Pornography	Should there be laws against the distribution of pornography whatever the age?★★	62 (no)	38 (yes)
Sex education	Do you favor sex education in the public schools?†	87 (yes)	13 (no)
Prayer in schools	Should prayer be permitted in public schools?‡	30 (no)	70 (yes)

Sources: ★National Election Studies, 2003. ★★National Election Studies, 1996. †General Social Survey, 1998. ‡CBS/*New York Times*, 1997.

On social issues, the public is generally thought to be rather conservative. Many but not all the divisions shown in Table 4.2 support this perception. One obvious limitation on the public's social conservatism is a willingness to support sex education in public schools.

Even on school prayer, the public's conservatism should not be exaggerated, though when offered only the choice between prayer and no prayer a substantial majority choose prayer (see Table 4.2). But consider responses to a 1997 CBS/*New York Times* survey in which respondents were offered three choices instead of two: (1) the Lord's Prayer or Bible verse said daily, (2) a silent prayer or meditation daily, or (3) no prayer or religious observation. Most (55 percent) preferred the "mild" solution that schools offer a moment of silence. The remainder split 22 percent in favor of a daily prayer or Bible verse and 21 percent favoring no religious observance. Interestingly, however, when it comes to the evolution controversy, a literal interpretation of the Bible holds sway with the public over the views of establishment science. A sizable plurality favors the creationist theory over evolution to account for the origin of human life. When asked to choose between these explanations, 48 percent opt for creationism and 28 percent opt for evolution (Gallup 2001).

Because the social issues presented in Table 4.2 have been on the public agenda for no more than a few decades at best, it is difficult to establish trend lines of any length. Nevertheless, some trend data are available. In the case of the legalization of marijuana, support has grown steadily but slowly. When Gallup started polling on legalization in 1969, opinion was 84–12 against legalization. By 2003, the division narrowed to about only 2–1 against, or 64–34 percent. For pornography laws, the trend has been stable at least since 1973, with those favoring laws against its distribution ranging between 57 and 63 percent. The same stability occurs for sex education and prayer in the public schools. Opinion in these two areas has been more or less constant for the last twenty years (Niemi et al. 1989; NES 1996; CBS/*New York Times* 1997). Support for gay rights has increased in recent decades. For instance, support for laws protecting homosexuals against job discrimination went up by 10 percentage points between 1988 and 1996 alone. Surveys generally show an increasing tolerance for gay lifestyles. Still, in most (but not all) contemporary surveys, more respondents oppose than support civil unions by gay couples. The public remains divided on whether homosexual behavior should be "legal."

Law and Order   One set of issue opinions that shows a decidedly conservative trend is that dealing with law and order (Flanagan and Longmire 1996; Soss, Langbein, and Metelko 2003). Opinion on the death penalty (which had trended liberal from the 1930s to the 1960s) provides the clearest example. As can be seen from Figure 4.6, support for the death penalty for convicted murderers rose from around 50 percent in the 1950s and 1960s to over 70 percent in the 1980s and 1990s, with 66 percent favoring the death penalty in 2002. However, if respondents are offered an option of "life imprisonment with no possibility of parole" in addition to the death penalty, support for the death penalty drops to 56 percent (Gallup 1999). Figure 4.6 also shows considerable

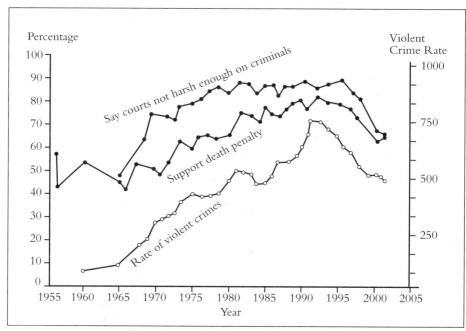

Figure 4.6 Law-and-order opinion and the rate of violent crime. *Source:* Richard G. Niemi, John Mueller, and Tom W. Smith, *Trends in Public Opinion* (New York: Greenwood, 1989), General Social Survey (1989–1998), Harold W. Stanley and Richard G. Niemi, *Vital Statistics of American Politics, 2003–2004* (Washington, D.C.: Congressional Quarterly, 2003).

public sentiment for the view that the courts do not deal harshly enough with criminals. In 2002, 67 percent endorsed that position, up 22 percentage points from 1965, but down from its all-time high of 80 percent in 1998. Interestingly, the public's apparent taste for greater punitiveness has not caught up with the actual trend toward longer criminal sentences (Sharp 1999). It is not clear whether the public mistakenly perceives that judges go easier on criminals than is true or whether people generally know the level of conviction and sentencing but insist on even harsher treatment of criminals. Conceivably some respondents confront the survey question about harshness toward criminals in a factual vacuum and respond simply as if it were a referendum on the goodness or badness of crime.

Figure 4.6 also shows that increases in support for the death penalty and beliefs that the courts do not deal harshly enough with criminals roughly tracked the rate of violent crime up to 1990. Some (Mayer 1992) have claimed that the increase in support for the death penalty was a reaction to the increase in violent crime. But as Figure 4.6 demonstrates, beginning about 1990 the rate of violent crime fell dramatically. There has, however, been a more modest decline in support for the death penalty or a preference for the harsh treatment of criminals. This trend suggests that political rhetoric and media attention are more proximate causes for opinion about crime than the level of crime itself (Sharp 1999). In the 1980s, elected officials clearly reacted to changing opinion on crime with policy innovations such as mandatory sentences and life terms for people convicted of three felonies. Although violent crime is decreasing, there is no discernible move to modify these harsher policies, which suggests there is no simple connection between the crime rate, public opinion, and the penal code.

Equality for Women   If law-and-order questions have shown a strong conservative trend, opinion about equality for women shows an equally strong liberal trend. From Gallup and GSS, we have data spanning fifty years on the question of whether or not the public would vote for a qualified woman for president—the ultimate nontraditional role. As shown below, we see a strong leftward flow of opinion on this issue, beginning with the advent of the women's movement in the late 1960s. The trend then abated somewhat in the late 1970s with the defeat of the Equal Rights Amendment and the organization of opposition to legal abortion. Beginning in the late 1980s, support in polls for the possibility of a woman president surged toward near unanimity.

Percentage Who Would Vote for a Qualified Woman for President

1937	33	1958	54	1972	70	1991	87
1945	38	1963	55	1975	78	1993	91
1949	50	1967	57	1978	79	1996	94
1955	52	1969	59	1983	83		

Over the decades, the public shifted from general opposition to the idea of a woman president to a general consensus accepting the idea in principle. Other opinion indicators on the role of women show a similar pattern. Since 1972, the NES has been asking respondents if women should have "an equal role with men in running business, industry, and government" or whether a "woman's place is in the home."[12] In 1972, a mere 59 percent (of opinion-holders) chose the "equal role" option. By 1980, 75 percent did. By 2000, support stood at 88 percent, with only 12 percent of opinion-holders saying women should stay home.

Abortion   The most salient of the social issues from the 1980s on into the twenty-first century has been abortion. Americans tend to oppose abortion on moral grounds while supporting the right to abortion as a matter of public policy. In 1998, for example, 57 percent of respondents said they "personally believe that abortion is wrong." But in the very next question, 69 percent said that regardless of their personal view, they favor the right of a woman to choose an abortion (Gallup-*Newsweek* poll, Oct. 30, 1998).

The public debate on abortion tends to stress the extremes, with the "pro-life" advocates demanding an end to all abortions and the "pro-choice" advocates demanding abortion on request. But most Americans favor neither polar position. In a 2003 Gallup survey, 26 percent said that "abortion should be legal in any circumstances" and 17 percent said that "abortion should be illegal under all circumstances." The majority, 54 percent, said abortion should be legal, but only under certain circumstances. (Three percent were undecided.)

We can discover the circumstances under which the public feels abortion should be allowed. Since 1965, the General Social Survey has been asking respondents if "you think it should be possible for a pregnant woman to obtain a legal abortion . . . " and then specifying six different circumstances. We can group these circumstances into "traumatic" and "elective," with traumatic being external circumstances beyond the woman's control (Cook et al. 1992), including danger to her health, damage to the fetus, and rape or incest. Elective reasons include personal and economic considerations—for example, if a married woman wants no more children, the family cannot afford more children, or if an unmarried pregnant woman does not wish to marry the father. Opinion on these items has been remarkably stable since the Roe v. Wade decision in 1973 (Shaw 2003). Public support for abortion rights in traumatic and elective circumstances in the 2002 General Social Survey was:

Traumatic Abortion		Elective Abortion	
Defective fetus	78%	Married, does not want children	41%
Health danger	85	Cannot afford children	40
Rape/Incest	76	Does not want to marry	37

Obviously, circumstances are crucial for the public's willingness to support abortion. Less than an absolute majority favor abortion for any of the elective reasons, while support is overwhelming in traumatic circumstances.[13] However, only about 7 percent of all abortions are done for traumatic reasons (Torres and Forrest 1988).

Given these mixed feelings, it is therefore not surprising to find that only a minority of the public favors reversing Roe v. Wade (which in some states would effectively outlaw abortions). When the public was asked in 1998 if the Roe decision should be overturned, 64 percent said "let it stand" compared with 36 percent who wanted the ruling overturned.[14] On the other hand, Americans favor some restrictions on abortion rights. In 1998 a CBS/*New York Times* poll showed that 78 percent favored a law requiring parental notification before a pregnant teenager under eighteen could get an abortion, and in July 1996, Gallup reported that over 70 percent of the public favored a law requiring physicians to inform patients about alternatives to abortion, notification of husbands if a married woman wants an abortion, and a 24-hour waiting period before the procedure. It seems clear that the public wants abortion kept legal, but with regulations and restrictions.

Measured by Gallup's standard abortion question, asked every year since 1975, pro-choice support peaked in 1994 when 33 percent said "abortion should be legal under any circumstances." The subsequent decline is probably a result of the highly charged debate over "partial birth abortions." Twenty-eight percent supported abortion for any reason in October 2003. When given a choice in May 2003 between the labels "pro-choice" or "pro-life," 48 percent chose the former and 45 percent chose the latter (Gallup).

Many politicians who once took hard-line stands against abortion moderated their positions in the late 1980s, apparently because they saw the tide of public opinion had turned in favor of abortion rights. Pro-choice advocates became much more active as they responded to the Supreme Court restrictions on abortion in cases like Webster v. Reproductive Health Services. But the mild trend in opinion away from "abortion on demand" has not much altered the balance of power between the two opposing groups. Pro-choice partisans still hold a numerical advantage in public opinion, but pro-life partisans are more likely to communicate their opinions to elected leaders. Verba, Scholzman, and Brady (1995) show that politically active citizens who hold pro-life preferences on abortion are about five times more likely to focus that activity on the abortion issue than are politically active citizens who are pro-choice. Politicians are known to pay greater attention to people who actively voice their convictions.[15]

4-2 GENERAL IDEOLOGICAL MOVEMENT

The preceding sections have shown trends on specific survey items. For a particular issue, opinion might become more conservative over time, or more liberal—or, as is often the case, it may just stay the same from one survey reading to the next. If there is a general ideological trend from the data we have examined, it would seem to be lost in the details. A challenging question is whether the public regularly undergoes changes in its "ideological mood." Conceivably, one could detect broad currents of opinion that sometimes flow in the liberal direction and sometimes in the conservative direction. We do know that any general ideological movement cannot be large. From one year to the next, net opinion on any issue rarely changes more than a few percentage points. And large movements generally are responses to events unique to the issue, such as when defense spending preferences once fluctuated in response to the momentary intensity of the cold war.

One way to locate trends in liberalism or conservatism on the part of the public is simply to record changes in the degree to which people call themselves liberals or conservatives. However, as shown in the previous chapter, self-ranking as liberal or conservative is sometimes questionable for the reason that many people lack adequate understanding of these terms. At a minimum, though, changes in how people describe themselves ideologically should reveal shifts in how fashionable are the terms *liberal* and *conservative*.

In polls taken between the late 1930s and the mid-1960s, respondents remained about evenly divided between self-declared liberals and self-declared conservatives. But then a conservative shift began so that by 1970, conservatives clearly outnumbered liberals, typically by a ratio of about 3 to 2. This change is puzzling, as the public's stands on issues did not obviously become more conservative at the same time. Why did the liberal label go into disfavor so suddenly in the late 1960s?

To some extent, the sudden shift toward "conservatism" reflected an increased public concern about issues on which people saw themselves as conservative (e.g., law-and-order issues) and less public concern about issues on which people saw themselves as liberal (e.g., New Deal social welfare issues). Also, in the changing 1960s, opponents of civil rights legislation frequently justified their position in terms of conservative ideology rather than opposition to the equal-opportunity goals of the civil rights movement. Finally, the mid-1960s were a time when much liberal legislation (Medicare, federal aid to education, major civil rights protection) was enacted. As policy became more liberal, people's ideological frame of reference changed. To be a liberal was to seek even more liberal policies rather than simply to support the new status quo.

In any case, the growth of conservative self-identification in the late 1960s was a one-time event. Table 4.3 shows the distribution of the electorate's ideological self-identification since 1976. Compiled from CBS/*New York Times* surveys, the table is notable for the absence of any trend. In terms of ideological identification, the electorate showed the same distribution in the Carter years of the late 1970s as the Reagan-Bush 1980s and the Clinton years of the 1990s. Most people choose the "moderate" option, with conservatives outnumbering liberals about 34 to 22 percent.[16]

A second way to monitor changes in liberalism/conservatism is to carefully estimate movement by combining responses to multiple survey items containing left-right political content. Two ambitious sets of estimates have been reported that somewhat contradict both each other and the trend (or, recently, lack of it) in ideological identification. After assessing a variety of political and social issues, Tom Smith (1990) argues that opinions became gradually more liberal between World War II and the mid-1970s, and then leveled off in a "liberal plateau."

James Stimson (1999) made a similar investigation, restricted to a narrower set of strictly policy opinions. Stimson's updated findings, shown in Figure 4.7, indicate a more oscillating movement of what he calls the electorate's ideological "mood." His mood index shows an increase in liberalism in the 1950s and early 1960s, followed by a decline in the late 1960s and 1970s, followed again by a liberal surge in the 1980s, leveling off again in the 1990s. The scale shown represents movement on the scale of the percentage of liberal (among opinion-holders). Thus, the maximum difference in "mood" is a 17-point range from the liberal "high" of the early 1960s to a conservative "low" around 1979.

One can read the fluctuation in the national mood as the ebb and flow of the electorate's net demand for policy change. This demand is sensitive to changes in public policy. When Congress passes major liberal legislation in response to a liberal mood, as in the 1960s, the demand for liberalism is satisfied and the electorate's mood turns conservative. Similarly, when congressional action turns conservative in response to mood, as under Reagan's presidency in the 1980s, the demand for conservatism is satiated and national mood turns more liberal (Erikson, MacKuen, and Stimson 2002).

4-3 GENERAL PARTISAN MOVEMENT

From an electoral standpoint, one of the most important indicators is the distribution of party identification among the categories of Democrat, Republi-

TABLE 4.3 | **Ideological Identification of the U.S. Public, 1976–2003**

Question: "How would you describe your views on most political matters? Generally, do you think of yourself as liberal, moderate, or conservative?" Don't know/no answer responses are excluded.

Year	Liberal	Moderate	Conservative
1976	26%	40%	35%
1977	22	45	33
1978	24	40	36
1979	23	40	37
1980	21	46	33
1981	20	43	36
1982	21	45	34
1983	21	44	35
1984	21	46	33
1985	22	44	34
1986	21	44	36
1987	23	42	35
1988	20	45	35
1989	22	42	36
1990	23	44	34
1991	23	43	34
1992	22	45	34
1993	21	43	36
1994	21	44	36
1995	20	44	37
1996	18	47	34
1997	21	44	35
1998	21	44	34
1999	23	44	34
2000	24	43	33
2001	22	44	34
2002	22	44	33
2003	20	44	35

Source: Pooled surveys by CBS News/*New York Times*. Yearly readings are composites of multiple surveys.

can, and Independent. The conventional view among political scientists regarding trends in party identification is that macrolevel partisanship is quite stable except for the rare shock of a "partisan realignment." Partisan realignments are precipitated by political parties making major changes in their policy orientations. As parties' policy images change in fundamental ways, the electorate responds with surprisingly large shifts in party identification.

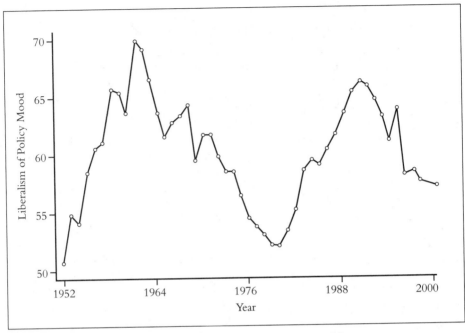

Figure 4.7   The public's policy "mood," 1952–2000. *Source:* James Stimson.

The classic example of a realignment was the New Deal of the 1930s, when the electorate transformed from predominantly Republican to Democrat. (Burnham 1970, 119–20; Sundquist 1973, 183–217). This change came in response to the Great Depression under a Republican president and Democratic president Franklin Roosevelt's response. Roosevelt was first elected in 1932, as the electorate demanded change with the onset of the Great Depression. Once in office, Roosevelt's policies, known as the New Deal, greatly expanded the role of the federal government to deal with the national emergency. People tended to align their partisanship anew based on their preferences for or against Roosevelt's economic liberalism. Although no polls were available until 1936, trends in election outcomes and voter registration clearly showed a major electoral shift in favor of the Democratic Party (Ladd 1970; Sundquist 1973, 183–217). To some extent, the electorate's division into Democrats and Republicans even today can be traced to the New Deal realignment.

If there had been polls in the 1920s, they would have shown a Republican dominance in partisanship. By 1937, when a national poll asked the party identification question for the first time, the Democrats predominated. In 99 percent of national polls conducted between 1937 and the present, Democrats outnumbered Republicans. On paper at least, the Democratic Party has had a decisive edge in identification.

In theory, the party system is stable for long periods punctuated only by realignment shocks such as the New Deal. Looking back on a half-century of political history, some scholars see signs of a more recent realignment (or something like it) in the 1960s, when issues like civil rights and social policy began to divide the parties nationally (Aldrich and Niemi 1996; Aldrich 2003). Others question the value of conceiving partisan history as equilibrium punctuated by sharp realignments (Mayhew 2002). In any case, it is now clear that the net direction of partisanship within the electorate is constantly moving over time.

As discussed in chapter 3, individual-level party identification is quite stable over time, as individuals rarely change their party preference. Still, when people do change partisanship (even if momentarily), they move in one-sided fashion in response to events. Figure 4.8 shows the annual reading of party identification in the Gallup poll since 1945. Measured as the percentage of Democrats among Democrat and Republican identifiers, this macrolevel index has been dubbed "macropartisanship" (MacKuen et al. 1989). The graph shows palpable movement, with what usually is a Democratic edge that is sometimes quite narrow but at other times a hefty 2–1 advantage in the count of partisan identifiers.[17] The partisan landscape changes via gradual evolution as well as realignment shock.

There were several changes in the nation's party identification over the last half of the twentieth century. The Democrats generally gained from World War II to a peak of support around 1964. Then the Republicans rebounded, only to show precipitous losses following the Watergate revelations of 1973 and 1974. The Democratic gain was followed by a strong Republican trend in the 1980s. As we enter the twenty-first century, the electorate is much more

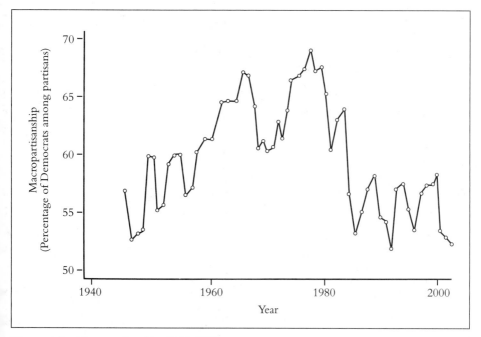

Figure 4.8   Macropartisanship, 1945–2003.

evenly divided between Democrats and Republicans than in the previous half-century, with the two parties deadlocked in a virtual tie in terms of citizen identification.

Close investigation of partisan trends shows that macropartisanship tracks both presidential approval (or, more accurately, the causes of approval) and economic conditions (MacKuen et al. 1989; Erikson, MacKuen, and Stimson 1998, 2002; but see Green, Palmquist, and Schickler 1998, 2002 for another view). For instance, the combination of economic recovery and the positive appeal of President Reagan helped the Republicans gain in the 1980s. Some observers at the time even foresaw the emergence of a permanent Republican realignment. Republican gains following the first President Bush's successful prosecution of the first Gulf War only solidified such expectations. But then Republican support skidded with the economic misfortune late in the first Bush presidency. Then, with the prosperity of the Clinton years, the Democrats began to slowly regain some of their earlier partisan edge. However, helped by the positive evaluation of President George W. Bush following 9/11, the Republicans surged again.

Interestingly, movement of party identification bears no resemblance to the movement of ideological mood or ideological identification previously discussed. The electorate's relative favor for Republicans or Democrats is totally unrelated to the electorate's swings between conservatism and liberalism. Although many people choose their partisanship based on ideology, the macrolevel movement of partisanship responds more to perceptions of party performance in office than to ideological preference.

One further trend of note in party identification is the growth in the proportion of the electorate who reject each major party, preferring to call themselves Independents. From World War II to about 1966, only between 22 and 25 percent of the public typically called themselves Independents. Then, as the nation faced the Vietnam War, youth unrest, and the peak of the civil rights revolution, a major rejection of the parties began. Since the late 1960s, about one-third of the electorate has called itself Independent.

Some observers call this trend beginning in the mid-1960s a general "dealignment," as people seemingly disengaged from formerly strong partisan ties. But the growth of Independents is often exaggerated in discussions of the topic. Although the proportion who say they are Independents clearly grew in the late 1960s, it has not appreciably grown since then. Further, there is considerable contrary evidence that people became increasingly more rather than less partisan during the Reagan-Bush-Clinton-Bush years (Bartels 2000).

4-4 PRESIDENTIAL APPROVAL

Without a doubt, the most closely watched political indicator in the United States is the president's approval rating. Unlike the other macrolevel attitudinal indicators we have discussed, presidential approval shows fluctuations so large as to attract attention from both politicians and the general public. The president's approval rating takes on importance because it is widely believed to measure the president's degree of political support at the moment. Congress may be more likely to enact the policy proposals of a president who shows popular support (Canes-Wrone and deMarchi 2002; Bond, Fleischer, and Wood 2003). Presidential approval also provides a guide to reelection prospects (Lewis-Beck and Rice 1982; Brody and Sigelman 1983; Wlezien and Erikson, 2000).

While many polling organizations ask some variant of the presidential approval question, the standard measure is Gallup's question, asked regularly for over fifty years. When the Gallup Organization polls the American public, it regularly asks its respondents whether they "approve" of the president's performance, "disapprove" of the president's performance, or have no opinion. Attention generally focuses on the percentage (of all respondents) who approve of the president's current performance.

Gallup's sampling of presidential approval began with sporadic monitoring of Franklin Roosevelt in the late 1930s, when public opinion polling was in its infancy. However, regular readings of Roosevelt's approval rating were interrupted by World War II. Beginning with Harry Truman, presidents have been monitored in terms of public approval on virtually a continuous monthly basis. This database provides enough information that, in general terms at least, we now know which kinds of circumstances increase a president's popularity and which lead to its decline. Figure 4.9 depicts the history of presidential approval polling over a half-century, from Truman to Clinton. (Later, we focus on President George W. Bush's popularity.)

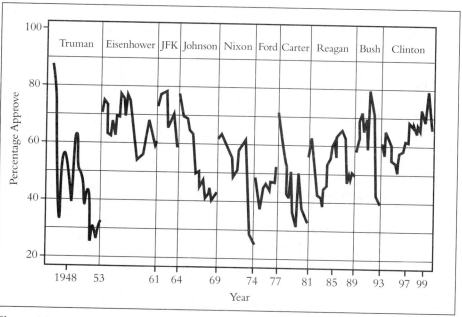

Figure 4.9   Presidential approval, Truman to Clinton. *Source:* Gallup Poll.

All presidents enjoy some time above 50 percent approval, and most have unhappily spent some time below the 50 percent baseline. Presidents Truman, Nixon, and Carter all spent time below the 30 percent approval level. Three sources account for most variation in a president's approval rating: (1) the honeymoon effect, (2) the rally-round-the-flag effect, and (3) the economy.

The Honeymoon

Every president starts the term with a rather high level of political support, with approval ratings in the 70 percent range not unusual. Then, as the term unfolds, the approval rating undergoes a gradual but inevitable decline. It is not surprising to find that presidents start out with an aura of goodwill, with even supporters of the defeated opponent offering their approval. The more interesting question is why this honeymoon eventually fades. Some say the reason presidents lose support over time is that they cannot please all segments of society all the time. Eventually, so this theory goes, the president must upset the expectations of some supporters, and this disillusionment creates a spiral of declining approval (Mueller 1973). Indeed, one might imagine a general rule that political support decays over time, with leaders inevitably becoming less popular the longer they govern. The implication is that no matter what presidents do to solve national problems, their political support will continue to erode.

A second interpretation is more optimistic. A president's early loss of popularity is best considered a retreat from an artificially high starting point rather than the erosion of a natural base (Kernell 1978). About a year into a presidency, the president's popularity reaches its natural, lower equilibrium level. By the second year, a president's popularity level stabilizes at about 50 percent. From this point on, approval is as likely to rise as it is to fall. The approval rating continues to vary around the usual average of about 50 percent—a function of events that reflect sometimes positively and sometimes negatively on the president's stewardship.

The basic reason presidents begin with an artificially high approval rating is that newly elected presidents start out free of criticism—either from other politicians or from the media. This grace period arises in part because the president has just proved his popularity at the ballot box. It also arises because the new president is a blank slate; he has conducted few official acts to be second-guessed. Instead of criticizing a new president, politicians and the media respond with words of support. Ordinary citizens take their cue from these expressions of goodwill—they, too, express approval (Brody 1990).

As the term evolves, however, the president must take actions that are subject to second-guessing and criticism from the media and from political opponents. The result is a natural decline in support. But after the first year, a new president's popularity generally stabilizes at a more natural level. Still, popularity continues to move in response to perceptions of how the president copes with events and the task of national leadership. We examine next some sources in this variation.

Rally-Round-the-Flag Effect

From time to time, public attention focuses on some foreign policy event—perhaps an unexpected crisis or a major treaty or U.S. intervention abroad. In the past, most of these were related to the cold war. Early examples include the Soviet shooting-down of a U.S. spy plane (the Francis Gary Powers U-2 incident) in 1960, the Cuban missile crisis in 1962, and seizures of U.S. ships by communist foreign governments in 1968 (the U.S.S. *Pueblo* by the North Koreans) and in 1975 (the *Mayaguez* by the Cambodians). However, not all salient foreign policy events are anxiety-provoking. Examples include events such as major treaties (e.g., Nixon's Moscow Treaty of 1972), summits (starting with Eisenhower's Geneva summit conference with Soviet leaders in 1955), and peace efforts such as Johnson's bombing halt (1968) and Carter's Camp David accords (1978) establishing the foundation for peaceful relations between Israel and Egypt.

What these events have in common is a focus on foreign policy. Generally, major foreign policy events are followed by a short-term surge in support for the president—what is called the rally-round-the-flag effect. These are special moments when eyes turn to the president, and the media and national politicians are seen to unite behind the chief executive.

Going to war is a special case. In the short term, wars traditionally result in the showering of approval on the president. One example comes from the early days of polling. While Roosevelt's approval ratings in the late 1930s were no more than respectable (typically in the mid-50s), entry into World War II saw his numbers rise into the 70s. More recent wars show similar patterns. Truman gained 9 points following the start of the Korean War in 1950. Johnson gained 8 points following a major escalation of the Vietnam War in 1966. Lesser conflicts, such as Johnson's 1965 invasion of the Dominican Republic and Reagan's invasion of Grenada, also were followed by surges in presidential popularity. Until 9/11 (see below), the biggest gain from a war certainly was the first President Bush's popularity surge to Gallup's record high of 87 percent in March 1991 following the brief first Gulf War against Iraq.

But the political rewards from wars and invasions can be short-lived (Mueller 1973, 1994). The Johnson administration, for example, miscalculated the American public's taste for a prolonged war in Vietnam. Johnson fell in a few short years from the 70s to the low 30s in approval. During the Korean conflict, Truman declined even further—into the 20s—as did Carter during the Iran hostage crisis. Both Truman and Johnson declined to seek reelection, and Carter was defeated in 1980. The first Bush's unique popularity after the first Gulf War shows what a short successful war can do to presidential popularity. But his approval decline in the war's aftermath (from 67 percent in August 1991 to 46 percent by January 1992) provides another lesson—that the political benefit from any presidential success may be short-lived.

The Economy

It is common knowledge that the president's approval rating rises and falls with the state of the economy. When unemployment or inflation rises, the president is blamed. When these indicators of economic gloom decline, the president is praised. Naturally, approval ratings reflect these tendencies. It is as if the electorate reads the state of the economy as a sign of the president's competence.

The exact mechanism by which the electorate converts economic perceptions into presidential approval has been the subject of considerable scholarly investigation. The simplest mechanism would be the straightforward response of personal pocketbook considerations—that when people face good economic times they support the president, and when they face hard times they do not. By this interpretation, presidential approval tracks the economy in direct response to the electorate's collective personal economic experience.

Consider, however, that most people, most of the time, know that they do not owe their current economic fortune to the president. If the economy is thriving, a person who just got fired or laid off is not likely to blame the president for his or her personal misfortune. Similarly, if the economy is clearly troubled, a person who earns a big raise and promotion is not likely to attribute this good fortune to the president.

But people *do* recognize the state of the general economy as having some relevance to their personal economic well-being. Consequently, citizens reward or punish the president not on the basis of their personal circumstances but rather their perceptions of the national economy. Such responses are called *sociotropic*, as people respond to how *society* is faring rather than how they personally are doing economically (Kinder and Kiewiet 1979). But the motive is still largely personal. People care about the national economy because they personally can be affected.

Sociotropic evaluations of presidential performance tend to be prospective rather than retrospective—that is, people update their evaluations based on prospects for the economy's future rather than evaluating its recent performance. We know this because, statistically, presidential approval tracks consumer expectations about the nation's economic future rather than consumer evaluations of current conditions (MacKuen, Erikson, and Stimson 1992; Erikson, MacKuen, and Stimson 2002).

In part, people base their prospective economic evaluations on the current economy. In other words, they use retrospective judgments to predict the future. But the electorate is also sensitive to signs of the future that are independent of the past, such as what economists call *leading economic indicators*. It works this way. When economists look into their crystal balls, they are reading leading indicators. The trend of these indicators is reported in the newspapers and on the evening news. In this way, knowledgeable people gain reasonable expectations of how the economy is going to behave. They do so not because ordinary people hold some special economic intuition; they learn about the economic future because they learn what economists say will happen.

Presidential Approval and George W. Bush

So far we have ignored the approval record for President George W. Bush. Figure 4.10 tracks Bush's popularity month by month over the first three years of his presidency. Bush began his presidency with a relatively weak honeymoon, thanks to the dispute over the outcome of the 2000 election. Then, following the catastrophe of 9/11, his approval numbers shot upward to the record level of about 90 percent. This was an extreme rally-around-the-flag response in public appreciation of Bush's response to the unprecedented terrorist attack. Then, inevitably, the numbers eroded as if they were seeking the usual equilibrium of about 50 percent approval. Bush's numbers surged upward again as the start of the second Gulf War initiated a predictable rally effect. They then went into another descent, as if this President Bush were tracking his father's popularity decline after the first Gulf War. But whereas the economy slumped toward the end of the first Bush's presidency, it began to recover in late 2003 and early 2004 under the second Bush. Early in 2004, the second Bush's approval level was holding steady in the 50 percent range.

Presidential Approval and Presidential Success

Each president's record of approval follows its own arc, reflecting the public's often changing judgment of his performance. Approval is more volatile than other indicators of public opinion—one would not want to predict a president's approval numbers a year ahead from the president's numbers today. Approval is distinct for each president—one would not want to predict a new president's approval numbers based on those of his predecessor. And a president's approval numbers are not always a measure of his actual level of success, objectively measured.

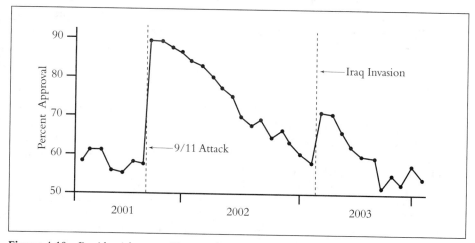

Figure 4.10   Presidential approval by month, George W. Bush. (Values for 9/01 and 3/03 include only polls post–9/11 and post-invasion respectively.) *Source:* Gallup Poll.

A useful lesson is the approval record of President Harry Truman. Based on Gallup's numbers, Truman was one of the least popular presidents. But historians judge (and the public feels in retrospect) that Truman was among the most successful.

4-5 CONCLUSION: WHAT MOVES PUBLIC OPINION?

We have seen that public opinion has changed dramatically on many issues over the seventy years or so since the advent of reliable public opinion polling. Large shifts have sometimes occurred over short periods, or incremental moves have aggregated over the years to a fundamental reversal in American political sentiment.

Abrupt changes in public opinion normally can be traced to the public's reaction to current events. Explaining incremental change is more complex. Cohort replacement is certainly one factor. Almost 50 percent of the American electorate is replaced every twenty years (Abramson 1983, 54). When we see dramatic change in support for the ideals of the civil rights movement between 1960 and 1980, it is important to understand that only about half of those comprising the adult population in 1960 were still part of that population in 1980. The new 50 percent enter the electorate often socialized to a different set of political values. Thus the change that appears in support for the ideas of the civil rights movement does not necessarily mean that people have changed their minds, although that may have happened as well.

Finally, the effects of modernization have certainly affected the political opinions of the American public. Included here are demographic trends such as rising levels of education, the decline of the rural population and growth of large cities, and the increasing penetration of the national mass media to all sectors of society. The advances of education, urbanization, and media penetration have undoubtedly played a role in the public's changing political attitudes and preferences.

NOTES

1. Responses to the services and spending question are based on a 7-point scale (see Appendix), where 1–3 are combined at one end, 4 is the midpoint, and 5–7 are combined at the other end.
2. See Charles Murray, *Losing Ground* (1985, ch. 1), for a discussion of the deserving and nondeserving poor. One survey showed that 37 percent of the public believed people were poor because of "lack of effort," 29 percent said circumstances beyond his or her control, with the remainder saying both played a role (Mayer 1992, 90).
3. See Smith (1987) for a report on this experiment using earlier data.
4. On the 7-point scale, points 1, 2, and 3 are collapsed to indicate preference for a government health plan, and points 5, 6, and 7 are collapsed to indicate preference for a private plan.

5. *Time*/CNN/Yankelovich Partners Poll (Jan. 19, 1998); *Time*/CNN/Yankelovich Partners Poll (Mar. 11–12, 1997); Mayer (1992, 444–445).

6. For an additional discussion of rationality in public opinion given seeming inconsistencies on taxing and spending, see Page and Shapiro (1992, 161–162).

7. For more on trends in affirmative action attitudes, see Steeh and Krysan (1996), Sharp (1999), and Stoker (2001). Questions about affirmative action were rarely asked by pollsters in the 1960s and early 1970s, when affirmative action policies were pioneered.

8. According to this view, the racially prejudiced find a respectable outlet for expressing their views on symbolic issues such as the busing of school children for racial balance. It has been demonstrated, for example, that the most vocal opponents of busing often are nonparents with little direct stake in the matter (Sears et al. 1979).

9. White racial attitudes are difficult to measure (Kuklieski et al. 1997), and because racial appeals are often subtle. See Mendelberg (2001) regarding racial appeals to whites during election campaigns.

10. Transatlantic Trend Survey, June 10–June 25, 2003, in the Roper Archive.

11. The question reads: "You will notice that the boxes on this card go from the highest position of 'plus 5' for a country which you like very much, to the lowest position of 'minus 5' for a country you dislike very much. How far up the scale and how far down the scale would you rate the following countries?" The plus scores are combined for the positive rating and the minus scores are combined for the negative rating. In October 1953, 72 percent of the public gave Russia a "minus 5"; by 1991 that percentage had dropped to 10.

12. Respondents place themselves on a 7-point scale in answering this question, with 4 being neutral. Responses 1–3 were combined to indicate preference for an equal role of men and women in government and society. Respondents at 5–7 were combined to indicate a preference for women staying home.

13. Additional information can be gained through combinations of six abortion items. Thus, 76 percent of the public favors abortion for all three of the traumatic reasons, while only 7 percent oppose abortion in all three of these instances. For elective abortion, 37 percent of the public say they favor abortion for all three reasons, while 47 percent say they oppose abortion for all three of these circumstances.

14. Survey by USODFOX.

15. For example, in a Harris poll conducted between July 7 and 11, 1989, voters who favored and opposed Roe v. Wade were asked, "If a candidate for political office stood for most of the things you believe in but took a stand on abortion that you disagreed with, you would certainly not vote for that candidate. . . . " Of those who favored Roe v. Wade, 12 percent said they would certainly not vote for the candidate; of those who opposed Roe v. Wade, 23 percent would certainly not vote for that candidate.

16. For a thorough discussion of trends in ideological identification and whether or not they can be explained, see Box-Steffensmier, Knight, and Sigelman (1998).

17. The percentages shown in Figure 4.7 are adjusted for "telephone-survey bias"—a well-known but little-understood acknowledgment that Gallup's phone surveys record more Republicans than Gallup's in-person surveys. Results from telephone surveys are adjusted to estimate the partisan distribution for in-home surveys.

5 | Political Socialization and Political Learning

Just as one learns to read and write and identify fashionable clothing, one learns about politics. A considerable portion of this learning occurs before one is old enough to enter the voting booth. Children, for example, tend to share the same partisan preference as their parents. A central premise of political socialization holds that what one learns as a preadult affects one's later political life. This assumption is crucial, for there is little reason for interest in the reaction of preadults to their political environment except insofar as it affects their adult attitudes and behaviors.

To *socialize* someone means "to make social, make fit for life in companionship with others" (*Random House Dictionary*). Thus one perspective on political socialization focuses on the learning of attitudes, values, and acceptable forms of behavior necessary to fit into the political order. It is the learning or failure to learn the lessons of being a good citizen, as defined by the political status quo (Easton and Dennis 1969). Another perspective sees the field as more akin to generic political learning. The emphasis is on individual political development rather than on molding the person to fit the political community (Jennings and Niemi 1974). In this chapter we discuss both these perspectives on the socialization of citizens to political life.

This chapter presents a journey through the political life cycle, with an emphasis on the formative years. It first traces the evolution of political learning from earliest childhood to the approach of adult life, evaluating the agents of socialization along the way. It then discusses aspects of political socialization during adulthood itself.

5-1 THE PREADULT YEARS: SOCIALIZATION TO CITIZENSHIP

Every political system attempts to indoctrinate its children to accept and support the ongoing political order. From the perspective of systems theory, Easton and Dennis (1969, 5) advance the hypothesis "that the persistence of some kind of [political] system may in part be dependent upon the success of a society in producing children most of whom acquire positive feelings about it." But socialization is more encompassing than just encouraging the young to identify with the regime and inculcating a benevolent view of the authorities. It is the transmission of the political culture from one generation to the next. From a systems perspective, the purpose of socialization is to maintain a stable political order. According to Easton and Dennis (1969, 31):

> If the socialization process raises children who upon reaching adulthood have among themselves conflicting aspirations, conceptions of the rules of the system, attitudes toward compliance, and feelings about authority, it is assumed that this will probably build social and political cleavages into the system and that instability will result.

Of course, if political training results in a total commitment to socially acceptable beliefs, the forces for change and improvement in society are greatly diminished. For instance, if political socialization of youngsters in the 1950s had been a complete success in terms of imprinting them with the dominant beliefs of the time, the change we have seen in the status of women and minorities could not have occurred.

To analyze the development of preadult political orientations, we divide the early years into four periods: preschool (ages three to five), early childhood (ages six to nine), late childhood (ages ten to twelve), and adolescence (ages thirteen to eighteen). These are approximate categories, for just as children differ in their physical development, they differ in their political development. In conclusion, we discuss the consequences of socialization for citizenship.

Preschool

The dawning of political recognition begins before children commence their formal education. Political impressions are often vague and inaccurate, but early awareness may lay the foundations for later political development.

Preschoolers frequently confuse political authority with religious authority. In a study of kindergarten children in California, Moore et al. (1985) report that when asked "Who does the most to run the country?" 30 percent responded "God" or "Jesus." Perhaps the most important public figures for the young child are the president and the police officer. One school of thought contends that both officials play a major role in shaping the child's attachment to the political order. Schwartz (1975) found that 90 percent of her preschool sample were able to recognize the "man in the picture" as being "the policeman," and 75 percent were able to answer correctly when asked "What does the policeman do?" The responses most frequently given concerned regulating traffic, helping lost children, and "catching bad people." The children, for the most part, saw the police officer as a benevolent authority figure. Less visible was the police officer's punitive and prohibitive role. Less than 10 percent of the preschool sample recognized a picture of the incumbent president. When asked "What does the president do?" only a few could give an accurate or specifically political characterization. The president is not viewed by these young children as particularly benevolent, especially when compared to the policeman (Schwartz 1975, 236–237). This may be due simply to the president's lower visibility—a situation that, along with perceived benevolence, changes dramatically at the next stage of political development.

Public servants are not the only political symbols visible to the preschool child. Even at this early age, children manifest a sense of political community. When presented with a picture showing nine different flags, the vast majority were able to identify the American flag. When asked "Which flag is your favorite?" 60 percent chose the American flag and another 19 percent the Liberian flag, which closely resembles the American flag (Schwartz 1975, 242–243). Thus preschool children both know and identify with the symbol of the American political community.

Early Childhood

With the onset of early childhood, the content of the young person's political world begins to expand rapidly. However, the increase in content is almost entirely in terms of feelings and affect. Political understanding and critical thought have yet to emerge. The young child now becomes aware of the existence of the president. Government is personalized—that is, the child becomes aware of political authority by becoming aware of certain individuals—notably the president and the police officer. The child sees these figures as possessing great power and is aware that they stand above the family in the obedience hierarchy. Unlike adults, who tend to be cynical about politics, the young child sees the president and the police officer (and political authority) as trustworthy, helpful, and benevolent. This outlook is illustrated by the following excerpt from an interview with a third-grade boy (Hess and Torney 1967, 42).

Q. What does the President do?

A. He runs the government, he decides the decisions we should try to get out of, and he goes to meetings and tries to make peace and things like that.

Q. When you say he runs the country, what do you mean?

A. Well, he's just about the boss of everything. . . .

Q. And what kind of a person do you think he is?

A. Well, he's an honest one.

Q. Anything else?

A. Well, loyal and usually pretty smart.

Q. Who pays him?

A. Well, gee, I don't know if anybody pays him; he probably doesn't get too much money for the job—I don't know if he gets any money.

Q. Why would he take the job?

A. Well, he loves his country and he wants his country to live in peace.

To a surprising extent, young children believe that the policeman and especially the president "would always want to help me if I needed it," that "they almost never make mistakes," and that "they know more than anyone." Reasoning from the primary principle and the benevolent leader hypothesis, students of political socialization attach considerable importance to the idealization of authority by young children. According to the primary principle, "what is learned early in life tends to be retained and to shape later attitudes and behavior" (Easton and Dennis 1969, 9). According to the benevolent leader hypothesis, the image of the president (the most visible symbol of political authority) that is formed in early childhood has a direct effect on the formation of attitudes and beliefs about other political figures and institutions. There is a hypothesized "spillover effect" from this early view of the president to later perceptions of other political authorities. Because the president is favorably viewed, they too tend to be viewed favorably. It is believed, therefore, significant that the child's introduction to politics is a positive one. Later in life, when the individual is able to make critical judgments about politics, this early idealization builds what David Easton (1965) refers to as "diffuse support"—a reservoir of goodwill toward the political system that is independent of any benefit the individual might receive. It helps legitimize the political order and, in times of political stress, the residue of this early idealization helps maintain a positive attitude toward government.

Late Childhood

Beginning about the age of ten or eleven, children start moving away from a personalized view of government to one based on a more sophisticated understanding. During this period the child learns the "civics book" norm of not always voting for the same political party but for the best person. In a national sample, 49 percent of fourth-graders say a good citizen would join a political party and vote for its candidates instead of voting for the best person. But by the eighth grade, only 26 percent endorse this strategy (Hess and Torney 1967, 96). Views of what constitutes "good citizenship" also undergo change. Young children tend to see the good citizen as someone who is "helpful to others" and "always obeys the laws." But by late childhood, good citizenship is defined more in terms of adult conceptions: political interest, voting, and getting others to vote (Hess and Torney 1967, 37). Sigel and Brookes (1974, 110) investigated conceptions of democracy among fourth-graders. They found only 17 percent answered "yes" to the question "Is a democracy where the people rule?" ("I don't know" was the most frequent answer.) They interviewed the same students two years later (then in the sixth grade) and found that 44 percent could respond correctly. However, definitions of democracy in late childhood and even through adolescence seldom include the right to criticize government. Only 54 percent of the eighth-graders in Hess and Torney's sample checked the option "you can say things against the government" as one possible definition of democracy. And fully 84 percent of eighth-graders agree that "the government usually knows what is best for the people." Such open acceptance of government and intolerance for dissent are generally regarded as unhealthy for democracy (see chapter 6). But from a systems theory standpoint, one can ask, "Do not such attitudes indicate successful socialization?" Acceptance of government and intolerance for dissent surely promote "system stability." It is implications such as these that have led to trenchant criticism of the systems perspective on political socialization (Connell 1987).

It is in late childhood that young people begin to separate individuals from their institutional roles. They begin to understand the difference between the office and the man or woman who holds the office. The presidency and the president are no longer seen as the same. Children also display the beginnings of critical judgment; they are sensitive to partisan and policy considerations. For example, those raised in Democratic households are more critical of a Republican president than children raised in Republican households. The president also becomes associated with certain policy positions (Weissberg 1974, 54). Still, political understanding is basically immature. Children revert back to personalization if asked about something they cannot comprehend.

Adolescence

The major spurt in a child's political learning usually comes during adolescence. An important aspect of this growth is the ability to comprehend the abstraction of community interest apart from self-interest. Ideals such as *community* and *society* are usually beyond the grasp of eleven-year-olds but not fifteen-year-olds (Adelson and O'Neil 1966). By midadolescence, the individual is in many ways politically beginning to resemble an adult. By the ninth grade, children have some ability to think along a liberal-conservative continuum. Adult levels of political efficacy are also reached by the ninth grade (Merelman 1971; Hess and Torney 1967). One orientation that shows surprisingly little growth is support for democratic values (free speech, minority rights, rules of the game, etc.). Merelman (1971, 79) finds no increase in support for democratic values between the ninth and twelfth grades. As we note below, many blame the failure of this development on the shortcomings of the public schools.

An orientation that begins in early childhood and, for the most part, continues unchanged through adolescence is the positive view most preadults have of the political system. Despite a "de-idealization" of the authorities brought about by exposure to the seamier side of politics, such as the impeachment of President Clinton amid accusations of lying under oath about a sexual affair with a White House intern, American adolescents retain a positive perspective on the political order. But they can be quite negative about government officials. Table 5.1 presents the views of high school seniors in 1974 (shortly after the Watergate scandal resulting in the resignation of President Nixon) toward the political community, the constitutional system, and the current government at the time (Sigel and Hoskin 1981, 73–5).

Note that 59 percent were very positive about "the flag," and 57 percent were very positive about "the U.S.," with the negatives for both items being minuscule. The "constitutional system" does not fare as well, with 32 percent very positive (although 68 percent are either positive or very positive), but still the negatives are small. On the other hand, just 16 percent felt very positive about Congress and only 5 percent felt very positive about the "current government," while 24 percent felt very negative. During one of the darkest political periods in the twentieth century the data show, among adolescents, a substantial erosion in positive views of those running the government but a strong fundamental commitment to the ongoing political order.

Fast-forward to the first week in February 1999, after President Clinton was impeached by the House and just before he was acquitted by the Senate on February 12, 1999. Based on a Gallup poll of adults and of adolescents between eleven and eighteen years of age, we see a pattern that is in many ways similar, but with some twists.[1] Like the Watergate adolescents, the Monicagate youth cohort is critical of those running the government—more so than a representative sample of adults. While 36 percent of the adult sample would have convicted the president, 47 percent of the youth sample would have done so; 55 percent of the adult sample had a favorable view of President Clinton, but only 43 percent of the youth cohort shared that opinion.

TABLE 5.1	The Views of High School Seniors Toward Political Objects					
	The U.S.	The Flag	Constitutional System	Congress	The Courts	Current Government
Very negative	1%	3%	3%	6%	8%	24%
Negative	4	3	10	16	17	35
Neutral	8	13	20	32	27	19
Positive	31	22	36	31	31	17
Very positive	57	59	32	16	17	5
	100%	100%	100%	100%	100%	100%

Source: Roberta S. Sigel and Marilyn B. Hoskin, *The Political Involvement of Adolescents* (New Brunswick, NJ: Rutgers University Press, 1981), 73.

But once the questions moved away from the president to more abstract opinions about government, the younger sample was more positive than their elders. While 34 percent of the adult sample said they could "trust government to do what is right" all or most of the time, 55 percent of the youth sample said they trusted government. Beyond personalities, Monicagate adolescents are a good deal less cynical about government than are adults, as can be seen below.

Do you personally think most public officials today are liars . . . ?		Do you think George Washington ever lied to the public . . . ?		Do you think Abraham Lincoln ever lied to the public . . . ?	
Adults	*Youth*	*Adults*	*Youth*	*Adults*	*Youth*
Yes 55%	34%	72%	49%	65%	53%

Like the Watergate findings, these data cast doubt on the notion that idealization of the president is necessary to build diffuse support of the political system. When compared with adults, adolescents were critical of the incumbent president, but more positive once we move past current officeholders. However, the socialization theory of diffuse support stresses the consequences of idealizing authority among younger children, usually between kindergarten and the eighth grade (Easton and Dennis 1969).

Socialization to Citizenship and Its Consequences

The most dramatic findings in the literature on early socialization of citizenship are the extent to which young children (kindergarten through eighth grade) personalize government and the remarkable degree to which they idealize authority, notably the president. But do these findings really mean anything for adult behavior? The theory of diffuse support, born of childhood idealization, is an appealing one, but difficult to verify empirically. The theory seems not to be general, as not all children idealize authority. African American (Greenberg 1970), Mexican American (Garcia 1973), and poor, isolated, rural white Appalachian children (Jaros et al. 1968) tend to see political authority as much less benevolent than do middle-class white children.

Children clearly learn about politics by exposure to political events. Even regular political occurrences, such as presidential elections, lead to substantial gains in preadult political socialization (Sears and Valentino 1997). It is therefore not unexpected that a traumatic event like Watergate would have a deep impact on those under eighteen, whose political identities for the most part are not yet fully formed. Several studies show that during the Watergate era, even middle-class white children came to see the president as almost sinister. Several studies done during the Watergate scandal (1972–1974) showed a "dramatic decline" in the positive image of the president (Arterton 1974; Dennis and Webster 1975; Hawkins et al. 1975; Rodgers and Lewis 1975). Christopher Arterton reports that, based on a Boston area sample, attitudes toward the president in fall 1973 "could only be described as wholly negative." The benevolent leader was transformed by Watergate into a "malevolent" leader. In the early 1960s, anywhere from 50 to 66 percent (depending on grade) reported the president was their "favorite of all" or "of almost all." By 1973, the range was 5 to 23 percent, with the older children (fifth-graders) being the least positive. Children in 1962 and 1973 were asked to "compare politicians" with "most people" in terms of power, selfishness, intelligence, honesty, and trustworthiness. The "spillover effect" of the president's image to other political authorities, which was positive in 1962, was negative in 1973. Particularly large differences between 1962 and 1973 exist on selfishness and trustworthiness. Fifty-four percent of the fifth-graders in 1962 thought politicians were less selfish than other people; only 19 percent thought so in 1973.

If the systems theory of childhood socialization would predict that the cynicism of schoolchildren exposed to the Watergate drama would persist over their lifetime, we might expect to see substantial differences between the narrow generation of Watergate babies—say, those who were in the fourth through the eighth grades between 1973 and 1975—and birth cohorts both older and younger. Exploring a more broadly defined generation, Delli Carpini (1986) reports that those socialized during the antiwar period of the late 1960s were somewhat more cynical as they entered the electorate than those socialized earlier. However, using the 1996 NES, we find those between ages thirty-two and thirty-eight (who would have been in grade school during Watergate) are no more or less trusting of government than other age cohorts.[2] However, we should not make too much of a weak test. As we show later, in some issue domains there is convincing evidence to support the persistence hypothesis—that is, what is learned about politics early in life persists into late adulthood.

5-2 THE AGENTS OF PREADULT SOCIALIZATION

Having traced the development of political attitudes through the preadult years, we now attempt to sort out the agents most responsible for this development. The family seems to be the most influential source of preadult attitudes, but it certainly is not the only source. Schools make an effort to indoctrinate children, and it seems unlikely that the effort is totally unsuccessful. Other possible agents of early political socialization include childhood friends and the mass media. (See chapter 8 for a discussion of the mass media.) Finally, when important historical events occur, it seems likely that they leave an imprint on the young.

The Family

Political influence is a function of two factors: communication and receptivity (Williams and Minns 1986). Parents score high on both these dimensions. Children, particularly young children, spend a large amount of time with their parents. The opportunities for children to learn parental attitudes and for parents to exert influence on children is considerable. Also, in terms of receptivity, few bonds are as strong as the affective tie between parents and children. The stronger this tie and the more personal the relationship, the greater the parents' ability to exert influence.

A common assumption is that the political attitudes of family members are highly similar, with the presumed causal flow being from parent to children (rather than from sources outside the family that affect all family members alike). Evidence to support this belief came from a number of early studies (pre-1960) in which parents and children were not independently interviewed.[3] Children (normally students) were interviewed and then asked to report the political attitudes of their parents. The parents themselves were not actually interviewed. We now know that this methodology grossly overestimates the amount of parent-child similarity on most political issues. In reporting parent attitudes, children tend to project their own attitudes onto parents, artificially inflating attitude correspondence. In actuality, the similarity in political attitudes between parents and their offspring could at best be described as moderate. Table 5.2, taken from the Kent Jennings and Richard Niemi 1965 study of high school seniors and their parents, displays the relationships between the attitudes of seniors and their parents on four policy issues.

Reading across the rows in the table, we can see that the students are much more likely to be pro–school integration and pro–school prayer when their parents favor these positions. For example, of the pro-integration parents, 83 percent have children who also favor integration, but when parents oppose integration the percentage of children favoring integration drops to 45—a difference of 38 percent. This relationship weakens considerably for the question of an elected Communist being allowed to hold office and virtually disappears on the question of allowing speeches against churches. In the case of the latter, knowing the parent's attitude is of no use in predicting the student's attitude. Most students favor allowing speeches against churches regardless of what their parents think. One can infer that parents had little influence on these latter two issues. Similar low relationships exist for attitudes about a "legally elected Communist" and a "speech against churches." Also, parents seem to have little influence on more diffuse orientations like political efficacy and political trust.[4] However, Altemeyer (1997) and Peterson, Smirles, and Wentworth (1997) report strong links between the authoritarianism personality syndrome in parents and the same syndrome in their children.

The most thoroughly documented successful transmission of an attitude from parent to child involves partisanship. Again using Jennings's and Niemi's 1965 data, Table 5.3 documents the widespread agreement between parents and children on the question of party preference. Reading across the rows of the table, when we move from parents who are Democratic to those who are Independent to those who are Republican, the percentage of Democratic children drops dramatically. The reverse holds for the case of Republican parents. When parents agree between themselves on partisanship (74 percent do agree), 76 percent of the adolescents follow the preferences of their parents. Interestingly, when parents disagree on partisanship (one is a Democrat, the other a Republican), the child is more likely to adopt the mother's partisanship than the father's (although the number of Independent children rises substantially, as

TABLE 5.2 | Relationship Between High School Student and Parent Opinions on Four Policy Issues, 1965

Students	Federal Role in School Integration* (Parents)			Prayers in Public Schools* (Parents)			Elected Communists Can Hold Office (Parents)			Allow Speeches Against Churches (Parents)		
	Pro	Depends	Con	Pro	Depends	Con	Pro	Depends†	Con	Pro	Depends†	Con
Pro	83%	64%	45%	74%	62%	34%	45%	—	32%	88%	—	82%
Depends	7	17	14	3	8	7	1	—	0	0	—	0
Con	10	18	41	23	30	59	53	—	67	12	—	18
Total	100%	99%	100%	100%	100%	100%	99%	—	99%	100%	—	100%
	(961)	(202)	(453)	(1253)	(68)	(238)	(1337)	—	(1,337)	(1,376)	—	(523)
	$Tau_b = 0.34$			$Tau_b = 0.29$			$Tau_b = 0.08$			$Tau_b = 0.08$		

Source: M. Kent Jennings and Richard G. Niemi, *The Political Character of Adolescence* (Princeton, NJ: Princeton University Press, 1974), 78. Reprinted by permission of Princeton University Press.

*Based on pairs in which both parents were "interested enough" to give a pro or con response.

†Ten or fewer cases.

		Parents		
Student	**Democrat**	**Independent**	**Republican**	**Marginals★**
Democrat	66%	29%	13%	(43%)
Independent	27	55	36	(36%)
Republican	7	17	51	(21%)
Total	100%	100%	100%	
Marginals★	(49%)	(24%)	(27%)	100%

TABLE 5.3 | **High School Student Party Identification by Parent Party Identification, 1965**

Source: M. Kent Jennings and Richard G. Niemi, *The Political Character of Adolescence* (Princeton NJ: Princeton University Press, 1974), 41. Reprinted by permission of Princeton University Press.

★The marginal totals present the proportion of parents and students holding a particular party preference. For example, looking at the column marginals we can see that 49 percent of the parents call themselves Democrats. Looking at the row marginals we can see that 43 percent of the students in the sample call themselves Democrats.

one would expect given the cross-pressures).[5] This generational continuity is important because it helps perpetuate existing party divisions across generations. One explanation for the dominance that the Democratic party once held in terms of party identification (see chapter 4) is simple parental transmission. People were Democrats because that is what they learned to be at the family dinner table.

However, there is clear evidence that parents are not currently as successful in transmitting partisanship as they were in the 1940s, 1950s, and into the early 1960s. In 1958, 79 percent of children with Democratic parents and 72 percent with Republican parents adopted parental partisanship. By 1976, these figures had dropped to 62 percent and 56 percent respectively. In 1992 it was 57 and 56 percent (NES). In most instances, the nature of the partisan rebellion against one's parents' partisanship is a declaration of being an Independent rather than converting to the party opposite one's parents. The decrease in successful parental transmission is a function of an increasing conflict between parental partisanship and the issue preferences of the offspring. When these predispositions complement each other, transmission is successful. But when cross-pressures exist (e.g., parents are liberal Democrats but the offspring is opposed to abortion, affirmative action, and gay rights), the response on the part of the younger generation is political independence (Carmines et al. 1987; Luskin et al. 1989; Green, Palmquist, and Schickler, 2002).

Even with transmission in decline, party identification is still passed from parent to child with much more success than other political orientations. The best explanation seems to be that most political questions are remote from the day-to-day concerns of the family. Few parents hold their political opinions strongly, and few children have an accurate perception of those opinions. In this regard, party identification is unique. It is one attitude that is normally of some consequence to parents and highly visible to children. At election time, young children often ask if "we" are Democrats or Republicans. In a study of high school seniors, Tedin (1974) found that while 72 percent were aware of parental party identification, no more than 36 percent were aware of parent attitudes on any one issue. But when issue attitudes were about as salient and well perceived as partisanship, parent-child correspondence approached that for partisanship. Anders Westholm (1999) finds a similar pattern in socialization study in Sweden. If children accurately perceive the political attitudes of their parents, socialization is quite successful. But misperception is frequent. A variation in this point is illustrated by Beck and Jennings (1991). They found that the high school seniors interviewed in 1965 for the study described above who came from politicized homes were much more likely to share their parents' 1965 partisanship when reinterviewed seventeen years later, in 1982, than were students from nonpoliticized homes. Thus parents seem to have the potential to exert more influence on issue attitudes than they often do. Perhaps in an era like the depression of the 1930s, when politics were polarized and certain issues were seen by many as being highly important, parents used considerably more of their available resources to politically socialize the young.

The Peer Group

Like parents, the peer group enjoys considerable opportunity to influence attitudes and behavior. Strong affective ties are involved, and young people normally spend a substantial part of their time with friends. Parents and peers differ, however, at the point in the preadult's life when influence is greatest. Parents dominate the lives of their offspring until adolescence, at which point peers become increasingly important (Beck 1977). Despite the considerable attention paid to peer groups in the United States, there is relatively little research and (perhaps as a logical consequence) little agreement on the role of peers as an agent of political socialization. Some scholars argue that peer groups are the most important of all adolescent socialization agencies, while others assert that the influence of peers is largely redundant.[6] Peers are seen as simply reinforcing the lessons learned in the family and school. It is clear, however, that adolescent peers can be influential in areas involving the individual's status in the group. But these areas usually involve matters of taste in music, clothing, and hairstyles rather than politics. In the Jennings–Niemi national study of parents and students, a subset of the students were asked to indicate their best friend of the same sex, who was then included in the sample. As expected, for party identification the correlation between students and parents greatly exceeded that between students and peers. On the other hand, in the case of changing the voting age from twenty-one to eighteen (one had to be twenty-one to vote at the time of the survey), the student-peer correlation exceeded the student-parent correlation.[7] This is the pattern one would expect. Partisanship is learned during early childhood and is not a particularly youth-oriented issue. On the other hand, preadults were more likely to become aware of the eighteen-year-old vote issue during adolescence, and the issue is particularly relevant to high school seniors. We would therefore expect more peer influence in the latter instance. In situations in which parents and peers disagree on partisanship, the student is more likely to follow the parent. But when parent and peer disagree on voting age, the student is more likely to follow his or her best friend (Sebert et al. 1974). Thus peer versus parent influence seems to be issue-specific.

It is difficult to make any absolute assessment of peer influence, but it seems certain that even in adolescence, peers are not as important as parents. When politics are remote from one's day-to-day concerns, and when family social harmony as well as one's status in the peer group are only slightly affected by politics, parents probably have an advantage over peers in the socialization process. We have noted that one important precondition for influence is communication. Politics are more important to the thirty-five–fifty-year-old group (the common age of parents with adolescent children) than to those eighteen years old and under (Eskey 1995). If one assumes all other things are equal, adolescents are more likely to be aware of and receptive to parent attitudes simply because most contemporary political issues are more important to parents (Tedin 1980). But when a matter is important to the esteem with which an adolescent is held by the peer group, parents usually cannot compete with peer influence. For most American youth, however, everyday political issues are rarely of consequence for their standing in the peer group.

The Primary and Secondary School

Many political theorists, practical politicians, political reformers, and political revolutionaries believe or have believed that the school is an instrumental agent in the political training of the young. Examples abound. After the 1917 Russian revolution, children were removed from the family (presumably still attached to the old order and unsympathetic to Communist values) and required to spend long periods in school for political retraining. The Allied Powers followed a similar policy after the defeat of the Nazis in World War II. The schools were "de-Nazified," and German youths were instructed in the principles of democratic government as defined by the West. The same beliefs are reflected in the fierce debate over a multicultural curriculum in American schools. The school is seen as the appropriate vehicle for instructing students in the values necessary for life in a multiethnic society.

A popular assumption is that some nations spend an inordinate amount of time politically indoctrinating their young. Communist nations are usually singled out in this regard, most notably the former Soviet Union during the cold war. One study showed, however, that during the cold war period of the 1950s, American schools expended more time on "political education" than did the schools in the Soviet Union (Bereday and Stretch 1963). Regardless, it is important to understand that virtually all nations charge the public schools with the responsibility of teaching obedience to political authority. The practice is nearly universal, and from the standpoint of maintaining political stability and continuity, it is a necessity. One need only observe the difficulties encountered by nations in which primary loyalties do not reside with the national government. For example, in some nations ethnic or tribal loyalty comes before national loyalty. Political stability is highly dependent on the ability of the agents of socialization to produce in children feelings as to the rightness, the oughtness, the legitimacy of the political order. In virtually all nations, this task is assigned to the schools. They are the one agent of political socialization over which the government has considerable control.

There can be little doubt, as we noted in the section on childhood political development, that preadults in the United States generally learn the lessons of patriotism and obedience. What is not clear is the relative role of the family and school in teaching these orientations. In one major study of the public schools, Robert Hess and Judith Torney (1967, 126) concluded that "compliance [with] roles and authority is the major focus of education in elementary schools." Most readers are undoubtedly aware of the patriotic rituals that characterize most classrooms—pictures of American heroes, the display of the American flag and proclaiming one's allegiance to it, singing of patriotic songs, "young citizens leagues," and the emphasis on obedience to authority. Teaching methods change periodically in response to changes in thinking about what is and is not effective for student learning, but the goal of socializing the young to be loyal citizens is never divorced from changes in the curriculum. This goal, for example, is evident in *America 2000: An Educational Strategy*, a national civics curriculum for grades K–12 endorsed by both the first Bush and the Clinton administration.[8] As Richard Merelman (1997, 56) observes, "the proposed national civics standards are mainly a symbolic ritual masked as educational policy for reinforcing cultural hegemony." In other words, the curriculum is focused on teaching a common American culture and values as opposed to teaching individual and group differences.

Students of political education agree that teaching loyalty and obedience is only one aspect of political education. There are other goals as well, such as teaching political knowledge, political participation skills, tolerance of competing political views, and acceptance and support for democratic values. On these goals there is consensus that political education in the public schools is less effective than most would like. One disappointment is that political education does not seem to generate much political enthusiasm or eagerness to participate in adult citizenship. For example, a Gallup survey showed that 61 percent of high school seniors said they were "not very" or "not at all" interested in politics.[9]

High school students' factual knowledge is generally reported to be quite low. Niemi and Junn (1998) report that fewer than two-thirds of twelfth-graders were aware that it is legal to participate in a boycott, organize a recall election, and impeach legislators. According to the National Assessment of Educational Progress, often called "the nation's report card," only 26 percent of high school seniors in 1999 had a "proficient" knowledge of how the government worked, and fully 35 percent failed the national civics test (Hedges 1999). Anderson et al. (1990) report that only 61 percent of high school seniors recognized (in 1988) that having more than one political party was a fundamental difference between the United States and the Soviet Union; only 58 percent knew the United States has a two-party system, and just 50 percent knew the governor is a member of the executive branch.

Finally, surveys of high school youth suggest that support for democratic values is limited and fragile. A study of high school seniors in the 1960s found 60 percent willing to allow the police and other groups to censor books and movies (Remmers and Franklin 1963, 62), and another found only 36 percent in favor of allowing a legally elected Communist to assume office (Jennings and Niemi 1974). Niemi and Junn's (1998) study from the 1990s finds that only 52 percent of high school seniors knew the right to religious freedom is part of the Bill of Rights, and only 47 percent knew there is a constitutional ban on double jeopardy. With similar findings persisting over many decades, the inescapable conclusion is that adolescent youth typically are little interested in politics, possess little factual foundation, and are slow to learn democratic norms (Bennett 1997, 1998; Mann 1999).

Unprepared as high school students are for political adulthood, we should ask whether high school civics courses work to add at least some incremental improvement in good citizenship. The thrust of the early empirical research indicated that the high school civics curriculum had little if any effect on the learning of political knowledge or political values. The most influential of these studies (Langton and Jennings 1968; Jennings, Ehrman, and Niemi 1974; Anderson et al. 1990), showed that whether or not students had taken any civics courses was largely irrelevant to their levels of political knowledge, political interest, political discussion, political efficacy, political trust, and participatory orientation. However, a detailed analysis of the data from the National Assessment of Educational Progress (NAEP) civics assessment by Richard Niemi and Jane Junn (1998) turned up significant effects of the civics curriculum on trust in government—the more courses taken, the most trusting the respondents (high school seniors)[10]—and substantial effects on political knowledge. In a multivariate equation with controls for factors strongly related to knowledge, such as parents' education and plans for college, the difference between little or no civics education and at least some increases political knowledge by 4 percent. While at first blush this increase may seem modest, almost all students have at least been exposed to the civics curriculum, which certainly dampens the effect. In addition, if one looks at all factors relevant to civics instruction—amount and recentness of course work, variety of topics studied, and discussion of current events—there is a combined effect of nearly 11 percentage points in amount of political knowledge (Niemi and June 1998, 122–123). Although the analysis of the NAEP data is mostly limited to gains in political knowledge, it serves to rehabilitate the civics curriculum as a significant contributor to political learning.[11]

However, it is not entirely clear how the curriculum in high school leads to higher levels of political knowledge or support for democratic values. There is, for example, no doubt that the better educated are more politically tolerant. The 1998 GSS shows that while only 51 percent of those with a grade school education support free speech for an atheist, 70 percent of those with a high school degree are supportive. Similarly, while only 45 percent of those with a grade school education would allow a homosexual to teach in college, 69 percent of those with a high school degree would be willing. Numerous other examples can be offered. It may be that a high school education simply slots people into social, economic, and political positions in which they have a greater opportunity to learn democratic norms. Or it could be that high school itself does have an impact, but we simply have not come up with the appropriate research designs to definitively identify effects and unravel the causal connections.

College: Higher Education and Its Impact

Although most students are legally adult when they enter college, the college experience is for many a transition period between life with the family and being on one's own. Today almost one of every two high school graduates goes to college. At the turn of the century, most young people did not even graduate from high school, let alone contemplate attaining a college degree.[12] Consequently, the proportion of the adult population with college experience has been rising steadily. For example, between 1950 and 1990, the proportion of adults with at least some college rose from 16 percent to 45 percent. In the short period between 1972 and 1998, the proportion of adults over twenty-five with college degrees rose from 13 percent to 27 percent (GSS). It is, however, important to understand that most of this recent increase is due to the departure of older, less educated citizens rather than an increase in the number of citizens receiving college degrees. In fact, there is currently little growth in the educational attainment of the youngest age cohort. Thus, in future years we will likely see little gain in the overall percentage of the population that is college educated (Nie et al. 1998, 112–118).

What are the political implications of the growth in the college-educated public? As we discuss at greater length in the following chapter, education is strongly correlated with political tolerance and support for democratic values. As the population has become better educated, its expression of support for these values has also increased. In addition, college generally has a liberalizing effect on noneconomic political opinions. Evidence in support of this view can be found since the 1920s. College seniors are consistently found to be less conservative than entering freshmen.[13] An example taken from the mid-1970s is presented in Table 5.4. The obvious inference is that students track to the left as they move through the years in college.

Three explanations are commonly advanced for these gains in liberalism: increased awareness, enlightenment, and indoctrination. None of these standing alone is entirely convincing. The awareness explanation is predicated on the fact that two of the stronger correlates of education are political knowledge and use of the media. Being informed about innovations and current events is directly related to education. One scholar advances the hypothesis that "thanks largely to wider personal contacts and greater exposure to the media of opinion, the better educated are the first to sense changes in the

TABLE 5.4 | Ideological Self-Placement of College Students by Year in School, 1975

	Liberal	Moderate	Conservative	Don't Know
Freshman	30%	44%	24%	2%
Sophomores	40	38	20	2
Juniors	41	29	22	2
Seniors	40	24	20	3
All students	35	36	22	2

Source: The Gallup Opinion Index, Sept. 1975, 19.

climate of opinion and quickly respond to new fashions in social thought" (Stembler 1961, 172). For example, in a study of support for the civil rights of women and blacks, one investigator found a large increase in support for women's rights occurring among the educated shortly after the media began devoting considerable attention to the issue. However, no parallel increase was found in support for black civil rights (which received no attention out of the ordinary), indicating that increased liberalism on women's issues was due to an awareness factor (Schreiber 1978). Early in the 1990s this same pattern appeared for "black" as opposed to "African-American" in terms of the preferred identifier for members of this racial group. Among blacks in the mass public, the college educated were the most likely to prefer "African-American."[14] The media (much influenced by the college educated) moved steadily to favor the newer label (Smith 1992). Because conservatism has an important status quo component and liberalism an important change component, a critic might argue that the awareness explanation is confusing becoming liberal with simply being trendy. The explanation is also time-bound. What is trendy at one point may be quite different at another.

A second argument asserts that education leads to "enlightenment," which in turn leads to liberalism. According to William C. Stephens and C. Stephen Long (1970, 17):

> Students learn in school. They become more sophisticated, knowledgeable, broadened, and attuned to the world outside, and this is why they become more liberal and politically aware. . . . Education promotes enlightenment; enlightenment promotes liberalism, political interest, and participation.

This somewhat gratuitous statement presumes that with education the scales fall from one's eyes, enlightenment occurs, and the virtues of the more liberal political options become apparent. However, as we demonstrate in chapter 7, education is not always a correlate of liberalism. On economic issues, the better educated tend to be more conservative. But as education increases, so does one's ability to think analytically and critically. The consequence is likely to be the rejection of stereotypes and prejudice, an increased tolerance of diverse lifestyles, and an increased liberalism across a variety of social issues.

A third explanation holds that the "liberal" college faculty indoctrinates students in the direction of their own political views. As Table 5.5 shows, college faculty members are decidedly more liberal than college seniors. Moreover, this table underestimates the liberalism of the relevant American professorate. Those disciplines that directly deal with government, society, and the human condition have the most liberal faculty. For example, one study showed that 70 percent of social science faculty members considered themselves liberal, compared to 41 percent of engineers (Boyer and Whitelaw 1989). When asked, students report that the college experience has a considerable influence on their political values, and certainly the faculty makes an important contribution to the college experience.[15]

But the indoctrination explanation probably underestimates the ability of students to make independent judgments. As students become better educated, they become more adept at critical thought and consequently more resistant to indoctrination. When asked about changes in their political opinions, the most frequent reason students give is an "increased thinking about political questions."[16] Further, the degree of leftward movement among students varies across historical eras. Kesler (1979) demonstrates that students reported moving significantly to the left in 1969 and 1970 (the height of the Vietnam antiwar movement), but much less so in surveys done between 1961 and 1963 and in 1977 and 1978. These historical effects cannot be explained by changed attitudes among faculty.

Although the current crop of college students is more conservative in self-identification then students of the 1960s and 1970s, the popularity of the liberal label among college freshmen has been increasing in recent years. We see

TABLE 5.5	Political Orientations of College Faculty and College Seniors, 1984 and 1999		
Year	Liberal	Middle of the Road	Conservative
Faculty			
1984	42%	27%	31%	100%
1999	45	37	18	100%
Students			
1984	35%	39%	26%	100%
1999	36	31	33	100%

Sources: For 1984 students and faculty, Ernest Boyer and Mary Jean Whitelaw, *The Condition of the Professoriate: Attitudes and Trends, 1989* (New York: Harper, 1989); for 1999 faculty, Denise E. Magner, "Faculty Attitudes and Characteristics: Results of a 1998–1999 Survey," *Chronicle of Higher Education* (Sept. 3, 1999): A20–A21; the 1999 college seniors data are courtesy of Dr. Jerry Jacobs, Department of Sociology, University of Pennsylvania.

evidence of this in the University of California, Los Angeles (UCLA) survey of college freshmen reported in Figure 5.1. College freshmen are seen to be slightly more conservative at the end of the twentieth century than in 1970. Among freshmen in 1970, liberals outnumbered conservatives by about a 2–1 margin. By 1985, perhaps due to the Reagan Revolution, conservatives slightly outnumbered liberals. Since then, however, liberals have been gaining, and in 2002 they outnumbered conservatives by a 3–2 margin. This trend toward self-identified liberalism has been accompanied by an increasing liberalism on issues such as the death penalty, legalization of marijuana, and gay marriage.

The 2002 study also showed students claiming no religious preference to be at an all-time high (16 percent). The move away from the middle coincides with an increase in political interest among college freshmen. In 1966, 58 percent of freshmen said that "keeping up to date with political affairs" is very important; this number declined to 38 percent in 1979 and fell to an all-time low of 26 percent in 1998, increasing slightly to 31 percent in 2001, but then dramatically jumping to 51 percent in 2002—a likely consequence of the 9/11 terrorist attack (CIRP Freshman Survey 2002).

Most observers would agree that college has an impact on student political views. Not only do college students become more liberal with increased years of college exposure (as noted above) but also there are substantial differences between young people in college and young people who do not attend college. This can be seen from data in two periods, presented in Table 5.6. However, not

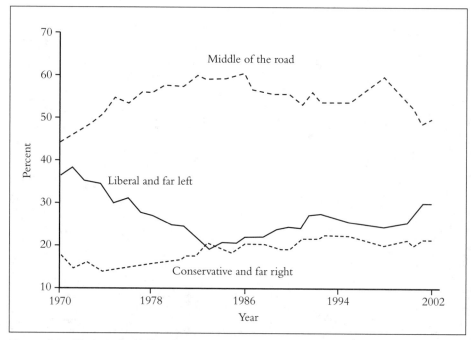

Figure 5.1   Ideological self-identification of college freshman, 1970–2002. *Source:* Institute for Higher Education, University of California, Los Angeles.

TABLE 5.6	Opinions of Youth Attending and Not Attending College		
Opinion		**College**	**Noncollege**
There is too much concern with equality and too little with law and order★		17%	42%
Patriotism is very important★		35	60
There should be more respect for authority★		59	86
Religion is very important★		38	64
Handgun permits should be allowed†		84	72
Abortion should be allowed if pregnant woman does not want to marry father†		57	40
A communist should be allowed to speak in local community†		89	72
Identify ideologically as liberals†		36	24

★Gallup Poll reported in Robert Chandler, *Public Opinion* (New York: Bowker, 1972), 6–13.

†1996–1998 pooled General Social Survey (eighteen–twenty-two-year-olds, whites only).

all these differences can be attributed to the college experience. We know from panel studies (where respondents are reinterviewed over time) that many of the differences we see between those who go to college and those who do not already exist when the two groups are still in high school. Jennings and Niemi reinterviewed their 1965 national sample of high school seniors eight years later, in 1973. With this panel design, it is possible to compare those who went to college with those who did not, and to compare the changes of the two groups from high school to their mid-twenties. The data show that college graduates were influenced both by their preadult socialization and their college experience. In some instances the opinion differences between those college-bound and those not were already apparent when the respondents were seniors in high school. On questions of civic tolerance, the college-bound were already more liberal than their noncollege age cohorts. But by 1973 these differences had increased even further. Thus, there seems to be both a self-selection factor at work as well as an impact of higher education. On the other hand, there was little difference in 1965 on questions of prayer in the public schools and support for racial integration. By 1973, however, there were substantial differences between those with a college degree and those who had not been to college, leading to an inference that college had caused opinion change in a liberal direction (Jennings and Niemi 1982, 257–260)

5-3 SOCIALIZATION DURING ADULTHOOD

Preadult (and college-age) socialization is important because it influences the values and beliefs people hold at the outset of their adult political experience.

But this takes the story only to the threshold of adulthood. What about subsequent socialization? In part, adult socialization is simply a story of stability. The political predispositions learned by one's mid-twenties persist to what might seem a surprising extent throughout adulthood. This fact only accentuates the importance of the early socialization experience. But early adulthood is also an important time of political awakening, as the political environment exerts a particularly strong pull during the first years of adult responsibility. The implication is that generations (or birth cohorts) differ politically based on the collective experiences around the onset of their adulthood in what are called *generation effects*. Another aspect of adult socialization is that people *do* change politically as they grow older. When these changes are age-dependent, we call them *life-cycle effects*. An example is when people seem to get more politically conservative over time. Finally, like children, mature adults change in response to commonly shared experiences, such as the turbulent 1960s, the end of the cold war, and the tragedy of 9/11. These time-dependent effects are called *period effects*. By definition, period effects exert a common influence on people at all ages in the life cycle. They are responsible for the bulk of the short-term changes in opinion discussed in the previous chapter.

A life-cycle effect exists when people's political views are influenced by maturation. As a reference point, assume each new political generation enters political life with identical political attitudes. Then, any difference across generations would be due to aging. When we find, as we often do, that the young are more liberal than their elders, these age differences are explained by life-cycle effects. The implication is that the young, having few responsibilities, can afford to be idealistic. As they age, however, they take on the responsibility of raising a family, paying a mortgage, and holding down a full-time job. The effect is nicely captured in a comment about partisan politics by Winston Churchill: "Those at 18 who are not socialist have no heart; those at 40 who are still socialist have no head." In addition, it is often noted that learning continues throughout life, but reevaluation seems more frequent early in life than later (Dawson et al. 1977, 73–92). Certain predispositions are reinforced over time, as people are more likely to expose themselves selectively to political stimuli with which they agree than to those with which they disagree. The life-cycle concept assumes a process that is similar for all age groups over time. It has been asserted, for example, that as people get older, political parties of the right become more attractive. This assertion (which we investigate below) posits an independent effect of aging on partisan predispositions.

A generational effect exists when a specific age cohort is uniquely socialized by a set of historical events. The logic of generational analysis dictates an interaction between age and experience. The usual assumption is that certain events in history make an indelible imprint on the young (defined approximately as the cohort of people age seventeen to twenty-six). It is argued that a generation's singular personality is shaped when its members leave the family and step out into the world on their own. Those that are younger remain shielded, to a certain extent, from the trauma of external events by the family. Those who are older are better equipped to resist its influence by their previous life experiences.

For a distinct political generation to exist, something of historical consequence must have happened during their "impressionable years" (about the ages seventeen to twenty-six).[17] It is difficult to imagine anything occurring in the 1950s that would have distinctively stamped a generational cohort. On the other hand, one can easily conceive of the Vietnam War era (1965–1972) or the Great Depression of the 1930s as defining unique generations.

Period effects complicate matters further. Strong political shocks can affect young and old alike; for example, when the cold war ended, all age groups relaxed their interest in further defense spending. When we observe all birth cohorts change in tandem as they grow older, we are tempted to see the changes as manifestations of life-cycle effects. But if the changes across all cohorts are time-bound, they can simply be "period effects" of shared experience rather than aging.[18]

Generations, the Life Cycle, and Party Identification

Much of the research on generational politics has been concerned with change in party identification. Generational effects are most important in the direction of party identification (Republican, Independent, Democrat), but variation in the strength of partisanship (strong partisan, weak partisan, Independent) responds more to life-cycle effects.

Partisanship can often be imprinted on a political generation by historical events. We can see examples in Figure 5.2, which displays the relationship between age and the direction of party identification for an accumulation of Gallup polls. The data are presented separately for 1990 and 1998. Comparing age groups for each year reveals clear generation effects.[19]

Let us look first at the data collected in 1990. We see those citizens who were in their impressionable years during the 1930s depression (those between sixty-six and seventy-seven) were the most Democratic age cohort in the electorate. But note also the partisanship of those in their impressionable years during the boom times of the 1920s, when Republicans were ascendant. These citizens, in their eighties in 1990, were the most Republican age cohort. The difference in partisanship between those seventy-four to seventy-seven in 1990 and those eighty-two and over illustrates the profound effect of being socialized in the Roaring Twenties versus the Great Depression of the 1930s. The gap in partisan preference between these groups, who differ only modestly in chronological age, is quite startling, especially considering that the differentiation in the two groups' experiences had occurred decades earlier.[20]

At the other end of the age spectrum, the youngest cohorts in 1990 were more Republican than their elders (save those over eighty), having been socialized under the beleaguered President Carter and the optimistic years of the early Reagan administration. For those under thirty, the Republicans averaged about a 10 percent edge over the Democrats in partisan attachment. From data such as these, Republicans were seeing visions of a Republican realignment.

Moving forward to 1998, the youthful Republicans in 1990 are now between twenty-six and thirty-seven years old. They are still the most Republican

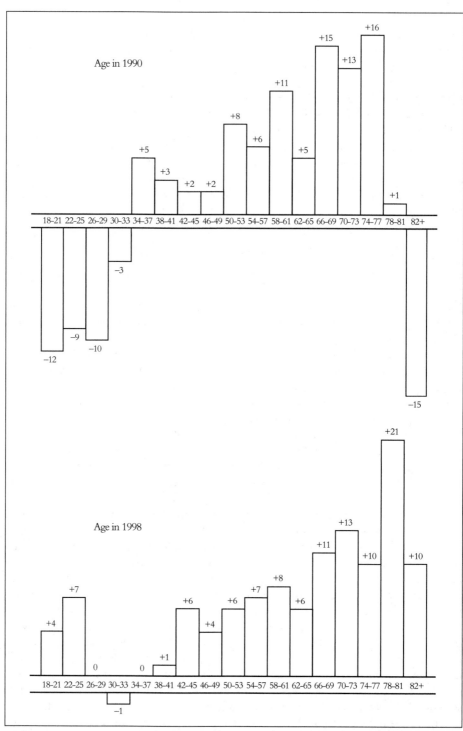

Figure 5.2   Party identification by age in 1990 and 1998 (percentage Democratic minus percentage Republican). *Source:* "America's Views and Mood 1998," *Public Perspective* (Dec./Jan. 1999): 65.

cohort in the electorate as of 1998, but the fact that they experienced the good times of the 1990s while still in their impressionable years undercut their earlier more Republican leanings. Unlike in 1990, the new entrants into the electorate now lean decidedly Democratic. They were socialized at a time the bloom had worn off the Reagan Revolution and during the economic prosperity of the Clinton administration.

The most Republican cohort in 1990—those eighty-two years old and over and socialized under presidents Harding, Coolidge, and Hoover—has now exited the electorate. The New Deal generation is also getting older. The most Democratic age group—those between seventy-eight and eighty-one years old—would have been in their teens and early twenties during the Great Depression. Early in the twenty-first century, this group too will mostly exit the electorate, and the age differences we currently see in Figure 5.2 will likely smooth out.

The responses of new generations of young voters are particularly relevant to the understanding of partisan realignments. As discussed in chapter 4, the United States has periodically undergone a partisan realignment. During realignments, the pace of partisan change quickens, with unusual numbers of voters changing their partisanship in response to new issues and events. The classic realignment occurred during the 1930s in response to the depression and New Deal, and it featured dramatic gains for the Democratic Party. Since the 1960s, pundits have occasionally forecast a massive new partisan realignment around the corner. If one arrives, what will it look like?

There is reason to believe that the vanguard of a new realignment will be young voters. Young voters lack strong partisan attachments, so they are particularly susceptible to political trends. (Note, for instance, in Figure 5.2 the quite different outcomes in 1990 and 1998 of the youngest cohorts as they reacted to the political events that occurred during their childhood and adolescence.) Moreover, young voters who have come of political age since the mid-1960s have shown an unusual degree of partisan independence. Many of these young Independents now face middle age. Perhaps they are still waiting for the right political movement to represent them.

The idea that young voters lead realignments is labeled the *mobilization theory* of realignment because it involves the mobilization of new voters. However, period effects also contribute to realignments, with both new voters and old voters showing equal rates of partisan conversion. If events are strong enough to cause a realignment, they may be strong enough to convert both old and young from one party to another. This view is known as the *conversion theory*.[21]

Will young voters lead the next realignment? Predictions based on the 1930s realignment are difficult because that realignment happened just as public opinion polling began. We saw, however, that the depression cohort, which began voting in the 1930s, even today leads other age groups in allegiance to the Democratic Party. But young voters in the 1930s were not numerous enough to account for a massive realignment by themselves. Examining early Gallup polls and *Literary Digest* polls (see chapter 2), Erikson and Tedin (1981) found evidence of considerable voter conversion during the realignment era. Realignments, it seems, are events of such force that even older generations of voters find the pressures difficult to resist.

Today it is recognized that partisan change occurs constantly, even without realignment-level shocks. The electorate's net party identification (or macropartisanship) constantly undergoes small changes, largely in response to whether the political and economic news favors the presidential party (Erikson, MacKuen, and Stimson 1998, 2002). In the short run, almost all the changes are due to period effects, as all age groups (generations) shift their partisanship more or less in tandem.[22]

Not all age differences in partisan direction are generational. Some scholars see a life-cycle effect—a tendency for the electorate to become more Republican as it ages (Abramson 1983, 124; Delli Carpini 1986, 208–211; Knoke and Hout 1974, 700–713). For example, the parents in the socialization panel showed a slight Republican increase (39.5 percent in 1965 to 43.3 percent in 1973), although no Republican increase was evident among their children, who were then entering adulthood. Thus there is some support for the contention made by the authors of *The American Voter* (Campbell et al. 1960) that Republicanism, because of its "air of respectability, conservatism, and social status," may have an increasing appeal to people as they mature. Much caution must be imposed on this interpretation, however, as the data can be confounded with pro-Republican period effects over the time of analysis. If people grow slightly more Republican from one period to the next, is it due to their maturing or the times changing?

Life-cycle effects are particularly operative for the strength of partisanship. Any survey will show that young adults have weaker partisan attachments than their elders. For example, the 1996 NES data showed 38 percent of those over age fifty-five claiming to be "strong" partisans, compared to only 22 percent under thirty. Similarly, only 23 percent of those over fifty-five were Independents, compared to 38 percent of those under thirty. With figures such as these, one might forecast a general decline in partisanship as older cohorts with firm partisanship exit the electorate and are replaced by younger cohorts with weaker partisan attachments. But this does not happen—at least under equilibrium conditions—because each new generation acquires stronger partisan attachments as it ages. Under equilibrium conditions, the electorate's net partisan strength is stable, with each age cohort showing the same strength of partisanship as previous cohorts at the same point in the life cycle.

Maturation brings about a hardening of partisan commitment. Young adults start out disproportionately Independent in partisan choice, unsure of both parties. With age, they harden their choices. When they become senior citizens, the proportion calling themselves Independent is cut in half. By the time it is necessary to enter a nursing home, most Americans have figured out whether they are Democrats or Republicans.[23]

Generations, the Life Cycle, and Policy Issues

Understanding of generation and life-cycle effects is far less advanced when we turn from partisanship to policy issues. For one thing, policy issues are many, with a likelihood that each tells a different story. In chapter 4 we saw a variety of trends (often stationary) in opinion on many issues. The presumption is that these trends are due mainly to period effects, as all birth cohorts move in tandem to the ethos of the times. In rare cases there may be generation effects, as each new batch of adult citizens brings a new perspective to old problems like taxing and spending or the death penalty. We might expect to find life-cycle effects, with people starting out liberal but becoming more conservative as they age. But in some instance, such as the rise of white acceptance of racial integration in the 1960s and 1970s, change is so fast that the liberalism of the times must offset any conservatizing life-cycle effect, making specific birth cohorts become more liberal with age.

The supposedly liberalizing (or radicalizing) effect of the 1960s on the generation that came of age in that decade has been the focus of some study. Delli Carpini made an intensive study of the 1960s generation and isolated a number of instances in which this generation differed from surrounding age cohorts. What we would expect among this generation, of course, is a leftist bent to their political ideology. For the most part, Delli Carpini finds that the generation of the 1960s was more supportive than other cohorts of government involvement in the issues of race, civil liberties, economics, and social concerns. But the differences were not large, and as the generation has aged, its distinctiveness has begun to erode. Society exerts a pull toward the political center as one moves through the life cycle (Delli Carpini 1986, 120–138).

If lasting effects of the 1960s generation are to be located, they would most likely be found among the subcohort of antiwar activists. An analysis was performed by Jennings (1987) using the famous socialization panel. From this group starting out as 1965 high school seniors, Jennings compared college graduates who protested the war and the matching sample of college graduates who were not protesters. An advantage of the panel approach is that one can look back to high school and see if the differences are explained by self-selection. On many issues there were substantial generational effects. In 1965, while in high school, the (future) protesters were 8 percent less favorable to prayer in the public schools than the nonprotesters, but seventeen years later they were 30 percent less favorable than the nonprotesters. The protesters were 13 percent more supportive of a federal role in school integration in 1965 but 43 percent more supportive in 1982. On many other issue orientations, however, the once liberal protesters began to move in a conservative direction. While 83 percent of the protesters considered themselves liberals in 1973, only 63 percent did so in 1982. Declines of at least 20 percent also occurred on questions of government responsibility for providing jobs, legalization of marijuana, rights of accused, helping minorities, and equality for women. The protesters were still considerably more liberal than the nonprotesters in 1982, but they had lost at least some of their distinctiveness.

By 1982, the protesters' attitudes had been shaped by both generational and life-cycle effects. Their experience as antiwar protesters stamped them with an indelible liberal print, while life-cycle effects pushed them back in a conservative direction. Furthermore, their liberalism had been eroded by a period effect—exposure to the conservative ethos of the 1980s.

Thanks to extensive collection of data on the ideological preferences of Americans, ideological identification (as a liberal, moderate, or conservative) is the one issue-related variable for which we have strong evidence to document the nature of change and stability over time. Opposite the pattern for party identification with its clear generational effects but no certain life-cycle effects, ideological identification shows clear life-cycle effects and no generational effects. As one might expect, each new generation starts out more liberal than average but then drifts toward the conservative with age. Moreover, each generation starts out with the same level of liberalism and drifts rightward at about the same rate. A regular pattern of newly entering liberals who then turn conservative works to keep the electorate's net division of ideological identification constant, at least under equilibrium conditions. We saw this in chapter 4, where unlike party identification, the division of ideological identification has been remarkably stable for over a quarter of a century.[24]

Table 5.7 illustrates showing the combination of birth cohorts and age cohorts for respondents in cumulated CBS/*New York Times* surveys for three years at eight-year intervals: 1984, 1992, and 2000. In each year, conservatism increases with age. Showing life-cycle effects, each "generation" changes with the time. For instance, the youngest group (age twenty-five and under) in 1984 was only 3 percentage points more conservative than liberal in self-identification. Eight years later, when they became twenty-six to thirty-three, they already moved (to +10 points) in a conservative direction. The cycle of entry by the new and exits among the old keep the balance of liberals and conservatives more or less at a constant level. Interestingly, in recent years the oldsters who are the most conservative in ideological identification are also the most Demo-

TABLE 5.7 | **Ideological Identification (% Conservative Minus % Liberal) by Birth Cohort, 1984, 1992, 2000**

Birth Year	1984	1992	2000
1975–1982			– 2 (18–25)
1967–1974		0 (18–25)	4
1959–1966	4 (18–25)	10	9
1951–1958	4	10	9
1943–1950	10	12	13
1935–1942	17	19	17
1927–1934	19	20	20
1919–1926	21	22	16
1911–1918	19	19	17 (82–89)
1903–1910	29	25 (82–89)	
1895–1902	22 (82–89)		

Source: CBS News/*New York Times* polls. Birth years are approximated from respondents' reported age.

cratic in terms of party identification. The generational effect of the depression apparently marked them for life.

5-4 THE PERSISTENCE OF POLITICAL ORIENTATIONS

At the outset of this chapter, we noted that a key assumption justifying the study of political socialization is that orientations formed early persist over time. There is a good deal of evidence that many important political predispositions do endure over a considerable span. There is also a good deal of evidence that people continue to learn and adjust their political perspective in response to their adult environment and the events in their lives.

When we speak of long-term persistence, it is helpful to think of persistence as relative to one's peers rather than as an immunity from period effects—the impact of commonly shared events. Consider the mental experiment of imagining a group of young people at the onset of adulthood. Some are Democrats and some are Republicans, some are liberal and some are conservative, with further variation in other attitudes and opinions as well. The mental experiment to ask is whether or not the relative political positions of these young people stay the same throughout their lifetime. For instance, would the young liberals still be the most liberal and the young conservatives still be the most conservative during their old age? Obviously people can change, but the answer to this mental experiment is "yes." The young conservatives remain the most conservative among their peers in old age (likewise for liberals).

It is important to understand that when we speak of persistence, what mostly persists are core values and predispositions rather than specific opinions on issues of the day. Thus overarching values such as partisanship, liberal-conservative orientation, and racial attitudes tend to persist, while trust in government or attitudes about defense spending tend to be more fleeting. Regarding persistence, two major points merit elaboration. First, political attitudes are malleable through the impressionable years. The basics of political socialization are not completed by the end of grade school, as some argue (Hess and Torney 1967). Second, after the impressionable years, political orientations harden considerably. Change still occurs, but stability markedly increases.

Once the impressionable years leading up to adulthood end, the stability of core political values increases greatly. There now exist three long-term panel surveys, all of which demonstrate this same point. The longest of these, and the most dramatic example of persistence, is the Bennington study originated by Theodore Newcomb. Young women (sixteen to twenty years old), mostly from conservative homes, matriculated at Bennington College, which at the time (in the 1930s) had an avowedly liberal faculty. Students were first interviewed between 1935 and 1938, then reinterviewed in 1960 and again in 1984. The data thus stretch over almost fifty years. Using a number of items to create a scale of liberal-conservative political orientations, Alwin et al. (1991) found a high level of persistence over the fifty-year period. The authors concluded that 60 percent of the variance in the 1984 political predispositions could be predicted from the predispositions in the 1930s when the students were attending Bennington, whereas the remaining 40 percent reflected attitude change (Alwin et al. 1991, 265). A second long-term panel survey (spanning thirty-seven years) is the Terman study of gifted children (Terman and Oden 1959). Respondents were interviewed four times, beginning in 1940 and ending in 1977 (when they were about thirty and sixty-seven years old). A reanalysis of these data by Sears and Funk (1999) showed that 65 percent held the same party preference and 54 percent held the same political ideology in 1977 that they did in 1940.[25] One conclusion is that socialization to core values for many people is largely complete by the late twenties.

Both the Newcomb and the Terman studies suffer from using highly unusual and nonrepresentative samples. The parent–child socialization study begun by M. Kent Jennings in 1965 (when respondents were eighteen) has a much stronger claim to overall generalizability.[26] The fourth wave of this study was completed in 1997 (when respondents were fifty), so it now spans thirty-two years. These data clearly support the impressionable years—later persistence hypothesis. Attitudes were subject to considerable change between eighteen and twenty-six years of age but became considerably more stable in the following years. The correlation between partisanship in 1965 (at age eighteen) and partisanship in 1973 (at age twenty-six) is 0.50. However, between ages twenty-six and thirty-five it rises to 0.65, and it remains at 0.65 from ages thirty-five to fifty. For civic tolerance, the correlations for the three time points are 0.41 (ages eighteen–twenty-six), 0.60 (ages twenty-six–thirty-five), and 0.65 (ages thirty-five–fifty) (Jennings and Stoker 1999).[27] Once the respondents had passed through their impressionable years, their attitudes stabilized. The cohort data presented in Figure 5.2 make the same point using a different methodology. Those respondents in adolescence and early adulthood during the Roaring Twenties (before the Great Depression) are markedly different from those who spent their impressionable years during the Great Depression—despite the fact that more than fifty years had passed since they were adolescents and young adults. This evidence, as well as other data (see Sears 1991 for a review), supports the general proposition of openness and change during the impressionable years, followed by a stabilizing and persistence of core political attitudes.

5-5 CONCLUSION

In this chapter we focused mainly on the preadult sources of political learning. Some political learning takes place in childhood, although the impressionable years (ages seventeen–twenty-six) seem to be the most important. While attitudes crystallize in later adulthood, political learning still takes place as individuals respond to their environment and life events. Even partisanship, the most stable of political predispositions, responds in adulthood to issues and political personalities (Markus 1979; Fiorina 1981; MacKuen et al. 1989). But generally speaking, political change in adulthood is incremental. It is the impressionable years that offer the greatest potential for a radical break from the past.

NOTES

1. Gallup conducted a survey between February 4 and 8, 1999, of 1,022 adults and 305 young people between the ages of eleven and eighteen for CNN/*USA Today*. For an additional discussion of the poll results, see Owen and Dennis (1999).
2. To make this a fair test that avoided overlap, we compared the levels of trust in government among those between the ages of thirty-two and thirty-eight, those between eighteen and twenty-eight, and those between forty-six and fifty-four. A one-way analysis of variance revealed no difference. The trust items used are reported in chapter 6, Figure 6.1.
3. Many of these studies are reviewed in Hyman (1959).
4. Another explanation for low relationships is measurement error. Dalton (1980) corrects for measurement error and finds a substantial increase in parent-adolescent relationships using the Jennings-Niemi data.
5. Following conventional wisdom, the evidence indicates that when husbands and wives disagree on party preference, wives are more likely to change in the direction of the party preference of their husband. However, most data on this issue are from the 1960s and 1970s and may not reflect gender relationships in the twenty-first century (Weiner 1978).
6. The former point is made by Harvey (1972, 601); the latter point is made by Silbiger (1977, 174).
7. For party identification, the student-parent correlation was .66; the student-peer correlation was .26. For the eighteen-year-old vote, the student-parent correlation was .08; the student-peer correlation was .29.
8. The U.S. Department of Education and the Pew Charitable Trusts awarded grants to the Center for Civics Education to develop a comprehensive, standardized curriculum for teaching civics education in grades K–12. For a discussion of the proposal, see Mann (1996) and Dry (1996).
9. "Gallup Survey: Six of Ten Teenagers Show Little Interest in Politics, Politicians," *Houston Post*, Oct. 19, 1977. For similar findings for college freshmen, see Mann (1999).
10. The principal difference is between little or no civics education to any degree. Students having more than a small amount of civics education were about 10 to 15 percent more trusting of government (Niemi and June 1998, 72).
11. In a seven-nation study (including the United States) of twelve- to eighteen-year-olds, Flanagan et al. (1998) found democratic school climates had a weak but significant effect on the civic commitment of their respondents.
12. It is important to appreciate that the meaning of a college education in the twenty-first century is quite different from the 1930s or earlier. Prior to World War II, someone with a college education was a rarity. Now such education is an everyday part of the social landscape. Thus, the impact of a college degree today may be quite different than fifty years ago, particularly when it comes to slotting people in social and economic networks. For an extended discussion of this point, see Nie, Junn, and Stehlik-Barry (1998, ch. 6).
13. For a summary of the extensive literature on this point, see Feldman and Newcomb (1969). A research project sponsored by William F. Buckley's conservative journal, *The National Review*, came to the conclusion that "attending college still makes it more likely that a student's thinking will be deflected leftward" (see Kesler 1979). For a view challenging the notion that education leads to liberalism, see Jacob (1956). The most recent statement on the matter can be found in Nie, Junn, and Stehlik-Barry (1998).

14. In a reading of preferences for this term in March 1997, 30 percent of the racial group preferred "Black," 30 percent preferred "African-American," 8 percent preferred some other term, and 32 percent said either term was acceptable (Hart and Teeter for the *Wall Street Journal*).

15. A 1969 poll for CBS News asked students: "Which of the following events, if any, have had a great effect on your life and values, which have had a moderate effect, and which have had no effect?" Sixty-six percent of the college students said the "college experience" had a "great effect." This was the highest percentage of the nine possible options (Kesler 1969).

16. On the question of the influence of college on political attitudes, 42 percent attributed their change in attitudes to either "lectures or course readings" or "personal contact with faculty" (Kesler 1979, 1488).

17. There is no agreement about exactly what ages constitute the impressionable years, other than that they extend from adolescence through to early adulthood.

18. The alert reader of this section will learn, correctly, that the accounting of change in terms of generation, life cycle, and period effects is fraught with more difficulties and ambiguities than one might think at first glance. When scholars study generation and life-cycle effects, they divide survey respondents by birthdate or age. Dividing by birthdate yields a set of birth cohorts, or people born during specific spans of years, like 1940–1944. Dividing by age yields "age cohorts," or people of specific age segments, like people fifty-six–sixty years old. Suppose we check the survey responses of a birth cohort over time as it goes through the political life cycle. Any change that is observed could be manifestation of either a life-cycle effect due to people changing as they grow older or a period effect due to people of all cohorts changing due to common experiences. Suppose we compare the survey responses of different age groups in a survey conducted at one specific period. Any observed variation by age could be a manifestation of life-cycle effects due to respondents at different stages of the cycle or to generation effects whereby respondents of different ages are affected by different experiences.

19. The 1990 data are a compilation of Gallup polls from 1989–1991 that contain 12,600 cases. The 1998 data are based on a single year. The exact number of cases was not reported in the original source.

20. A slightly different interpretation of differences between generations like the predepression and the post-depression generations is found in chapter 5 of Erikson, MacKuen, and Stimson (2002). Instead of dwelling on the unique events occurring different generations came of age, they emphasize the extra experience of the older generation. For instance, the more experienced pre-depression generation differed from the post-depression generation mainly due to their added years of exposure to the "good" Republican years of the 1920s, before the depression. Both groups moved Democratic during the depression, but the older group's starting point was more Republican.

21. The best statement of the mobilization theory is found in Andersen (1979); an argument for the conversion hypothesis is found in Erikson and Tedin (1981); for a critique, see Campbell (1985); see Erikson and Tedin (1986) for a response. For a somewhat different approach to generations and changes in party identification, see Beck (1974).

22. Although not depicted in Figure 5.2, the 1960s generation (socialized between 1965 and 1973) also uniquely responded to the events of the time. If we look at a very special subcohort, those college graduates who protested the Vietnam War, and compare them to college graduates who did not protest, we find a strong,

persistent generational impact. Jennings (1987) has made this analysis using a subset of the parent-child socialization panel. The panel contained 129 college graduates who had protested the war and a matching sample of college graduates (about twice as many) who had not been war protesters. These two groups differed little when they were in high school. Protesters-to-be were 39 percent Democratic; nonprotesters were 38 percent Democratic. By 1973, the two groups had shifted in opposite directions, with the protesters 48 percent Democratic and the nonprotesters 27 percent. By 1982, these percentages had changed little. The antiwar movement had clearly left its partisan mark on those who were actively involved.

23. The socialization panel study provides a clue to why strength of partisanship increases throughout the life cycle. In the later life of the 1965 high school seniors, an increase in partisanship was found—but mainly among those who voted. Those who did not vote tended to remain Independents. Thus, one aspect of age that may lead to the acquisition of partisanship is simple learning based on experience (Jennings and Markus 1984).

24. The current steady state of ideological identification was preceded by a surge in conservative identification in the late 1960s and 1970s, contrary to the atmosphere of societal change at the time (see chapter 4). The possible role of different generations for this shift has not been systematically explored.

25. For party identification, 59 percent were perfectly stable over the four waves between 1940 and 1977, and another 6 percent moved around between waves but ended up in 1977 at the same place they started in 1940. For ideology, 42 percent were perfectly stable and 12 percent moved around but returned to their 1940 position by 1977.

26. But the panel is still not representative, as the sample of eighteen-year-olds in 1965 was limited to high school seniors. Those who dropped out of high school were not included. And, as in all panels, those who fail to be reinterviewed usually differ in some ways from those who remain in the panel.

27. It is important to distinguish between absolute and relative continuity. By *absolute continuity* we mean those who were strong liberals at Time 1 remain strong liberals at Time 2. By *relative continuity* we mean those who were most liberal at Time 1 are the most liberal at Time 2, but they may not have maintained their exact position on the scale. Correlation coefficients measure relative continuity, so what we are referring to in this section is the tendency, over time, for the most liberal respondents at Time 1 to be the most liberal at Time 2, not that they maintain the exact position on issues between time points. It would be unreasonable, for example, to think that in the Bennington study respondents would maintain the same issue position over a fifty-year period.

6 | Public Opinion and Democratic Stability

In a democracy, public opinion is important because it can influence the decisions political leaders make. Certain aspects of public opinion take on special importance because they can influence the functioning of democratic government. In this chapter we analyze those attitudes and predispositions generally thought necessary to maintain a democracy and examine the degrees to which Americans appear to hold these attitudes.

Ideas about what is vital for the functioning of democratic government can be divided into four groups. First, there should be widespread tolerance of opposing points of view and support for the rules of democracy. An apt analogy here is the rules of the road for driving an automobile. If most people did not accept the rule that one must stop when the light is red, chaos would ensue. The rules of democracy involve guarantees that the civil liberties of all shall be protected—that majorities rule, but minorities have rights.

Second, democracy's stability may rest on a social consensus regarding values and goals. Disagreements must not be so fundamental that neither resolution nor compromise can be gained by institutionalized procedures. Too great a division may overtax even the best procedures for resolving conflict. Contemporary examples include the Protestant-Catholic division in Northern Ireland, the Tamil (Hindu)–Sinhalese (Buddhist) conflict in Sri Lanka, and the Serb-Croat-Muslim division in Bosnia. Strong cultural divisions are particularly vexing for the design of new democracies, as in Iraq, with its divisions between Shiites, Sunnis, and Kurds.

Third, it is important that people find reasons to trust their government and believe that their democratic participation is meaningful. For people to accept government decisions, they must believe their political actions can be effective and they can trust the government to respond to their interests. If political alienation becomes sufficiently intense and widespread, it may pose a threat to democratic stability.

Fourth, democracy is often thought to work best when people have certain kinds of what might be called *political personalities*. For instance, people should be open-minded rather than seek comfort for their problems by blaming others. They should accept the complexity of democratic decision making rather than seek solutions from a strong leader to override democratic discussion. When antidemocratic personalities are common, so the theory goes, minority rights become fragile and the stability of democracy is threatened.

6-1 SUPPORT FOR DEMOCRATIC VALUES

One of the great threats to any political system, democracies included, is the desire on the part of those who hold political power to maintain it and to work their will free from constraints imposed by others. Ambition in political leaders is not, in and of itself, an undesirable trait. But history is strewn with examples of people in government warding off competition by the expeditious route of eliminating it. Consequently, democracies must anticipate that leaders may not suffer criticism gladly and may not want to share or give up political power if there is a way to avoid it. One solution to this problem, developed by the framers of the U.S. Constitution, was to build in a series of mechanisms designed to protect the rights of people outside government who aspire to political influence from those on the inside who hold political power. But constitutions can only go so far in making good on these protections. As Judge Learned Hand (1959, 144) once observed, "Liberty lies in the hearts and minds of men and women; when it dies there, no constitution, no laws, no court can save it." Some commitment to democratic values on the part of both political leaders and the public is essential.

In using the term *democratic values*, we are referring to procedural norms. These norms do not refer to the substance of legitimate political conflict, such as the desirable trade-off between inflation and unemployment or the distribution of government spending, but to the rules of the game in which that conflict takes place. One important set of procedural norms is found in the Bill of Rights. Here Americans are guaranteed the right to freedom of expression, freedom from unreasonable search and seizure, protection from self-incrimination, a speedy and public trial, free exercise of religion, and so on. Two related democratic values of great importance are majority rule and minority rights. At regular intervals the population is mobilized into opposing camps. Each camp proclaims its own virtue and criticizes the opposition. An election is then held, and the winners take control of the government. The losers remain free to rouse popular hostility toward the new leaders in the hope of embarrassing them and ultimately replacing them in office. This procedure is normally the way decision makers are chosen in the United States. One therefore hopes to find an understanding among the electorate that these are the methods that should be employed to select public officials.

As shown in Table 6.1, survey evidence does in fact demonstrate that when democratic values are stated in the abstract (e.g., "public officials should be chosen by majority vote"), there is an overwhelming positive consensus of support for them. But note that these assertions are very general, with no reference to any specific person or group. These statements basically constitute an official American political ideology—the sort of lessons that are taught in a variety of both political and nonpolitical contexts by the family and the school and reinforced by the mass media.

However, when statements about the rules of the game have a double stimulus, with references both to democratic principles and to unpopular groups, support for these rules declines.

Relevant evidence is presented in Table 6.2, in which the statements are two-pronged. Each refers to a democratic norm plus some specific group or activity. For example, in the statement "Members of the Ku Klux Klan should be banned from running for public office," individuals are asked to respond to both the norm of free elections and feelings about the Klan.

One interpretation of these data is that public support for procedural rights is less than ideal. In the cases of elections and the Ku Klux Klan, 70 percent would ban a Klan member from running for public office. The pattern in Table 6.2 is clearly one of a lack of enthusiasm for the values of democracy when items refer to protests, demonstrations, or unpopular groups such as American communists. Of course, we might avoid getting overly alarmed if we keep in mind that this evidence is not drawn from actual behavior and may simply represent ill-considered survey responses to hypothetical situations. However, when ordinary citizens are given the power to directly legislate using the ballot

TABLE 6.1	Support for Democratic Values Stated in the Abstract		
Statement	**Democratic Response**	**Uncertain Response**	**Undemocratic Response**
People in the minority should be free to try to win majority support for their opinions.	89%	9%	2%
Public officials should be chosen by majority vote.	95	3	2
I believe in free speech for all, no matter what their views might be.	85	7	9
No matter what a person's political views are, he is entitled to the same legal protections as anyone else.	93	4	3

Source: John L. Sullivan, James Piereson, and George E. Marcus, *Political Tolerance and American Democracy* (Chicago: University of Chicago Press, 1982), p. 203.

TABLE 6.2 | Support for Democratic Values, by Specific Application

	Democratic Response	Undecided	Undemocratic Response
[Should] people who want to overthrow the government by revolution [be] allowed to hold public meetings to express their views? (GSS 1996)	66%	5%	29%
[Should] books that contain dangerous ideas be banned from public libraries? (PEW 1997)	47	4	49
Should X-rated movies be totally banned for sale to adults? (Gallup 1985)	54	3	43
Freedom of the press should be protected under all circumstances. (WP 1997)	34	1	65
If the police suspect that drugs, guns, or other criminal evidence are hidden in someone's house, should they be allowed to enter a house without first obtaining a search warrant? (CBS 1970)	66	2	32
If a man is found innocent of a serious crime but new evidence is uncovered, do you think he should be tried for the same crime again? (CBS 1970)	38	4	58
Forcing people to testify against themselves [prohibited by the Fifth Amendment] may be necessary. (CLS 1978–1979)	40	26	35
If a person is suspected of a serious crime, do you think the police should be allowed to hold him in jail until they can get enough evidence to charge him? (CBS 1970)	38	3	58
[Should] someone who believes blacks are inferior be allowed to speak in your community? (WP 1998)	63	1	34
Judges should be able to censor the press in criminal cases so jurors are not biased. (FF 1997)	42	7	51
If someone is suspected of treason or other serious crimes, he should not be entitled to be released on bail. (Gibson 1987)	21	14	65
Members of the Ku Klux Klan should be banned from running for public office. (Gibson 1987)	23	7	70
People ought to be allowed to vote even if they cannot do so intelligently. (McClosky 1958)	48	N/A	52
[It is] . . . a good idea for the government to keep a list of people who take part in demonstrations. (Harris and Weston 1979)	25	26	50

Sources: John Sullivan et al., *Political Tolerance and American Democracy* (Chicago: University of Chicago Press, 1982); General Social Survey (GSS), 1985; CBS: Robert Chandler, *Public Opinion* (New York: Bowker, 1972); Herbert McClosky, 1958; Herbert McClosky, "Consensus and Ideology in American Politics," *American Political Science Review* 58 (June 1964); CLS: Herbert McClosky and Alida Brill, *Dimensions of Tolerance* (New York: Russell Sage Foundation, 1983); Louis Harris and Alan F. Westin, *The Dimensions of Privacy* (Stevens Point, WI: Sentry Insurance, 1979); James L. Gibson, *Freedom and Tolerance in the United States* (NORC: unpublished codebook, 1987); *Washington Post* 1997; Pew Research Center 1997; the Freedom Forum 1997.

box, they often use that power to deprive unpopular minorities of their civil liberties and rights. Barbara Gamble (1997) looked at seventy-four ballot initiatives on public accommodations for minorities, school desegregation, gay rights, English language laws, and AIDS policies. She found that more than three-quarters of these elections resulted in the defeat of policies designed to protect minority rights.

A Growth in Democratic Tolerance?

Table 6.3 shows the change in Americans' tolerance of selected unpopular groups from 1952 to 2002. One point attracts immediate attention: the appearance of a substantial increase in political tolerance over the half-century of polling. For example, note that tolerance for someone "speaking out against churches and religion" rose from 38 percent in 1954 to 77 percent in 2002. A simple conclusion is that the American public has become more tolerant of opposing points of view. A common explanation for this change is based on social learning theory. The assumption is that increases in exposure to social and cultural diversity lead to increases in support for democratic norms. Two changes of consequence for this explanation are rising levels of education and the move from rural to urban areas. The proportion of people who have been to college has more than doubled since the 1950s (NES 1952–2000). Educated people are more likely to understand the importance of protecting democratic liberties, if only in their own self-interest. Also, social and cultural diversity,

TABLE 6.3	Public Tolerance for Advocates of Unpopular Ideas, 1954–2002								
	Person Should Be Allowed to Make a Speech			Person Should Be Allowed to Teach in College			Person's Book Should Remain in the Library		
	1954	*1972*	*2002*	*1954*	*1972*	*2002*	*1954*	*1972*	*2002*
An admitted communist	28%	52%	70%	6%	39%	62%	29%	53%	71%
Someone against churches and religion	38	65	77	12	40	61	37	60	74
Someone who favors government ownership of all railroads and large industries	65	77	★	38	56	★	60	67	★
Someone who believes that blacks are genetically inferior	★	61†	63	★	41	53	★	62	62

Sources: 1954 data are from Samuel Stouffer, *Communism, Conformity, and Civil Liberties* (New York: Wiley, 1954); 1972 and 2002 data are from the General Social Survey.

★Question not asked.

†General Social Survey, 1976.

such as that found in the city, brings individuals into contact with people who are not like them. They learn that those who are different are not always dangerous (Williams et al. 1976).

A less obvious explanation for the rise in support for democratic values holds that there has been little real change between 1954 and 2002; rather, what we see is nothing more than an artifact of the question—that is, the groups used in 1954 to elicit tolerant or intolerant responses are not as threatening as they were in 1954. At the time of the 1954 survey, the climate of opinion in the United States was strongly influenced by the scare tactics of the ultra-right-wing junior senator from Wisconsin, Joseph McCarthy. He claimed to have proof that communists had infiltrated the American government, and more than a few people believed him (Goldstein 1978). The groups identified in the 1954 survey are those usually associated with the left—communists, atheists, and socialists. Tolerance may appear to have gone up simply because these groups no longer appear to pose the danger many once thought.[1]

In an ambitious project, Sullivan, Pierson, and Marcus (1982) devised a test to determine if the increased tolerance one sees in Table 6.3 is real or simply an illusion. They suspected that support for the civil liberties of a specific group was largely driven by emotion rather than considered judgment. If someone liked atheists, that person would have no problem allowing them the right of free speech. It takes no tolerance to put up with someone with whom one agrees or someone who is promoting a political agenda with which one concurs. On the other hand, the same person might heartily dislike members of the Ku Klux Klan and be quite willing to deny them free expression. The acid test for tolerance, according to Sullivan and his colleagues, is putting up with those whose ideas one finds repugnant. In other words, they suspected that support for procedural rights depended on whose ox was being gored.

Sullivan et al. (1982, 60–63) devised a "content-controlled" question in which respondents were given a list of groups and asked which one they liked least (with an option to supply a group not on the list). Respondents were then queried as to whether they would "put up with" (i.e., be tolerant of the procedural rights of) their least-liked group.

As Table 6.4 demonstrates, tolerance using a least-liked approach does not seem to have improved much since 1954.[2] For example, only 18 percent would allow a member of their least-liked group to teach in the public schools. These levels of tolerance are not much different from the 1950s. If true, this finding has disturbing implications. It calls into question the inherent willingness of Americans to embrace one of the pillars of democratic thought: tolerance. It also seems to offer little hope for improvement. The early studies showed a strong relationship between education and support for democratic values. One might suppose, then, as aggregate levels of education increased, so would political tolerance. However, the revisionist thesis holds this is not the case, as Americans are no more tolerant now than they were during the McCarthy era of the 1950s. Thus improvements in the general level of education, according to this viewpoint, are not the answer to what is seen as a dangerously low level of support for democratic values.

TABLE 6.4 | **Levels of Tolerance Using Content-Controlled Items**

	Percentage Tolerant of Least-Liked Group
Members of the [least-liked group] should be allowed to teach in public schools.	19
The [least-liked group] should not be outlawed.	31
Members of the [least-liked group] should be allowed to make a speech in this city.	50
The [least-liked group] should not have their phones tapped by our government.	63
The [least-liked group] should be allowed to hold public rallies in our city.	32

Source: James Gibson, *Freedom and Tolerance in the United States* (National Opinion Research Center: unpublished codebook, 1987).

Not surprisingly, this line of research has been subject to substantial criticism. Among the most telling critiques is a claim that the questions used are inherently incapable of determining the true level of support for democratic values. The questions are flawed because by their very nature they have double stimuli—support for a general principle and reactions to an unpopular group or political act. Further, these stimuli are not balanced. A strong stimulus (one's single most disliked group) is contrasted to a much weaker stimulus (abstract democratic values).

In the typical survey setting, in which respondents must give answers in a few seconds, it is not unexpected that the strong stimulus frequently overwhelms the weak one (or first comes to mind). Most people know whom they do and do not like, and whom they do not like they often find threatening. Coming to grips with an abstract principle is more difficult (Brady and Sniderman 1985; Zaller and Feldman 1992). Thus, initially, the strong stimulus dominates. But importantly, several studies show that people can often be talked out of—or talked into—antidemocratic positions (Chong 1993; Cobb and Kuklinski 1997). Gibson (1996) demonstrates that of Americans who initially gave an intolerant response, 38 percent changed their minds when given subsequent counterarguments for the tolerant alternative. But counterarguments were even more effective among those initially giving a tolerant response. Sixty-three percent changed their minds and gave the intolerant response. Davis and Silver (2003) show a similar pattern in their study of the trade-off between civil liberties and national security following 9/11. It was easier to get people to abandon pro–civil liberties attitudes than to abandon pro-security attitudes. It seems quite clear that people have great difficulty reconciling their desire to support the principles of democratic procedure with their fears and apprehensions about unconventional groups and national security.

Democratic Values and 9/11

It is real and not hypothetical circumstances that provide the acid test for citizen commitment to democratic values. In everyday life, concerns over civil liberties are usually remote. In that regard, the 9/11 terrorist attack on the World Trade Center in New York and the Pentagon near Washington, D.C., provides a unique circumstance to test the willingness of citizens to trade off liberties protected by the Bill of Rights for more domestic security. In the wake of 9/11, the government proposed and enacted a number of measures to increase national security, but at a cost in terms of personal liberty. The public debate has turned on the need to protect civil liberties as the government seeks greater powers to defeat a mostly foreign enemy, but one that also poses risks to domestic security.

To properly test for the effect of 9/11, we must examine data both before and after the terrorist attack. As shown in Figure 6.1, starting with the Oklahoma City bombing in 1995, the public has been repeatedly asked "In order to curb terrorism in this country, do you think it will be necessary for the average person to give up some civil liberties, or not?" Immediately following the Oklahoma City bombing, 49 percent thought it would be necessary to give up some civil liberties. As time passed, the percentage taking this position declined. However, shortly after 9/11, 63 percent thought it would be necessary to give

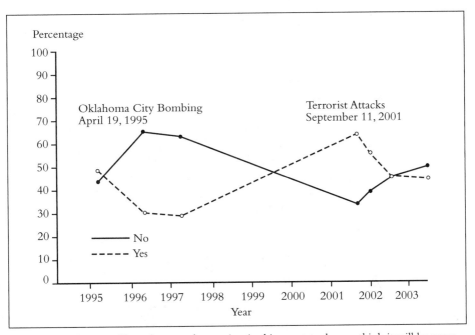

Figure 6.1   *Question:* "In order to curb terrorism in this country, do you think it will be necessary for the average person to give up some civil liberties, or not?" *Sources:* Surveys by *Los Angeles Times, Newsweek,* Pew Center.

up some personal liberties to fight terror, but again these percentages declined over time. Still, as of July 2003, 44 percent think we may have to give up some civil liberties to fight terrorism, which is only 5 percentage points lower than just after the bombing of the Murrah Federal Building in Oklahoma City on April 19, 1995.

The data in Figure 6.1 underscore the persistent finding in the literature on democratic values that the perception of threat against society or cherished beliefs is the single most important factor that drives people to cede fundamental liberties to government (Markus and MacKuen 2001). For their study of post–9/11 attitudes toward civil liberties, Davis and Silver (2004) constructed a nine-item scale that addressed the trade-off between civil liberties and personal security. In addition to the items shown in Figure 6.1 they asked, for example, if high school teachers should "have the right to criticize America's policies toward terrorism" or should high school teachers "defend America's policies in order to promotion loyalty to our country." Sixty percent of a national sample said teachers should promote loyalty. On the other hand, 77 percent opposed the government being able to search a suspected terrorist's property without a warrant. Davis and Silver conclude that on the whole Americans are not unreasonable on these matters. Among the best predictors of a willingness to yield liberal liberties to the government was the perception of threat and trust in government. The more people feared the possibility of another terrorist attack in the next three months and the more they trusted government, the more likely they were willing to cede fundamental liberties to the government in order to fight terror.

The Theory of Democratic Elitism

If the public is as equivocal about or nonsupportive of democratic values as many believe, how does democracy in the United States survive? American colleges and universities contain substantial numbers of atheists (Gibson and Bingham 1985, 15). In 2002, 39 percent of the public would not allow atheists to teach in these institutions (GSS). Why has there been no mass movement to root out the nonbelievers? Beyond the obvious observation that what people say has no one-to-one link with actual behavior, the most influential accounting for this circumstance is "the theory of democratic elitism" (McClosky 1964; Rose 1964; Stouffer 1955).

The starting point for the theory of democratic elitism is the observation that support for democratic values is not evenly spread throughout the population. Perhaps not surprisingly, surveys show the least commitment to democratic values among the least educated and the politically inactive. Conversely, surveys show the most support for democratic values among the highly educated and politically alert, and especially among public officials. For example, Nunn et al. (1978) demonstrated that 83 percent of a community leader sample could be classified as "more tolerant" compared to only 56 percent of a comparable mass sample. While as recently as 2002 General Social Survey data show only 70 percent of the mass public favoring free speech for a communist and only 69 percent favoring free speech for a militarist, samples of elite groups going back to the 1980s and before show that well over 90 percent of the respondents demonstrated a firm (verbal) commitment to these democratic values (Gibson and Bingham 1985; McClosky and Brill 1983).

Perhaps the most important predictor of support for democratic values is education. Several investigators have presented data showing people who are better educated tend to be more supportive of democratic procedures than those with less education (Stouffer 1955; Nunn et al. 1978; Nie et al. 1998). The 2002 General Social Survey shows that 63 percent of those with a grade-school education would allow a homosexual to teach at a college or university, while 93 percent of those with a college degree would do so. Nie and his colleagues (1998) argue a causal link between education and support for democratic values runs through verbal cognitive proficiency—the ability to gather, analyze, and comprehend information and discover where one's self-interest truly lies.

In addition, some go even further and argue that within categories of education, political elites are more tolerant than the public. One author inferred from the Stouffer data (part of which is presented in Table 6.3) that the "differences between leaders and the community at large does not seem due simply to education, since 79 percent of the college-educated leaders are among the more tolerant as compared to 66 percent for the general college-educated population" (Kornhauser 1970, 67). According to theory of democratic elitism, political leaders are more tolerant than their education alone would predict because of their exposure to the democratic values that permeate the American elite political culture (McClosky 1964; McClosky and Brill 1983). The system works, therefore, because those who are least attached to democratic values are unlikely to be active or influential in politics. On the other hand, those most committed to democratic tolerance are the ones who have the most influence on actual political outcomes because of their high interest and high levels of political participation. Proponents of democratic elitism can point to countries like Argentina, where government has been unstable, and find confirmation of their theory in the fact that educated political activists in that nation are very low in their support for democratic values (Dahl 1971, 139). That American political elites score high on these values is then interpreted as an explanation for democratic stability in the United States.

In the words of one of the more influential writers on the subject, "Democratic viability is . . . saved by the fact that those who are the most confused about democratic ideas are also most likely to be politically apathetic" (McClosky 1964, 365). The implication would seem to be a cautionary note that too much democracy is a bad thing if, once actively engaged, the masses can pose a substantial threat to democratic values. Democracy works best, it would seem, when people are content to passively vote for competing sets of elites who control the political parties but to otherwise leave political decisions to elected leaders.

Considerable criticism has been directed at this theory. Any explanation of democratic stability that portrays political activists and officeholders as saviors and common people as potential saboteurs of democratic government will be found immediately suspect by many. Reanalysis of the Stouffer data by Robert Jackman (1972), for example, casts considerable doubt on the claim that political influentials are more supportive of democratic values than are others who share their education, gender, region of origin, and other distinguishing characteristics. The Sullivan et al. (1982) least-liked-group analysis found that the differences in tolerance between political activists and nonactivists were spurious, caused by other factors related to both support for democratic values and tolerance. Sniderman et al. (1996), in an analysis of mass and elite opinion in Canada, found no support for the theory of democratic elitism. Over a host of individual rights issues, they found mass and elite opinion essentially indistinguishable. In their study of post–9/11 attitudes, Davis and Silver (2003) conclude those who in normal times are the strongest defenders of civil liberties are among the most willing to make concessions to the government under threat of terror.

Critics also note that despite the survey evidence and an occasional ballot initiative (usually with an unclear message), the actual record of tolerance for democratic rights by the mass public has not, in the view of most people, been unduly alarming. On the other hand, one can point to certain elite behaviors that many find dangerously undemocratic. Among the examples are the internment of Japanese Americans during World War II, the failure of political elites to respond critically to violations of traditional norms of free speech and due process during the persecution of alleged communists in the McCarthy era of the early 1950s, and the events surrounding the break-in at the Watergate by persons in the employ of the president of the United States.

In the case of the McCarthy era, James Gibson (1988) has correlated the tolerance scores of the mass and elite samples from the 1954 Stouffer survey, aggregated by state, with an index measuring repressive legislation passed by the states during that period. He found no evidence of demands for the repression of American communists emanating from the mass public, but he did find evidence of a link between intolerant state elites and repressive state legislation.

A different type of analysis holds that the survey evidence supporting the elitist theory is itself invalid. Critics argue that the better educated simply learn what are socially desirable and "appropriate" answers to questions about democratic tolerance (Jackman 1978; Weissberg 1998). In the language of cognitive psychology, educated survey respondents may learn and retain a greater number of democratic (versus nondemocratic) "considerations" to sample from memory when being interviewed. Thus they have a greater probability of giving democratic responses (Zaller and Feldman 1992; Chong 1993). That does not, however, necessarily mean they are more committed to democratic principles.

Doubts about the tolerance-inducing effect of education can be drawn from the often-noted pressure for "political correctness" within certain provinces of higher education. In the 2002 GSS, a surprisingly high 39 percent of the college educated would not allow someone who believed blacks are genetically inferior to teach at colleges or universities. They have apparently learned that it is now socially *chic* to condemn racists, even though their rights of free expression are no different than those of American communists or any other group. But this learning is of a very superficial sort. When it comes to endorsing the ideals of the civil rights movement, the well-educated are considerably more supportive of the ideals than those with less education. However, in demanding applied situations (such as government action to benefit racial minorities), the well-educated are no more likely to be supportive than are the less-educated. (For details, see chapter 7.) Jackman and Mulha (1984) stress that education does not so much increase tolerance as it increases the ability of those in the privileged class to develop sophisticated rationales for their privileged position.

Pluralistic Intolerance

In another approach to reconciling an intolerant public with continuing democratic government, Sullivan et al. (1982) offer a theory of "pluralistic intolerance." While the public may be quite intolerant, their data show no consensus as to what group should be suppressed. There was a great deal of diversity among the groups Americans like least. In the Sullivan et al. (1982) survey, the least-liked group was American communists at 29 percent, followed by the Ku Klux Klan at 24 percent. The most recent survey by Gibson (1987) reverses this order, with the Klan at 32 percent and American communists at 24 percent.[3] Because there is no agreement on what groups to suppress, elites receive mixed signals and consequently have the freedom to act on the basis of their own (presumably democratic) preferences. In other words, with no intolerant consensus, there is no demand for political repression of any particular group.[4]

The theory of pluralistic intolerance might seem to imply that when one vulnerable group is very unpopular among the general public, political repression will occur. In the 1950s, intolerance was focused on communists and people of the political left. Repression of those persons has been amply documented (Goldstein 1978). Following the decline and fall of McCarthyism in the mid-1950s, intolerance became unfocused and repression was much less evident. The post–9/11 atmosphere presents concern about a new focus of public intolerance on Muslims and people of Arab extraction.

But is public hysteria over out-groups the major factor when repression occurs? The direction of causation here is very much open to question. It is possible that both the policy of repressing the left during the McCarthy era and mass public opinion opposing communists and the like were determined by political elites.[5] In fact, a common interpretation of mass–elite linkage is that independent of any effect of opinion on policy, elite opinion and behavior shapes mass opinion (e.g., Zaller 1992; Jacobs and Shapiro 2001). The danger in focused intolerance at the mass level may be that demagogic elites can find a receptive audience to fuel an antidemocratic political movement.

Intolerant Beliefs and Intolerant Behavior

How much significance should we allot to responses to survey questions about tolerance and civil liberties? Intolerant beliefs may be of consequence only if they lead to intolerant behavior, and there is little evidence of any meaningful link. It is important to realize that behavior has multiple causes, of which attitudes are only one (Deutscher 1973). For example, a person would probably look for group support before attempting to prevent an atheist from speaking or before removing books by a communist from the public library. The opinions measured in studies of political tolerance are so uniquely distant from intolerant behavior as to render them little more than hypothetical (Weissberg 1998). For instance, do the expressed fears of some citizens in an opinion survey about libraries stocking their shelves with inflammatory books by Marxists really capture an enduring predisposition for antidemocratic behavior? Translating antidemocratic beliefs into behavior is likely to be a much less frequent occurrence than translating a preference for a political candidate into the behavior of casting a vote for that candidate

6-2 POLITICAL CONSENSUS

Clearly, a democracy is more stable if citizens agree, or are in consensus, on basic values and goals. Some conflict over issues is inevitable in a democracy because public policies generally cannot benefit or penalize all persons or groups equally. Intense or severe political conflict, however, is undesirable because it may threaten the stability of democracy. Robert Dahl defines *intensity of conflict* as a function of the extent to which each side sees the other as an enemy to be destroyed by whatever means necessary (Dahl 1971, 335). As issues become more intensely debated, the language of conflict becomes harsher; opponents are accused of acting out of less than honorable motives, and tactics that were once regarded as illegitimate are given serious consideration. The Protestant-Catholic split in Northern Ireland and Muslim-Christian split in Lebanon are classic examples of a political division that makes democratic government and the protection of civil liberties virtually impossible.

The United States has clearly experienced political conflict, but unlike many other countries, there has not been significant controversy over a number of fundamental issues. Evidence from several surveys indicates that (1) the broad elements of the constitutional order are widely endorsed; (2) there is a consensus that defects should be remedied by legal processes of change; (3) most people are satisfied with the economic order, with 94 percent agreeing that we "must be ready to make sacrifices if necessary . . . to preserve the free enterprise system"; few want to nationalize large corporations; big business is widely accepted; labor unions are less popular, but few want to see them eliminated; (4) Americans believe that opportunities exist for personal achievement—the doors of success are open for those willing to work; and (5) most people are content with their lot.[6] When asked, 85 percent say they feel extremely good or very good when the see the American flag fly, and 92 percent profess extreme or very strong love for their country (NES 1988). Eighty-six percent are proud to be American (GSS 1994), and 89 percent say they would rather be a citizen of the United States than of any other country (GSS 1996).

Traditional sources of cleavage that have posed problems in other countries have, for the most part, been moderate in the United States. Among the most important of these are class, regionalism, and religion. Particularly important is the fact that political attitudes are only weakly related to these divisions (see chapter 7). Regional differences (at least currently) also tend not to be intense. The American public is mobile. The Bureau of the Census reports that in a typical year, 20 percent of the population moves, with about one-third moving a considerable distance. Even the South, on the question of race, is beginning to lose some of its uniqueness. Religious antagonisms, too, do not lead to severe issue conflicts. One reason is that religious preference is only slightly related to social class. One's religion does not determine one's opportunities or economic well-being. The low salience of these conflicts is evidenced in that 92 percent of opinion-holders said they would vote for a Jew for president, 95 percent said they would vote for a black, and 94 percent said they would vote for a Catholic (Gallup 1999).

Despite these observations, there have been two important divisions within American society. The most persistent is race. Another is the divisiveness in the 1960s and 1970s over the Vietnam War.

Race

Racial divisions have, of course, existed since the beginning of the Republic and have been the principal threat to the survival of democratic rights in the United States. Recent violent manifestations of this cleavage were the urban riots that occurred in virtually every city between 1965 and 1968, then again in several cities in the 1990s in response to several high-visibility assault and murder trials in which victim and accused were of different races. Today there still exists a wide gap between the opinions of whites and blacks on a substantial range of issues. These differences are most pronounced on questions of what constitutes fair treatment for blacks (again, see chapter 7) but exist in other domains as well. The possibility for conflict between the races is intensified by the fact that socioeconomic differences reinforce issue disagreements. Compared to whites, blacks are disproportionately working class and unemployed.

While blacks clearly have specific policy grievances and tend to view partisan politics from a different perspective than whites, they do not reject the central tenets underlying the American political system. In 1981, 76 percent of a national sample of black respondents thought the United States had a special role to play in the world; 86 percent said the United States was the best place in the world to live (Gallup 1986); and in 1988 (NES), 87 percent of blacks were "extremely proud" or "very proud" to be Americans. Less than 3 percent were "not proud at all."

Vietnam

Unlike most wars of America's past, U.S. involvement in the Vietnam War (fought at its height between 1965 and 1972) drew intense opposition that grew as the war progressed. The war polarized Americans along ideological lines between pro-war "hawks" and antiwar "doves." Disagreement was so intense that it resulted in a number of actions at the fringe of legality and some that went considerably beyond. There were demonstrations, riots, occupation of buildings, violence (police and hard-hats versus protesters), and the shooting of unarmed demonstrators. As a counter to the perceived threat of leftist protesters, the government engaged in a number of illegal practices, such as wiretapping and surveillance.

The Vietnam War caused the display of many traits characteristic of intense political conflict. The stakes were high, substantial numbers on both sides had strongly held beliefs, and no compromise was acceptable to competing sides. While relatively few people were directly affected by the war, a vocal minority was outraged over the notion of American boys being required to fight and sometimes die in someone else's civil war. Another sizable minority saw the war resisters as traitors. Compromise was extremely difficult; both sides were committed. In addition, the North Vietnamese would accept only one solution—total American withdrawal from South Vietnam.

While attitudes about the war threatened a very serious cleavage, two factors served to diminish its polarizing effect. First, the entire population was not divided into two extreme camps. Rather, after 1968, the majority tended toward the middle position. They viewed the war as a mistake but did not want it ended by an immediate withdrawal or an all-out military attack. There also existed cross-cutting cleavages. Extreme conflict becomes more threatening when an individual's attitudes and group memberships reinforce one another. However, attitudes toward the Vietnam War were not highly associated with other attitudes or with group membership. For instance, doves were not necessarily pro-abortion, college educated, or under thirty. Rather, views on the war cut across these divisions. The existence of cross-cutting cleavages served to mute the intensity of the conflict.

6-3 POLITICAL SUPPORT: TRUST AND EFFICACY

A common assumption is that political systems work better when citizens both trust their fellow citizens and trust their government. Social trust (trusting fellow citizens) is a key component of *social capital*, often cited as the lubricant that makes democracy work. *Political trust* (trusting government) is the affective component of support. Those high in political trust are satisfied with the procedures and products of government. The opposite of trust is *political cynicism*, or the evaluation that the political system is not producing policies according to expectations. *Efficacy* is the cognitive or belief component of support; it is the extent to which a person believes his or her political activities will influence government.

Political Trust

No government has the complete trust of all its citizens. However, many argue that it is important for democratic government to maintain some minimal (usually unspecified) level of trust among its citizens. One argument is pitched at the normative level. If the distinctive character of democracy is the substitution of voluntary consent for coercion, it is no small moral shortcoming when citizens withdraw trust out of a conviction that the government is not acting in their best interests (Sabine 1952; Nye 1997). Others make claims of a more practical bent. Levels of trust are thought to affect the leadership strategies available to political decision makers. Leaders must be able to make decisions and commit resources without first consulting those persons who will be affected by the decisions and called upon to supply the resource materials. According to William Gamson (1968, 45–46), when trust is high, "the authorities are able to make new commitments on the basis of it and, if successful, increase support even more. When it is low or declining, authorities may find it difficult to meet existing commitments and govern effectively." Thus, when trust was high in 1964, the government could draw on its credit rating with the electorate and send troops to fight an overseas police action in Vietnam with little public debate. That sort of freedom was considerably constrained after 1972.

Weatherford (1987) argues that levels of trust are particularly important in the economic area, where the government needs maneuvering room to pursue long-term policy goals. For example, if inflation becomes entrenched, the government must sometimes call upon citizens to endure the pain of recession for the promise of stable prices at a point in the indeterminate future. Citizens must have faith in the fairness and competence of government and not demand a premature accounting based on a short-term appraisal of cost and benefits. More concretely, Nye (1997) sees low trust among citizens as undermining their willingness to provide tax dollars, the willingness of bright people to go into government, and the willingness to voluntarily comply with the law.

If trust drops sufficiently low, some contend the result may be social disruption. Disruption may serve as an impetus to needed reform, or it may threaten the stability of an existing regime. At the very least, a portion of state resources must be diverted to cope with the disturbances. Almond and Verba (1965, 354) write that insufficient trust is particularly dangerous when the system is not performing in an adequate fashion—as, for example, in an economic depression. Lipset (1960, 69) provides evidence from the 1930s showing that when many democratic governments ceased to be effective it was those with a reservoir of trust among its citizens that were able to withstand the strain, while those not so advantaged (such as Austria, Germany, and Spain) succumbed to antidemocratic movements.

Levels of political trust may serve as a barometer indicating how well government is performing. It is, therefore, no surprise that scholars have paid considerable attention to the fluctuations in trust over time.[7] Figure 6.2 presents the trend in political trust between 1958 and 2002 taken from the National Election Studies. The data from 1958 to 1966 reflect the tranquility of the Eisenhower years, the Camelot years of Kennedy, and the landslide election of Lyndon Johnson. After 1966 trust began to decrease at a steady pace until 1980. Common explanations include the government's handling of the civil rights movement, the Vietnam War, Watergate, the pardon of Richard Nixon, and

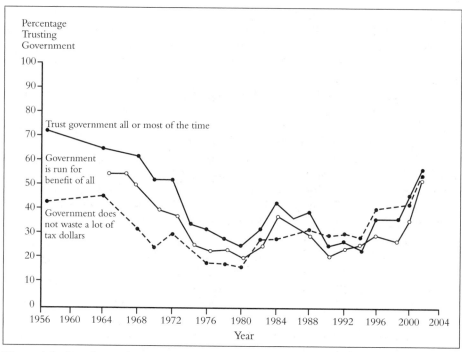

Figure 6.2   Trends in public trust by item. *Source:* National Election Studies (1958–2002).

the economic and foreign policy problems associated with the Carter administration. The decrease in trust during this period came about equally from the dissatisfied left and the dissatisfied right. For example, cynics on the left tended to think the government had moved too slowly on civil rights; cynics on the right tended to think it had moved too rapidly (Miller 1983).

The most severe decline in trust came between 1972 and 1974. The most plausible explanation is Watergate. Daily accusations of break–ins, slush funds, wiretapping, extortion, cover-ups, etc., are not designed to encourage enthusiasm for government. But even after President Nixon left office there was no immediate decline in cynicism. In fact, trust did not rebound until Ronald Reagan took office and proclaimed it was "morning in America." The Reagan administration's attack on big government may also have helped boost the level of trust. By 1984, trust had rebounded considerably, although it was nowhere close to the levels of the late 1950s and early 1960s. Following this uptick, trust again declined, mostly in response to the Iran-Contra scandal and the breaking of the "read my lips—no new taxes" pledge by the first President Bush. At the close of the twentieth century, there was again an upward movement in political trust that began in 1996. One might think the robust economy is the most plausible explanation, but that is not the case. Rather, the cause was an improvement in perceptions of government effectiveness and evaluations of congressional job performance (Hetherington 1998).

With the events of 9/11, trust in government skyrocketed. In January 2001 a CBS/*New York Times* poll showed a mere 31 percent of Americans claiming to trust the government in Washington to do what is right "most of the time" or "just about always." Two weeks after 9/11, an ABC News/*Washington Post* poll showed 64 percent trusted government "most of the time" or "just about always." A CBS/*New York Times* poll in early October 2001 found 55 percent trusted government. The *New York Times* proclaimed "Suddenly Americans Trust Uncle Sam" (Langer 2002). One had to go back the presidency of Lyndon Johnson in 1966 to see trust at this elevated level. However, the surge in trust was not to last. CBS/*New York Times* polls showed trust in government at 46 percent in January 2002, at 45 percent in June 2002, and falling to 36 percent in July 2003—about where it stood before 9/11.

The rapid surge and decline in trust following 9/11 forced students of public opinion to reconsider the meaning of political trust. The long decline in trust starting in 1966 already had been subject to a good deal of speculation. Inglehart (1997a) saw the decline simply as part of an overall decline in confidence in all major institutions due to a rise in postmaterialist values, which encourage the denigration of authority. Confidence in American business over the three decades prior to 2000 had dropped from 55 to 21 percent, in universities from 61 to 30 percent, and in medicine from 73 to 29 percent.[8] Government is simply part of this overall pattern. Some, however, saw causes more closely aligned with government itself.

Contemporaneous with the general decline in trust was a change in the role of the media from mostly presenting the news and supporting the political establishment to interpreting the news in a highly negative and personalized fashion (Patterson 1994, 2002). Many see this change as going beyond the critical to the condescending and the contemptuous, with candidates and public officials portrayed as duplicitous, disingenuous, and self-serving (Orren 1997). Television journalism is particularly prone to this practice, and those who rely mostly on television for their political information are decidedly more distrustful of government than those who rely on newspapers (Hetherington 1998). According to this perspective, trust declined after 1966 because most of what people heard about government was negative.

Of course, it is possible to argue that distrust in government can be directly traced to poor performance by government and public officials.[9] The perceived competence of government is a strong predictor of political trust (Hetherington 1998). A 1997 study by the Pew Research Center on the causes of political distrust showed that while people are not angry with government, they are frustrated with government.[10] This frustration is primarily directed at the politicians who lead government rather than the civil servants who administer it. Dissatisfaction with political leadership is the most frequent reason (40 percent) people gave for distrusting government.[11]

According to this perspective, the increase in trust after 9/11 can be easily explained by a change in the object of trust. Prior to 9/11, most people thought about trust in terms of leadership on domestic policy. After 9/11, the focus of leadership evaluations turned to the war on terror. Here public officials got high marks—at least early on. The media, instead of being critics, suddenly became cheerleaders. Trust now meant trusting the government to "do the right thing" when it came to fighting terrorism (Bishop 2002).

However, approval of President George W. Bush's handling of the war and the economy began to decline by January 2003. Soon the media stopped cheerleading. As the president's approval declined, so did levels of political trust.

Most scholars now conclude that low political trust does not mean rejection of the political order. Nevertheless, there may still be worrisome consequences. Orren (1997) argues that people turn to quick, simpleminded fixes—for example, direct legislation, third parties, and term limits—for perceived problems when trust is low. In two-party presidential elections, the distrustful are more likely to vote for the challenger than the incumbent. In three-party contests, the distrustful are more inclined to vote for third-party candidates than the Republican or the Democrat. In voting for president, those low in trust opt for candidates promising the most far-reaching change (Hetherington 1999). A similar pattern appears on the issue of term limits for elected officials. The strongest predictor of those voting for term limits in state referenda is low political trust (Karp 1995). Scholz and Lubell (1998) show trust in government significantly influences compliance with tax laws. Those scoring low on trust in government tended to underreport their taxable income. Others insist that the decline in political trust is an important contribution to the decline in voting turnout since 1960 (Abramson and Aldrich 1982). One common interpretation of these claims is that the distrustful do not find the institutionalized choices the political system offers its citizens acceptable.

None of the possible consequences listed above, however, threatens democratic stability. How low, then, must political trust fall before it makes a difference? One obvious observation is that in the mid-1970s, when trust was at its nadir, the process of government did not operate with any appreciable difference from the 1950s. The weapons of war were still being built, pensions were paid, and the garbage was collected. On some of the items reported in Figure 6.2, the level of trust had fallen below 30 percent. One author speculates that the support of 15 percent of the population is enough (Wright 1976, 269). But the social location of the group is important. In the United States, support is highest among the white, non-Southern, non-Jewish, middle-aged upper middle class. In other words, trust is concentrated people who are most rewarded by the existing system. Extending broad trust beyond this group may be a key to democratic stability.

Political Efficacy

The concept of *political efficacy* was originally developed in the early 1950s to explain variations in voting turnout. The four questions used to measure it have been repeated frequently and over a longer period than almost any other survey indicator. Efficacy can be best described as a belief that one can influence the political process. It is a feeling that an active citizen can play a part in bringing about social and political change, and that one's input counts (Campbell et al. 1954, 187). Since it was first developed, the concept has been generalized to account for a wide variety of political activities. Given its long use and history, the original four-item efficacy scale has been the subject of an extensive methodological review. Some of the original items proved to be poor indicators of the concept, but in recent years considerable effort has gone into the development of more reliable items (Niemi et al. 1991).

Data from two large-scale studies of political participation show a strong relationship between political efficacy and many types of political activity (Verba and Nie 1972; Verba, Scholzman, and Brady 1995). Beyond its relationship to voting, these studies generally show that the higher the sense of political efficacy, the greater the likelihood that one will participate in political activities of a relatively demanding sort. Conversely, a low sense of efficacy is one of the factors normally associated with political apathy (Verba and Nie 1972, 133).

It should come as no surprise that political efficacy and trust are related—that those who feel they can influence government also tend to trust it (Walker and Aberbach 1970; Abravanel and Busch 1975). However, according to the 1996 NES, about 14 percent of the American public scored in the top 25 percent in efficacy but also in the bottom 25 percent in political trust.[12] Thus there seems to be a nontrivial segment of the population that could be mobilized for active opposition to the status quo given the appropriate circumstances. It might be noted, for example, that the low-trust/high-efficacy group voted at almost twice the rate for third-party candidate Ross Perot in 1992 than did the rest of the population.[13]

Considerable research has been conducted on the behavior patterns of those low on trust but high on efficacy. Shingles (1981), in a reanalysis of the Verba-Nie participation data, finds the combination of low trust and high efficacy overcomes the disadvantages of low income and low education in motivating political participation. This combination was a particularly important antecedent of political activity among African Americans. The data set, however, allowed only for examination of conventional political behavior. The research on unconventional political behavior has taken two approaches. The first is to look at the predisposition to engage in unconventional or violent behavior and infer a likelihood of disruptive or violent behavior under certain conditions. The second is to study riot participation after it occurs.

Abravanel and Busch (1975) find, for a sample of college students, that high-efficacy/low-trust respondents are likely to employ nontraditional forms of exerting political influence. Schwartz (1973) reports a repudiation of conformist modes of political participation among both students and urban blacks. Jennings and Andersen (1996) find the same pattern in support for the confrontational tactics used by the AIDS Coalition to Unleash Power (ACT-UP), which demanded that the Food and Drug Administration (FDA) release experimental AIDS drugs.[14] The most sophisticated and extensive analysis of unconventional political behavior has been carried out over a thirty-year period by Edward Muller and his colleagues. In a variety of research settings, Muller has demonstrated that collective violence is most likely to occur among people who are distrustful of and alienated from government and who also believe that their actions (often violent) will get them what they want.[15]

Although there is little doubt about the reliability of these relationships, there is considerable uncertainty about the links between these attitudes and behavior. Those studies that investigate predispositions are subject to the same criticism we made earlier (see section 6-1) about the linkage between statements of intent and political action. These studies of riot participation raise the question of the direction of causation. The respondents were interviewed after the riots were over. Did the attitudes cause the behavior, or did participating in the riot lead to a change of attitude? One can well imagine someone feeling considerably more efficacious after than before a violent outburst. Also, there is the possibility that riot behavior may be motivated by narrow local grievances (for example, the refusal of a supermarket chain to cash a check) but later justified by indictment of the entire political order. The linkages between efficacy, trust, and political action are provocative, but not all scholars agree that they provide a satisfactory explanation for nonconventional political participation.

Social Trust

Social trust can be differentiated from political trust. Social trust is generalized trust in others. It is trust in other people, people you have never met. It is often measured with the question "Do you believe that most people can be trusted or that you can't be too careful in dealing with people?" Social trust has little in common with political trust, as the two have different origins (Uslaner 2002). Looking across a variety of nations, the level of social trust is strongly related to the existence of democratic institutions. The higher the level of interpersonal trust among citizens, the more likely a nation will have democratic institutions and the more likely a nation is able to maintain long-term democratic stability (Inglehart 1999). Among the reasons are that democratic institutions depend on a trust among citizens that those voted into power will not use extralegal methods to stay there or use the power of state to suppress political opposition. People who trust others tend to be tolerant, participate in politics, contribute to charity, serve on juries, have high levels of confidence in political institutions such as Congress and the Supreme Court, and generally display the hallmarks of civic virtue (Putnam 2000). According to some, generalized trust is the oil the lubricates democracy (Warren 1999; Uslaner 2002).

Like political trust, social trust has been declining. In 1960, 57 percent of the public said they trusted most people (Almond and Verba 1963). By 1978, social trust had dropped to 40 percent and by 1994 to 33 percent, a range where it has more or less stayed (GSS 1972–2002). Almost all of this decline can be attributed to generational replacement (Putnam 2000, 140). Trusting seniors are being replaced in the electorate by less trusting new entrants. With the events of 9/11 came an increase in social trust, but it did not skyrocket like political trust. In November 2001, 42 percent said they trusted most people (Pew Research Center), but by February 2002 social trust had dropped to 34 percent (GSS 2002). Still, compared to other nations, Americans tend generally to trust others. Only the Scandinavian countries routinely exceed the United States when it comes to generalized social trust (Katzenstein 2000, 123).

Social trust also matters because it is an essential component of social capital. Many students of democracy believe that the development and maintenance of a civic culture is greatly aided by high levels of social capital. Robert Putnam (1993, 182) writes that "democratic government is strengthened, not weakened, when it faces a vigorous civil society." Social capital involves membership in voluntary associations and networks that create a sense of political efficacy. It allows people to work together effectively to influence government, which in turn mitigates the intensity of conflict that can threaten democratic government (Verba, Schlozman, and Brady 1995; Fukuyama 1995). Associational life in civil society, in the words of Verba and his colleagues, "operates as the school of democracy" (Brady, Verba, and Scholzman 1995, 285).

Levels of social capital have attracted much attention in recent years because of the provocative claim by Putnam (1995a; 1995b; 2000) that civic engagement in the United States has undergone a serious decline (see also L. Bennett 1998). As evidence, Putnam notes that membership in voluntary associations ranging from the Red Cross to bowling leagues has declined from 25 to 50 percent over the last three decades. The primary culprit, according to Putman, is the widespread appeal of television beginning in the mid-1950s.[16] The more one watches television, the less time one has for life in voluntary associations. In addition, data show that the more one watches television, the lower one's level of interpersonal trust. Television emphasizes violence, crime, and duplicitous personal relationships. According to the "mean world" thesis of George Gerbner (1998), heavy television users confuse its content with the real world. They see the world as unrealistically mean and dangerous, which has a negative effect on social trust. Not everyone, however, is convinced by the decline-in-social-capital thesis. Some have challenged the evidence of a decline (Pettinico 1996; Ladd 1998a); others doubt its connection to democratic stability (Jackman and Miller 1996; Tarrow 1996).

6-4 PERSONALITY AND PUBLIC OPINION

Individual political opinions can have their roots in the entire spectrum of human existence. For instance, the reason most personal injury attorneys oppose tort reform seems fairly obvious. They do not think the financial limitations on insurance claims proposed by insurance companies and their soulmates are in the best interest of the legal professional or in the best interest of the average American. It is not as easy to understand why some people are adamantly opposed to the fluoridation of drinking water while others accept it as a desirable form of preventive medicine. One explanation that received considerable attention is that certain attitudes and behaviors are possibly influenced by personality.[17]

Although there is no agreed-upon definition, we follow Eysenck and define *personality* as "the more or less stable and enduring organization of a person's character, temperament, intellect, and physique which determines his unique adjustment to his environment."[18] The basic element is the enduring, abstract perspective that a person uses to order the world and meet personal needs—for example, constructing a self-image in which one is an attractive and socially useful individual.

While trait psychologists have tried to associate personalities with specific attitudes and behavior, most researchers interested in personality dismiss such efforts as simplistic and naive. Rather, they pursue investigations across a wide range of attitudes and beliefs. As might be expected, such extensive and time-consuming assessments for each individual result in few persons being evaluated. The most frequently cited studies of personality and political behavior usually examine fewer than thirty persons. Such groups can in no way be considered a meaningful sample of any segment of the population. If the dynamics of personality and behavior noted in these limited groups were universal or identical to those of other people, as is sometimes claimed, these works would be more definitive. As it is, their primary contributions are insight into the psyches of people other than ourselves and the comfortable feeling that we know them personally, as opposed to the formality of a tabular presentation of a thousand faceless survey respondents. One study, however, that combines both a clinical and a survey perspective is *The Authoritarian Personality*.

The Authoritarian Personality

Influenced by events in Germany during Hitler's rule, a group of psychologists from the University of California at Berkeley began a systematic investigation into the personality structure of individuals particularly susceptible to anti-Semitic and fascist political appeals. Was there something about the personality of some individuals that led them to actively support or passively sympathize with a program of genocide against Jews, homosexuals, and gypsies, and the replacement of democratic government by dictatorship (as happened in Germany between 1932 and 1945)? The study (Adorno et al.) was completed in 1950 and has had a profound influence on all branches of the social sciences.

The thesis of the book is straightforward. Prejudice, suspicion, distrust, and hostility are manifestations of attempts to resolve deep-seated psychological conflicts. At the heart of these conflicts is a highly ambivalent and tense orientation toward authority. Authoritarians are submissive to those above them in the social order and condescending toward those below. As depicted in German folklore, they are like a person on a bicycle—above they bow, below they kick. While such persons are outwardly deferential, they in fact harbor considerable hostility toward authority. This hostility, however, is mostly unconscious, and authoritarians are only intermittently aware of the hate side of this love-hate amalgam. Rather, negative feelings are repressed by primitive ego defensive mechanisms. Authoritarians are extremely servile toward authority, driving from consciousness the malice they feel toward those above them. But repression has its costs, and the tensions created seek an outlet. To compensate for feelings of personal weakness, authoritarians present a tough façade. They are critical of those they see as beneath them, particularly those who are different, such as members of minority groups (Greenstein 1969, 106–107). Other characteristics of the authoritarian syndrome include: (1) conventionalism—a rigid adherence to conventional middle-class values; (2) anti-intraception—opposition to the tenderhearted, subjective, and imaginative; (3) superstition—a belief in mystical determinants influencing one's fate; and (4) ethnocentrism—a strong attachment to one's own group and hostility to outgroups (Kirscht and Dillehay 1967, 5–6).

Authoritarianism is thought to originate primarily with childhood family relationships.[19] Peterson, Smirles, and Wentworth (1997), for example, demonstrate the strong tendency for authoritarian parents to have authoritarian children.[20] Persons displaying the authoritarian syndrome often describe parental affection as being given only as a reward for good behavior. Their parents employed rigid, punishment-oriented disciplinary practices, as opposed to discipline based on love withdrawal. Family roles were clearly defined in terms of dominance and submission (Milburn, Conrad, and Carberry 1995). According to Adorno and his colleagues, "Forced into submission to parental authority, the child develops hostility and aggression which are poorly channelized. The displacement of a repressed antagonism toward authority may be one of the sources, and perhaps the principal source, of his antagonism toward outgroups" (1950, 482).

The implications of *The Authoritarian Personality* for public opinion and democratic stability became obvious to students of politics soon after its publication. One of the first tasks investigators set for themselves was to determine the political correlates of authoritarianism. (Are authoritarians prejudiced toward minorities? Do they hold antidemocratic political beliefs? and so on.) This undertaking was greatly aided by the fact that *The Authoritarian Personality*, unlike other such studies, provided a ready-made paper-and-pencil test to measure the extent to which the syndrome exists. This instrument, the *California F-scale* (the *F* is for fascism), has become virtually synonymous with authoritarianism. Typical agree/disagree items from the F-scale include the following (Adorno et al. 1950, 167):

- What young people need most of all is strict discipline by their parents.
- Most people who don't get ahead just don't have enough willpower.
- Sex criminals deserve more than prison; they should be whipped in public or worse.

Investigators soon discovered severe methodological problems with the F-scale. Among the most difficult to resolve was response set. All twenty items in the original F-scale were worded in a positive direction (to agree was authoritarian). As we indicated earlier, people with low education tend to be yea-sayers, making it difficult to separate the effects of education from the effects of personality when all questions in a scale suffer from response set. One solution is to reverse some of the items so that disagreeing with the question is the authoritarian response. While this strategy has merit, it is less than a completely satisfactory solution. Also, one essential requirement of a personality measure is that it not be contaminated by political content. It is now generally agreed that the F–scale is biased in the direction of right-wing authoritarianism. For example, one agree/disagree item from the F–scale states: "Homosexuals are hardly better than criminals and ought to be severely punished." Such a question may tap both personality traits and right-wing political outlooks. Consequently, the F–scale might not be sensitive to authoritarians of the left (such as American communists).

There have been two important attempts to deal with the problem. The first, by Milton Rokeach (1960), was the development of a new measure—the *dogmatism scale*—which Rokeach claimed could tap authoritarianism of both the left and the right. Currently, the dogmatism scale is one of the most frequently used measures of authoritarian tendencies (although it also suffers from response set, because to be "dogmatic" is to agree with scale items). The second solution was simply to recognize the problem and reformulate the concept as "right-wing authoritarianism." Bob Altemeyer (1981; 1988; 1997) argues that authoritarianism naturally leads to right-wing political views. He reorganizes the concept into three domains: submission to established authorities, aggression toward outgroups, and adherence to traditional social conventions. Thus, for example, research in the former Soviet Union showed that authoritarians (using Altemeyer's scale) tended to be more supportive of the old communist regime than nonauthoritarians (McFarland et al. 1992).

One aspect of authoritarianism that is clear is its association with social conformity (Feldman 2003). For instance, in a typical study a persuasive message was presented (from a variety of sources) to a number of different groups. Those scoring high on the F–scale were particularly likely to change their attitude when the message was delivered by a high-status source (Harvey and Beverly 1961, 125–130). Interestingly, authoritarians generally claim to hold their political opinions strongly, even though they tend not to be particularly informed politically (Peterson, Duncan, and Pang 2002).

Researchers studying democratic values have found authoritarianism (measured with Rokeach's dogmatism scale) to be related to political intolerance. Sullivan et al. (1982) found "large and significant" differences (in the predicted direction) between those scoring high and those scoring low on the D-scale with regard to the toleration of respondents' least-liked group, as did McClosky and Brill (1983, 342) using the traditional F-scale. Gibson and Tedin (1988) report similar findings in a study of tolerance for gay rights. They found dogmatism contributed to an intolerance for gays by reducing support for norms of democracy. Feldman and Stener (1997) find authoritarianism contributes to intolerance by increasing the perceived threat of disliked groups.

Decades of research have found a linkage from authoritarianism to racism. The correlation between these constructs is one of the most enduring in the social science literature. John Ray (1988, 673), one of the most trenchant critics of the concept, concedes that "despite all the other failures of their theory, Adorno et al. would appear to have succeeded in at last one of their basic aims—to find something that would predict who is a racist and who is not." Most recently, Meloen et al. (1996) have demonstrated strong relationships between authoritarianism and voting for political parties with a racist agenda.

Sniderman and Piazza (1993) have shown that authoritarian values among whites lead to the negative stereotyping of both Jews and African Americans. These groups are so different from each other in terms of educational accomplishment, material success, intact families, and other characteristics that factual considerations can hardly explain why the same people who hold negative stereotypes about Jews also hold them about blacks. Rather, the explanation is authoritarian values. It is not the actual characteristics of blacks, any more than it is the actual characteristics of Jews, that evoke prejudice and dislike. Rather, it is the ethnocentric dimension of the authoritarian personality—the generalized hostility to outgroups—that is part of the syndrome.

One particularly interesting study on authoritarianism involved the classic experiment developed by Stanley Milgram (1969) to measure obedience to authority. In this experiment, a naive subject ("the teacher") is required by the study director ("the authority figure") to administer an electrical shock each time "the learner" fails to perform a rote memorization task satisfactorily. The teacher is not aware that the learner is in league with the person running the experiment and is in fact receiving no shock at all. However, each time the learner fails the task, the authority figure (the experimenter) orders the teacher to shock the learner at an ever higher level of voltage. As the shocks presumably become stronger, the learner cries out in pain. The object is to see how long the teacher will obey the authority figure and continue to administer the shocks. One disturbing feature of this study is that many subjects continue to administer the shocks until the learner is in an apparent state of unconsciousness. Alan Elms administered the "teachers" the F-scale before conducting the Milgram experiment. He found that those who scored high on authoritarianism were highly reluctant (as predicted) to disobey the authority figure and terminate the experiment. Elms (1972, 113) explains:

> The relationship between obedience and some elements of authoritarianism seems fairly strong; and it should be remembered that the measure of obedience is a measure of actual submission to authority, not just what a person says he's likely to do. Too much of the research on authoritarianism . . . has been on the level of paper and pencil responses, which don't necessarily get translated into behavior. But here we have a realistic and highly disturbing situation. . . . So it does look as if those researchers in the late 40s had something, something which can be translated from abstract tendencies into actual authoritarian behavior: submitting to the man in command, punishing the weaker subordinate.

Is There a Democratic Personality?

Considerably less attention has been paid to the possibility that certain personality traits might promote support for democratic principles. Much of what has been written is either speculative or consists of inferences based on intensive interviews with small samples. Authors like Lasswell (1951), Lane (1962), and Inkeles (1961) wrote about the democratic character as being warm, outgoing, high in self-esteem and ego strength, flexible, and tolerant of ambiguity. One characteristic of this literature is a rather cavalier tendency to portray the democratic personality as the "healthy" personality and the nondemocratic personality as having psychological maladjustments.

It is misleading to talk about a democratic personality as if it were a distinct psychological type. But there may be certain personality traits that elicit support for democratic values as these values interact with particular environmental situations. The emphasis on environment is important because personality traits that encourage support for democratic principles (the accepted norm) among citizens of the United States probably encouraged support of totalitarian communism (the accepted norm) among citizens of the former Soviet Union. In other words, some personality types work well within the given rules of the political game—whatever those rules might be. It is not surprising, therefore, that many politicians who were successful when communism was the accepted norm in the Soviet Union are also successful under the norms of democracy in Russia and the Independent States. For example, Russian president Vladimir Putin is a former colonel in the Soviet KGB (the intelligence agency).

6-5 CONCLUSION

There seem to be two fundamental prerequisites for the existence and maintenance of democratic rights and freedoms. One is economic and the other is psychological. In the former, considerable research indicates that some minimal level of economic affluence and development is necessary before a democracy can operate successfully. If people must worry about feeding themselves and their children, concern about democratic government will be a low priority for most (Inglehart 1990; Huntington 1991). Beyond simple sustenance, the most relevant factor associated with democratic development is communication networks. Without sufficiently developed channels of communication, interests cannot be articulated and aggregated; conflicting groups cannot exchange information on goals and desires (Lipset 1959). But once a minimal level of economic development has occurred in tandem with associated communication networks, psychological and cultural factors become important (Inglehart 1997b).

This chapter has analyzed a number of political attitudes commonly thought to affect the stability of democracy. All may be of consequence, but none alone, or even in combination, provides a total explanation for the continued protection of democratic values in the United States. America has perhaps been most fortunate in that it has experienced few intense group or issue cleavages dividing the population. As long as a modest consensus exists and most of the population has a minimal degree of economic security, the system seems able to tolerate a wide variety of personality types, a relatively low level of trust in government, and considerable lack of enthusiasm (although perhaps not outright hostility) for procedural democratic norms.

NOTES

1. One bit of evidence for this thesis is the rather substantial increase in support for the civil rights of communists that occurred between 1988 and 1993, the period surrounding the fall of the communist Soviet Union. According to the GSS, in 1988, 60 percent would allow an admitted communist to speak; in 1993, 71 percent would. In 1988, 59 percent would allow an admitted communist's book to remain in the library; by 1993, 70 percent would. Increases in tolerance for other groups addressed in this battery of questions (e.g., atheists, militarists) were not nearly as large, so the explanation must be that with the fall of the Soviet Union, communists do not seem so dangerous.

2. Sullivan, Piereson, and Marcus (1982, 67) concede that tolerance may have increased somewhat between 1954 and 1978, but not as much as the items in Table 6.3 would lead one to believe.

3. The data presented here are a module in the 1987 GSS.

4. A point first noted by Herson and Hofstetter (1975).

5. For additional critiques of the theory of pluralistic intolerance, see Gibson (1986) and Sniderman et al. (1989).

6. Surveys reported in Dahl (1982), Ladd (1989), McLean (1999).

7. The literature on trust is voluminous. Among the better, more recent studies are Craig (1993), Nye, Zelikow, and King (1997), and Hetherington (1998).

8. Based on Harris polls, cited in Nye (1997, 283).

9. Not surprisingly, survey respondents are more trusting of government when their party is electorally triumphant. After the verdict in the disputed 2000 election, Gore supporters became less trusting while Bush supporters became more trusting (Anderson and LoTempio 2002).

10. "How Americans View Government: Deconstructing Distrust." Pew Research Center survey report, released March 10, 1998. http://www.People-Press.org.

11. The second reason for distrust (24 percent) concerns the poor performance of government; money is spent frivolously, nothing gets done, government is too intrusive. Policy dissatisfactions (15 percent) are also of consequence (Miller 1991). For example, people who support term limits tend to distrust government (Karp 1995). Finally, 13 percent in the Pew study said they distrust government because it does not pay attention to or care about ordinary people. This is only a partial list of possible reasons for distrust of government. For a more comprehensive list (seventeen in all), see Nye and Zelikow (1997).

12. The 1996 efficacy scale is based on three agree/disagree items: "Sometimes politics and government seem so complicated that a person like me can't really understand what's going on"; "People like me have no say in what government does"; and "I don't think public officials care much what people like me think." For each, to disagree is to give the efficacious response.

13. In 1992, 27 percent of those scoring low on trust and high on efficacy voted for Ross Perot. Perot support fell off within this group in 1996, with those low on trust and high on efficacy voting only 4 percent more for Perot than all others.

14. The tactics used by ACT-UP members included stopping trading on the floor of the New York Stock Exchange, disrupting political speeches, locking themselves inside the offices of major pharmaceutical companies, and conducting "die-ins" on streets with heavy traffic (Jennings and Anderson 1996, 313).

15. The best statement of this perspective can be found in Finkle, Muller, and Opp (1989).

16. In 1950, only 10 percent of all households had television. By 1960, 90 percent of all households had television. Americans typically watch three to four hours of television a day. The more television they watch, the less active they are in voluntary associations (Putnam 1995a).

17. For a review of the field, see Greenstein (1992).

18. Cited in Sniderman (1975).

19. For an argument that the authoritarian syndrome originates in Darwinian evolution, see Somit and Peterson (1997).

20. Peterson et al. (1997) report a significant path coefficient ($r = 0.47$) between authoritarianism in parents and authoritarianism in children. Altemeyer (1997) finds a similar relationship ($r = 0.40$).

7 | Group Differences in Political Opinions

$$P$$eople often think of themselves as belonging to a specific group. This group identification may influence political opinions, as people see certain policies as being beneficial to the group with which they identify. Thus we are not surprised if blacks are more favorable to affirmative action than whites, or people with high incomes more opposed to social welfare programs than those living near the poverty line. However, not all group differences are the result of calculated self-interest. Many political opinions are based on sociotropic considerations—that is, on the well-being of the nation as a whole rather than on that of the individual or the group (Kinder and Kiewiet, 1981). Life experiences can also shape political outlooks. For instance, individuals with a college education differ sharply from those without on a variety of cultural or social issues, such as abortion. Growing up as a white person in the South once virtually ensured an allegiance to the Democratic Party, although obviously no longer.

In this chapter we explore the validity of generalizations made about group differences in public opinion. Most of these differences we find to be correct but sometimes overdrawn. Although it is often thought that group differences in opinion and partisanship have been fading with time, recent evidence suggests that groups in different economic, religious, racial, age, and gender categories have been growing farther apart rather than closer politically (Manza and Brooks 1999).

7-1 SOCIOECONOMIC CLASS AND POLITICAL OPINIONS

Because a great many issues in political life concern the distribution of benefits within society, the rich and the poor often seem to have quite different economic interests. The haves and the have-nots are expected to disagree, for example, on questions involving taxation and government services.[1] In most European democracies, the major political battle lines are drawn between working-class parties and parties of the middle class. As indicated by the fact that the United States has never had an appreciable socialist movement, America has escaped the more extreme forms of class polarization and conflict. There are, nevertheless, class differences on many political issues.

How do we measure economic or social class? One approach, called *subjective social class*, is simply to ask people into which social class they fall—the lower class, working class, middle class, or upper class. When asked, almost everyone is willing to place himself in one of these classes. In the 2002 GSS, 5 percent identified with the lower class, 45 percent with the working class, 46 percent with the middle class, and 4 percent with the upper class. An alternative to the subjective approach is to use the objective indicators of occupation, income, and education. Each indicator has its problems. The connections among the three are often far from perfect. Many blue-collar workers have greater incomes than white-collar workers. Also, education is an imperfect predictor of income because many college graduates often have lower incomes than skilled manual workers. We could focus on income, but the same dollar amounts buy distinctly different lifestyles in various parts of the country. A $40,000 annual income in rural Montana might allow a pleasant middle-class lifestyle, while a family would have to struggle to live on that amount in New York City. Subjective class identifications actually are quite predictable from education, income, and occupation (Jackman and Jackman 1983). Still, analysts worry about how accurately survey respondents perceive their social reality. We proceed by employing what we see as the most appropriate indicator for the question at hand, with a sensitivity to the difficulties and imperfections of measuring socioeconomic class.

Class Differences on Economic Issues

Income is more concentrated at the upper levels of society in the United States than it is in any other Western democracy (Phillips 2002). In 1999, the richest 1 percent of all Americans had more money than the bottom 50 percent (Johnstone 1999). Rather than decreasing, the level of income concentration in recent years has been increasing, fueled significantly by wealth generated through the technology revolution. In 1991, conservative analyst Kevin Phillips (1991, 10) wrote that "no parallel upsurge of riches has been seen since the nineteenth century, the era of the Vanderbilts, Morgans, and Rockefellers." With the advent of the dot.com boom and the tax cuts of the second President Bush, that upsurge is even more pronounced in the twenty-first century (Phillips 2002, 157–161). In 1977, the richest one-fifth of the population took home 44.2 percent of all income; in 1999 they took home 50.4 percent. In 1997, the richest 1 percent received 7.3 percent of all income; in 1999 they received 12.9 percent (Johnstone 1999). To some extent, this growing inequality is recognized by the public. An increasing number of Americans see society as divided into the haves and have-nots. In 1988, just 26 percent said the nation was split along these class lines, compared to 46 percent in 2001.[2]

Yet by European standards, political cleavages along class lines in the United States are rather muted. Perhaps one reason is a belief among Americans that the opportunity to succeed financially is readily available to those with the energy and ability. For example, one poll found only 12 percent saying there is little or no chance of becoming rich in the United States if one is willing to work hard. When a British sample was asked a similar question, 63 percent said they did not think they had a chance to become rich if they really wanted to.[3]

Typically, the poor in the United States are more favorable to social welfare programs designed to raise living standards than are the more well-to-do. They are even more favorable if the program affects them directly. To take an early example, Gallup found in 1949 that 57 percent of the poor favored government action to improve the lot of the poor, compared to 28 percent of the prosperous.[4] This pattern has continued through the years and is reflected in the 1996 NES study. Respondents were asked if government should provide more services in the areas of health and education, even if it meant an increase in government spending. Among opinion-holders, 61 percent of blue-collar workers favored this position compared to 38 percent among business executives and professionals.

Table 7.1 shows the relationship between subjective social class and beliefs regarding whether the government should spend more money on programs such as student loans, child care, retirement benefits, aid to the homeless, and science and technology. For most of these programs, the working class is the group most likely to favor increased government spending. The greatest opinion difference among

TABLE 7.1	Subjective Social Class and Opinions About Spending on Selected Government Programs		
Percentage Wanting to Spend More On	Working Class	Middle Class	Upper Middle/ Upper Class
AIDS research†	60	51	38
Public schools†	80	75	70
Aid to poor people†	62	52	44
Roads and bridges★	36	37	36
Social Security†	74	62	45
Child care†	70	61	52
Unemployment assistance★	43	28	35
Preventing crime★	62	54	50
Science and technology★	36	37	49
Foreign aid★	08	06	05

★General Social Survey, 2002.

†National Election Studies, 2000.

the classes is on Social Security benefits, unemployment, child care, and AIDS research. Obviously the working class has real concerns about the well-being of their children when they are away from home, for their own financial security after retirement, and the AIDS epidemic. On the other hand, there is no difference in opinion on spending for roads and bridges, which benefits all classes. The opinions on these spending increases seem predictable from one's station in life. Social security and unemployment are of much more concern to the working class than the more affluent classes. On the other hand, the most affluent class is a potential beneficiary of increasing spending on science and technology, and its members tend to support such spending increases. There is virtually no constituency for an increase in spending on foreign aid.

The effects shown in Table 7.1 are, for the most part, quite modest. However, if we compare actual recipients of program benefits with nonrecipients, we find the differences increase dramatically. Cook and Barnett (1992, 150) report that 75 percent of those receiving Aid to Families with Dependent Children (AFDC) favored increasing such spending, compared to only 32 percent of nonrecipients. The same is true for food stamps, with 53 percent of recipients favoring an increase compared to 24 percent for nonrecipients. The same pattern holds for Medicaid, Social Security, and unemployment insurance.

For the 2000 NES, Figure 7.1 shows how family income, an objective indicator of social class, is related to opinion on the issues of increasing domestic

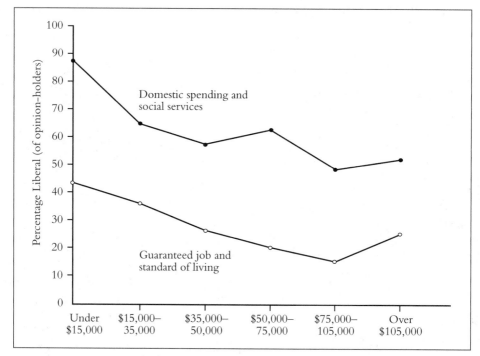

Figure 7.1   Social welfare opinion by family income (whites only). *Source:* National Election Studies, 2000.

spending and services and to support for a government-guaranteed job and good standard of living. (Nonwhites are excluded here in order to show the effect of income independent of race.) We would expect for reasons of simple economic self-interest that people in the lower-income categories would support public policies designed to promote employment and fund social programs, with a commensurate lack of support among the more financially secure. As one goes from poor to affluent, one does in fact see a decline in the percentage of people holding liberal positions on these economic issues.

Despite the repeated findings that rich and poor divide on redistributive issues like taxing and spending, it may seem puzzling that this class division is not stronger than shown in surveys. Clearly, more than direct self-interest is at work. Many wealthy individuals support government programs, paid for by their tax dollars, for which the direct benefits go to those less fortunate, while many of the less fortunate oppose programs for which they pay little tax but receive benefits.

One instance of this puzzle is the general public acceptance of President George W. Bush's tax cuts, which predominantly benefit the wealthy. According to polls, a plurality accepted Bush's tax cuts, including even repeal of the estate tax, which benefits only the wealthiest 2 percent. Why did ordinary people not object? Analyzing respondents in the 2002 NES survey, Bartels (2003) found that those who feel their personal tax burden is too great supported the Bush tax cuts regardless of their own personal economic circumstances. It is apparently of little consequence that the primary beneficiaries are the rich. The results raise intriguing questions. What is the reason for the disconnect between opinion and economic self-interest? Would more voters oppose tax cuts for the rich if they were better informed? Or, as some say, is it simply that voters favor benefits for the rich because they hope to be rich someday?

Class Differences on Noneconomic Domestic Issues

On noneconomic issues, liberalism tends to increase rather than decrease as one goes up the status ladder. Typical are the relationships between social class and opinions on equality for women, prayer in the schools, gays in the military, and the rights of the accused, shown in Table 7.2.

While the differences are not large, they are consistent. Reading the table across the columns, we see that support for women's issues rises as one moves up the status ladder, as does support for the rights of the accused and allowing gays in the military. Similar relations between status and opinion are found when people are asked about whether communists, socialists, or atheists should be granted the full range of civil liberties. Among whites, high-status respondents express less racial prejudice than do low-status respondents (Marcus et al. 1995; Kinder and Sanders 1996; Schuman et al. 1997; Sniderman and Carmines 1997).

Those with higher incomes tend to be conservative on economic issues, but on issues outside the economic realm status differences are complicated by the role of education. We saw in chapter 5 that educational achievement promotes political tolerance and political liberalism. This liberalizing effect of education is,

TABLE 7.2 | Opinions on Noneconomic Domestic Issues by Social Class
(Percentages of Opinion-Holders)

Opinion	Working Class	Middle Class	Upper Class
Favor equal role for women★★	78%	83%	80%
Oppose law requiring parental consent for preadult abortion★★	18	20	28
Allow gays in the military★★	72	77	83
Support rights of the accused★	39	41	47

★National Election Studies, 1976.
★★National Election Studies, 2000.

however, almost entirely limited to noneconomic issues. If we separate the effects of income and education on political attitudes, we find different patterns for economic and noneconomic issues. On noneconomic issues, high education but not high income is associated with liberalism. On economic issues, high income is negatively related to liberalism, but education is not.

Table 7.3 shows relevant examples. This table indicates that within each of the three income categories, liberal opinions on the noneconomic issue of abortion increase with educational attainment. Notice, for example, the large differences in support for abortion in the low-income group with varying amounts of education. Only 45 percent of those whose education stopped with high school graduation support abortion, moving to 55 percent with some college and 71 percent among college graduates. The reverse pattern can be seen on the economic issue of domestic spending. As family income goes up, individuals become more conservative on domestic spending. Seventy-five percent of college graduates with low incomes want increased spending, compared to only 47 percent of college graduates with high incomes. The third issue—aid to blacks—taps both the economic dimension of financial aid and the noneconomic dimensions of attitudes toward minorities. On this issue we can see the joint effect of higher education (which affects the noneconomic part of the issue) and the conservative effect of income (which affects the economic part of the issue). Thus we see that among those of low income, college graduates are the most favorable to aid for blacks. But among college graduates, those with the highest incomes are the least favorable.

Class Differences on Foreign Policy

The major class differences on foreign policy attitudes is that people in the lower educational strata more readily take the isolationist position than the more internationally minded, better-educated strata. These sorts of class differences can be traced to the 1930s and 1940s, when isolationism had great appeal to the working class, while the middle and upper classes favored an active role for the

TABLE 7.3	Joint Effects of Income and Education on Selected Issues, Whites Only

		Education		
		High School Only	Some College	College Graduate
For legal abortions in most circumstances				
Family income	High	58%	61%	68%
	Medium	58	58	64
	Low	45	55	71
For more domestic spending				
Family income	High	68	57	47
	Medium	59	64	60
	Low	72	67	75
For more government aid to blacks				
Family income	High	6	21	19
	Medium	7	15	22
	Low	18	12	29

Source: National Election Studies, 2000 election data. Percentages are based on opinion-holders among white respondents. For the full text of opinion questions, see the Appendix.

United States in world affairs (Mueller 1977). In 1948, for example, 92 percent of the college educated favored an active role for the United States compared to only 59 percent with less than a high school education (Page and Shapiro 1992). This same pattern is revealed in the more recent data shown in Table 7.4. There we see that the better educated have a more favorable view of the United Nations, are more willing to normalize relations with Cuba, believe that treaties with other countries would better protect the United States than a missile defense system, did not (in 1993) view communism as harshly as those with less education, and are decidedly more willing to endorse an active role for the United States in solving the world's problems.

We might expect that high-status people would be more willing to support military action abroad, as it is in some ways a logical extension of internationalism, just as isolationism implies keeping the troops at home. The accumulation of survey evidence shows only a modest tendency on the part of those with high economic status or high education to support American military adventures. In the case of Vietnam, support for the war in 1968 among the college educated may seem surprising because the most visible war opponents were found on college campuses. Only if we refine the educational index to isolate the small segment of people with graduate degrees or four-year degrees from the most prestigious universities do we find disproportionate antiwar sentiment at the top of the educational ladder (Rosenberg et al. 1970, 54–65). During the mid-1980s,

TABLE 7.4 | Education and Internationalism

	Less Than High School	High School Graduate	College Graduate
Have a favorable view of United Nations*	50%	67%	73%
U.S. should normalize relations with Cuba†	42	56	61
U.S. should be active in world affairs and help solve problems***	48	68	87
Communism worst kind of government**	63	49	36
Treaties better than missile defense system to protect U.S.***	39	53	62

*Princeton Survey Research Associates, 1996.

†CBS News, 1996.

**General Social Survey, 1993.

***Pew Research Center, 2001.

the United States was deeply involved in a guerrilla war against Marxist elements in Central America. Table 7.5 shows the better educated were only slightly more likely to support this effort than were those with less education. The education differences are somewhat larger when respondents were asked if they agree that "all things considered, the [1991 Persian] Gulf War was worth the cost." In the 1990s, as Table 7.5 shows, the college educated were the most supportive of sending peacekeeping troops to Kosovo. But also as Table 7.5 illustrates, the educated were the most reluctant to endorse the second Iraq war in 2003.

We must be careful in extracting significance from the class differences on questions of foreign policy, as the "no opinion" rate increases dramatically as one goes down the status ladder. Quite understandably, lower-status people are more concerned with the economic issues of day-to-day living than more abstract questions of foreign policy. We may particularly suspect that poor people and those with little education often grope for what they perceive to be the official policy when asked to give their foreign policy views (Ladd 1970).

Class Differences in Voting and Party Preferences

Ever since the 1930s, socioeconomic class has been the principal factor dividing people into Republicans and Democrats. We can see this division persisting into the 1990s, using data from the 2000 National Election Study. Figure 7.2 divides white respondents into five income groups from low to high, arranged as quintiles, with each group representing roughly one-fifth of white voters. As one would expect, the figure shows that as one moves up the income ladder, the frequency of identification and frequency of Democratic presidential voting both increase.

TABLE 7.5 | **Education and Opinion on U.S. Involvement in Foreign Countries**

Issue	Less Than High School	High School Graduate	College Graduate
U.S. should expand the Vietnam War (1968)★	24%	21%	25%
U.S. should be more involved in Central America (1986)★	19	21	25
The Persian Gulf War was worth it (1992)★	48	56	61
U.S. should commit peacekeeping troops to Kosovo (1999)†	44	49	63
Iraq War was worth fighting (2004)★★	57	55	54

★National Election Studies.

†Gallup.

★★*Washington Post* poll.

Let us first look at the 2000 presidential vote, Gore versus Bush. Among the poorest quintile (fifth) of white voters, 55 percent voted for Gore. Gore received a plurality of the white vote only among this lowest quintile. Among

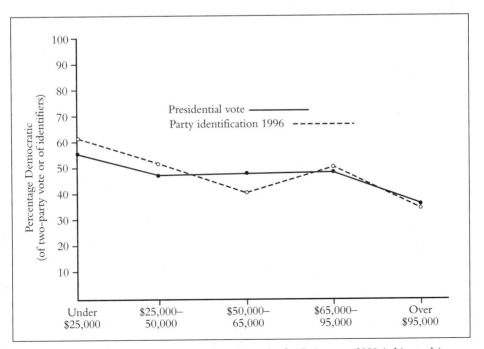

Figure 7.2   Party identification and presidential vote by family income, 2000 (whites only). *Source:* National Election Studies, 2000 election data.

the richest quintile, Gore won a mere 36 percent of the vote. (The middle quantities were in between—slightly pro-Bush.) The income gradient is slightly steeper for party identification than the vote. Among the poorest fifth, 62 percent of the partisans call themselves Democrats. And among the richest fifth of white voters, Republicans outnumber Democrats 2–1.

Estimating the impact of socioeconomic status or class on the vote over time is a tricky matter because of measurement issues. The conventional measure of class based on occupational status (usually of the household "head") is less relevant today and confounded by the surge of women in the workforce. If we consider the high-status category of professionals (doctors, lawyers, teachers, etc.) we see a movement from the Republican to the Democratic camp over the past half-century or more. While this might seem to indicate a decline in the importance of income differentials, it reflects mainly changes in the effect of education. Whereas college graduates used to be the most Republican of groups, they are now no more Republican than high school graduates.

As measured by family income, itself an imperfect measure, class differences in politics have clearly grown. Figure 7.3 shows the trend, with a comparison of the voting behavior of the top and bottom thirds of family income (for whites only) from 1952 through 2000. As a general trend, clearly the rich and poor have grown farther apart politically. Even as noneconomic issues have become more salient to voters, the partisan polarization of the rich and poor has actually increased. (See also Stonecash 2000.)[5]

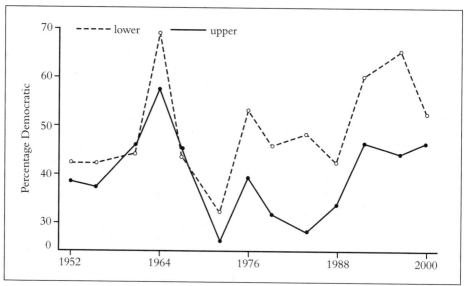

Figure 7.3   Major party presidential vote (whites only) by top third and bottom third of family income, 1952–2000. *Source:* National Election Studies Cumulative File.

7-2 RACE AND POLITICAL OPINIONS

The most profound political division between groups in the United States is between blacks and whites. In 1968, the Kerner Commission (U.S. National Advisory Committee on Civil Disorders 1968, 1) concluded that "Our nation is moving toward two societies, one black, one white—separate and unequal." While progress has surely been made since that date, there is a wide gulf between blacks and whites on most political issues, particularly on those involving discrimination and its remedies. Of course, blacks are not the only racial or ethnic minority in America. The proportion of Latinos (Hispanics) and Asians is growing at a rapid rate, and the former now outnumber blacks as the largest minority group in the United States. However, neither group has the distinctive political opinions that characterize the black population.[6]

Blacks, Whites, and Political Opinions

Until the late 1970s, the central division of opinion in the United States concerning the role of African Americans was the very issue of a racially integrated society. In a 1964 NES survey, respondents were asked if they favored "strict segregation" of the races, "desegregation," or "something in between." Not surprisingly, 73 percent of blacks favored desegregation, while only 6 percent favored segregation, with 21 percent favoring something in between. In the case of whites, about equal numbers chose strict segregation (25 percent) as desegregation (27 percent), with the remainder choosing something in between. But by 1978 (the last year this question was asked), only 5 percent of whites favored strict segregation—about the same as among blacks (6 percent). In 1964, the NES shows 74 percent of whites thought civil rights leaders were "pushing too fast" compared to 11 percent among blacks. But by 1980 the percentage had dropped to 40 percent among whites, with blacks remaining essentially unchanged.

By the late 1970s, the political agenda on race shifted to the question of whether the government should actively help blacks move into the economic mainstream through preferences in education and employment or whether blacks themselves were responsible for their economic well-being. We can compare the distribution of these sentiments among blacks and whites using a NES question asked in 1974 and 2000 as to whether the government should "make every effort to improve the economic and social condition of blacks and other minorities" or whether they should help themselves.

	Whites		Blacks	
	1974	*2000*	*1974*	*2000*
Government should help blacks	25%	16%	63%	36%
Unsure	26	26	25	31
Blacks should help themselves	50	58	12	33
	101%	100%	100%	100%

There are substantial differences between blacks and whites on this issue in both 1974 and 2000. But the trend for both racial groups is in a conservative direction. While there has been a 9 percent drop in support among whites for government assistance to blacks and other minorities, there has been a larger 27 percent drop among blacks. The fact that blacks and whites have moved in the same direction suggests a declining belief among both racial groups in the ability of government to solve problems—including those that may stem from the consequences of America's past racial practices.

In recent years, much of the debate over racial policies has shifted to the arena of affirmative action. Given the dual emphasis in the American political tradition on equality and individualism, many well-intentioned citizens appear caught in a dilemma. First, there is a recognition that blacks historically have not had the same opportunities as whites, but there is also a belief that educational opportunities and jobs should be filled on merit, without reference to race, sex, or religion.

As one would expect, blacks are more supportive of affirmative action than whites. In 2000, the GSS asked if due to past discrimination blacks should be given preferences in hiring and promotion, or whether such preference is wrong because it discriminates against whites.

	Whites	Blacks
Favor preferences for blacks in hiring and promotion	18%	50%
Undecided	7	12
Oppose preferences for blacks in hiring and promotion	75	38
	100%	100%

As seen here, programs that imply preferences or quotas for minorities are highly unpopular with whites while dividing blacks.[7] As we noted in chapter 4, questions on affirmative action are sensitive to question-wording effects, as many of the terms employed, such as *quotas* and *racial preferences*, are politically charged. We can see this from the divisions in responses to a very similar question to the one above (this one from the NBC News/*Wall Street Journal Poll*, 2003), where the affirmative action alternative rejects "rigid quotas."

	Whites	Blacks
Affirmative action programs needed "as long as there are no rigid quotas"	43%	79%
Not sure	6	12
Affirmative action programs "should be ended because they unfairly discriminate against whites"	49	14
	100%	100%

In this instance, whites are divided while blacks are one-sidedly favorable.[8]

These opinion gaps are rooted in much larger differences between blacks and whites concerning perceptions of the continued existence of racial discrimination. In 1995, 68 percent of African Americans said that racism is a "big problem" in American society compared to 38 percent of whites and, in 1997, 65 percent of blacks said they saw no real improvement in their position in recent years, while only 36 percent of whites agreed with that sentiment.[9] About four times as many blacks as whites perceived discrimination against blacks in education, and 57 percent of blacks believed they get lower wages because of discrimination, while only 14 percent of whites believe such discrimination exists. Sigelman and Welch (1991, 59) write that blacks today "see racial discrimination as an everyday occurrence, not a historical curiosity."

Even on issues that are tangential to civil rights, blacks are more likely than whites to take the liberal position. Some examples are shown in Table 7.6. As we would expect, there are substantial black–white differences on economic issues such as the pace of domestic spending and whether or not the government should guarantee everyone a good standard of living. For whites, social class is a consistent correlate of opinion on these social welfare issues. However, for blacks there is no relationship. Upper-income blacks are about as supportive as lower-income blacks. The reason for this nonrelationship is that greater income among blacks is related to greater racial identification (Tate 1993, 27–29). In other words, upper-income blacks are more likely to identify with their race than with their social class. Upper-class whites, on the other hand, are more likely to identify with their social class.

Blacks are also much less supportive of the death penalty than are whites, perhaps because those on death row are disproportionately black. Note, however, that the death penalty is still supported by a majority of black citizens. Blacks are also less supportive of American military action abroad. For example, we see a sizable difference in support for American involvement in the two Iraq wars of 1991 and 2003. Blacks were much less supportive of the Vietnam War than were whites and have been less enthusiastic about other American military

TABLE 7.6	Race and Opinion on Selected Non–Civil Rights Issues (Percentage of Opinion-Holders)		
Issue	Whites	Blacks	Difference
Government should provide more services and increase spending (2000)*	61%	91%	+ 30
Government should see that people have jobs and good standard of living (2000)*	27	51	+ 24
Oppose death penalty for those convicted of murder (2000)*	24	49	+ 25
Homosexual marriage should be legal (2004)†	41	47	+ 6
War in Iraq was not worth fighting (2004)†	38	74	+ 36

*National Election Studies.

†*Washington Post* poll.

adventures, whether in Nicaragua, Grenada, and Panama in the 1980s or in Bosnia and Kosovo in the 1990s. These racial differences may stem from the Vietnam War, where a disproportionate number of African Americans bore the brunt of the fighting. In conflicts since then, the Pentagon has been careful to ensure that blacks and other minorities are not overrepresented (given their numbers in the armed services) among those assigned to combat zones.

Despite the existence of an undeniable racial divide in the United States, there is evidence that points toward an easing of strains in racial relations. Between 1981 and 1997, there was a 14 percent increase in the number of blacks who said they had a "close personal friend" who was white and a 17 percent increase among whites saying they had a "close personal friend" who was black.[10] American neighborhoods have become more racially integrated. Between 1980 and 1998, the GSS reports a 14 percent increase in black respondents saying they have white neighbors and white respondents saying they have black neighbors. Perhaps the acid test of race relations is approval of intermarriage among blacks and whites. In 1958 Gallup asked, "Do you approve or disapprove of marriage between blacks and whites?" Among whites, 5 percent approved. By 1980, white approval had risen to 48 percent, and in 1997 it was 67 percent. Among blacks in 1997, 83 percent approved of intermarriage among blacks and whites (Schuman et al. 1997, 245).

Racial Groups and the Vote

In terms of the vote and party identification, there are major differences between blacks and whites. For instance, in 2000, 90 percent of African Americans but only 42 percent of whites cast their vote for Al Gore. We present below the 2000 vote choice, as reported in VNS exit polls, for the four major ethnic groups in the United States.

2000 Vote	Asians	Blacks	Latinos	Whites
Gore	53%	90%	60%	42%
Bush	41	8	35	54
Nader	5	1	4	4
Buchanan	1	0	1	1
	100%	100%	100%	100%
	(n=211)	(n=1461)	(n=858)	(n=10,147)

We see Latinos voted heavily Democratic, although not to the same extent as blacks. Between 1996 and 2000, the largest Republican gain in presidential voting was a 14 point increase among Latinos. Asians, we see, voted mainly for Gore in 2000. This is a reversal from 1996, when a plurality of Asians voted for Republican Bob Dole over Democrat Bill Clinton. Asians account for about 2 percent of the votes cast, blacks 12 percent, and Latinos 7 percent, with whites holding a 79 percent majority.

The voting differences we see among the races are also found in terms of the underlying attitude of party identification. Among whites in the 2000 National Election Study, 33 percent were Democrats, 30 percent were Republicans, and 37 percent called themselves Independents. Among blacks in the sample, 65 percent were Democrats, 6 percent Republicans, and 29 percent Independents. Using the VNS exit poll, we can expand our analysis to include Asians and Latinos. The data reported below represent only the 51 percent that voted on election day, not the overall adult population.

Party Identification	Asians	Blacks	Latinos	Whites
Democrat	43%	82%	58%	34%
Independent	25	12	17	20
Republican	32	7	25	41
	100%	100%	100%	100%
	(n=211)	(n=1461)	(n=858)	(n=10,147)

Over time, American blacks have undergone a long-term reversal in their party allegiance. Between the Civil War and Franklin Roosevelt's presidency, most blacks who could vote opted for the Republican Party because it was the party of Lincoln. From the 1930s to the present, however, most blacks have supported the Democratic Party. Initially this shift was a response to economic issues rather than any consequential attempt on the part of the Democratic Party to remove racial barriers or explicitly appeal to blacks. Only in recent years could the Democratic Party be identified as the party with clearly greater sympathy for the civil rights cause. As a result of the Democrats' increasing image as the more pro–civil rights party, Democratic voting among blacks at the presidential level has changed from a tendency to near unanimity. The solidifying event was the 1964 election, in which President Lyndon Johnson took a strong stand in favor of the Civil Rights Act and Republican challenger Barry Goldwater opposed and voted against it in Congress (as an infringement on states' rights). The change over time is shown in Figure 7.4.

Clearly the black vote is a pivotal factor for the Democratic Party in presidential elections. In only one such election since World War II (1964) has the Democratic candidate received a majority of the total white vote. The usual predictors of party preference among whites do not work in the case of blacks. Higher-income blacks are not more likely to be Republican, as is the case in the white population. In fact, black Republicans and black Democrats are remarkably similar, both demographically and in their policy preference (Tate 1993).

7-3 AGE AND POLITICAL OPINIONS

If one examines a breakdown by age of the scores of political issues that might interest the student of public opinion, three patterns stand out. On the majority of issues there are no meaningful age-group differences; on a sizable minority of issues, those older are more conservative than those younger; and on a small number of issues, the young are more conservative than their elders. As discussed in chapter 5, there are two major reasons why older cohorts might

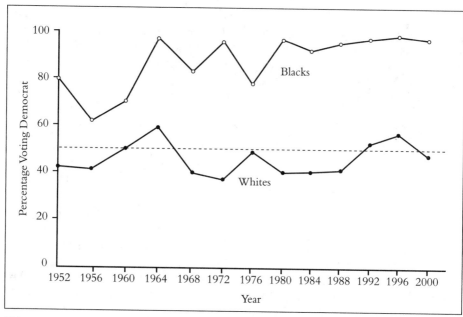

Figure 7.4 Race and the two-party presidential vote, 1952–2000. *Sources:* Gallup Poll, 1952–1976; National Election Studies, 1980–1992; Voter News Service, 1996–2000.

differ from younger ones:. First, there may be life-cycle effects in which the process of maturation results in changes throughout adulthood. People growing more conservative with age is the typical example. Second, there may be generational effects, with each group of young voters differing from those in the past. While increasing conservatism with age creates an age gap in opinions, so do generational differences.[11]

The Politics of Age

To the list of reasons for age groups to differ in their political opinions we can add the politics of self-interest. Advocates for children often blame inadequate funding for programs benefiting youngsters on the political power of older Americans, whom they accuse of greedily siphoning off more than their fair share of government dollars, or voting against school bond referendums to keep their property taxes low (Tedin, Matland, and Weiher 2001). Recently, many have voiced concern that the Social Security and Medicare benefits enjoyed by older Americans will bankrupt the system before those currently paying the bill are eligible to receive benefits. Issues such as these have raised the specter of intergenerational political conflict.

We do in fact see meaningful differences between the age groups on at least some economic issues. Younger adults are more likely to feel the government should provide increased services to its citizens and see to it that everyone has a good job. Reflecting its self-interest, the younger cohort is considerably more liberal on the issue of increased spending for student loans.

On the issue of government health insurance, the generational difference closes, reflecting the self-interest older Americans have in health care benefits. Nevertheless, the younger generation remains slightly more liberal.

When we turn to social issues, where society is in a state of flux, we find younger cohorts consistently more liberal than older ones. The young are more receptive to new ideas since they are, for the most part, not committed to old ones. This point can be illustrated using the 25 percent gap in the open housing item in Table 7.7. No one under thirty-five has lived during a time when refusing to sell your home to someone because of race or

TABLE 7.7	Age and Opinion on Selected Issues		
	Percentage Support Among Opinion-Holders		
	Under 30	**55 and Over**	**Difference**
Economic Issues			
Government should provide more services, even if it means increased spending (2000)★	77%	62%	+ 15
Government should see to it that everyone has a good job and standard of living (2000)★	39	22	+ 17
Government should cover all hospital and medical expenses (2000)★	67	53	+ 14
Increase spending on student loans (1996)★	70	42	+ 28
Social Issues			
Homeowners should not refuse to sell home to someone because of race or color (1998)†	79	54	+ 25
Marijuana should be made legal (1996)†	35	17	+ 18
Allow homosexuals to teach in college (1996)†	88	61	+ 27
Allow abortion for any reason (2000)★	40	33	+ 7
Favor English as official language (2000)★	75	56	+ 19
Foreign Policy/Military Issues			
U.S. should decrease military spending (2000)★	29	43	− 14
Disapprove of going to war in Iraq (2002)★	35	30	+ 5
Civic Orientations			
Watch campaign TV shows (1992)★	53	64	− 11
Read news about 2000 campaign (2000)★	40	69	− 29
Pay attention to national news (1998)★	33	57	− 24
Liberal/Conservative Ideological Identification (2002)‡			
Liberal	30	18	
Moderate	42	46	
Conservative	28	35	

★National Election Studies.

†General Social Survey.

‡CBS News/*New York Times* Surveys.

color was legal. For most people, this prohibition is simply taken for granted. Alternatively, those over fifty-five may recall when such practices were not only legal but quite common. To endorse the more liberal position for the older generation may mean changing an opinion that was once viewed as legitimate.

On foreign affairs, it is often thought that the young are more dovish than their elders. However, the evidence for that proposition is mixed and often depends on circumstances. In past conflicts, including World War II, Korea, Vietnam, and the two Iraqi wars, the younger cohort has in fact been more supportive of U.S. involvement than those over fifty-five (see Wittkopf 1990). Yet the older generation is more likely to say that the war objectors should have served regardless of their beliefs.

Most of the issue differences reported in Table 7.7 show the older generation to be more conservative than the younger. In some instances, the proper inference is that people get more conservative as they get older. But a contributing factor in some instances is a growing liberalism over time on the part of successive generations (Davis 1992). As we saw in chapter 5, the relationship between partisanship and age looks different depending on the year examined. The partisan preferences of each generation reflect both the partisan landscape during the generation's impressionable years of their youth and the period effects of events in the years since their early adulthood.

Finally, younger Americans in general tend to be less interested and involved in politics than older generations. Several investigators have noted that the current young generation seems uniquely turned off by political affairs. Bennett (1998, 535) observes that "today's youth are more withdrawn from public affairs than earlier birth cohorts when they were young." They are simply going to the polls less frequently than their age group peers in the 1970s. Currently, voters under thirty are less likely to cast their ballots than those over sixty-five by about a 4–1 margin (Goldstein and Morin 2002; Wattenberg 2002). With data such as these, it is small wonder that politics often seems to center disproportionately on issues such as Social Security and prescription drug benefits.

Younger adults are also less engaged with the political news. A 1996 Pew Research poll found that while 76 percent of those over thirty had read a newspaper on the day of the interview, only 31 percent of those under thirty had done so. As seen in Table 7.7, young respondents in the NES 2000 survey were much less likely to have read news stories about the campaign or follow the national news. In the 2000 presidential campaign, only 40 percent of those under thirty had done so; 57 percent of those over fifty-five paid a lot of attention to the national news, compared to 33 percent of those under thirty. This lack of interest in political affairs among the young has a quite predictable result—elevated levels of political ignorance (Bennett 1998). The causes of political disinterest in the youngest generation are multifaceted and may involve everything from political scandals to the increasingly negative tone of political coverage by the media (Bennett 1997). At the dawn of the new century, the youngest age cohort seems uniquely indifferent to politics.

7-4 RELIGION AND POLITICAL OPINIONS

Compared with other nations, Americans are religious. Between 1990 and 1993, respondents in the World Values Survey were asked if they were or were not a religious person.[12] As we can see from the following table, the United States stands out in the high proportion of its citizens who find religion important in their lives.

	Am a Religious Person	Am Not Religious	Other/Don't Know*
United States	82%	15%	3%
Mexico	72	22	6
Canada	69	26	5
Spain	64	27	9
Britain	55	37	8
Germany	54	27	19
France	48	36	16
Sweden	29	56	9

Volunteered.

Americans also tend to belong to churches, although that was not always the case. At the time of the American Revolution only 17 percent were church members. By the end of the Civil War the number had doubled to 35 percent, then increased to 53 percent by 1916 and to 63 percent in the 1990s (Finke and Stark 1994). This increase in church membership is important, as religion and church membership have an important influence on public opinion.

Protestants, Catholics, Jews, and "Nones"

In terms of religious preference, 53 percent of American adults are Protestant, 26 percent are Catholic, 2 percent are Jewish, and 14 percent profess no religious preference ("Nones").[13] On what basis would we anticipate religious denominations to differ politically? Although Protestants are a pluralistic group, we might expect they would be the most conservative. Protestants once held higher-status jobs and enjoyed higher incomes than did Catholics (there is no difference today among the white population). But the fact that Catholic immigrants arrived more recently and were subjected to a certain amount of discrimination may have left traces of liberal sentiment. Also, doctrinal differences exist that might have political relevance. The Catholic Church has taken a strong position against birth control and abortion, mainstream Protestant churches less so. Further, the Protestant focus on individual responsibility for one's own economic and spiritual well-being (the "Protestant ethic") may predispose Protestants to be conservative on economic questions and issues of affirmative action. The high-status, high-income occupations of Jews compared to other religious groups, plus their concern for the well-being of Israel, might lead us to anticipate that Jews would be the most conservative and internationalist of religious groups. Counterbalancing these forces is the unique history of the Jewish people as a persecuted minority, which drives them in a liberal direction, particularly on civil liberties and civil rights.

Finally, a group that received little attention but now constitutes 14 percent of the adult population (up from 7 percent in the early 1990s) is the Nones (see Hout and Fischer 2002). This residual category consists of atheists, agnostics, those indifferent to religion, and those believing in a Supreme Being but disenchanted with organized religion. We would expect them to be liberal, as to be unchurched is to be outside the American cultural mainstream. Such marginality tends to result in a liberal political outlook.

We limit our initial analysis to Northern whites so as not to confuse the effect of denominational preference with region and race. The South is largely Protestant and conservative; blacks are largely Protestant and liberal. Table 7.8 shows Protestants to be slightly more conservative on issues than Catholics, but the margins are not large. On economic matters, Catholics and Nones are somewhat more liberal than Protestants, with Jews being the most liberal. On civil and moral issues, Jews and Nones are decidedly more liberal than the two major faiths. Note that on the key issue of abortion there is no difference between Protestants and Catholics—they are equally likely to endorse the statement that abortion should be allowed for any reason. Claiming a denominational affiliation is, of course, an easy response. However, if we look at differences between Catholics and Protestants among those who attend church once a week or more, there is still almost no difference between the two groups. On the other hand, Jews and Nones are much more supportive of abortion on demand than are Protestants or Catholics. On foreign and defense policies, Catholics and Protestants differ only marginally. Jews are somewhat more internationalist than other groups—as expected. But they were less supportive of the 1991 Persian Gulf War than the other two major religious groups and less likely than all others to say the government should spend more on defense.

Turning to the more general orientations of partisanship and ideology, note that (among Northern whites) Protestants constitute one large group that is far more Republican than Democratic. Catholics still tilt slightly Democratic, while Jews and Nones are decidedly Democratic in partisan tendency (although the Nones, with no religion, gravitate to Independent or nonalignment in party identification). Protestants are also the most conservative group in terms of ideological identification, followed slightly by Catholics, with Jews and Nones the two religious groupings that tilt more liberal than conservative. Finally, we can contrast the voting patterns of the major religious groupings. There were once substantial differences between Protestants and Catholics, but in recent years these have narrowed. Religious divisions were at their clearest in the 1960 presidential election, when the Democrats broke with tradition and nominated a Catholic, John F. Kennedy, for president. Among Northern whites in the 1960 NES, the vote broke down by religion as follows:

Northern Whites	Protestant	Catholic	Jewish
Voting Democratic (Kennedy)	28%	83%	83%
Voting Republican (Nixon)	72	17	7
	100%	100%	100%

| TABLE 7.8 | Religious Denomination and Political Opinion, Northern Whites |

Issue	Percent Support Among Opinion Holders			
	Protestant	*Catholic*	*Jewish*	*None*
Economic Issues				
Government should provide more services, even if it means increased spending (2000)★	57%	68%	88%	71%
Government should see to it that everyone has a good job and standard of living (2000)★	28	28	23	29
Government should pay for medical care (2000)★	40	59	62	67
Civil/Moral Issues				
Abortion allowed for any reason (2000)★	33	30	80	51
Favor legalization of marijuana (1996)†	20	26	44	45
Disapprove of prayer in public schools (1996)†	32	41	85	65
Favor government aid to blacks (2000)★	14	17	46	17
Men, women equally suited for politics (1996)†	71	77	84	79
Foreign/Defense Issues				
Communism not worst form of government (1992)†	49	48	68	69
Decrease military spending (2000)★	20	20	29	35
Take less active role in world affairs (2000)★	24	29	14	32
Did the wrong thing in sending troops to 1991 Persian Gulf War (1992)★	12	16	29	28
Ideological Identification (2002)‡				
Liberal	17	21	34	36
Moderate	47	48	54	44
Conservative	36	31	12	20
Party Identification (2002)‡				
Democrat	27	36	56	39
Independent	29	33	31	44
Republican	44	31	13	17

★National Election Studies.

†General Social Survey.

‡CBS News/*New York Times* Surveys.

(*Note:* 1996 GSS readings are for pooled 1994–1998 data.)

Almost three-fourths of the Protestant vote among Northern whites was for Nixon, while over 80 percent of the Catholic and Jewish vote went for Kennedy. In more typical elections, without a Catholic candidate, the same ordering exists, but the differences are smaller. The table below shows the presidential vote divisions among (Northern white) Protestants, Catholics, Jews, and Nones among respondents in the 2000 VNS Exit Poll. Protestants voted the most Republican, followed by Catholics and those with no religious preference; Jewish voters were the least Republican.

Northern Whites	Protestant	Catholic	Jewish	None
Voting Democratic (Gore)	35%	45%	80%	57%
Voting Republican (Bush)	62	51	18	30
Voting Green (Nader)	3	4	3	13
Voting Reform (Buchanan)	1	1	0	1
	101%	100%	100%	100%

The temporal stability of partisan differences between Protestants, Catholics, and Jews is shown in Figure 7.5. The data show the percentage of Democratic (among identifiers only) among Northern whites beginning in 1956. The most remarkable aspect of Figure 7.5 is the stability over time in partisan preference. Typically, Jews are about 80 percent Democratic, Catholics about 65 percent (and slowly declining), and Protestants about 40 percent. Of those declaring no religious preference, about 65 percent identifying are Democrats.[14] The long-term trend shows little loss of religious distinctiveness in party preference.

Many of the reasons advanced earlier to explain issue differences among the religions also apply to the differences we see in partisanship and voting. However, we should note that the Democrats have traditionally wooed immigrant voters, most of whom were Catholic. The payoff of this policy for the Democratic party has been the continued allegiance of many members of Catholic ethnic groups—the Irish, Italians, Poles, East Europeans, and Mexicans—who often

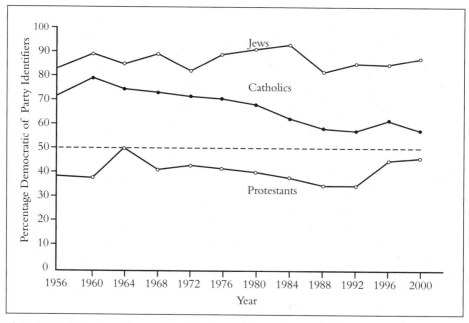

Figure 7.5   Religion and party identification (Northern whites only), 1956–2000. *Source:* National Election Studies.

continue to identify and vote Democratic despite having incomes that place them solidly in the middle class. One explanation for the continued Democratic voting among Catholics is that in the past American Catholics were less affluent than their Protestant neighbors—a condition that would naturally cause them to gravitate to the Democratic party for economic reasons. But there is more than economics at work, because during the 1940s surveys showed that even affluent Catholics tended to be Democratic, much as affluent blacks are today (Berelson et al. 1954, 64–66). Besides, the Protestant-Catholic gap in income closed decades ago. And as we saw earlier, Catholics are slightly more liberal than Protestants, but with differences certainly not of the magnitude to prevent them from comfortably embracing the Republican Party. Perhaps the best explanation for the Democratic allegiance of Catholics is simply the socialization of partisanship from one generation to the next. Even though the social and economic reasons for remaining Democratic no longer exist, there is a family tradition of Democratic partisanship among Catholics that keeps them from turning Republican.[15]

Protestant Denominations and Evangelicals

On many issues there is greater disagreement among Protestants of various persuasions than between Protestants and Catholics. Theological differences between denominations often show up as differences in political opinion. For example, the emphasis on personal salvation in the Baptist church and other fundamentalist groups seemingly makes their members conservative, while the more worldly involvement in social problems on the part of nonfundamentalist groups (Presbyterians and Episcopalians, for example) ought to make their members relatively liberal. Also, the theology of some fundamentalist Protestant denominations condemns departures from traditional lifestyles, while more liberal denominations are more accommodating. Very sharp differences on these issues have been found between the political attitudes of Protestant clergymen of fundamentalist and nonfundamentalist churches and among church members who are very politically involved. Wald and associates investigated the possibility that active membership in a specific congregation can have a direct effect on the political attitudes of parishioners. Based on a sample of twelve Protestant churches in a Florida community, they found parishioners from the more theologically conservative congregations were also more politically conservative, particularly on social issues. This relationship is attributed directly to "messages from the pulpit and social interaction [among] the congregants" (1989, 542; see also Jelen 1992 for an extension of this research). Leege and Welch (1989), in a study of Catholic parishioners, came to a similar conclusion about the role of theology in political outlook.

Since the mid-1970s, evangelical Christian groups have interjected a new dynamic into American politics, due both to the uniqueness of their political beliefs and the grass-roots activism among their members. These groups are mostly Protestant, but they cut across denominations. Two major evangelical subgroups have been especially politically active: the fundamentalists and charismatics/Pentecostals. Fundamentalists emphasize personal experiences with the Holy Spirit (being "born again"), a literal interpretation of the Bible, and rejection of the Social Gospel (salvation through good works). Charismatic or Pentecostal Protestants are fundamentalists with a focus on the mystical, such as faith healing, prophecy, and speaking in tongues. Many in the fundamentalist movement are critical of charismatics, arguing their focus on spiritual gifts undermines the doctrine of the Bible's inerrancy. Fundamentalists tend to be more conservative on political issues than are Pentecostals (Jelen 1993). Evangelicals currently constitute about 27 percent of the population and 56 percent of all Protestants (Wald 1997, 173). Comparatively speaking, they tend to be rural, Southern, less affluent, and less educated than the rest of the population (Reichley 1985, 312).

Table 7.9 presents evidence of how Protestant fundamentalists differ from more secular Protestants in their political views, according to the 1996 NES survey. The table is limited to white Protestants, as blacks tend to be more theologi-

TABLE 7.9	Religious Fundamentalism and Political Views, White Protestants Only, 1996		
		Religious Orientation	
Political Opinion	Secular (36 percent)	In Between (39 percent)	Fundamentalist (25 percent)
Want more domestic spending	61%	76%	76%
For national health insurance	38	39	20
Guarantee good standard of living	23	24	11
Decrease spending on welfare	61	61	77
Always permit abortions	57	29	8
Allow gays in military	72	61	35
Equal role for women	88	76	54
Punish criminals to reduce crime	47	60	65
Protect environment at cost of jobs	57	39	28
Favor gun control	44	46	29
Gone too far pushing equal rights	53	62	77
Willing to use force abroad	17	24	29
Increase defense spending	48	69	76
Oppose Persian Gulf War†	17	11	10
Percentage Democratic (of party identifiers)	50	40	23
Percentage liberal (of ideological identifiers)	36	12	6
Percentage for Clinton (of 1996 two-party vote)	49	40	20

1996 National Election Studies Data.
†National Election Studies, 1992.

cally conservative than whites but more politically liberal due to their racial identification. Fundamentalism is measured in terms of a variety of religious beliefs (such as being "born again"). The table contrasts the views of the 36 percent most secular (or religiously indifferent) of Protestants with the 25 percent most fundamentalist (with the remaining 39 percent classed as "in between").[16]

Overall, the fundamentalists are very conservative, with almost all ideological identifiers choosing the "conservative" label versus one-half of the secular. While the fundamentalists are somewhat more conservative on economic issues than are the other groups, and somewhat more hawkish on defense issues, it is social and cultural issues that most clearly distinguish the religious right from other Protestants. Compared to the secular, fundamentalists are much more likely to oppose gays in the military, oppose an equal role for women in business and government, and favor harsh punishment for people convicted of crimes. We see a particularly large difference on abortion, perhaps the most salient issue on the new right agenda. Only 8 percent of fundamentalists favor abortion rights. These differences are, for the most part, unaffected by controls of social background variables. It is no coincidence that membership in anti-feminist groups tends to be heavily drawn from evangelical religions, while pro-feminist activists tend to be secular or belong to worldly denominations (Tedin et al. 1977). The politics of the evangelical cause at the mass level is mostly limited to a focus on social and cultural issues, although fundamentalists also are strong supporters of Israel. Rebuilding the Old Testament Jewish Temple in Jerusalem is an essential component of evangelical apocalyptic prophecy. Evangelical movements are found primarily, but not entirely, among Protestant denominations. Some Catholics also share this theology. However, Leege and Welch (1991) find Catholic evangelicals differ from Protestants, with the former being noticeably more liberal.

Given their lower-status demographic characteristics, we might expect white evangelicals to favor the Democratic party. They clearly did so in 1976, when evangelical Christians voted overwhelmingly for born-again Democratic presidential candidate Jimmy Carter (Reichley 1985). Since then, however, fundamentalist Christians have moved notably in the direction of the Republican party in their presidential voting (Layman 1997). In 1980, born-again white Christians gave Ronald Reagan 61 percent of their vote—a not insignificant proportion, given the much greater tendency for others with similar background characteristics to vote Democratic. By the end of the century, most evangelicals saw the Republican party as most sympathetic to their social agenda, as seen from the following tabulation from VNS exit polls.

	Republican Percentage of Presidential Vote			
	1988	1992	1996	2000
Catholic	52	43	37	47
Jewish	36	26	16	19
White (nonevangelical) Protestant	66	57	53	54
White evangelical	81	68	65	84

7-5 GEOGRAPHY AND POLITICAL OPINIONS

People commonly think of American public opinion as differing along regional lines. The South stands out in particular for its political conservatism, particularly on civil rights and cultural issues. Outlandish fads (political and otherwise) are thought to start in the West, most notably in California. The East is often characterized as being liberal (the land of Ted Kennedy and Hillary Rodham Clinton). There have been other regional stereotypes that once may have been valid but seem less so today. The South, for example, was once the most international-minded region in foreign policy, largely because of the cotton growers' interest in free trade with other nations. The Midwest at one time had the reputation, seemingly deserved on the basis of poll results, for being the most isolationist (least internationalist) region of the country.[17] The long-term trend shows little loss of regional distinctiveness in party preference.

Several factors, however, serve to undermine the impact of region. Americans are mobile (20 percent move each year) and dilute the native citizenry. Only 39 percent of adults say they currently live in the same locale as they did when they were sixteen years old (GSS 1990–1996). The near-universal penetration of the national media would seem to have a homogenizing effect on regionalism. But we should not overstate the case. On many issues meaningful regional differences persist, especially between the South and the remainder of the country.

Ladd's (1998b) analysis of GSS and NES data from the 1990s is perhaps the most thorough evaluation of regional variation in opinion, with results that still hold for more recent survey data. On virtually all social issues—such as school prayer, gay rights, allowing communists to speak in one's community, abortion, and gun control—the South is markedly conservative. The South is also uniquely conservative on foreign policy issues. Its residents want to spend more on defense and are more likely to endorse the use of military force to settle international conflicts. These distinctive opinions represent the cultural conservatism of the South. On economic questions, however, the South has not been historically conservative. As the poorest region in the nation, the South has a vested interest in government spending. Currently, it either does not stand out from the rest of the country on issues like more government services and welfare reform and, on some economic issues, is slightly more liberal than the rest of the nation—for example, spending for the public schools.

On some of the same issues on which the South is uniquely conservative, the West and New England are uniquely liberal. For example, Ladd found only 43 percent in the deep South favoring legal abortions, compared to 78 percent in the West and 73 percent in New England (Ladd 1998b). Similar patterns can be found for gay rights, prayer in the schools, the legalization of marijuana, and gun control. In 1997, 51 percent of Southerners said they wanted to amend the Constitution to allow for school prayer, compared to 35 percent in the West and 41 percent in the East.[18] The West is also slightly more liberal on questions of foreign policy than the rest of the nation and slightly more conservative when it comes to economic issues (Mayer 1992). Finally, the stereotype of the East as a bastion of liberalism is certainly exaggerated. The East (New England plus the mid-Atlantic states) is the most liberal on most issues, but only by a small margin (Ladd 1998b).

But are regional differences in fact related to a regional culture, or are they simply compositional effects? For instance, perhaps the South is less supportive of civil liberties because its residents have comparatively little education. While there is certainly some truth to this view, individual state culture does make a large contribution to one's partisanship and political ideology (Erikson et al. 1994). For example, with demographic factors controlled, living in Minnesota instead of Indiana results in a partisan difference of about the same magnitude as being in the lowest income category versus being in the highest. There is something about state residence that affects partisanship and ideology beyond the fact that residents may differ in their religion, income, education, or union membership.

Other than state residence and regional groupings, the most common geographical division is between cities, suburbs, small towns, and rural areas. It is generally thought that urban areas are sources of liberal and nonconventional political attitudes, with rural and small-town America being the bastions of conservatism. An analysis of GSS data by Yang and Alba (1992) focusing on nonconventional opinions, such as those toward the legalization of marijuana, the role of women in politics, and government regulation of pornography, shows the residents of urban areas are much more liberal on these domains than those living in small towns and rural areas. A study by Wilson (1985) also shows urban residence has a positive association with political tolerance—those living in urban areas were the most tolerant across all the target groups included in the General Social Survey. However, at least part of this variation is due to composition effects. City residents show up as more liberal in surveys because they have a large proportion of people with liberal group characteristics, such as blacks, Jews, and Catholics. Small towns and rural areas are conservative because they are predominantly Protestant and, outside the South, contain few blacks. But not all these urban/rural differences disappear when controls for composition effects are introduced. In fact, most remain statistically significant, although reduced in magnitude. Fischer (1975, 1320) advances an "urban subculture" theory, which holds that urban residents are more nonconventional in their political opinions because urban life provides a *critical mass*, meaning "the congregation of numbers of persons sufficient to maintain viable unconventional subcultures." In other words, there is something about urban life—perhaps social diversity or the existence of support groups—independent of the social background of the residents that makes them more liberal or nonconventional than those living in small towns and rural areas.

The Changing American South

The once distinctive South (the old Confederacy) is gradually losing its unique political character. The reasons are complex but certainly involve the economic boom that began after World War II, migration (many blacks left the region in search of jobs, while many Northern whites moved into the region for the same reason), plus rapid industrialization of the region with attendant liberalizing consequences.

The South's original distinctiveness spans many elements of opinion and political behavior. We have discussed the South's conservatism on cultural issues. The uniqueness of the South was associated even more with a conservative stance on racial questions and overwhelming support for the Democratic party. Currently, however, most surveys show only small differences between white Southerners and the rest of the nation on race.

Over the past half-century, the white South has adapted to the end of racial segregation. Table 7.10 shows the dramatic decline in the difference between Southern and non–Southern whites in response to the question of whether or not one favors the principle of black and white children attending the same school. In 1956, the differences between the South and the rest of the nation were substantial. By 1985 (the last year the question was asked), there was almost no difference of consequence between the whites in the South and whites in the rest of the nation on whether black and white children should attend the same schools.[19] For the 1994 NES question on whether "the federal government should see to it" that blacks and whites attend the same schools, there was no difference between whites in the South and the rest of the nation (38 percent in both regions favored government action).

Not all are convinced by the New South argument. Measuring racial hostility is difficult, given the social norms that surround the race issue. The most racially prejudiced may in fact be the most likely to hide their true feelings. Using a method to disguise racially sensitive questions, Kuklinksi, Cobb, and Gilens (1997) report considerably more racial resentment among white Southerners than among whites outside the South.[20] For example, 42 percent of

---

TABLE 7.10 | School Integration Opinion Among Whites by Region and Education, 1956 and 1985

Favor Blacks and Whites Attending the Same School

Non–South	1956	1985
Less than high school	58%	86%
High school	67	98
Some college or more	79	99
South		
Less than high school	8	67
High school	20	93
Some college or more	30	98

Sources: 1956 data adapted from Howard Schuman, Charlotte Steeh, and Lawrence Bobo, *Racial Attitudes in America* (Cambridge, MA: Harvard University Press, 1985), p. 78; the 1985 data are from the General Social Survey.

white Southerners expressed anger at the thought of a black family moving in next door, compared to 10 percent of non-Southern whites (Kuklinksi, Cobb, and Gilens 1997, 329–330). Their conclusion is that many white Southerners are giving insincere answers when asked directly about racial issues.

The initial attachment of the South to the Democratic party goes back, of course, to the Civil War, but it was reinforced by economics. The South was long the poorest region of the country—a plus for the Democratic party, given its image of providing jobs and benefits to the average person. Until the Voting Rights Act of 1965, blacks were effectively disenfranchised in much of the South, meaning that the Democratic party of the South was largely a white party. Strategically, the white South had gained by staying with the Democrats because its prominent position stymied the party's Northern liberal wing to act on blacks' pressing demands for civil rights legislation. Then, as discussed in chapter 3, the parties began to diverge on civil rights at about the moment that blacks began voting in heavier numbers. The next forty years or so saw a rapid decline in the white South's allegiance to the Democratic party. Today, whites are more Republican in the South than in any other region, and the South has become the most dependably Republican region in terms of voting, first only for president but now more generally for other offices as well.

Figure 7.6 documents Republican gains in the white South in terms of party identification. In 1952, Democrats outnumbered Republicans by an 8–1 ratio in the white South. As can be seen in Figure 7.6, the major Republican gain followed the presidential candidacy of Republican Barry Goldwater in 1964. Goldwater voted against the 1964 Civil Rights Act on the grounds that it violated states' rights. Since then, the decline has been gradual but steady. By

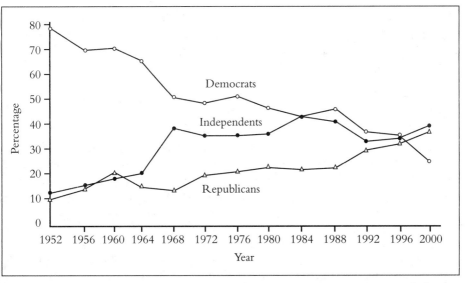

Figure 7.6 Party identification among white Southerners, 1952–2000. *Source:* National Election Studies.

the dawn of the twenty-first century, more white Southerners were calling themselves Republican than Democrat.

The survey evidence regarding the white South's growing Republicanism reveals the importance of long-standing party attachments. Older Southern whites who grew up during the Democratic era are more resistant to Republicanism than young Southerners, who flock to the Republican party unburdened by the habits of lifelong Democratic identification (Wattenberg 1998; Erikson, MacKuen, and Stimson 2002). This contrast between the party identifications of old and young white Southerners has important consequences in the voting booth. For instance, in the 2000 presidential election, older white Southerners were held back by their Democratic heritage from voting for Bush at the same high rate as their younger counterparts. This age gap was unlike the trend in the non-South, where voting differences across ages were virtually nonexistent among white voters, as seen in the following table drawn from the 2000 VNS exit poll.

2000	% Bush (of two-party vote)				
	18–24	25–39	40–59	60–74	75–
Southern Whites	76%	68%	67%	61%	54%
Non-Southern Whites	54%	55%	52%	51%	52%

It is not just that young white Southerners have become more Republican; they are now even more Republican than their white counterparts in the North. It is paradoxical that younger Southerners show the most movement to the Republican Party even though polls have shown them to be more liberal on racial and cultural issues than their elders. The nature of this attraction has been debated by scholars. Some emphasize a latent racism among Southern whites as the cause, at least for the initial bolt to the Republican party (Carmines and Stimson 1989). Others insist that the source is the white South's cultural conservatism on social issues and foreign policy (Abramowitz 1994). The matter remains unresolved.

7-6 GENDER AND POLITICAL OPINIONS

Since the early days of survey research, it was thought that there were few differences between the sexes in political opinions. Although women participated less than men, they were thought to be indistinguishable from them on questions of party and voting, with perhaps a few minor differences on issue positions. That situation changed in 1980, when considerable media attention was devoted to the gap between male and female voting for president. Women voted about equally for Reagan and Carter, but men gave Reagan 19 percentage points more than they gave Carter. Since that time, much attention has been devoted to the study of gender differences in political orientation.

The Gender Gap

Before 1980, either there were no gender differences in the vote or women more than men tended to vote Republican. For example, women favored Dwight Eisenhower by 7 points more than men in 1956, and had the 1960 presidential election been decided by women alone, Richard Nixon would have been elected president (Kenski 1988, 50). The large gender gap that first appeared in 1980 weakened through the 1992 election but reappeared strongly in 1996 and 2000. In 2000, according to the VNS exit poll, George W. Bush received 53 percent of the male vote; Gore received 42 percent. Women gave 43 percent of their vote to Bush while giving Gore 54 percent. The gender gap was 11 percentage points—arguably a gender gap record.[21] The gap is nearly as large (9 percent) in voting for the U.S. House and appears as a key variable predicting party identification. The NES shows that in 1980 women were 3 percent more Democratic than men, but they were about 10 percent more Democratic than men between 1988 and 2000. This Democratic tendency in identification is particularly noticeable among unmarried and well-educated women.[22]

The conventional wisdom about the gender gap is that over the years women became more Democratic as greater numbers entered the workforce and became more attuned to their own political agenda. As women entered the workforce, they became more liberal on social welfare issues, while men became correspondingly more conservative, contributing to the gender gap in partisanship and the vote (Kaufmann and Petrocik 1999). Some also see the decline in the institution of marriage as a factor; the increasing number of unmarried women face economic disadvantage that pushes them toward the Democratic party (Edlund and Pande 2002).

Last, the notion that the gender gap was created by women becoming more Democratic in their partisan preference and vote choice is wrong. The data show just the opposite. The voting behavior and partisan behavior of women has remained essentially stable since 1980. Meanwhile, men have moved in the Republican direction. It is this movement among men that accounts for the gender gap partisanship and vote choice.

Gender and Issue Differences

As our discussion has implied, women and men often differ in their opinion on issues. Table 7.11 presents gender differences in selected issue domains. Since the 1930s, surveys have shown that women are less prone to endorse violence and aggression in any form, be it at the personal level, regarding capital punishment, or in foreign affairs. We see in the table a ten-point gender gap on the issue of sending U.S. ground troops to Kosovo. These gender differences have also appeared in other conflicts. Women were 12 percent more likely than men to say it was wrong for the United States to get involved in the 2001 Gulf War (NES 1992). There was a similar gender difference in support of the Korean

TABLE 7.11 | Gender and Political Opinions

Opinion	Percent Among Opinion-Holders		
	Men	Women	Difference
Force, Violence, and Aggression			
Oppose U.S. ground troops to Kosovo (1998)★	54%	64%	+ 10
Oppose military action against Iraq over refusal to allow site visits (1998)★	45	65	+ 20
Want stricter gun control laws★★(2000)	50	70	+ 20
Oppose death penalty over life in prison for capital murder (1999)★	38	62	+ 24
Iraq War not worth fighting (2004)‡	38	46	+ 8
Compassion			
Spend budget surplus on social programs, not tax cut (1999)★	49	64	+ 15
Government should provide health insurance (2000)★★	53	58	+ 5
Government should see to good jobs/standard of living (2000)★★	28	31	+ 3
Increase spending for the homeless★★ (1998)	52	63	+ 11
Gender-Related Issues			
Allow abortion for any reason (2000)★	41	43	+ 2
Men and women should have equal role (2000)★★	87	92	+ 5
Men and women equally suited for politics (1998)†	42	41	− 1
Draft men only into the military (1998)★	56	51	− 5
Increase spending for child care (2000)★★	58	67	+ 9
Civil Liberties/Civil Rights			
Legalize gay marriage (2004)‡	39	47	+ 8
Favor legalization of marijuana (1996)★★	35	24	− 11
Favor affirmative-action programs (1994)††	42	45	+ 3
Allow communists to speak (1998)†	74	62	− 12
Reduce crime by solving social problems (1996)★★	27	33	+ 6
Favor government aid to blacks (2000)★★	19	18	− 1

★Gallup Poll.
★★National Election Studies.
†General Social Survey.
‡*Washington Post* poll.
††Roper.

War and the Vietnam War, with women typically being 8 to 10 percent less enthusiastic than men. Finally, a long-running series of questions dating to the late 1940s relates to issues surrounding the development, testing, and possible use of nuclear weapons. Women have consistently been more dovish (or perhaps more compassionate and concerned with human life) than men. For example, in 1989 women were 16 percentage points more likely to believe it was morally wrong to use the atomic bomb on Japan to end World War II (Brandes 1992). Miller (1988) argues that this gender difference on foreign affairs has important electoral consequences. When elections tend to turn on questions of human rights and issues of war and peace, the gender gap in voting increases, with women moving to favor Democratic candidates.

These differences on violence and aggression are probably due to the interplay of socialization and biology. Though not conclusive, there is some research showing that men have a greater predisposition than women do to use force. Caldicott (1986) describes men as "insecure aggressors," while women are more nurturing and pacifist because "their bodies are built anatomically and physiologically to nurture life." Also, the socialization of young boys frequently emphasizes aggression (witness playground games), while such aggression is discouraged in young girls (Miedaian 1991). Another possible explanation is that women are more risk-adverse than men (Tedin and Yap 1993). For example, 31 percent of men but only 5 percent of women favor building more nuclear power plants (1991 NES Pilot), and 33 percent of men say nuclear power plants are "very safe" compared to 15 percent of women (Gallup 1999).

There are also gender differences on compassion issues relating to jobs, education, income redistribution, and protection for the vulnerable in society. Women are generally more supportive of a compassionate approach than men, but the differences are not large. When large differences appear, they are usually on issues that address specific hazards rather than more general society-wide problems. For example, in addition to differences in support for building nuclear power plants, there are substantial gaps in support for the 55-mile-per-hour speed limit, for state laws requiring seatbelts, and for stiff jail terms for drunk drivers (Shapiro and Mahajan 1986).

On civil rights issues, white men and white women usually do not differ. One exception is that women are considerably more supportive of gay rights than are men. Even though women sometimes benefit from affirmative action programs, Table 7.11 shows them only slightly more supportive of such programs than men. There are, however, consistent gender differences on civil liberties. On most of the 1998 GSS civil liberties items, men are more supportive than women. These differences are not limited to the United States but show up in Western Europe and the former Soviet Union as well (Norris 1988; Tedin and Yap 1993; Tedin 1994a). Controls for background factors reduce, but do not eliminate, these differences.

On most gender-related issues the gender gap is small to nonexistent. Women are more in favor of increased spending for child care, but on most other gender issues there are either no gender differences or, occasionally, differences that seem to run counter to self-interest. In twenty-one successive readings of the General Social Survey, men have been at least as supportive of abortion "for any reason" as have women. In some GSS surveys, men have been as much as 10 percentage points more supportive, although the gap has declined in recent years (as shown in Table 7.11). The gender differences are in the unexpected direction in other instances when the question of women's equality is addressed. For example, in the late 1970s men were consistently more favorable to the passage of the Equal Rights Amendment than were women (Simon and Landis 1989, 275).

One reason for this pattern is that on many issues that directly concern women there is a greater gap among women themselves than between women and men. Take, for instance, the label *feminist*. In 1998, 26 percent of adult women answered "yes" to the question "Do you consider yourself a feminist?"[23] Women accepting this label tend not to be "average." Rather, they are highly educated and affluent (Keene 1991). Their voting patterns are also atypical. In 1996, non-feminists voted 24 percent for Bill Clinton while feminists gave him 84 percent, a much greater gap than one would ever find between men and women.[24]

We see clearly the class division among women by looking at the 1996 NES question that asks if "women should have an equal role with men in running business, industry, and government," or whether "women's place is in the home." Women disagree among themselves on the answer to this question more than they disagree with men. The line of stratification divides working women and homemakers and divides on level of education. Sixty percent of working women chose the most equalitarian category (option 1 on a seven-point scale; see the Appendix), compared to only 42 percent of the homemakers. Among working women with a college degree, 74 percent chose the most egalitarian option. Only 43 percent of homemakers with no more than a high school education chose this option. Although support for women in the workforce continues to increase as full-time working women have become commonplace, there are nevertheless clear lifestyle distinctions about what makes one an important and worthwhile person that split women on the issues at the heart of the women's movement.

7-7 CONCLUSION

Group characteristics can clearly make a difference in how people see the political world. Belonging to a group is part of one's self-identification. Many groups have a vested political interest. Belonging to the upper social class encourages one to believe that through one's own effort success can be achieved, and government should be limited in its ability to spend tax money to aid those who have not been successful in life's competition. Race, gender, region, and age also intrude on one's life in a fashion not entirely neutral, consequently coloring the way one sees the desirable organization and ends of the polity.

Over time, certain group distinctions may increase or decrease in importance. For example, the distinction between urban and rural has declined with the rapid industrialization of society. Group distinctions that may increase in importance are those between the young and the old, the Sun Belt and the Frost Belt, and the technologically skilled and unskilled. These potential cleavages may at some point replace traditional sources of voting alignments, such as partisanship or class. If that happens, the benefits that government bestows on its citizens, as well as the obligations it demands, may also change.

NOTES

1. When asked by Gallup in July 1988 if they belonged to the "haves" or the "have-nots," 59 percent of Americans said they belonged to the "haves" and 17 said they belonged to the "have-nots," with 15 percent saying neither or both and 9 percent unsure. When asked in March 1988, 41 percent of British respondents said they belonged to the "haves," while 37 percent said they were part of the "have-nots."
2. The Pew Research Center, "Economic Inequality Seen as Rising, Boom Bypasses Poor" (June 21, 2001).
3. "Public Opinion and Demographic Report," *Public Perspective* 4 (May/June 1993): 85.
4. "The Polls," *Public Opinion Quarterly* 12 (1949): 781.
5. The growing division of the vote based on income also survives if one restricts the analysis to Northern whites. The increased partisan divide based on income also is found when party identification is substituted for the vote. Even occupational class has held its own as a predictor of the vote when multivariate controls are imposed (Manza and Brooks 1999).
6. On contemporary public opinion among Latinos, including variations by nation of origin, see Uhlaner and Garcia (2002) and Barreto et al. (2002).
7. There is greater racial division on questions involving racial preferences in education than on jobs, with blacks more one-sidedly favorable to affirmative action in the realm of education opportunities. More blacks, as well as more whites, are more likely to endorse programs that create equality of opportunity rather than equality of outcomes.
8. Sigelman and Welch (1991) analyzed answers to a large number of affirmative action questions and found, depending on question wording, that as much as 96 percent of blacks and 76 percent of whites were favorable, or as few as 23 percent of blacks and 9 percent of whites were favorable. They also found that those affirmative action programs that get the most support from blacks also get the most support from whites.
9. *Washington Post* Survey (Sept. 28, 1995); Princeton Survey Research Associates (Nov. 5, 1997).
10. Data from polls taken by the *Washington Post* reported in *The Public Perspective* (Oct./Nov. 1997): 17.
11. Generational differences can be a function of compositional effects, as when more recent political generations hold opinions different from their elders because of their greater levels of education.
12. Reported in *The Public Perspective* 6 (Apr./May, 1995): 25.
13. An additional 5 percent chose some other religion, such as Islam. These estimates are based on the 1998 GSS.
14. Due to a small sample size in 1996, the percentage for Jews in Figure 7.5 is taken from the combined NES data for 1994, 1996, and 1998.
15. It should be emphasized that just as Catholics are held to the Democratic party by tradition, so too are Protestants drawn to the Republican party by tradition. If the Protestant-Catholic gap in partisanship were to close, it is just as plausible that

Protestants would turn Democratic as that Catholics would turn Republican. In other words, the gap implies no particular edge to either party.

16. For the scale of religious orientation, each respondent received one point for each of the following: saying that they were fundamentalist, evangelical, or charismatic, that religion provides a great deal of guidance in life, that they pray and read the Bible several times a day, that the Bible is the actual word of God, that they are a born-again Christian. The items were coded as 0, 1 being secular; 2, 3, 4 as in between; and 5, 6, 7 as fundamentalist.

17. To take an example of one-time regional differences in foreign policy isolationism, Southerners, when asked in 1945 whether the United States and Russia "should make a permanent military alliance," responded favorably by a ratio greater than 2 to 1. At the other extreme, a slight majority of Midwesterners opposed such an alliance (Cantril 1951, 961). By the late 1950s, such disparities had largely disappeared (Key 1961a, 134).

18. *New York Times* poll, Jan. 17, 1997.

19. As almost everyone now endorses the principle of white and black students attending the same school, the question has not been asked by the GSS since 1985.

20. Kuklinski et al. randomly gave one-half of the sample a list of three nonracial items and asked how many of the items make them angry—importantly, not *which one*, just *how many*. The other half of the sample got the same three items plus an additional item addressing race, such as "a black family moving in next door." Again, the respondents were asked how many make them angry. Only the additional item for half of the sample getting four options addresses race. Thus respondents saying two of four items anger them assumes the interviewer cannot know which two—which indeed he or she cannot. However, statistical methods can be used to determine the level of anger about "a black family moving in next door" among Southerners and non-Southerners as a group.

21. The 2000 gender gap is 10 points in terms of voting for Bush and 12 points in terms of voting for Gore, averaging out as 11 points. (The difference is accounted for by the minor party vote.) According to exit polls, in 1984 men voted 62 percent for Reagan, 38 percent for Mondale; women voted 54 percent for Reagan, 46 percent for Mondale; in 1988 men voted 57 percent for George H. W. Bush and 41 percent for Dukakis; women voted 50 percent for Bush and 49 percent for Dukakis; in 1992 men voted 41 percent for Clinton, 38 percent for Bush, and 21 percent for Perot; women voted 45 percent for Clinton, 37 percent for Bush, and 17 percent for Perot; in 1996, men voted 44 percent for Clinton, 45 percent for Dole; women voted 55 percent for Clinton and 35 percent for Dole.

22. This trend was already evident in the 1980s. See Weisberg (1987) for a statistical demonstration.

23. Based on a survey by Yankelovich Partners (May 18, 1998) for *Time* and the Cable News Network.

24. The non-feminists were defined as all women who rated on the NES feeling thermometer the "women's movement" below 50 degrees (14 percent). Feminists were defined as all women who rated the women's movement at 85 degrees or higher (30 percent).

8 | The News Media and Political Opinions

O ur political beliefs are shaped by the political information we receive, and most of this information originates—directly or indirectly—from the mass media. In totalitarian political systems, the regime
attempts to shape this information by controlling outlets for the news. In
democracies, the mass media are relatively free of government control. Indeed,
it is difficult to imagine free democratic elections without a free flow of competing information in the mass media.

However, the proper flow of political information requires more than simply the government allowing an unfettered mass media to print or broadcast
free from political interference. Today, most of what we read, see, or hear in
the mass media comes from newspapers, magazines, television, radio, and Internet outlets that are owned by large private conglomerates, such as General
Electric, Disney, and Viacom. Within these institutions, individuals with complex motives and incentives decide what to print or what to broadcast. These
motives and incentives range from a commitment to report the news thoroughly and objectively, to packaging the news for profit like any other commercial product, to using corporate power over the media to preserve the
economic and political status quo.

Defined most broadly, the content of the mass media extends beyond matters of politics to include all aspects of information and entertainment. Although it can be tempting to read political implications in the entertainment
portions of media content, that is not our concern here. Our focus is on political news and commentary in newspapers and on the radio, television, and the
Internet. In this chapter we discuss the nature of the news media, their possible biases, and the effect of the media on public opinion.

8-1 THE EVOLUTION OF THE AMERICAN MEDIA

The evolution of the media can be divided into four eras (West 2001). The first is the Era of the Partisan Press (1787–1832). During this period, the press was simply an arm of the political parties, with parties or factions reaching out to their supporters via newspapers. At one time, the newspaper of the Federalists, the party of Alexander Hamilton, was the *Gazette of the United States*. For the Democrat-Republicans, the party of Thomas Jefferson, it was the *National Intelligencer*. It was the parties who arranged financial support and appointed the editors. The job of each newspaper was to promote the party's issue positions and criticize opponents. The *Gazette*, for example, ran numerous stories about sexual misconduct between Thomas Jefferson and his slave Sally Hemmings. Due to limited population literacy and high subscription costs, these were not mass circulation newspapers. Rather, they were directed at the elite of each party, providing some news and instructing the faithful about the issue positions the party championed. It was fully understood that objectivity was not a goal in reporting the news.

The Era of the Commercial Media began in 1833 with the advent of the penny press. Newspapers now sold for a penny (versus 6 cents in the earlier era), which—along with rising literacy—allowed for mass circulation. With the invention of the telegraph, newspapers in 1848 organized the Associated Press, which gathered information from around the world. Political news could be delivered to newspaper editorial desks from all parts of the country hours or even minutes after it happened.

The penny press also entertained its readers with human interest stories and sensational reports of crimes and disasters. Importantly, the press now made a profit—often a substantial profit. This financial success allowed the press to free itself from control by the political parties and gave rise to powerful independent editors who could package news stories as they saw fit. However, this packaging was often strongly partisan and sensationalistic, a practice referred to as *yellow journalism*.[1] Among the most flamboyant practitioners of yellow journalism was William Randolph Hearst. He used his newspapers to promote his politics. By claiming the explosion which sunk the U.S. battleship *Maine* in Havana harbor was the work of Spanish agents, he provoked a public outcry for a war between the United States and Spain.[2] The practice of yellow journalism tended to undermine the credibility of the press. The media would have to transform itself yet another time before gaining the confidence and respect of the public (Bettig and Hall 2003).

The new century (1900) saw the dawning of the Era of the Objective Media. Previously, reporters were not professionals; they had no specialized training or professional values that guided their work. Recognizing a need, newspaper magnate Joseph Pulitzer provided funding to establish a school for journalism at Columbia University. Other schools soon followed. Journalists were trained to be *objective*, defined by the American Society of Newspaper Editors as "free of opinion or bias of any kind." Commensurate with their new status, reporters now had bylines—that is, the reporter's name appeared along with the story. This innovation allowed the public to hold reporters accountable for what they wrote.

The coverage of the Vietnam War and Watergate represented the high point for the objective press. The glaring light of publicity was brought to bear on matters of the highest importance by investigative journalists. Woodward and Bernstein became household names for their investigations that ultimately brought down the Nixon White House (West 2001; Jameison and Campbell 2001). Walter Cronkite, anchor of the CBS evening news, was once the most trusted man in America (Robinson and Kohut 1988). Public confidence in the media was at an all-time high. There was talk of the media establishment as a coequal "fourth branch of government."

The current period, starting about 1985, is often referred to as the Era of the New Media (Davis and Owen 1998). Three trends in this era have fundamentally changed the way the news is processed and delivered. The first is a move away from objective journalism toward interpretative journalism, second is the absorption of the once numerous independent media by a small number of huge media conglomerates, and third is the fragmentation of the media brought about by cable TV and the Internet.

Interpretive Journalism

The trend toward interpretative journalism reflects a general skepticism about the possibility of holding to a standard of strict objectivity that arose in intellectual circles in the 1980s. Facts do not speak for themselves; rather, they need to be understood in context.[3] This development coincided with the career aspirations of journalists, who want to add their independent and unique contribution to the political debate—their "journalistic voice." They do not simply want to report the news; they want to analyze it. In the Era of the New Media, reporters are less inclined to behave as lapdogs for politicians, as some have characterized their role during the Era of the Objective Press (Sabato 1993).

This trend is not simply a changing taste on the part of working reporters; it reflects a change in how editors and executive producers see the market for news. In the realm of politics, news consumers demand more than hearing and reading what the politicians have to say (Iyengar, Norpoth, and Hahn 2004). Journalists today do not see their job as helping politicians get their story out directly to the public. Rather, journalists see themselves as standing between politicians and the public. Politicians do not talk to citizens; politicians talk to journalists. In the Era of the New Media, it is the journalists who talk to the public. They see their job as analyzing and interpreting for the public the often ambiguous or misleading messages being delivered by political leaders. Thomas Patterson (1996) argues that this interpretative style empowers journalists by giving them significant control over the news message. It places the journalist at the center of the news story.

There is substantial empirical data to document this change. For example, journalists increasingly speak for candidates rather than candidates speaking for themselves. The average length of the candidate sound bite (candidates speaking for themselves) on the network news has decreased dramatically. As seen in Figure 8.1, in 1968 these sound bites averaged 43.1 seconds. By 2000 they averaged only 7.8 seconds. In fact, Democratic presidential candidate Al Gore got more speaking time during his one appearance on David Letterman's TV show than he did on the news broadcasts of all three major networks combined during the month of October.[4] On the other hand, speaking time allotted to journalists has increased commensurately (Owen 2002). Patterson (1993, 82) found the same pattern in the print media. For the *New York Times* in the 1960s, the vast majority of the news stories (91 percent) were descriptive. In the 1990s, the vast majority (84 percent) were interpretative. Rather than direct communication from politicians, much of what the public hears today is the analysis of journalists.

The New Media Conglomerates

Newspapers were the first medium to become a quasi-monopoly. In 1920 there were over 700 cities with competing daily newspapers. By 1953, that number had shrunk to 91, and by 1996 only 19 U.S. cities enjoyed the rivalry of two or more newspaper competing head-to-head. In 1940, 83 percent of newspapers

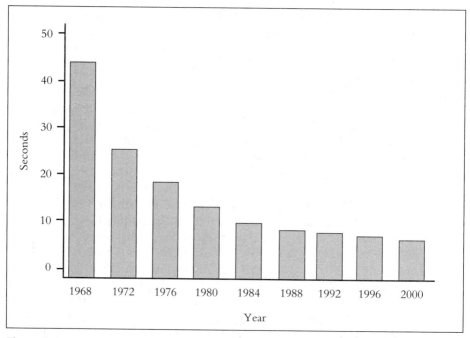

Figure 8.1 Sound bites in seconds by presidential candidates on network television, 1968–2000. *Sources:* Daniel Hallin, "Sound Bite News: Television Coverage of Elections," *Journal of Communications* 43 (Spring 1992), 12; Diana Owen, "Media Mayhem: Performance of the Press in Election 2000." In Larry Sabato (ed.), *Overtime* (New York: Longman, 2002), 130.

were independently owned; by 1990 the figure had dropped to 24 percent. In that same year, three large chains, Gannett, Knight-Ridder, and Newhouse, accounted for 23 percent of all newspapers sold in the United States (Bagdikian 1997). This consolidation has significantly improved the corporate bottom line. In the 1980s, the average profit for newspapers was 14.5 percent; in the 1990s it was 21.5 percent—despite a 47 percent drop in overall newspaper circulation between 1976 and 1998 (Laventhol 2001; West 2001). Lance Bennett (2003) claims these mergers have cheapened news quality. With little competition and a corporate stress on maximizing profits, newspapers have cut staff, printed more stories taken directly from the wire services or the national dailies, and made decisions about what is newsworthy based on what appeals to audiences desired by advertisers rather than professional journalistic criteria. We should not, however, overstate the case. There do exist independently owned national daily newspapers, such as the *New York Times*, the *Washington Post*, and the *Wall Street Journal*, that cater to the audience for hard news.

Until recently, the major television networks were oligopolies. CBS, NBC, and ABC once accounted for 90 percent of the television audience. Importantly, prior to the current era they were also independent entities (Bennett 2003, 93). Lacking competition, the networks could afford to run their news divisions at a loss. Profits were made by the entertainment division. Because television used the public airwaves, the Federal Communications Commission (FCC) required some minimal civic affairs programming.[5] The networks saw the news division as an important public service and a way to build prestige for the new medium. The network news division enjoyed considerable autonomy from the profit-making entertainment side of the industry. In 1962, William S. Paley, owner of CBS, told his news division: "You guys cover the news; I've got [comedian] Jack Benny to make money for me" (Baum 2003, 34).

Beginning with the Reagan administration, deregulation brought an end to network independence. It became legally possible and financially attractive for large corporations to own multiple media outlets—including television networks. Today, the five major networks are all owned by large multinational corporations. NBC is owned by General Electric; ABC is owned by Disney; CBS is owned by Viacom; Fox is owned by Rupert Murdoch's NewsCorp, and CNN is owned by Time-Warner. Each network is but a single component among a large number of components making up the corporation.[6] The goal of each component is to maximize profitability; for the networks, that means attracting and holding a large, demographically desirable audience for advertisers (Berger 2003, 187).[7]

The television news is now accountable for the bottom line just like the entertainment division. This has led to a transformation in the way the news is processed and presented. The first direct effect of the mergers was to cut staff and close many expensive international news bureaus. Until 9/11 made the importance of international events clear to all, the foreign news attracted the smallest news audience. The second effect was to make the news attractive to a larger audience. This has meant blending news and entertainment into a format called soft news. Where once the primary purpose of the news was to inform viewers, now the primary purpose is to entertain viewers. The result is more focus in the news on human interest stories, natural disasters, and crime (Baum 2003, 37). For example, Media Monitor (2000) reports the number of stories in the network news about murder increased fivefold between 1990 and 2000, despite a decline in the overall murder rate during this period. In summer 2001, before the terrible events of 9/11, the story that dominated the national news was the disappearance of an intern in the office of Congressman Gary Condit.

Some claim a third effect of the mergers is a censoring of the news so what is reported as news does not reflect badly on the parent corporation or its subsidiaries (Bagdikan 1997; Bennett 2003). In a study by the Pew Research Center (2000), 33 percent of local news directors said they felt the need to self-censor the news lest they offend corporate sponsors, and 21 percent said they were pressured to avoid negative stories about advertisers. At the national level, when a story broke about Disney theme parks hiring convicted pedophiles, ABC News (owned by Disney) killed the story. According to Disney CEO Michael Eisner, "I would prefer ABC not to cover Disney. . . ." That declaration has not, however, prevented ABC from presenting news coverage favorable to Disney (Bennett 2003, 99).

The Fragmentation of the Media

Even with the decline in independent ownership of the media, thanks to deregulation and technological innovation the actual number of media outlets has skyrocketed over what was available just a few years ago. Cable and satellite TV gave rise to channels like MSNBC, CNN, and the Fox News Network, which cover the political news twenty-four hours a day, seven days a week. The Internet revolution, beginning in 1991, offers unlimited access to political information any time of day. Depending on one's preferences, there is news with a liberal slant (such as at www.salon.com) and news with a conservative slant (such as at www.freerepublic.com).

Table 8.1 shows the change in audience size for the "traditional media" outlets and the "new media" between 1993–1994 and 2002. Respondents were asked if they "regularly" used a particular medium. The local television news remains the most frequently used source for political information, but its numbers are declining. However, the major change since 1993 has been the audience for the evening network news, which declined by half between 1993 and 2002. The bulk of those defectors have moved to new media sources, such as cable television and the Internet.[8]

Of course, some of these trends started before our first data point in 1993. The percentage of households subscribing to a daily newspaper peaked in 1950. The percentage getting news from the network television peaked in 1970 (West 2001, 131). Meanwhile, the first cable news channel came on line in 1980. Talk radio was not a major factor for political discourse until 1988, when it was reinvented by Rush Limbaugh. And almost no one got their news from the Internet prior to 1990.

TABLE 8.1 | **Audience for Traditional Media and New Media**

Traditional Media

	1993–1994	1998	2002
Local TV news	77%	64%	57%
Nightly network news	60	38	32
Newspapers	58	48	41
Radio news	47	49	41
Print news magazine	16	15	13
Network TV magazines	52	23	22

New Media

	1993–1994	1998	2002
CNN	35	23	25
Fox News Channel	—	17	22
MSNBC	—	08	15
Talk radio	16	13	17
National Public Radio	09	15	16
Online news	—	13	25

Source: Pew Research Center, "Public's News Habits Little Changed by September 11" (June 9, 2002) http://www.people-press.org.

While the trend toward new media is clear, it is still important to note that in the dawn of the twenty-first century most people still get their news from traditional sources. As just noted, the local TV news remains the primary source of information for most people. It is also important to understand that television as a news source is not in decline; it is, in fact, the reverse. Rather, in the Era of the New Media, there is simply a wider menu from which to choose.

The fragmentation of news media outlets has had several important effects on how people get the news. One consequence of the greater competition among news outlets may be the quality of news reporting and the amount of information about current events that people receive. With twenty-four-hour news channels and Internet news sources, interested news consumers can catch up with current events at a speed previously unimaginable. Yet, despite the new diversity of choices and contrary to American culture's celebration of the virtues of competition, some observers conclude that the fragmented media has actually lowered the quality of the news. John Zaller (2004) presents evidence that in-depth coverage of issues decreases as competition increases. He concludes that journalists produce better-quality news when insulated from market pressures. His point echoes media critic Walter Goodman (1994), who earlier foresaw a "creeping tabloidization" in the national network news (see also McChesney 2000).

The diversity of choices has had further consequences. Today's consumer of television news can choose from a menu of cable all-news outlets that includes "mainstream" CNN, conservative Fox, and upstart MSNBC. For more information, opinion, and analysis, the avid news consumer can turn to the incredible diversity of the Web, where each network and major newspaper has its Web page, plus Web sites for political opinions and analysis of all ideological stripes. Obviously, this heterogeneity limits the power of conventional news sources to mold opinion and provides news consumers of virtually any ideological disposition the opportunity to gravitate to news sources congenial with their point of view. But the ramifications may not all be positive. When people rely solely on news sources that fit their ideological niche, they become less open to alternative viewpoints. As a result, initial opinions intensify and are reinforced, possibly contributing to an increased polarization and rancor in public discourse that had previously been absent.

Still another consequence of news fragmentation is a decline in the power of the president and other leaders to hold the people's attention. Matthew Baum and Samuel Kernell (1999) claim that cable/satellite TV had ended the "golden age" of presidential influence via television. The multiplicity of media options has significantly diminished the president's ability to reach a large national audience. Previously, when presidents chose to address the nation they had a monopoly on prime-time television. Viewers could either watch the address or seek entertainment other than television. In 1969, a routine press conference of President Richard Nixon drew 59 percent of the potential national TV audience. In 1995, a major prime-time news conference by President Clinton attracted only 6.5 percent of households with television. While access to cable news may allow greater attention to the details of contemporary politics, television viewers are freed from reliance on the broadcast networks. Analyzing the 1996 presidential debates, Baum and Kernell found when controlling for key background variables, those without cable television—a captive audience— were 7 percent more likely to have watched the first debate and 9 percent more likely to have watched the second debate than those with cable television.[9] This fragmentation is not lost on network executives, who appreciate that the cost of carrying a prime-time presidential address is the loss of audience share to cable competitors. "Going public" is an important leadership tool for the modern presidency. The current focus on audience share and profits may mean the president has lost an asset that will be difficult to replace (Baum and Kernell 1999).

8-2 BIAS AND NEGATIVITY IN THE NEWS

Although the news media pride themselves on the fairness of their news coverage, critics from both the left and the right complain that the news media are biased and lack objectivity. Could it be the case that the media *are* seriously biased, or are ideological critics too quick to blame the messenger when they dislike the message? *Objectivity* has proven notoriously difficult to define. Like beauty, it is very much in the eye of the beholder. Objectivity is so elusive that it was dropped from the code of ethics by the Society of Professional Journalists. It was replaced in the ethics code by "truth, accuracy and comprehensiveness" (Bennett 2003, 192). One reason is that objectivity can imply passing along messages from government officials without subjecting them to critical scrutiny—a practice some would say on its face is nonobjective, given the ability of those in government to dominate the news. But to what extent does the media cover the news with truth, accuracy, and comprehensiveness? Given the complexity of the question, it is not surprising there is no agreed-upon answer.

Critics on the political left charge that as business operations dependent on business advertising for their profits, the media tilt their coverage to the right. Critics on the political right see a liberal bias to the media, with liberal journalists slanting the news to the left. Both liberals and conservatives have nonprofit organizations with Web sites devoted exclusively to exposing press bias. Accuracy in the Media (http://www.aim.org) is devoted to exposing liberal bias in the news, while Fairness and Accuracy in Reporting (http://www.fair.org) is designed to ferret out bias in the conservative direction. Neither side lacks compelling examples. On the other hand, the academic literature has concluded—at a minimum—there is no systematic and pervasive ideological bias in the media (Patterson 1994; Groeling and Kernell 1998; Farnsworth and Lichter 2003).

Criticism of the news media is occasionally subtle and can extend beyond blanket charges of bias based on ideology. Some say because the mainstream media try to appeal to the broadest possible audience, they constrict the flow of ideas in the safe middle range (Bennett 1980, 304–344). Some see the media as too uncritical of government officials out of a need to protect their access to news sources (Hertsgaard 1988; Press and Verburn 1988). But others see the reverse, with journalists giving a particularly hard time to incumbent office-holders (Patterson 1993). As we discuss below, one of the more serious charges against the media is that to maintain the interests of its audience, news outlets promote an overly cynical outlook as they focus excessively on negative news.

In this section we discuss two sorts of claims about the content of the media. First, is the news biased in a liberal or conservative direction? Second, as some charge, are the news media unduly negative in their reporting?

Liberal Journalists

Is there a liberal bias to the news media? One foundation for the claim the news is biased in a liberal direction comes from the fact, confirmed by many studies, that journalists themselves tend to be much more liberal and Democratic than the American public as a whole. Further, the most liberal and most Democratic journalists tend to work for the prestige news sources, such as the *New York Times* or network news (Weaver and Wilhoit 1996). Shown in Table 8.2 is data contrasting the opinions of journalists and everyday citizens from a 1985 *Times-Mirror* survey and a 1992 survey sponsored by the Freedom Forum (see also Dautrich and Dineen 1996).

TABLE 8.2	Views of General Public and Journalists on Selected Issues		
		Public	**Journalists**
Consider Self	left (liberal)	18%	47%
	Right (conservative)	34	22
Consider Self	Democrat	34	44
	Republican	33	16
Sympathize with	business	33	27
	labor	32	31
Government should reduce income inequality	favor	55	50
	oppose	23	39
Increase defense budget	favor	38	15
	oppose	51	80
Allow women to have abortions	favor	49	82
	oppose	44	14
Prayer in public schools	favor	74	25
	oppose	19	67
Death penalty for murder	favor	75	47
	oppose	17	47

Sources: David H. Weaver and G. Cleveland Wilhoit, *The American Journalist in the 1990s* (Mahwah, NJ: Erlbaum, 1996), 15–18; William Schneider and I. A. Lewis, "Views on the News," *Public Opinion* 8 (Aug.–Sept. 1985), 7.

Journalists are in general a good deal more liberal than the adult population. The Freedom Forum survey shows that while 18 percent of the adult population "leans left" in politics, 47 percent of journalists "lean left" and 58 percent of those from "prominent organizations" lean left (Weaver and Wilhoit 1996, 17). On the other hand, while 34 percent of the public "leans right" only 22 percent of journalists "lean right." We see the same pattern for partisanship, with journalists disproportionately Democrat, especially among the prominent media (Weaver and Wilhoit 1996, 20). Perhaps the most liberal is the Washington press corps, where most stories about national politics originate. A Roper Center survey found in 1992 that Washington reporters voted for Clinton over the first President Bush by the overwhelming margin of 89 percent to 7 percent (Dautrich and Dineen 1996).

Journalists are particularly more liberal than the public on social issues like abortion the death penalty, as can be seen in Table 8.2. However, journalists may be more conservative than the public when it comes to economic issues. At a time when 23 percent of the public opposed government action to reduce income inequality, 39 percent of the journalists were opposed (Schneider and Lewis 1985). Journalism is a high-paying profession, and these data may be reflecting the class interest of those in the news business.

It is interesting to speculate why journalists lean to the left politically. Although some conservatives might argue differently, there is no evidence that news organizations reward reporters and other workers based on their political ideology. The reason news employees show a liberal political tendency is not that conservative aspirants are cast aside for their political views. To some extent, the liberalism of journalists, especially outside the economic sphere, simply reflects the values of young urban college-educated professionals—the class from which journalists are drawn. Another factor may be that journalism attracts people with liberal personality traits, much the same way that a military career (for example) attracts conservative personalities.

Conservative Ownership

If some claim that the media are biased to the left because of the political views of news media employees, what about the opposite charge that there exists a conservative bias to the news media? The foundation for the claim of conservative bias starts with media ownership. All five major networks are owned by giant multinational corporations—whose managers and major stockholders are not noted for their liberal sentiments. And while the *New York Times* and the *Washington Post* remain independent, most other newspapers are part of media conglomerates most interested in the financial bottom line. Gilens and Hetzman (2000) found significant differences on how newspapers covered congressional debate on the 1996 Telecommunications Act, designed to ease restrictions on corporate ownership of multiple media outlets. The newspapers owned by those who would benefit from the passage of legislation downplayed monopoly issues. The authors concluded that financial self-interest affected not only the editorial page but leaked into the straight news reporting as well.

If there is a conservative tendency to the American news media, the most obvious manifestation is on newspaper editorial pages. Unlike most television and radio stations, newspapers regularly take positions on the issues. And while television and radio stations do not formally endorse candidates during election season (due to FCC rules about equal time), newspapers routinely endorse political candidates on their editorial pages. Newspapers are far more likely to endorse Republicans than Democrats. In almost all presidential elections (1964 and 1992 being exceptions), the vast majority of endorsing newspapers favor the Republican candidate.

Two factors readily account for newspaper publishers' tendency toward Republicanism and conservatism. First, newspaper publishers are businesspeople. Their conservative Republicanism is a natural extension of the prevailing orthodoxy of the business community. Second, a newspaper's advertisers also represent the conservative business community. Although it is rare for major advertisers to threaten to withdraw their ads from newspapers because of their political stands, newspapers must depend on advertising for the major share of their revenue.

Biased News?

The liberalism of journalists does not necessarily mean that their ideological preferences filter into news stories, nor does the conservatism of their bosses (and newspaper editorial pages) necessarily spill over into the reporting of the news. It is plausible that both the liberalism of journalists and the conservatism of their bosses influence the presentation of the news, with each offsetting the other. Objective measurement of possible bias is difficult, complicated by loud voices on the left and right claiming to quantify the existence of bias by the other side.

The public discussion of bias tends to bog down in narrow debates between competing protagonists, with each side presenting its own mostly anecdotal evidence. For instance, the conservative former CBS newsman Bernard Goldberg (*Bias in the News* 2001) claims to have identified one way in which TV newscasts promote liberalism as the mainstream. He charges that network newscasts repeatedly label conservative political figures as "conservatives" while leaving their liberal counterparts unidentified ideologically. Goldberg claims the networks see liberal positions as the norm and identify those taking positions on the right as "conservative" to alert viewers they are out of the mainstream. Liberal media critic Eric Alterman (*What Liberal Bias?* 2003) dissents, saying Goldberg presents only anecdotal evidence to support his contention. Alterman cites counterevidence where the networks label conservatives and liberals evenhandedly. Even if it were true that network newscasts disproportionately pin ideological labels on conservative politicians more than liberal politicians, this would fall far short of proof that the network newscasts, or the media at large, routinely distort the news to favor the liberal point of view. On the other hand, critics say this tendency is simply one sign of a much larger problem.

Does the political ideology of reporters affect the way they cover the news? There is no conclusive answer to this question, but in their study of the Washington-based media, Dautrich and Dineen (1996) asked journalists for a self-assessment of whether their opinions ever affected their reporting. Seventy-eight percent said it did so at least "occasionally" and virtually no reporter said "never." Still, most reporters hold professional values that mandate a conscious effort to keep personal politics out of their reporting. In one experimental study, a sample of reporters was asked to describe how they would cover a variety of hypothetical stories. Political ideology had only a minor (but statistically significant) effect (Patterson and Donsbach 1996). In addition, while stories are written by reporters, editors responsible to CEOs and owners decide what gets published or aired. These gatekeepers, who themselves are decidedly less liberal than their reporters, are unlikely to be promoting a liberal agenda.

Academic studies of network news coverage of presidential campaigns show that the networks attempt to achieve balance. Networks devote roughly equal time to both major party candidates and tend to give both candidates about equal positive versus negative coverage (which, as we see in the next section, is mostly negative). In-depth studies of the 1996 and 2000 election campaigns showed that the stream of information presented by the media about candidates did not favor one party over the other (Domke et al. 1997; Farnsworth and Lichter 2003).

There exists no such balance, however, when we turn from the reporting of the news to opinion, or commentary. Any liberal favoritism in news reporting is offset by the conservative tilt of media commentary. Particularly in the era of fragmented media, conservative voices have come to significantly outnumber liberal voices. To the conservative dominance of newspaper editorial pages, which has long been in place, one must add talk radio and cable news punditry. Talk radio, in particular, is dominated by conservatives. On national radio there is no liberal equivalent to Rush Limbaugh, Michael Reagan, or G. Gordon Liddy. Much the same is true for opinion shows on cable news channels. The left has no one to match Bill O'Reilly or Joe Scarborough. One must look elsewhere for liberal equivalents.

The public has concluded that the media are not entirely objective in covering the news. When people were asked about "bias in the media" in a September 2003 Gallup poll, 45 percent said the "news media" were "too liberal," while only 14 percent said it was "too conservative" (39 percent said it was "about right"). However, when asked about "bias in election coverage," the public sees the media as more evenhanded. A Pew Research Center poll in early 2004 shows 22 percent say the media are biased toward Democrats and 17 percent say the media are biased toward Republicans. Not surprisingly, 47 percent of conservative Republicans see a Democrat bias, while 36 percent of liberal Democrats see a Republican bias.[10]

As we detail in the following section, it is apparent why some people at both ends of the political spectrum might see the news as biased. In the 2000 election, a content analysis showed 60 percent of the media evaluations of George W. Bush were negative and 63 percent of the media evaluations of Al Gore were negative (Farnsworth and Lichter 2003, 114). As citizens look at media content through the colored glasses of partisanship, it is easy to conclude that one's own political values are not getting a fair shake.

Negativity in the News

While there remains disagreement about ideological bias in the news, a much stronger case can be made that in recent years the tone of the media has turned profoundly negative. Where once the media affirmed political authority they now denigrate it. According to Thomas Patterson, the real bias in the media is an "ingrained cynicism" (Patterson 1996). In an analysis of stories in *Time* and *Newsweek* about presidential campaign coverage, Patterson (1994) found the negative content of this coverage increased dramatically beginning in 1980. In 1960, only 25 percent of the stories were negative, but by 1976, 40 percent were negative. Over half were negative in 1980, and in 1992, 60 percent of the stories were negative. In 1991, when the popularity of George H. W. Bush stood at 88 percent in the Gallup Poll, barely half his media coverage was positive (Groeling and Kernell 1998).

It is not just presidential candidates that get negative coverage but politicians and public officials in general. Following approval of the "Contract with America" by House Republicans in 1994, both House Speaker Newt Gingrich and other top Republican leaders were rewarded with biting negative press coverage. More than 60 percent of the stories about Republican leaders were negative. While one might think this is but another example of liberal bias in the news, it is worth noting that in 1992, newly elected Democratic President Bill Clinton was not even accorded the courtesy of a brief honeymoon from negative innuendoes in the press. During his first two months in office, 60 percent of his press coverage was negative (Patterson 1996).

We see the same pattern when it comes to coverage of presidential candidates on the major television networks. In past four elections, the nonpartisan Center for Media and Public Affairs has conducted a content analysis of all campaign stories that appeared on networks from Labor Day through Election Day. As can be seen in Table 8.3, by 1988 the majority of television coverage was negative. Although Republicans seem to get somewhat more negative press than do Democrats, the data show clearly that both the right and left are denigrated on the evening television news (Farnsworth and Lichter 2003, 120).

Clearly something has changed with the press, as there is little evidence of any change in ethics or honesty among politicians over the past thirty years. One explanation for the change holds that relations between politicians and the press have become increasingly adversarial. In recent years, politicians have aggressively tried to control the flow of the news, which detracts from the ability of journalists to do their job. A mutual dislike has arisen resulting in the negative coverage of political personalities (Zaller 2004). A second explanation is economic. The conviction in financial quarters that the news must be entertaining to be profitable has led to a focus on sensational stories, scandal (real or imagined), and "gotcha" news coverage of those in public life (Sabato, Stencel, and Lichter 2000; Farnsworth and Lichter 2003).[11] Whatever the reason, the media are a good deal more aggressive in exposing potentially embarrassing actions by public officials than they were in past.

While there is agreement that cynicism in the news has increased substantially when compared to the past, there is disagreement about how this trend affects public opinion. As we noted earlier, the effect of the media is rarely massive. In 1976, Michael Robinson coined the term *videomalaise*, which linked the rise in political cynicism to negativity in the news. Some make the controversial claim that the decline in political trust and/or the continuing low levels

TABLE 8.3	General Election News: Tone of Coverage, 1988–2000			
	Percent Negative			
	1988	**1992**	**1996**	**2000**
Democratic nominee	59%	48%	50%	60%
Republican nominee	62	71	67	63

Source: Adapted from Stephen J. Farnsworth and S. Robert Lichter, *The Nightly News Nightmare* (New York: Roman-Littlefield, 2003), 117.

of political trust can largely be blamed on the negative media (Patterson 1994, 22; but for a different view, see O'Keefe 1980). According to some, constant denigration of political authority breeds cynicism among the public.

Experimental studies show people exposed to negative stories about government are more likely to be distrusting than an equivalent control group (Robinson 1976; Cappella and Jameison 1997). Others have used survey evidence to show that the more one is exposed to the political news, the greater the mistrust of government (Miller, Goldenberg, and Erbring 1979; Hetherington 2001). Farnsworth and Litcher (2003) used tracking polls (polls conducted weekly or daily) to demonstrate in the 2000 primaries that when the network coverage of a candidate shifted to the negative, that candidate's poll ratings declined. It was once rare for candidates of either political party to end the campaign season with a negative favorability rating (Barry Goldwater in 1964 was an exception). According to Patterson (1996), between 1980 and 1992 all major party candidates ended their campaign with a plurality of negative ratings by the electorate. Another claim is that the approval rate of Congress suffers due to relentless negative portrayals of the institution in the media (Mann and Ornstein 1994, 4). About nine out of ten media evaluations of Congress are negative. Hibbing and Theiss-Morse (1998) found the greater exposure to the media, the more likely people had a negative emotional reaction to Congress. However, others are not so convinced. While the decline in political trust coincides with the rise in media negativity, cause and effect have yet to be clearly demonstrated.

8-3 MODELS OF MEDIA EFFECTS

In the 1938 radio broadcast "War of the Worlds," Orson Welles described an invasion of New Jersey by Martians from outer space. Although the story was fiction, many believed it to be true, causing somewhat of a panic in the New Jersey area. For many scholars, this was an example of the powerful sway the media can have over citizens. The use of media propaganda by Benito Mussolini in Italy and Adolf Hitler in Germany to gain and hold political power was seen as another example of pervasive media effects. This model of media influence has been dubbed the *hypodermic effect*, as it is similar to getting a drug injection. The effect is immediate and powerful. However, with the advent of scientific public opinion surveys, scholarly consensus shifted in the opposite direction. Early studies found media influences in political campaigns to be trivial, giving rise to a new perspective, called the *minimal effects model*. In recent years, the minimal effects model has also fallen into disfavor. Current media scholars favor a more nuanced approach that emphasizes the search for subtle but meaningful consequences of media exposure, including some that are easy to overlook.

The Minimal Effects Model

The first attempts to examine empirically the political influence of the mass media were the early studies of voting behavior: panel studies of voters in Erie

County, Ohio, in 1940 and voters in Elmira, New York, in 1948 (Lazarsfeld et al. 1948; Berelson et al. 1954). These early studies presented a viewpoint regarding the influence of the media that has since become known as the minimal effects model of media influence. Perhaps because the researchers for these projects moved into voting research from market research, they expected to find campaign messages in the mass media (at that time, essentially newspapers and radio) to be quite influential on individual voters. They envisioned voters waffling in their choice of candidates somewhat in the way a consumer might change his or her choice of toothpaste from purchase to purchase, depending on the effectiveness of the latest advertising.

These early researchers on presidential choice, however, made three discoveries that seemed to dismiss the mass media's influence. First, they discovered the anchor of partisanship. A substantial number of citizens interviewed as early as May of election year had already decided how they were going to vote in November. This suggests that most voters had a "product loyalty" to one or the other of the two major political parties. Second, the researchers discovered perceptual screening. Voters paid particular attention to the messages from the candidate they preferred, which served to maintain their "product loyalty." They avoided exposure to campaign messages for the opposition, even misperceiving these messages when exposure was unavoidable. Third, the researchers discovered the importance of personal conversations. When someone was about to change his or her viewpoint due to a persuasive message in the media, that person would often return to the original opinion after talking to others who shared that original opinion.

For these reasons, the messages on the mass media are less influential than they might appear. Because people's political views are anchored by their past beliefs, perceptual screening, and interpersonal communications, it is not likely that any particular revelation in the evening news will create massive changes in people's political likes and dislikes. Two interesting examples are the responses to President Reagan's Iran–Contra scandal in 1986 and 1987 and the scandal involving President Clinton and Monica Lewinsky in 1998 and 1999.

In late 1986, the American public was first shocked to learn that President Reagan was selling arms to Iran and then shocked again to learn that one purpose was to illegally fund the Contras in Nicaragua. The national media gave this scandal the coverage and the treatment usually reserved for a constitutional crisis on the order of Watergate. In one month, popular approval of Reagan's performance dropped about 20 percentage points, which (until 9/11) perhaps defines the outer limit of how quickly public opinion can respond in the short run. Twenty percentage points is the greatest one-month drop in presidential approval ever recorded. Yet if one sets a high threshold regarding what constitutes a "major" opinion change, an upper limit of 20 percentage points may seem like not much at all. At least two-thirds of those who approved of Reagan before the scandal broke continued to do so despite the Iran–Contra revelations.

The 1998 Lewinsky scandal surpassed the Iran–Contra scandal in shock value. Within days of the first revelations, pundits were discussing whether the president would be or should be impeached. The news being reported appeared disastrous for the president at a time when Clinton was basking in the glow of a record level of popularity for a president so late in his presidency. Given the new revelations involving sex, lies, and audiotape, most political experts were sure that Clinton's standing with the public would plunge like a rock. Instead, it rose. In fact, over the first week of the scandal, Clinton's approval rating rose 10 points, close to a record for short-term presidential gain. What occurred was a seeming disconnection between the negative media stories and the public's evaluation of the president—a development that is far from fully understood (Zaller 1998; Owen 2000; Fischle 2000; Just and Crigler 2000). What is now clear is that public opinion does not automatically flow in the direction of the news. People judged the facts of the Lewinsky case in a way that allowed them to support the president in spite of negative revelations and speculation in the media.

Contemporary Perspectives on Media Effects

The Iran-Contra and Lewinsky examples illustrate the obvious limits of the media's power. Consistent with the minimal effects interpretation of media influence, shifts in public evaluations are limited even in response to one-sided news stories, and sometimes not even in the expected direction. However, many mass media researchers reject the minimalist interpretation. They concede the media has limited ability to change vote preferences in partisan elections or change opinions deeply rooted in partisanship or group identification. Instead, they search for more modest influences on political beliefs that perhaps can be detected only by experimental designs, imposing complex statistical controls on the data, or by isolating influences that exist only under restricted circumstances. (e.g., see Bartels 1993; Finkel 1993).

It is well understood that media effects are circumscribed because message awareness and message acceptance push in opposite directions. Consider that the possibility of opinion change in response to a new political message depends on both the likelihood of becoming aware of the message and the likelihood of accepting it once becoming aware. For many people, when the likelihood of accepting a message from the media is high, the likelihood of hearing it is low—and vice versa. For instance, those low in political sophistication might have a .90 probability of accepting a new message if they receive it but only a .10 probability of actually hearing (receiving) the message. The probability of opinion change for that person is only .09 (.10 × .90). On the other hand, a person high in sophistication might have a .90 probability of hearing a message but only a .10 probability of accepting it. His or her political sophistication leads to resistance for those messages at variance with currently held opinions. Again, the probability of opinion change is .09. On the other hand, a person at the midrange of sophistication might have .50 probability of hearing a message and .50 probability of accepting it. The probability of opinion change for that person is .25 (.50 × .50). Thus, individuals most susceptible to media effects are those with moderate levels of political sophistication. They are sufficiently interested to be aware of media content but lack the sophistication to completely resist media messages (Converse 1962; Zaller 1997).

Finally, there is a recognition that the net influence of the mass media so often seems to be slight because it represents a balance among conflicting points of view (Zaller 1992, 1996). If the media messages were truly one-sided, like the flow of propaganda in a nondemocratic regime, their cumulative impact might well be substantial. Even in a democratic society, there is often a consensus at the elite level that results in a one-sided media message. Examples include the president's honeymoon period and rally effects following crises, both discussed in chapter 4. In these instances, presidents receive exceptional popularity levels because media voices are uniformly supportive (Brody 1991).

Contemporary thinking about media effects focuses on three processes by which the media are believed to influence public opinion: agenda setting, where the media influences the issues citizens think are most important; priming, which influences the how citizens use these issues to evaluate political figures, and framing, which can influence opinion by the way issues are presented to the public.

Agenda Setting

The potential influence of the mass media on political thinking is not limited to influence on policy preferences. As Bernard Cohen famously remarked, the media "may not be successful much of time in telling people what to think, but it stunningly successful in telling [people] what to think about" (Cohen 1963). A small study of the 1968 presidential election conducted by McCombs and Shaw (1972) is the precursor to a growing body of research on agenda setting. McCombs and Shaw asked their survey respondents to name the "main things . . . government should concentrate on doing something about." The issues named turned out to be the same issues stressed in newspaper and television coverage of the campaign. McCombs and Shaw argued that this relationship is more than a sharing of concern by the public and the media decision makers because the public obtains its information from the media. They suggest that the media set the political agenda for the public.

Ideally, the best way to ascertain the degree to which the mass media influences the agenda is to experimentally manipulate what people read or watch. This approach was used by Iyengar and his associates (Iyengar et al. 1982; Iyengar and Kinder 1987) in a study of the network news. Ordinary citizens were divided into four groups, and for six consecutive days they watched the nightly news. Unknown to the subjects, each group saw a different version. For one group, a news story about defense preparedness was edited into each news program. For a second, a news story about pollution was inserted. The third group saw an economic inflation story, and a fourth group saw an unedited version of the news. Thus, each group got a weeklong dose of messages concerning one particular problem.

The most interesting result was the set of responses to the "most important problem" question before and after the experiment. Those given pollution stories and those given defense stories registered significant increases in concern about pollution and defense respectively. The inflation group did not change much, apparently because they already expressed a strong concern about inflation in their questionnaires prior to the experiment and could hardly increase the level of their response. Further analysis suggested the subjects in each group began to evaluate President Carter according to how they saw Carter's handling of their manipulated topic. Iyengar and his colleagues showed not only that the content of the media can influence the agenda but that the choice of issues for the agenda can influence people's evaluation of the president.

MacKuen (1981) studied agenda setting by using polling data. He conducted an elaborate statistical analysis of national responses to the "most important problem facing the nation" question over a fifteen-year period (1962–1977). MacKuen found that, for most issues, public concern tracked media attention as measured by the frequency of reporting of the issue in the newsmagazines. For some issues, MacKuen found the public's level of concern responding more to media concern than to the objective circumstances. For instance, media attention to crime predicted public concern about crime better than did the actual crime rate. Similarly, media attention to the war in Vietnam predicted public concern about the war better than did American troop levels (MacKuen 1981, 84–88).

An important issue is how individual political sophistication relates to agenda setting. Iyengar et al. report that their least sophisticated respondents were the most responsive to experimental manipulation of the agenda. This finding seems reasonable, as less sophisticated people lack the stored information that helps discount messages in the media at odds with their current opinions. However, the subjects were shown news programs under artificial experimental conditions. Would they have been as attentive and persuaded in a natural setting? MacKuen (1984) finds the least sophisticated respondents to be the most immune to changes in the media's agenda. As we noted earlier, at least a moderate level of political sophistication seems necessary for the media to lead. To be persuaded by the media requires some minimal attention to the media. In a natural setting, that attention apparently does not exist among the least sophisticated.

It is now understood that when an issue becomes the subject of media attention, the net public opinion change will be slight as long as both sides of the issue are presented (although people on each side may become more polarized). When the media present only one side of an issue, public opinion responds to the dominant message (Zaller 1992; Baumgartner and Jones 1993; Jacobs and Shapiro 2000). The door is thus open for possible media manipulation. However, objective circumstances mostly drive the media agenda. For example, the media cover inflation when inflation is high and therefore newsworthy (Behr and Iyengar 1985). Still, the media's choices that set the public agenda also reflect the voices of those who clamor to heard. Government officials, particularly the president, exert a strong influence on the media's agenda. At the local level, officials sometimes avoid making decisions elites oppose, but the public favors, by keeping certain issues off the agenda (Berkman and Kitch 1986; Graber 1997).

Priming Issues

By setting the agenda, the media not only increase the perceived importance of an issue, they can also prime the public so the issue becomes a key ingredient in the way the president (or other relevant political figure) is evaluated. When an issue is primed by the media, the president is allocated blame or credit for how that issue is being resolved. Or, if the media pay no attention to an issue, it is usually not a factor for most citizens when evaluating the president (Iyengar 1991). For example, when the 1991 Gulf War was in the daily headlines, the popularity of the first President Bush soared to record heights. The public was being primed by the media to evaluate Bush based on how he was handling the war. However, by November 1991 the attention of the media shifted to the economy. By placing the economy at the top of the public agenda, the media was priming the public to evaluate Bush not on his past successes in the Persian Gulf but on an allegedly stalling economy (Krosnick and Brannon 1993; Hetherington 1996). When the media shifted its focus from the war to the economy, the president's approval rating rapidly declined (Zaller 1994).

There are two ways priming might work. First, it can increase the accessibility of information in short-term memory. When the media focuses attention on combating terrorism, "considerations" about the war on terrorism are at the top of the head for many when asked to evaluate the president (Iyengar and Kinder 1987). Second, when the media focus attention on an issue they make it clear, either explicitly or implicitly, that reporters and editors feel this issue is important. It is not unexpected that many people come to share this media perspective—at least if they place some minimal level of trust in the media. Once a person comes to believe an issue is important, it is only natural to place significant weight on that issue when evaluating the president (Miller and Krosnick 2000).

Considerable experimental and survey evidence is now available that supports the priming hypothesis (Iyengar 1991; Mendelsohn 1996; Mutz 1998; Miller and Krosnick 2000). One study capitalized serendipitously on the highly publicized revelation, which occurred midway through the interviewing during the 1986 NES survey, that the Reagan administration was selling arms to Iran and channeling the money to the Nicaraguan Contras.[12] President Reagan's approval dropped immediately. The prediction from the priming hypothesis is that opinions about foreign policy matters increase in importance as predictors of Reagan's approval, and opinions about domestic matters remain constant or decline. That is precisely what Krosnick and Kinder's (1990) statistical analysis of the data shows. After the press moved Iran-Contra to forefront, Iran-Contra surged to second place (after perceptions of the economy) as a predictor of presidential performance evaluations. Attitudes about government help for racial minorities, which had been the second-best predictor of Reagan approval prior to the Iran-Contra revelations, dropped to zero.

If the media can use its agenda-setting power to prime the public about the proper issues on which to evaluate the president, there is a possibility that significant damage could be done to presidential support if the media get the facts wrong. That appears to have happened in November 1991 when the media shifted focus from the Gulf War to the economy. The economy was recovering, but media coverage was consistently downbeat (Hetherington 1996).[13] Over 90 percent of all media references to the economy during the 1992 election campaign were negative (Patterson 1994). The economy was in reality getting better, but the networks relentlessly portrayed it as getting worse—a portrayal the public accepted. When asked in the 1992 NES postelection survey if the economy was better, worse, or about the same as one year ago, 72 percent said it was worse. The more people paid attention to the media, the more negative their assessment of the economy, and more negative their assessment of the economy, the more probable a vote for Bill Clinton over George H. W. Bush in the 1992 presidential election. Hetherington concludes that had "voters cast their ballots based on the actual conditions of the national economy in 1992, they more than likely would have returned George Bush to office" (Hetherington 1996, 383).

Framing Issues

A media frame provides meaning to unfolding events. It is the central or organizing theme in a news story. A frame highlights what is important about an issue, such its causes, morality, the people involved, and proposed solutions (Cappella and Jamieson 1997; Jamieson and Waldman 2003). While agenda setting and priming concern the importance the media place on an issue, framing concerns the way media present issue content to the public. A frame determines what is in the picture and what is left out. According to the framing hypothesis, the slant or angle journalists take on newsworthy issues can affect opinions about these issues. We are all familiar with the way news stories can be framed. News about poverty programs can stress a "helping hand" or a "government handout." Combatants in foreign conflicts can be "freedom fighters" (e.g., the Nicaraguan Contras) or "terrorists" (e.g., the Taliban). Antiabortion protestors can be portrayed as idealists committed to the sanctity of life or as religious zealots intent on enforcing their views on everyone else.

A number of studies have shown that how news stories are framed can affect political opinions (Iyengar 1991; Kinder and Sanders 1996; Nelson, Clawson, and Oxley 1997; Kellstedt 2000). Following a rally by the Ku Klux Klan in Ohio, investigators conducted an experiment in which one group of college students saw news clips that framed the issues involved as "free speech" (the Klan wanting to get out its message). Another group saw clips that framed the controversy as involving "public order" (the potential for violence). Those who saw the issues framed as free speech scored significantly higher on a scale of political tolerance than those who saw the issues framed as public order (Nelson; Clawson, and Oxley 1997).

Of course, there is always concern about the generalizability of a college sample and whether the experimental effect still existed a week or a month later. However, a sophisticated analysis by Paul Kellstedt (2000) of how the news media framed race issues from 1950 to the early 1990s lends support to the experimental studies. He coded over 2,000 news stories about race where the controversy was framed by the media either in terms of "individualism" (hard work leads to success) or in terms of "equalitarianism" (a level playing field for all). He then related these frames to shifts in public opinion. During periods when the equalitarian frame dominated the news about race, public opinion moved significantly in a liberal direction on race issues. However, during periods dominated by the individualism frame, opinion did not move in a conservative direction. Depending on circumstances, framing seems to work by making some considerations more accessible than others, by selectively enhancing the importance of certain beliefs, or by changing the belief content that underlies a particular opinion (Kinder and Sanders 1996; Nelson and Oxley 1999).

8-4 MEDIA CONTENT AND POLITICAL OPINIONS

While the minimal effects model holds that the media do little more than reinforce preexisting opinions, recent research has demonstrated meaningful media effects on political opinions among those who regularly follow politics on television and talk radio and in the newspapers. In this section we discuss the findings of some of these studies.

Television News

In an ambitious study, Page and Shapiro (1993) estimated the influence of television news reports on the content of public opinion. They collected eighty instances from the late 1960s into the early 1980s where the same survey question about an important question of public policy was administered to national samples over a period of years. They then determined whether television news content between the two surveys could account for the observed change in public opinion. This exercise involved extensive monitoring and coding for more than a decade's worth of network news programs.

On the average, opinion did not change much in the short run of even a few years. But when change occurred, the direction tended to be consistent with the preponderant direction of the messages on network news. The authors examined the impact of many sources of information on network news (e.g., presidents, the opposition party, interest groups). The source that best predicted opinion change was television commentary—from anchorpersons, reporters in the field, and special commentators. According to the estimates, each viewpoint presented in a commentary could bring about as much as 4 percentage points of opinion change. But Page and Shapiro are cautious when interpreting why television commentary predicts opinion change. They do not claim that individual newscasters are themselves the major source of opinion change. Rather, their message frequently overlaps or reinforces the dominant elite message that filters to the public via the media. Or news commentators and others with whom they agree may be perceived as simply reflecting an agreed-upon consensus that may strongly influence the formation of citizen opinions (Page and Shapiro 1993).

In other words, when the messages on television news are predominantly one-sided and advocate a particular change of policy, it is a good bet that public opinion will change at least modestly in the same direction. But instead of television messages *causing* the opinion change, another possibility could be that both television messages and public opinion are both *responding* independently (but in a common direction) to the same events. In this way, public opinion and elite opinion (via the media) could be moving in tandem but with neither causing the other.

We saw earlier that more people get their political information from the local news than from any other source. Media scholars agree that the content of the local news presents an unrealistic picture of life in America. In Los Angeles County, for instance, 17 percent of all crime stories were about murder when in reality less than 1 percent of all crime in the country was murder. Since people learn about crime from the media rather than personal experience, this is an important exaggeration. Most crime is property crime, but on the local news most crime is violent and the perpetrators frequently are minority males.[14]

Using actual footage from local Los Angeles television, Gilliam and Iyengar (2000) conducted an experiment that demonstrated that the local news content affects political opinions. One group watched a news script where the alleged perpetrator of a crime was a black male, another saw the same script but the alleged perpetrator was a white male, and a third group saw a crime story but with no perpetrator. When asked to recall the race of the perpetrator, 70 percent of the group that saw the black perpetrator correctly recalled he was black, compared to 64 percent of the group that saw the white perpetrator correctly recalling him as white. However, for the group that saw no perpetrator at all, 60 percent falsely recalled the person committing the crime was black. Given the prevalence on the local news of blacks and violent crime, people inferred the perpetrator must be black, even though no such information was contained in the news clip they saw. As Kuklinksi et al. (2000) have demonstrated, when information is missing, people use stereotypes to fill in the blanks.

In addition, whites who saw the news clip with either the black perpetrator or no perpetrator at all endorsed more punitive measures to contain crime and displayed more negative sentiments toward blacks when compared to a control group. In a follow-up survey, the same results were found. The more people watched the local news, the more likely they were to endorse punitive measures to deal with crime and to express negative opinions about blacks.

Talk Radio

In the era of the new media, nowhere has the merger of the news and entertainment been more been more successful than talk radio. Thirty-six percent of Americans say they listen to talk radio at least occasionally (Barker 2002, 19). Its champions claim talk radio serves to empower everyday people. However, as Davis and Owen (1998) forcefully note, talk radio is first and foremost about making money. The content of talk radio is simply a byproduct of what sells best to the public. Currently, conservatives dominate the talk radio format. However, if some other format drew a larger audience, many conservative talk shows would quickly disappear.

The audience for talk radio tends to be older white males—particularly in the case of conservative talk radio. For the medium's best-known personality, Rush Limbaugh, 67 percent of listeners are male, 45 percent are over fifty years old, and 95 percent are white. Those who listen to talk radio tend to be more conservative than nonlisteners, but not by a large margin. Davis and Owen (1998, 168–1970) found that 57 percent of listeners call themselves conservative, compared to 42 percent of their public sample. Listeners were also more Republican (Davis and Owen 1998, 168–170). The fact that talk show hosts are generally a good deal more conservative than their audiences leads some analysts to conclude that entertainment is as big a drawing card as is political content (Lee and Cappella 2001).

One might think that the audience for talk radio leans atypically to the right because conservatives self-select to listen. Talk show hosts are essentially preaching to the choir. Mostly, that is the correct conclusion. However, several studies have shown that for issues frequently discussed on talk radio, hosts can have an independent influence on political opinions. In the mid-1990s, Rush Limbaugh spent considerable time bashing Ross Perot and Bill Clinton. David Barker (2002) found those who regularly listened to Limbaugh, when compared to nonlisteners, were more negative in their evaluations of Perot and Limbaugh—all other things being approximately equal. On the other hand, listeners and nonlisteners did not differ on issues rarely covered by Limbaugh, such as the death penalty or school prayer. In the 2000 Republican primary, Limbaugh came out early in favor of George W. Bush over his principle primary opponent, Senator John McCain of Arizona (who Limbaugh said was not a "real" Republican). Using a design where respondents could be tracked over time, Barker (2002) found the more one listened to Limbaugh, the more likely a change toward a favorable opinion of Bush and an unfavorable opinion of McCain. Because the sample was entirely composed of Republicans and tracked change over time, one can reasonably rule out the alternative explanation of self-selection.

Newspaper Endorsements

In principle, political reporting in newspapers is not supposed to reflect an ideological position. Professional ethics dictate that journalists not let their own political feelings color their reporting. However, for the editorial pages that is neither the expectation nor the case. Here, columnists such as conservative George Will and liberal Maureen Dowd analyze political events through an ideological prism. In addition, the owners and managers of newspapers often endorse candidates for public office—a rare practice for the owners of television and radio stations. Because they use the public airwaves, radio and television stations would have to provide equal time for other candidates to respond.

As in the case of television and talk radio, there is evidence that the editorial content of newspapers can effect the political opinions of its readers. One reason is that editorial opinion can leak from the editorial page to straight news coverage. For example, in an analysis of media coverage of seventy-nine senate races between 1988 and 1992, Kahn and Kenney (2002) found that when a newspaper endorsed an incumbent senator on its editorial pages, the tone of its campaign coverage of that senator was significantly more positive than when it made no endorsement. Thus, to the extent there is spillover from the editorial pages to the straight news, the potential is greater for newspapers to influence political opinions (but see Dalton, Beck, and Huckfeldt 1998 for a somewhat different take).

Based on a content analysis of diversity of opinion (an indicator of liberalism)[15] on the front page of the newspapers, and ideological liberalism on the editorial page, Robert Entmann (1989) demonstrated with an elaborate statistical model that the ideological tone of the paper read by NES respondents in 1976 influenced the ideological tone of some political evaluations and even their vote for president. An alternative causal interpretation of Entmann's data is selective exposure, with readers choosing their newspaper based on ideological affinity. This risk is minimized by the fact that contemporary readers typically have only one choice of a local newspaper; results were not weakened in a separate analysis of readers with one newspaper choice. Still another consideration, however, is that editors are aware of ideological opinion among readers and slant their stories accordingly.

Newspapers generally endorse Republicans for president, which makes it difficult to match voters who read Republican newspapers with those who read Democratic newspapers. But one exception to the Republican endorsement habits of American newspapers provided a unique opportunity to study endorsement effects. In the 1964 presidential election, more newspapers endorsed President Lyndon Johnson (42 percent) than his Republican opponent, Barry Goldwater (35 percent). With this relatively even division, Erikson (1976b) was able to compare the vote in communities where the local newspaper(s) endorsed the Democrat with the vote in communities where the local newspaper(s) endorsed the Republican. Statistical controls were imposed for the community's previous vote, the particular state, and the size of the city. Even with these controls, the 1960–1964 vote shift was about 5 percentage points more in the Democratic direction where the endorsements were Democratic than where they were Republican. In their statistical analysis of senatorial elections around 1990, Kahn and Kenney (2002) find that endorsements of senatorial candidates in the editorial pages of the paper affect how these candidates are covered in straight news stories, which in turn influences the opinion about the incumbent U.S. senators seeking reelection. In cases of heavy news coverage, an endorsed incumbent senator gained about 16 points in positive evaluation (on a 100-point scale) compared to one who was not endorsed.

8-5 THE NEWS SOURCE AND COMPREHENSION

As we have seen, the public gets most of its news from television, and the trend is increasing. People also say the news they see on television is more credible than the news they read in the papers (Roper 1997). But from which medium do people actually learn most? Table 8.4 shows evidence from the 2000 NES survey. People generally reported that they watched news on television more regularly than they read the newspapers. They also claimed to pay more attention to the presidential campaign on television than in the newspapers.

On the other hand, the evidence presented in Table 8.4 may exaggerate people's reliance on television for their news (Robinson and Levy 1986, 231–241; Robinson and Levy 1996). People pay different degrees of attention to the broadcast and the print media. Watching television news or listening to radio news is the most passive form of attention. Indeed, the set may be on, but without concentration from the viewer or listener.

Using the 2000 NES election data, we offer additional demonstrations of how newspapers and television news inform voters during presidential campaigns. We divided 2000 NES respondents into three categories of television news watching. "Regular viewers" claimed both to watch national news at least six days a week and to follow television news of the campaign with "quite a bit" or "a good deal" of attention. "Nonviewers" claimed to watch no national news or to pay no attention to campaign news. "Occasional viewers" were between these two extremes. We rated newspaper readership similarly. "Regular readers" claimed both to read newspapers at least six days a week and to follow the campaign in newspapers with "quite a bit" or "a good deal" of attention. "Nonreaders" claimed to not read newspapers or pay no attention to campaign news. "Occasional readers" were in between.

Rating respondents according to three categories on viewing and three categories on reading gives a combined set of categories with a total of nine cells. Frequencies with which people appear in each of the nine cells are shown in Table 8.5. This table reflects the growing dominance of television over newspapers as a news source. But the same individuals who attended to one medium generally attended to the other. Regular viewing and regular reading tended to go together. So did nonviewing and nonreading. Our interest is in sorting out the separate effects of reading and watching on political interest and information. At the same time, we must be aware that causality also flows the other way; while monitoring the media can stimulate interest and the growth of information, it is also true that interested and informed citizens seek out media information.

TABLE 8.4 | Media Usage in 2000 Presidential Campaign

National TV News		Daily Newspaper	
Days Watched During Week	**Attention to Campaign News**	**Days Read During Week**	**Attention to Campaign News**
None 27%	None, very little 41%	None 26%	None, very little 62%
1–6 47	Some, quite a bit 48	1–6 40	Some, quite a bit 31
7 days 29	A good deal 11	7 days 34	A great deal 7

Source: National Election Studies, 2000 election data.

We can see the basic results in part (a) of Table 8.6, which shows the percentage of respondents who said they were "very interested" in the campaign. As we move from nonviewers to regular viewers or from nonreaders to regular readers, we see that campaign interest increases. This relationship between media attention and campaign interest is clear for both viewing and reading. For each level of television news viewing, newspaper readers are more interested than nonreaders. For each level of newspaper reading, television news viewers are more interested than nonviewers. All this fits with common sense. Interest in the campaign should make one want to follow the campaign more

---

TABLE 8.5 | **Patterns of Attention to Newspaper and Television News, 2000**

		Television Viewing			
		Regular viewer	**Occasional viewer**	**Nonviewer**	**All cases**
	Regular reader	7★	5	2	14
Newspaper	Occasional reader	8	17	5	30
Reading	Nonreader	7	26	23	57
	All cases	22	47	31	100

★Cell entries are percentages of total sample.
Source: National Election Studies, 2000 election data.

TABLE 8.6 | **Responsiveness in the 2000 Presidential Campaign, by Media Attention**

(a) Percentage "Very Interested" in the Election

		Television News Viewing		
		Regular viewer	**Occasional viewer**	**Nonviewer**
Newspaper	Regular reader	79	62	68
Reading	Occasional reader	62	28	23
	Nonreader	53	14	9

(b) Percentage with High Information About Candidate Positions

		Television News Viewing		
		Regular viewer	**Occasional viewer**	**Nonviewer**
Newspaper	Regular reader	33	46	36
Reading	Occasional reader	33	22	29
	Nonreader	21	8	10

Source: National Election Studies, 2000 election data.

closely both in newspapers and on television, and following the campaign either in newspapers or on television makes one more interested.

In part (b) of Table 8.6, note what happens when we substitute percentages with "high" information about candidate policy positions for campaign interest. We define high scorers as those who correctly rated Bush to the right of Gore on all five issues examined. Newspaper reading is sharply related to information level, but only among people who are not regular consumers of national news reports on television. Viewing televised national news is modestly related to information level, but only among people who do not read newspapers. Taken together, these patterns suggest newspapers are more informative than television news and also that each medium is more effective in the absence of the other. Interestingly, the most informed of all are regular newspaper readers who do not watch television news. Obviously this must be a matter of self-selection rather than television causing information loss; people who choose newspapers over television are more cognitively skilled and therefore more informed to begin with.

8-6 AN INFORMED ELECTORATE? TELEVISION NEWS AND CAMPAIGN ADS

Surprising as it may seem at first glance, citizens learn a good deal more about substantive policy issues from the content of paid candidate campaign ads than they do from television news coverage. This pattern was first uncovered by Thomas Patterson and Robert McClure in a study of the 1972 presidential campaign, and reconfirmed in a study of the 1992 election by Brians and Wattenberg (1996).

During the 1972 election, Patterson and McClure (1976) interviewed citizens in the Syracuse, New York, area in early September and again in November. They found that people who claimed to regularly watch the network news increased their knowledge of candidate issue positions by 28 percent on average. But people who claimed to not watch network news at all gained about as much, 25 percent, indicating the network news had almost no effect. On the other hand, those who (by self-report) watched "many" political ads gained 36 percent in awareness of candidate issue position, compared to 25 percent among those who watched only "a few" ads. In 1992, Brians and Wattenberg found watching the network evening news was unrelated to knowledge of candidate issue positions, while watching political ads was a significant predictor (but only in October).[16]

While cynics often charge that political advertising is without substance and designed simply to fool the voters, research indicates that ads provide considerable information about candidate policy positions. Darrell West (2001) analyzed 429 prominent ads between the 1952 and 2000 presidential elections. Twenty-five percent of the ads addressed contained specific issue appeals; 26 percent of the ads for Republicans contained specific policy pledges, as did 20 percent of the ads for Democrats (West 2001, 48). While these are not large figures, they are sufficient to provide meaningful information to the electorate.

The reason the public learns virtually nothing about candidate issue positions from the network news is that the media frame the campaign not as a clash of ideas but as a strategic game. Issues are seldom covered, and even less often covered in any depth. Rather, the news media are fixated on the game of politics—the "horse race" (Patterson and McClure 1976). A consistent finding for elections in the past thirty years is that the primary focus of the network news is on who is leading, who is gaining, and who is losing electoral support, with stories often supported by polling data. Since television news pays little attention to issues, it is not surprising that viewers gain little substantive knowledge. As Larry Bartels (1988, 32) notes, "In covering a presidential campaign, the media tell us more about who is winning and losing than they do about who is fit to be president." Table 8.7 depicts the percentage of coverage of the horse race versus coverage of policy issues between 1988 and 2000 by the ABC, CBS, and NBC nightly news. If anything, television coverage of the game of politics is increasing. In 2000, 71 percent of the election news on these networks was essentially devoted to the horse race (compared to only 27 percent for the PBS *NewsHour with Jim Lehrer*). In the case of primary elections, in 1988, 49 percent of network news stories were devoted to the horse race, while in 2000 this increased to 78 percent (Farnsworth and Lichter 2003, 59).

The fascination of the media with election-year strategy and its disdain for serious analysis of candidate issue positions comes at a cost to the electorate. To the extent the media set the agenda—that is, tell the electorate what to think about—citizens are thinking about the game of politics and not about the issues. In fact, surveys show that while citizens are mostly ill informed about issue substance, they are quite well informed about who is ahead in the polls (Farnsworth and Lichter 2003). Candidates are thus hindered from promoting their qualifications and policy proposals, and citizens are hindered in learning them.

In elections, particularly primaries, horse-race journalism often leads to a bandwagon effect where candidates portrayed in the lead gain an advantage as undecided voters choose to go with the likely winner. Primary election winners receive a positive and dramatically disproportionate share of the post-election news coverage (Bartels 1988; Patterson 1994). In a democratic society,

TABLE 8.7	Horse-Race Coverage in Network News, 1988–2000 General Election News*			
Focus of Coverage	**1988**	**1992**	**1996**	**2000**
Horse Race	58%	58%	48%	71%
Policy Issues	40	37	32	39

*Stories can include a horse race and a policy focus (or neither focus); numbers therefore do not sum to 100 percent.

Source: Stephen J. Farnsworth and S. Robert Lichter, *The Nightly News Nightmare* (New York: Rowan-Littlefield, 2003), 51.

people need information in order to cast self-interested votes and hold office-holders accountable. The televisions newscasts, by focusing on strategy and largely ignoring the hard news, increase the disconnect between citizens' preferences and rational political action.

Horse-race journalism has not always characterized the media campaign coverage. Until the 1970s, reports on candidate issue positions more than held their own with reports of campaign conduct (Iyengar, Norpoth, and Hahn 2004). The most frequently identified reason for this change is the need the New Media have for novelty, currency, appealing pictures, and human interest stories—all of which feed into the corporate requirement to maximize profits. The proliferation of public opinion polls has accentuated this tendency. As we noted in chapter 2, two-thirds of all campaign stories include information from polls.[17] The evidence is mixed on whether the public really prefers horse-race journalism or wants the media to focus more on issue substance. Farnsworth and Lichter (2003) report a number of polls and other evidence supporting the claim that people really want more substance, while Iyengar et al. (2004) find that when given an unambiguous choice in a real-world setting, more people prefer strategic information than issue information.

Public Perceptions of the Media

Public perceptions of the media lean decidedly toward the negative. When the public was asked in 2002 and again in 2003 how much confidence it had in various American institutions, just 9 percent said it had a "great deal of confidence" in the news media, compared to 71 percent in the military, 49 percent in the president, 24 percent in the FBI, 18 percent in the public schools, and 12 percent in the IRS.[18] Negative perceptions of the press also seem to have risen over time. In 1985, only 34 percent said that "news organizations' stories and reports are often inaccurate." This increased to 62 percent by May 2003 (Gallup 2003). Other examples abound.[19]

Some degree of skepticism about the media is probably healthy. Still, if taken too far it can undercut the ability of the press to credibly inform the public in a fashion necessary for citizens to hold public officials accountable. Despite the numbers, there is reason to doubt the situation is as gloomy as it might appear. There is a tendency for partisans to see any unfriendly criticism in the media as media bias and, as we saw earlier, criticism is the norm in today's news. As we asked earlier, one can question whether perceptions of media bias conform to the facts.

Provocatively, Dalton, Beck, and Huckfeldt (1998) demonstrated there is a virtually no connection between the liberal-conservative tilt taken by newspapers and reader perceptions of that tilt. Dalton and his colleagues used content analysis and a representative sample of newspapers in forty counties to measure the actual ideological slant of the news and a survey to measure the perception of that slant by newspaper readers. They found no meaningful correspondence. What they did find was that strong Republicans saw their paper as slanted toward Clinton, and strong Democrats saw their paper as slanted toward Bush.

The results reported by Dalton et al. are consistent with a good deal of experimental research on the hostile media phenomenon, which holds that people are predisposed to see bias when the press covers topics important to them. In one study, two groups on opposite sides of the Middle East issue (either pro-Arab or pro-Israeli) were given a news story about conflict in the area and asked to evaluate it. Both sides tended to see the story as biased against their position. However, the two sides read exactly the same account (Vallone, Ross, and Lepper 1985).

8-7 CONCLUSION

Like citizens and politicians, the media has a crucial role to play in the American democracy. Self-government depends on the free exchange of ideas among reasonably well informed men and women. How the media provide the necessary information for this exchange of ideas in the years to come will have importance consequences for democratic accountability in the United States.

Developments in the past twenty years lend cause for both optimism and pessimism. The advent of multiple sources of political information can certainly be cause for optimism. Detailed information and in–depth analysis about political matters is there to be had for anyone who wants it. However, politics is a low priority for most Americans. They mostly look for shortcuts, and it is only rational for citizens to seek the minimal amount of information necessary to hold decision makers accountable. Unfortunately, in the Era of the New Media, the information that is easily found is often not very useful. The focus on candidate strategy and the horse race has almost no lasting educational value, it and provides virtually no useful policy insights upon which citizens might draw. And one cannot help but feel that the rampant negativity that characterizes the political news can only have a corrosive effect on the relations between citizens and government, although cause and effect have yet to be convincingly demonstrated.

The Era of the New Media is just beginning. With rapid advances in technology and some human ingenuity, it may yet be possible to make the political news appealing and profitable while at same time genuinely informative. However, even under the best of circumstances, one should not overestimate the influence of the media for either good or bad. There is virtually no convincing evidence that media effects are substantial. While the minimal effects model, taken to its extreme, is almost certainly not correct, the realistic alternative could perhaps be labeled something like *minimal effects plus a little bit more*.

NOTES

1. The term *yellow journalism* arose from the practice of the Hearst newspapers of presenting particularly inflammatory headlines in brightly colored print.
2. There is still debate over what actually sunk the *Maine*. The most plausible explanation is that the ship hit a mine, causing its munitions to explode. Other believe the cause was internal; perhaps its munitions were ignited by a spark from its boilers.

3. In academic circles, this school of thought is called *postmodernism*. In its most extreme form it is a philosophy that holds all knowledge is subjective. All that really matters is the interpretation placed on facts by those who hold political and economic power. So before Galileo, the "truth" was that the sun revolved around the earth because that was the "reality" forced on people by those who held political power.

4. Center for Media and Public Affairs, "Press Release," Oct. 30, 2000.

5. In 1960, the FCC asserted that news programming was "a major element . . . necessary to the public interest" (Baum 2003, 35).

6. For example, Viacom owns CBS, thirty television stations, the UPN network, five radio stations, Infinity Broadcasting, MTV, VH1, Nickelodeon, Showtime, Comedy Central, several movie companies including Paramount Studios, commercial Web sites, the book publishers Simon and Schuster, Free Press, and Pocket Books, theme parks, movie theaters, and advertising companies, just to name some of its holdings (Bennett 2003, 84).

7. When Westinghouse owned the CBS television network, the CEO of Westinghouse told *Advertising Age*, "We are here to serve advertisers. That is our raison d'être." It is not just the size of the audience that counts, it is demographic characteristics as well. Advertisers most desire an audience between ages twelve and thirty-five. These viewers have yet to make firm product choices, and advertising may affect those choices or convince them to try a new product. Those over thirty-five are thought to be more resistant to these messages (Berger 2003, 189).

8. As the size of the audience for network news declines, the remaining audience grows older. Between 1991 and 2003, the median age of television viewers rose from fifty-five to sixty. *Source:* Nielsen Media Research as reported in *New York Times*, Feb. 9, 2004, C6.

9. While households not wired for cable comprise a captive audience for television networks, the amount of news presented by broadcast networks has declined appreciably. Much political news of the type once reported by broadcast networks (e.g., coverage of party conventions) is now relegated to cable news networks.

10. The greater perception of a liberal than a conservative bias may be due to the louder voices on the political right who have complained for over thirty years that the media are too liberal. On the left, Alterman (2003) argues that conservative spokespeople have been "playing the ref," to use a basketball analogy. They keep calling fouls on the part of the media in the hope that a sensitized media will bend in their direction in the future.

11. Still another contributing factor to the news media's increased negativity is that they take the lead from the increased negativity of candidate advertising. As candidates increasingly run negative campaigns attacking their opponents, these attacks become part of the news story and hence reported by the media.

12. The Contras were fighting to overthrow the Marxist regime of Nicaraguan president Daniel Ortega.

13. In the 1992 election year, gross national product (GNP) grew by 2 percent, both inflation and unemployment were lower in 1984 when Ronald Reagan was reelected in a landslide, and the recession that began in July 1990 had ended by March 1991 (Hetherington 1996, 372).

14. Gilliam and Iyengar (2000) observe that while minorities were often presented as perpetrators of crime on the Los Angeles local news, their proportion of appearances closely matched their proportion of arrests in Los Angeles County.

15. Entmann (1989) says diversity of opinion on the front page is an indicator of liberalism because the majority of newspapers tend to be conservative in outlook. More diversity in stories mean a less homogeneously conservative tone to news coverage.
16. Patterson and McClure found reading about the campaign in the newspapers led to significant gains in political knowledge, although Brians and Wattenberg (1996) found no relationship. The latter speculate the policy content of newspapers was not as rich in 1992 as in 1972 when Patterson and McClure conducted their study.
17. As Stephanie Larson (2001) notes, one downside of the media's reliance on polls is inaccurate reporting, as many reporters do not properly interpret poll results. She gives a number of examples of how reporters come to wrong conclusions based on polling data.
18. Fox News Service polls. The FBI and IRS data are from 2002; the remainder are from 2003.
19. See the reports by the Pew Research Center at http://www.people-press.com, Media Monitor at http://www.aim.com, or the report by the American Association of Newspaper Editors (1999), *Examining our Credibility: Examining Credibility, Explaining Ourselves*, at http://www.asne.org.

9 | Elections as Instruments of Popular Control

In a democracy, the public supposedly controls the behavior of its public officials by exercising its influence at the ballot box in a rational fashion—in accordance with what we call the *rational-activist model*. Ideally, each voter selects the candidate who best represents his or her views on matters of public policy. At least in a two-candidate election, the collective choice is then the candidate who is closer to most voters on the issues. The policy result is the closest correspondence possible, given the choice of candidates, between the collective preferences of the electorate and government policy.

But representation of the public interest via democratic elections is not as simple in practice as it is in theory. It is possible, for instance, to hold elections in which none of the candidates on the ballot offer policy choices that voters find attractive. Even when the candidates present a relevant menu of policy choices, the electorate may—through some combination of misguidance, ignorance, and indifference—vote "irrationally" by voting into office a candidate who does not represent their interests. Also, if officeholders perceive that the electorate is not watching, or that it does not care, they may feel free to make policy decisions without consideration of public opinion.

Looking at the matter positively rather than negatively, we can state the conditions that *do* allow elections to be an effective instrument for inducing policy decisions that are responsive to public opinion. First, the candidates should offer a meaningful choice of policy options that appeal to voters, and once elected, the winner should try to carry out campaign pledges. Second, the voters should be informed about the issues that separate the candidates and vote for the candidate who best represents their own views. Clearly, the fulfillment of each of these conditions depends on the other. For example, political leaders pay the greatest attention to public opinion when they believe the public is alert enough to throw them out of office if they do not. Similarly, voters have the greatest opportunity to vote intelligently on the basis of policy issues when the politicians act on the assumption the public is going to do so.

In the present chapter, we examine the behavior of the electorate when it carries out its assigned responsibility. In chapter 10, we examine the responsiveness of political elites to public opinion.

9-1 POLITICAL CAMPAIGNS AND THE VOTER

During every political campaign, voters are bombarded with news and propaganda about the candidates who seek their favor. Judging by the attention politicians give to the voters at election time, one might conclude that the voter reacts to campaign stimuli in the same fluid manner as a consumer reacting to advertising stimuli in the mass media. Just as the person about to purchase a product, such as a detergent, might vacillate in his or her choice of brands until the moment of purchase, so might the voter waver between the candidates until entry into the voting booth forces a final decision. But as we saw in chapter 8, this image of the voting process underestimates the voter's ability to resist political messages.

As discussed in chapter 3, most American voters have a more or less permanent attachment to either the Republican or the Democratic party. It is through this filter of party identification that most voters view the partisan aspects of the political world. The anchor of party identification prevents most voters from wavering in their choice of candidates during a campaign, and they do not change the party they vote for from one election year to the next.

On a day-to-day or week-to-week basis over a campaign, vote choices tend to be stable. The greatest change is observed following major campaign events such as party conventions or candidate debates. Hillygus and Jackman's (2003) panel study of Internet respondents in the 2000 campaign finds only about 10 percent of prospective voters with a candidate choice prior to the two conventions or prior to the first debate changing their mind after the event. The vast majority of changers simply became undecided rather than switch to the other major candidate. Over the course of a fall campaign, few change from one major party's candidate to the other. Over a half-century of National Election Studies, 2,489 respondents were interviewed between forty-five and sixty days before the presidential election, offered a preference for a major party candidate, and then reported voting Democratic or Republican when interviewed again after the election. Only 7 percent of these respondents switched choices over the interval. Similarly, panel studies following voters over the four years between presidential elections show about 80 percent vote for the same party's presidential candidate both times (Converse 1962). In the NES's 1992–1996 panel, 21 percent of those who voted in both elections reported voting for the same presidential party both times. The percent deflates to 11 percent if third-party votes for Perot are excluded.

Below the presidential level, the percentage of voters who stick with their party's choice is even higher. For lower offices, the amount of information that reaches voters is often too slight to give them any reason to go against their party. Only in nonpartisan elections and primary contests (where party identification cannot be a criterion of choice) do voters vacillate in an erratic manner. In fact, vote preferences in primary contests are so fluid that pollsters have great difficulty predicting outcomes, even when they monitor opinion as late as a day or two before the election (Bartels and Broh 1989).

Of course, if party identification were the sole determinant of how people vote, election results would simply reflect the balance of Democratic and Republican identifiers. And since the ratio of Democratic to Republican identifiers changes only modestly in the short run, election results would be almost identical from one election to the next. In fact, election results often depart considerably from the voter division that would occur with a strict party-line vote.

When an election is decided on a party-line basis, the result is called the *normal vote*. At one time, the normal vote was considered a constant of politics. The calculation was that assuming a 50–50 split by Independents and a balanced, minimal defection rate by partisans (about 10 percent on each side), the nation-level normal vote would be a narrow Democratic win by about 54 percent Democratic to 46 percent Republican (Converse 1966; see also Petrocik 1989). This calculation reflects the Democratic edge in party identification that more than counterbalances the higher turnout rate among Republicans than Democrats.

Figure 9.1 presents a fifty-four-year approximation of the normal vote, between 1948 and 2002, derived from the national division of party identification.[1]

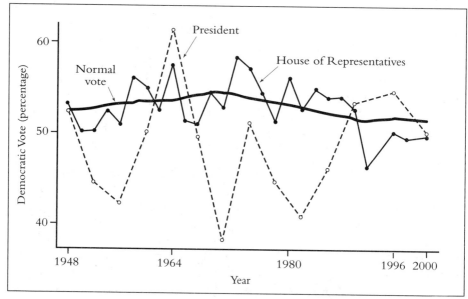

Figure 9.1   The national two-party vote (percent Democratic), 1948–2000.

Note the disappearance of the Democrats' once-dominant edge over the Republicans. Nationally, the normal vote is approximated by the national vote in congressional elections. As Figure 9.1 shows, the national House vote between 1948 and 1992 never varied from between 50 and 59 percent Democratic, averaging at the expected 54 percent Democratic. The Democrats' prior large advantage in party identification thus explains why the Democrats controlled the House of Representatives (and usually the Senate) for forty years running, from 1954 to 1994. In 1994 the Republicans suddenly gained control of the House after their forty-year drought. This could not have happened without a change in the normal vote brought about by Republican gains in party identification.

The difference between the actual vote and the normal vote represents the *short-term partisan forces* of the election. When it comes to voting for Congress, national issues are of only modest importance. National-level short-term forces are modest for congressional elections, so party control of Congress is largely determined by the normal vote. But for the presidency, short-term forces can be of major importance. As Figure 9.1 shows, the national vote for president often departs significantly from the normal vote. In fact, during the post–World War II era, the presidency has been won by the Republicans as often as by the Democrats.

Deviations of election results from the normal vote do not signify that the usual role of party identification in shaping election results has broken down. Instead, one finds that the party favored by short-term forces is the beneficiary of most of the short-term party defections, and it also wins the majority of the Independent vote. Figure 9.2 shows this pattern over the fourteen presidential elections from 1948 through 2000.

When short-term forces favor the Republicans, Democrats defect beyond their usual rate; Republicans are even more loyal to their party than usual, and Independents vote overwhelmingly Republican. With pro-Democratic short-term forces, the pattern is the reverse—with unusually frequent Republican defections and a Democratic trend among Independents.

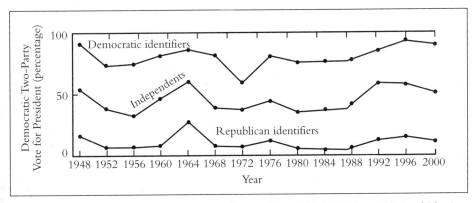

Figure 9.2 Party identification and the vote for president, 1948–2000. *Source:* National Election Studies election data.

Short-Term Forces Below the Presidential Level

For state and local elections, the normal vote reflects the partisan balance of the particular state or local constituency rather than the nation as a whole. Due to the kinds of people who reside in the area, the local normal vote often is one-sided in favor of the Republicans or Democrats. Election results reflect the local normal vote plus any short-term forces that carry over from national politics (or from higher-level state or local contests). In addition, the local vote reflects the short-term forces generated by the local candidates and their campaign. One way of thinking about local short-term forces is as the personal vote generated by the candidates themselves (Cain et al. 1987).

Although candidates for local office run less visible races than presidential candidates, their own campaigns help determine their electoral fate. The importance of local campaigns is indicated by the fact that as many as half the voters in a national election report that they split their ticket rather than vote for one party's candidate for all offices (Burden and Kimball 2002). Because of this ticket splitting, the same constituency often votes the Democratic candidate into one office and the Republican candidate into another.

As for president, election outcomes below the presidential level depend in large part on the short-term forces of the specific campaign. By one estimate, short-term forces for the statewide offices of governor and U.S. senator are about as large as for president (Erikson et al. 1994, ch. 9). The implication is that statewide (and perhaps local) outcomes readily depart by 10 or 15 percentage points from the state (or local) normal vote. Even where one party dominates, the disadvantaged party often can win when it fields the stronger candidate.

Who Are the Floating Voters?

Election outcomes are the result of both the normal vote and short-term partisan forces of the campaign. Voters whose choice is determined by the campaign rather than a long-term partisan commitment are called *floating voters*. An important question remains: How informed are the floating voters? If the floating voters were more politically informed than the average, we would think that election trends are essentially the response of the most politically alert segment of the public. But if the reverse is true—that floaters are *more* politically ignorant than the average—then we might be pushed toward the more dismal conclusion that election trends are largely the result of campaign propaganda of the sort that appeals to the voters least capable of making an informed evaluation.

Thanks to a classic article by Converse (1962) and a more recent elaboration by Zaller (1992; see also Alvarez 1997), we have a good but complicated theory regarding floating voters. Consider a candidate's decision to pitch the campaign at inattentive and unsophisticated voters or at attentive and sophisticated voters. On one hand, the more attentive voters are easier to reach with new campaign messages. On the other hand, these attentive voters are more hardened in their views. Their accumulated storage of political information helps bolster their initial views against intruding information. For example, a Republican who is highly informed about politics is better equipped to discount Democratic propaganda than one who is more politically ignorant. Less attentive voters are more easily swayed, but only if new information reaches them.

Given these complications, the information level of floating voters depends considerably on the intensity of the campaign and the flow of information. When the information flow is low, the least attentive voters are so uninformed that they lack any basis for switching between candidates. They vote according to their initial partisan predisposition, if they vote at all. Attentive voters, meanwhile, although more resistant to influence from campaign propaganda, sometimes change their candidate choice when new information reaches them. However, when the information flow is high, even the least attentive voters receive some information. Because these least attentive voters are the most influenced by new information they receive, they contribute disproportionately to electoral volatility.

The battle for the presidency attracts great interest and large voter turnout, with almost all voters receiving some campaign exposure. For example, awareness of the candidates' names is nearly universal during a presidential campaign. The universal intake of new information during a presidential campaign loosens a great number of voters from their partisan moorings—particularly among the least attentive voters. The tiny fraction of presidential voters who manage completely to avoid the campaign maintain stable candidate preferences throughout it. But setting these few cases aside, partisan defections and preelection wavering in candidate choice are most frequent among voters with the least exposure to the presidential campaign.

Table 9.1 illustrates the relationship between our information scale, introduced in chapter 3 and defined in the Appendix, and partisan defection in the 2000 presidential election. First, let us consider the Democratic identifiers in 2000. Although the vast majority voted for Gore, the few defectors were drawn mainly from "low" and "medium" information voters; "high information" Democrats were steadfast for Gore. Among Republicans too, the more informed were the most loyal to their party, with the least informed being more likely to defect from Bush to Gore.

Table 9.1 also shows the voting behavior of self-proclaimed Independents in the 2000 presidential election. In 2000, Independents were closely divided between Bush and Gore, a result that reflects the overall closeness of the election. In less close elections, Independents tend to flock to the winner, especially less informed Independents. In 1996, for instance, Clinton did well among all Independents, particularly the least informed. In 1988, the last time a Republican won a decisive presidential victory, the first President Bush did well among the Independents, especially the least informed.

Knowledgeable voters tend to sort as Democratic and Republican partisans based on their beliefs and stick to them. Less informed voters enter the campaign as relatively blank slates, available to persuasion by the short-term forces of the campaign. We see this when we follow the vote over the presidential elections from 1984 to 2000 separately for high-information voters and low-information voters. Among the NES's "highly informed" presidential voters

TABLE 9.1 | **Vote for President, 2000, by Information Level and Party Identification***

	Information		
	Low	**Medium**	**High**
Democratic identifiers			
Gore	92%	93%	98%
Bush	8	7	2
	100%	100%	100%
Independent identifiers			
Gore	41%	55%	40%
Bush	59	45	60
	100%	100%	100%
Republican identifiers			
Gore	11%	12%	5%
Bush	89	88	95
	100%	100%	100%

Source: National Election Studies, 2000 election data.

*Information scale based on correctness of relative placement of candidates on issues. For details, see the Appendix.

(by criteria similar to those used here for the 2000 election), the 1984–2000 trend in the two-party vote was slight:

	1984	**1988**	**1992**	**1996**	**2000**
% Dem. among High Info. Voters	44%	48%	56%	48%	48%

But among NES's low information voters, we see considerable volatility:

	1984	**1988**	**1992**	**1996**	**2000**
% Dem. among Low Info. Voters	44%	48%	61%	77%	63%

As Converse argues, it sometimes seems that "not only is the electorate as a whole quite uninformed, but it is the least informed members within the electorate who seem to hold the critical 'balance of power' in the sense that alternatives in the governing party depend disproportionately on shifts in their sentiment" (Converse 1962, 578).

We might even be tempted to conclude that the most effective presidential campaign would be one aimed directly at the voter who is normally inattentive and uninformed about politics. But recall that the inattentive voter is a less accessible target of campaign messages. Note, too, the tendency of the least informed to dilute their influence by not voting. Based on self-reports, the 2000 vote turnout within the least- and most-informed categories was as follows:

	Low Information	High Information
Voted	45%	85%
Did not vote	55	15
	100%	100%

The electoral contribution of the least-informed citizens is diluted by their low motivation to vote.

9-2 POLICY ISSUES AND VOTERS

Despite our current knowledge about voting behavior, scholars do not fully agree on the precise role of policy issues in elections. From what we know about the capabilities of average American voters, we are not surprised that many scholars are skeptical of the capacity of candidates' policy proposals and ideological leanings to affect many voter decisions. Among the most pessimistic are the authors of *The American Voter*, undoubtedly the single most influential book on voting behavior. They found the electorate almost wholly without detailed information on the issues of the day, unable to judge the rationality of government policies, and unable to appraise the appropriateness of the means necessary to arrive at desirable ends (Campbell et al. 1960, 543).

The American Voter, however, was based on the two Eisenhower elections from the quiescent 1950s. Several studies of more recent elections—most notably *The Changing American Voter*—offer a rather different interpretation of the capabilities of the American voter (Nie et al. 1976).[2] Beginning with the Johnson-Goldwater election of 1964, political issues and political ideology have become increasingly important as determinants of the vote in the United States. The reason for this growth of issue voting is that parties and candidates have become more polarized on liberal versus conservative lines. But just how important issues have become remains controversial.

For voters to be influenced by policy issues when they cast their ballots, two conditions must be met. First, the voters must be aware of the differences between the policy views of the candidates. Second, the voters must be motivated to vote on the basis of the issues that divide the candidates. Evidence of issue voting is strongest when the divergence between the candidate stances is strong and the issue is of considerable importance to the electorate.

Here, we examine the evidence of policy voting in presidential elections. Most of the data analysis that follows is from the National Election Studies (NES) survey of the 2000 presidential election. As measured via survey analysis, the degree of issue voting in 2000 was typical of recent presidential elections.

Voter Perceptions of Candidate Differences, 2000

A necessary condition for voting on the basis of candidates' policy positions is that the voters perceive actual policy differences between the candidates. Following the usual procedure of NES surveys, in 2000 the NES researchers asked respondents for their perceptions of the presidential candidates' positions on a series of seven-point scales representing several issues. Table 9.2 arranges these data to show how voters rated the Democratic candidate (and popular vote winner), Al Gore, relative to his Republican opponent (and electoral vote winner), George W. Bush.

Individuals could rate Gore to the left of Bush (correct), rate Bush to the left of Gore (incorrect), or place the two candidates in a tie (presumably incorrect). Additionally, on each issue scale some voters (generally around 25 percent) gave incomplete ratings, claiming not to know the position of one or both of the major candidates.

Table 9.2 shows that when voters perceived the candidates to be different on an issue, they almost invariably saw Gore to the left of Bush. Still, voters often rated the candidates the same or gave incomplete ratings. On all issues, however, a majority of voters ordered the candidates correctly. The sharpest perception was on the liberal-conservative ideology scale, where 71 percent saw Gore to the left of Bush.

The respondent ratings of candidate ideology shown in Table 9.2 provided the basis for classification on our information index. Among voters in the 2000 election, 25 percent were "high-information" scorers, meaning they saw Gore to Bush's left on all five items shown in Table 9.2. "Low-information" scorers constitute 33 percent of the voting total, and they score in the guess range regarding net candidate placement (see the Appendix). The remaining 42 percent were in between. Thus, roughly speaking, a fourth of the voting electorate is clearly tuned in to the candidates' ideological differences, another third is not, with the remainder somewhere in between. As usual, our picture of the electorate is mixed.

TABLE 9.2	Voter Perceptions of Issue Differences Between Presidential Candidates, 2000		
	Gore Left of Bush	Bush Left of Gore	Same or incomplete ratings
Liberal/conservative ideology	73	16	11
Domestic spending	71	10	19
Defense spending	53	15	31
Abortion	54	13	31
Environment	61	7	31

Source: National Election Studies, 2000 election data. Each percentage is based on voters only.

Policy Issues, Ideology, and Votes, 2000

In order to vote on the basis of policy issues, it is not enough for voters to become aware of the candidates' policy differences. In addition, they must find these choices sufficiently important to influence their vote choices. With policy voting, we would observe people voting for the candidate closest to their own views. This would usually mean liberals voting Democratic and conservatives voting Republican.

Table 9.3 presents simple evidence of policy voting in the 2000 presidential election. This table shows that over a variety of issues, voters who prefer the liberal position gave the most support to Gore, while voters preferring the conservative position gave the most support to Bush. Some of the issues shown were actively discussed in the 2000 campaign, with the candidates taking divergent stands. Of these, the one on which the candidates most sharply diverged during the campaign was the matter of spending and services by the national government. Reflecting the traditional positions of their parties, Gore favored more spending while Bush favored less spending, with lower taxes. It should not surprise, therefore, that of the issue items examined, opinions on government spending had the seemingly strongest impact on the presidential vote; while about three-quarters of spending liberals chose Gore over Bush, over 80 percent of the spending conservatives made the opposite choice of Bush over Gore.

Environmental policy, also an active issue of the campaign, was a distant second in terms of predicting candidate choice. Among the issues shown, the least division in presidential voting was found on the death penalty. Although capital punishment may be a major issue to many Americans, the two 2000 presidential candidates did not divide on this issue except for minor nuances (both favored the death penalty). Perhaps as a result, the differences in presidential voting by death penalty advocates and opponents were more muted than for other issues.

Because so many issues seem to matter, we should be able to improve our vote predictions by taking into account voter positions on many issues simultaneously rather than one issue at a time. Table 9.4 shows the relationship between general liberal-conservative ideology and the 2000 vote two ways.

First, the table shows the vote as a function of ideological self-identification, where ideological identification is measured using the full seven-point scale from "extremely liberal" to "extremely conservative." Ideological identification predicts fairly well, particularly for voters on the liberal side of the spectrum. Of the 23 percent who placed themselves at one of the three positions on the liberal side of the spectrum, 92 percent voted for Gore over Bush. Of the 37 percent on the conservative side, 84 percent chose Bush over Gore. Thus, for most voters with an ideological leaning, the vote choice was in line with the ideological preference. But not all voters identify with one of the ideological sides. Of the 40 percent of voters either moderate or without an ideological preference, almost two-thirds chose Gore over Bush.[3]

The second part of Table 9.4 shows the vote as a function of a ten-item composite liberal-conservative index introduced in chapter 3. Here the degree

TABLE 9.3	2000 Presidential Vote by Policy Opinions			
Policy	Gore (%)	Bush (%)	(%)	Difference
Domestic Spending				
More	76	24	= 100%	+ 50
Less	16	84	= 100%	
Environmental Regulation				
More	66	34	= 100%	+ 43
Less	23	76	= 100%	
Defense Spending				
Less	80	20	= 100%	+ 39
More	41	59	= 100%	
Guaranteed Standard of Living				
Favor	78	22	= 100%	+ 35
Oppose	43	57	= 100%	
National Health Care				
Favor	72	28	= 100%	+ 35
Oppose	37	63	= 100%	
Gun Control				
Favor	67	33	= 100%	+ 33
Oppose	34	68	= 100%	
Laws Protecting Gays				
Favor	63	37	= 100%	+ 31
Oppose	32	68	= 100%	
Abortion				
Permit	65	35	= 100%	+ 30
Restrict	35	65	= 100%	
Aid to Blacks				
Favor	74	26	= 100%	+ 29
Oppose	45	55	= 100%	
Death Penalty				
Favor	70	30	= 100%	+ 25
Oppose	45	55	= 100%	

Source: National Election Studies, 2000 election data. Votes for minor-party candidates are ignored.

of prediction is, if anything, even better. The ten–item scale has a 21–point range from −10 (perfect liberal) to +10 (perfect conservative). Among the 14 percent who are on the far left, from −5 to −10, more than 90 percent voted for Gore over Bush. Similarly, among the 17 percent who are on the far right, from +5 to +10, over 90 percent chose Bush.

TABLE 9.4 | Presidential Vote by Two Summary Measures of Liberalism–Conservatism, 2000

Self-Identification on Ideological Scale

	Extremely Liberal						Extremely Conservative	
	1	2	3	4	5	6	7	None
Gore (%)	95	96	84	64	23	12	9	67
Bush (%)	5	4	15	36	77	88	91	33
(Percentage of voters)	(2)	(12)	(9)	(25)	(13)	(21)	(4)	(15)

Ten-Item Composite Issue Index★

	Most Liberal						Most Conservative
	+10 to −8	−7 to −5	−4 to −2	−1 to +1	+2 to +4	+5 to +7	+8 to +10
Gore (%)	100	90	82	57	35	8	7
Bush (%)	0	10	18	43	65	92	93
(Percentage of voters)	(3)	(11)	(22)	(25)	(22)	(12)	(5)

Source: National Election Studies, 2000 election data.

★For construction of the ten-item composite issue index, see the Appendix.

From this demonstration, voters with consistently liberal or conservative views are highly predictable in their vote choice. But most voters are not at either ideological extreme. One-fourth are near the exact center—in the −1 to +1 range on the ten-point scale—and must be described as decidedly moderate or centrist. Many others appear only vaguely liberal or conservative, and their votes do not always follow from their ideological direction.

In part, the predictability of votes from ideology as shown in Table 9.4 is due to voters simply responding to their partisan background. Liberals tend to identify with the Democratic party and conservatives with the Republicans (chapter 3). Thus, just by voting their party identification, voters tend to support the candidates closest to their views. Issue voting is further enhanced by party defections and issue voting by Independents. Table 9.5 illustrates this by showing the relationships between ideology and the vote within the three categories of party identification.

Conservative Democrats and liberal Republicans, while rare, are the partisan groups most prone to defect in their presidential voting. Meanwhile, Independents present the clearest example of issue voting. Neutral in terms of partisanship, they generally vote Democratic if liberal and Republican if conservative.

TABLE 9.5	2000 Presidential Vote by Ideology with Party Identification Controlled								
	Democrats			Independents			Republicans		
	Ideological Self-Identification								
	Lib.	Mod.	Con.	Lib.	Mod.	Con.	Lib.	Mod.	Con.
Gore (%)	99	91	90	85	52	15	43	25	2
Bush (%)	1	9	10	15	48	85	57	75	98
(Percentage of voters)	(17)	(12)	(5)	(8)	(13)	(12)	(1)	(4)	(2)
	Democrats			Independents			Republicans		
	*Ten-Item Issue Index**								
	Lib.	Center	Con.	Lib.	Center	Con.	Lib.	Center	Con.
Gore (%)	95	96	78	77	51	17	55	17	1
Bush (%)	5	4	22	23	49	83	45	83	99
(Percentage of voters)	(15)	(19)	(8)	(4)	(16)	(2)	(10)	(9)	(17)

Source: National Election Studies, 2000.

*Ideology scale collapsed so -10 to -3 = liberal; -2 to $+2$ = center; $+3$ to $+10$ = conservative.

Information and Ideological Voting

As one would expect, ideological voting is most prevalent among voters who are highly informed about candidate positions. In surveys, the observed relationship between ideology and vote choice becomes most pronounced when we select the most informed voters (Knight 1985; Jacoby 1991; Lyons and Scheb 1992; Pierce 1993). Figure 9.3 illustrates how issue voting rises with information.

The figure divides year 2000 respondents into those low, medium, and high on our scale of information about candidate differences on issues. For each group, Figure 9.3 shows the relationship between the ten-item index of respondent liberalism-conservatism and the vote. Graphed percentages represent the Gore proportion of the two-party vote.

The graph shows that the sharpness of the tendency for liberals to vote Democratic and conservatives to vote Republican varies with the voters' level of information. Among the "high-information" voters, there were few exceptions to the rule that liberals voted Democratic and conservatives Republican. In fact, even a slight ideological tilt (in the -2 to -4 or $+2$ to $+4$ range) was sufficient to push most informed voters to vote consistent with their ideological tendency. Among "medium-information" voters, ideological voting is also present, although in a more muted form. Among "low-information" voters, we see the mildest tendency toward ideological voting.

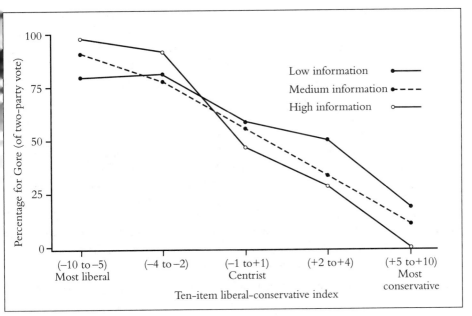

Figure 9.3   Issue voting by level of information, 2000. *Source:* National Election Studies, 2000 election data.

We learn from this exercise that when voters are informed about the ideological differences among candidates, ideology is a strong influence on vote choice. The degree to which voters choose candidates based on ideology depends in large part on the degree of ideological division between the candidates and the degree to which these differences are publicized. When Democratic and Republican candidates are similar ideologically, ideological differences between Democratic and Republican voters are also slight beyond those that derive from voting on the basis of party identification. Studies of different elections (e.g., Nie et al. 1976) show that the stronger the candidates' ideological differences, the more ideological voting follows. [4]

Easy Versus Hard Issues

For voters, questions of public policy are hard issues in the sense that they require a certain amount of attention and sophistication. Many voters lack the political resources necessary to monitor and evaluate the candidates' policy proposals. Recall from chapter 3 that no more than a quarter of the electorate (sometimes less) can be classified as sophisticated ideologues who evaluate parties and candidates in left-right policy terms. But even if unsophisticated voters do not make judgments about the desirability of specific policies, they can evaluate candidates in terms of relatively easy issues. One example of an easy issue evaluation is whether a candidate appears to favor or represent the interests of certain groups more than others. This, recall from chapter 3, is a group benefit response to voting. Another easy kind of issue evaluation is to decide whether conditions seem good or bad under the incumbent or incumbent party. This, recall from chapter 3, is nature-of-the-times voting. Neither group benefit nor nature-of-the-times voting requires direct knowledge of either specific policies or what the candidates claim they would do if elected. But each allows the voter to cast a seemingly informed vote with a minimum of information costs.

Group-Based Voting   Voters can orient themselves to parties and candidates on the basis of which groups they are for or against. In this way, voters must recognize which groups they like and dislike and learn the party with which each of these groups is aligned. No investment in determining candidate positions or the relative benefits from these is required. Group-based voting is voting on the basis of "ideology-by-proxy" (Campbell et al. 1960, 219–220). For example, a relatively prosperous citizen can learn to vote Republican simply by adopting the belief that Republicans favor the rich. In this way, our prosperous citizen votes the same as if he or she were able to develop a conservative ideology to rationalize economic self-interest.

Nature-of-the-Times Voting   Still another voter shortcut is nature-of-the-times voting—evaluating whether times are good or bad (or will improve or worsen) and rewarding or punishing the incumbent party accordingly. Especially when little other information is available, the recent performance of the incumbent (or incumbent party) may be the best forecast of future prospects under a continuation of the existing regime. Nature-of-the-times voters may not have specific policies in mind, but they can throw the rascals out if the obvious signs indicate that it is time, in Campbell's words, to let "a new bunch of fellows run things for a while" (1964, 755).

The National Election Studies (NES) regularly asks its respondents to evaluate the recent economy, asking whether over the previous year the nation's economy "has gotten better, stayed the same, or gotten worse." Responses to this question are usually consistent with vote choice, as in 2000:

Vote	Economy has gotten better	Economy has stayed about the same	Economy has gotten worse
Gore	69%	45%	33%
Bush	31	55	67
	100%	100%	100%
Percentage of voters	(39)	(46)	(14)

With far more voters acknowledging a growing economy (39 percent) than saying it has gotten worse (14 percent), the perception of a good economy worked in Vice President Gore's favor. Two-thirds of those saying the economy had grown voted for Gore, while two-thirds of the smaller group who insisted the economy was moving backward voted for Bush. Clearly, the perception of prosperity under President Clinton helped Vice President Gore at the polls. Still, these numbers may exaggerate the actual influence of economic perception on vote choice. One reason for the consistency between economic perception and vote choice in surveys is that respondents often respond to economic questions with rationalizations of their vote choice. For instance, a respondent who has signaled enthusiasm for the president may feel a need to praise the president's economy out of a need to appear consistent. But even allowing for this source of contamination, economic perceptions account for many vote choices. A bad economy allowed Clinton to defeat the first President Bush in 1992, and a good economy helped give Clinton a second term in 1996. In 2000, the economy helped Gore—but not enough to put him in the White House.[5]

Candidate Evaluations

Still another important set of voter motivations has nothing to do with issues. We refer to voters' evaluations of the personal characteristics and leadership abilities of the candidates. Simply put, voters tend to support candidates whom they like and trust. Whether a voter likes a candidate may transcend policy differences or even overcome a strong party identification.

To examine candidate evaluations in the 2000 presidential contest, we turn to the open-ended evaluations of candidates. NES respondents were asked to articulate up to five likes and dislikes about Gore and Bush. Here we consider only open-ended responses to a candidate's personal characteristics—from leadership and experience (e.g., "Bush is a proven leader") and personal characteristics (e.g., "Gore cares"; "Gore can't be trusted"). Respondents are coded as pro-Gore if their Gore-likes and Bush-dislikes outnumber their Bush-likes and Gore-dislikes. The opposite pattern was scored pro-Bush. Many respondents were neutral in their evaluations.[6] Net candidate evaluations predict year 2000 votes as follows:

Vote	Like Gore better	Neutral	Like Bush better
Gore	83%	59%	16%
Bush	17	41	84
	100%	100%	100%
Percentage of voters	(32)	(36)	(32)

In terms of personal attributes, Gore and Bush were equally attractive to the electorate, and most voters with a preference in terms of personal characteristics voted for the candidate they liked best. Among the 36 percent with neutral candidate evaluations, Gore slightly outpolled Bush.

Prediction and Causation

Policy issues, ideological identifications, group attitudes, retrospective evaluations, candidate evaluations, and party identifications all seem to predict the vote. The more variables we take into account, the better the prediction. To see that most votes can be predicted, let us simultaneously predict year 2000 presidential votes from the three best predictors: (1) party identification, (2) the ten-issue ideological scale, and (3) net candidate evaluations. We simply score each predictor as pro–Democratic, neutral, or pro–Republican, and sum them to make a scale from −3 (liberal Democrats who like Gore better) to +3 (conservative Republicans who like Bush better). The results are shown in Table 9.6.

Table 9.6 scores 17 percent at zero with balanced positions on the three predictors; these seemingly neutral voters gave a slight margin to Gore over Bush, 54 to 46 percent, evidently due to other factors such as the good economy. For the remaining 83 percent with a partisan tilt to their relevant attitudes, the vast majority—92 percent—voted in accord with the direction of their partisan attitudes. At the extreme, one-tenth of the voters found all three relevant attitudes in partisan agreement; they were either liberal Democrats who liked Gore better or conservative Republicans who liked Bush better. Of these 96 respondents, all but one (99 percent) voted in accord with their partisan attitudes. The lesson to be learned is that when voters possess consistent reasons to vote one way or another, their votes are usually consistent with those reasons.[7]

We must be cautious, however, in attributing causal connections. Voters have a need to maintain cognitive consistency between their partisan attitudes and their vote. Of course, the obvious way to achieve this consistency is to vote according to one's partisan attitude. The problem is that when people decide whom to vote for, they may also rearrange their political attitudes to fit their vote decision. Once citizens decide to vote Republican, for example, they tend to develop new attitudes even more favorable to the Republican point of view. Thus, when a Bush supporter asserts the economy is going well, that Bush is a great leader, or that Bush is right on the issues, we might suspect that some of these attitudes are generated to support the vote choice rather than the reverse. Of special concern is the voters' need to maintain cognitive

TABLE 9.6	Predicting 2000 Presidential Votes from the Summary of Partisan Attitudes						
	Pro-Gore			Neutral		Pro-Bush	
	− 3	− 2	− 1	0	+ 1	+ 2	+ 3
Gore (%)	98	96	87	54	16	2	0
Bush (%)	2	4	13	46	84	98	100
	100	100	100	100	100	100	100
(Percentage of voters)	(4)	(18)	(22)	(17)	(16)	(17)	(5)

Source: National Election Studies, 2000 election data.

Note: Index scores represent sum of partisan directions (+ = Republican, − = Democratic) on party identification, ten-item ideological scale, and net candidate evaluations. −3 voters are liberal Democrats who like Gore better. +3 voters are Republicans who like Bush better.

consistency between their issue stances, their perceptions of the candidates' issue stances, and their choice of candidate.

Consider the voter whose views are initially out of alignment—for example, the voter might have liberal views combined with an initial attraction to the more conservative Republican candidate. How this voter would resolve this dilemma depends on which of the three elements—perceptions of the candidates, policy views, and candidate preference—is the weakest link. If the voter feels strongly about his or her policy views and is certain the favored candidate opposes them, the voter could resolve the dilemma by reversing the candidate choice. This would be an example of policy voting. If the candidate's stands are only vaguely known, the easiest way out might be to shift one's estimate of the candidate stances. This process, known as *projection*, is a frequent way out of the dilemma. Voters who see conservative candidates as liberals or vice versa are often projecting their favored views onto their favored candidates (or projecting views they dislike onto candidates they dislike).[8]

A third possible resolution would be for the voter to change a relatively weak policy stance to make it consistent with the position of the favored candidate. Because of such *rationalization*, it becomes impossible to disentangle fully the causal process that produces a correlation between voters' policy views and their candidate choice. Consider, for example, the many voters in 2000 observed to be both conservatives and Bush supporters. Presumably conservatives supported Bush because they were attracted to his conservatism. But in theory, part of the explanation could be that liking Bush—for whatever reason—made his supporters think better of his policy positions.

Does rationalization seriously contaminate survey analyses of the vote? Every report of a relationship between voter attitudes and voter decisions should be read cautiously with an eye to the possibility that the seeming evidence of policy voting may be contaminated by widespread voter rationalization. Probably, however, electoral analysts err on the side of caution. Elaborate statistical analyses suggest that concern about voter rationalizations may be overdrawn (Page and Jones 1979; Markus and Converse 1979; Markus 1982). Still, we cannot be sure.

9-3 EXPLAINING ELECTION OUTCOMES

Explaining election outcomes requires a different level of analysis than explaining voter decisions. At the microlevel, analysts try to account for why people vote the way they do. At the macrolevel, analysts try to account for short-term forces and electoral trends—for example, why Clinton beat Dole in 1996. The variables that explain individual decisions at the microlevel are often insufficient to account for macrolevel electoral change. For example, we have emphasized the role of voters' liberal-conservative ideologies and party identifications for predicting microlevel voting decisions. But aggregated to the national level, shifts in macro ideology (e.g., mood; see chapter 4) and macro party identification ordinarily are dwarfed by the volatility of other electoral variables.[9] As we saw in chapter 4, the public shows some volatility in the liberalism or conservatism of the national mood. Similarly, the nation's aggregate party identification undergoes continual small shifts as the electorate responds to party performance. Although mood and partisanship can be shown to affect national elections via statistical analysis (Erikson, MacKuen, and Stimson 2002), their impact is limited in the short run. For instance, between 1996 and 2000 there was insufficient change in net ideology or net partisanship to account for reversal of party fortunes at the presidential level. To identify causes of electoral change, we must look to the variables that change the most from one election to the next: the nature of the times and the candidates themselves.

Changing Economic Evaluations

Recall that voters are often motivated by their reaction to the nature of the times—their personal evaluation of government performance and their attribution to the presidential party. The electorate's net evaluation of the nature of the times is partially captured by its evaluation of the president. Especially when the incumbent president runs for reelection, a useful electoral predictor is simply the incumbent president's popularity as Election Day approaches. An axiom of politics is that when presidents seek reelection, an approval rating above 50 percent (Eisenhower, Johnson, Nixon, Reagan, Clinton) is followed by victory, while an approval rating below 50 percent (Ford, Carter, the first Bush) augurs defeat. As we saw in chapter 4, foreign policy helps drive presidential approval. Presidents gain popularity when they are seen as coping with foreign policy crises. George W. Bush's boost in the aftermath of 9/11 is the most visible example. However, prolonged wars (e.g., Vietnam), prolonged crises (e.g., the Iran hostage crisis), and foreign policy folly (Iran-Contra) certainly do not help. The perceived management of the economy is a particularly important aspect of presidential popularity. Beyond its effect on presidential popularity, the degree of economic prosperity is a key determinant of presidential election results. Prosperity on Election Day benefits the incumbent presidential party regardless of whether the president seeks reelection.

The effects of the economy on presidential elections can be observed directly. For thirteen post–World War II elections, Figure 9.4 graphs the vote (for the incumbent party) as a function of per capita income growth in the election year. Clearly, the more the election year growth in per capita income, the stronger the national vote for the president's party. It might even seem that all a president must do for his party to win the next election is to time the upward swings of the economic cycle to coincide with election years in the political cycle. Perhaps fortunately, it is not always that simple. Some presidents (e.g., Carter and the first Bush) have found themselves presiding over election-year economic recessions instead of prosperity. And the incumbent party does not win with great regularity anyway. Of the fourteen presidential elections from 1948 through 2000, the incumbent party won seven and lost seven.

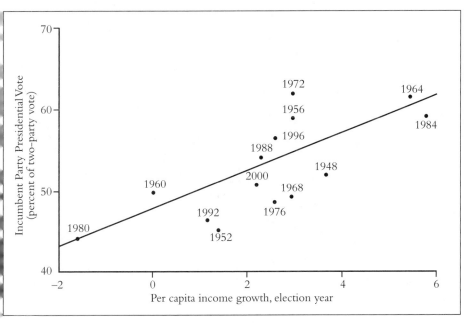

Figure 9.4   Presidential vote by income growth, 1948–2000.

Changing Candidate Evaluations

One important source of changing short-term electoral forces is the changing cast of candidates. For election to any level of office, the personal attractiveness of the major-party candidates can be a decisive factor. At the presidential level, the electorate's attraction to the Republican and the Democratic candidates can vary dramatically from one election to the next. Using multivariate statistical techniques, analysts have generated estimates of the net contributions of presidential candidates' personal attractiveness to presidential election outcomes.[10] The estimates are generated from NES respondents' candidate evaluations from the likes and dislikes expressed about candidates' personalities and leadership abilities.

Figure 9.5 presents the estimated candidate effects, 1952 to 1992. As the figure shows, the public's evaluations of candidate personalities and capabilities constitute a major determinant of electoral change. The most popular candidate of recent decades was Dwight ("Ike") Eisenhower, elected twice in the 1950s. Eisenhower was a popular World War II general who engaged the voters with his warm smile. Most candidates have been favorably viewed by voters, but not to the extent that the 1950s voters "liked Ike." Two candidates who were viewed particularly negatively were Barry Goldwater (Republican in 1964) and George McGovern (Democrat in 1972). According to the estimates, each cost their party about 4 percentage points just in terms of likeability and leadership. Each lost in a major landslide.[11]

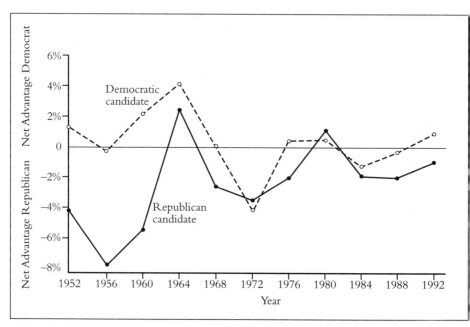

Figure 9.5   Partisan advantage accruing from candidate evaluations, 1952–1992. *Source:* Michael R. Kagay and Greg A. Caldeira, "A Reformed Electorate? Well at Least a Changed Electorate, 1972–1976," in William J. Crotty, ed., *Paths to Political Reform* (Lexington, MA: D. C. Heath, 1979); updated for 1980–1992 by Mark Wattier.

Candidate Issue Positions

Changing candidates provide more than a revolving set of personal attributes for the voter to judge. Each new candidate also brings a new set of policy positions. Even though the electorate is relatively fixed in its policy preferences, candidate positions do change. With each change of candidate, the shift in policy position can change the equation regarding which candidate is closest to the electorate's net preferences. Shifting candidate positions allow policy issues to affect election outcomes. Let us examine how.

Part of the popular lore of politics is that in a two-person race, the candidate who stakes out the middle ground of the political spectrum will win by virtue of appealing to the moderate voter. In terms of their personal views, candidates tend to be more liberal (Democrat) or conservative (Republican) than their electorate. Yet the belief that moderate voters decide elections pushes candidates toward the center of the spectrum.

This logic is spelled out in a model of the vote developed by Anthony Downs (1958, ch. 8) and illustrated in Figure 9.6. This figure presents voter positions as a bell-shaped distribution on the liberal-conservative spectrum. The Downs model assumes policy voters who prefer the candidate closest to their views on this spectrum. If both candidates are stationed near the center, as in Figure 9.6(a), neither will have the policy edge. But if one candidate veers

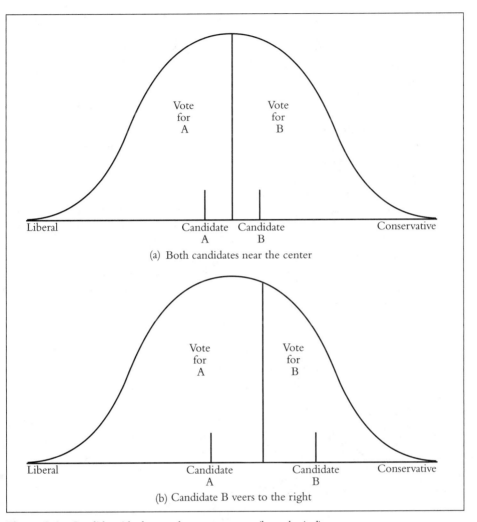

Figure 9.6   Candidate ideology and voter responses (hypothetical).

toward one of the ideological extremes—as does the conservative in Figure 9.6(b)—then policy voters in the middle will support the opponent, giving that more moderate candidate the victory.

The Downs model predicts that Democratic candidates get more votes when they take moderate rather than liberal positions and that Republican candidates get more votes when they take moderate rather than conservative positions. These hypotheses have received considerable support in research on congressional (U.S. House and Senate) elections (Erikson 1971; Johannes and McAdams 1981; Wright and Berkman 1986; Erikson and Wright 2001a; Erikson and Wright 2001b; Canes-Wrone, Brady, and Cogan 2002).

Legislators create their own record of roll-call votes, which can be arrayed on a scale from 100 percent liberal to 100 percent conservative. Both Democrats and Republicans usually get ideological satisfaction from voting with their party's ideological extreme, but they gain electoral benefit from moderation. By one estimate, this electoral benefit is almost 2 percentage points for each 10 percentage points of roll-call moderation (Erikson and Wright 2001b). One can extrapolate that Congress members in the middle of the ideological spectrum generate almost 10 percentage points more of the vote than they would at their party's ideological extreme.

Table 9.7 offers a simple illustration. The 2000 presidential election was both sufficiently close and sufficiently partisan so that in House districts, the presidential vote is a reasonable surrogate for the district normal vote. We can then compare extremist and moderate Congress members of each party to see how they fared in the 2000 election compared to the normal vote, as proxied by the district vote for president. Table 9.7 shows that for Republicans, the more liberal the member (as measured by the rating of the liberal Americans for Democratic Action), the greater the lead over Bush. Similarly, for Democrats, the more conservative the member, the greater the lead over Gore.

If congressional contests can be decided by candidate ideology, the same must certainly be true for presidential elections. We have already seen that citizens' votes are determined by their personal positions on the left-right scale. Presidential election outcomes are partially determined by both the voters' and the candidates' ideological positions—which candidates (and which parties) best reflect the preferences of the voting electorate.

To shed some light, we can examine NES survey data. Since 1972, respondents have been asked not only to place themselves on the seven-point version

---

TABLE 9.7 | **Vote for House Incumbents (as Lead over Presidential Ticket) by Incumbent Liberalism, 2000.**

Republican Incumbents' Liberalism (ADA Index)

	0–9% (most conservative)	19–19%	20–29%	30% and higher (least conservative)
Mean Lead over Bush in District (N in parentheses)	+ 7.0% (99)	+ 8.8% (35)	+ 13.2% (19)	+ 15.9% (13)

Democratic incumbents' liberalism (ADA index)

	91–100% (most liberal)	81–90%	71–80%	70% and less (least liberal)
Mean Lead over Gore in District (N in parentheses)	+ 5.6% (29)	+ 6.1% (59)	+ 10.2% (32)	14.1% (49)

Note: The ADA index measures the frequency of liberal votes on House of Representative roll calls in 2000, on a scale from 0 percent liberal (i.e., 100 percent conservative) to 100 percent liberal.

of the ideological scale but also to locate the two major presidential candidates as well. Figure 9.7 traces the historical record, comparing the mean positions over time of the electorate and also the candidates as they are perceived by the NES voters.

Of the eight elections shown in Figure 9.7, the 1972 contest stands out as one clear case where most voters were closer ideologically to one candidate than the other. In 1972, Richard Nixon was decisively reelected over the Democratic nominee, George McGovern, who most voters saw as too liberal. Figure 9.7 also shows that in elections since 1972, the average voter was close to the midpoint

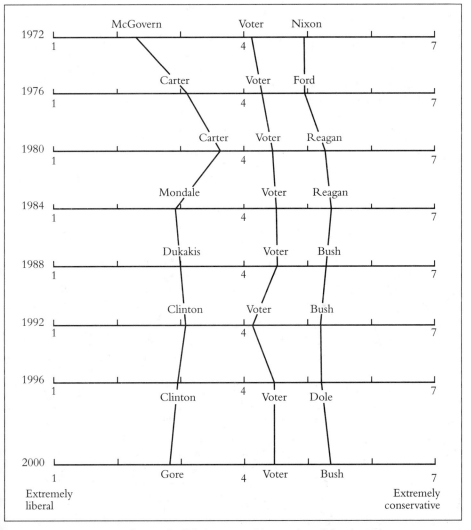

Figure 9.7   Mean ratings by voters of their own positions and candidates' positions on seven-point liberal-conservative scales, 1972–2000. *Source:* National Election Studies data.

between the mean perceptions of the two candidates' positions. A close scan of the figure also shows that in all but one contest (1980), voters were slightly closer ideologically to the Republican than to the Democratic candidate. But this may be deceptive. Voters comfortable with ideological language tend to vote Republican, and on average about as Republican as their relative ideological proximity from the candidates suggests. Some voters do not rate themselves or the candidates ideologically in NES surveys. Those voters are ideologically liberal, tend toward liberal positions on specific issues, and vote Democratic. Moreover, if we look at voter evaluations of candidate positions on specific issues rather than general ideology, they give the edge to the Democrats on some issues (e.g., abortion) and to the Republicans on others (e.g., affirmative action).[12]

In the final analysis, what can we say about the role of issues and ideology in deciding election outcomes? Most political analysts and candidates believe that ideological issues divide Americans and that voters evaluate the ideological positions of candidates when they go to the polls. Because issues and ideology matter, ideological mood swings by the public and the ideological responses of candidates and party leaders contribute to the relative fortunes of the Democratic and Republican parties in American politics. Moreover, the belief that issues and ideology matter drives politicians to respond to changes in public preferences when they become visible. We examine how politicians respond to public opinion in the next chapter.

9-4 CONCLUSION

When the rational-activist model is fulfilled, elections are decided by voters choosing candidates on the basis of their policy views. By this standard, the record of recent presidential elections is mixed. Tracing back to the 1964 presidential election, Democratic and Republican presidential candidates have polarized on liberal versus conservative grounds sufficiently to give the voters a clear ideological choice. At the microlevel, many individual voters are motivated by the ideological menu when they cast their ballots. But they are also motivated by nonpolicy considerations. At the macrolevel, the electorate's collective reactions to candidate positions help shape their electoral verdict, but in conjunction with other considerations.

Apart from policy issues and ideology are additional determinants of the vote. As we have seen, people sometimes vote for or against the incumbent party on the basis of its past performance. One would find difficulty condemning this behavior as irrational. In addition, two important predictors of individuals' votes are their party identification and their evaluation of the personal characteristics of the candidates. To the extent that people vote on the basis of a party identification that is grounded in policy or ideological considerations (as when a staunch conservative is committed to the Republican Party) and to the extent that the candidates are ideologically typical of their party (see chapter 10), party voting can be viewed as rational.

But what about voting on the basis of the candidates' personal characteristics? One of the best predictors of a person's vote is simply whether the voter likes the personal qualities of the Democratic candidate more than the Republican. We may be tempted to view voting on such a non-issue (or even apolitical) basis to be voting on the basis of irrelevant considerations. But this view may be mistaken. Morris Fiorina (1977, 618) puts the question well:

> Considerable misconception surrounds the discussion of the importance of candidate qualities for the voting decision. Various authors have suggested that voting on the basis of candidate qualities is irrational, or at least of lower order of rationality than voting on the issues. . . . Such suggestions apparently stem from the erroneous belief that attitudes toward the candidates reflect no more than Ike's smile, Nixon's beard, or Kennedy's accent. Actually, the bulk of the citizenry's impressions of the candidates focuses on qualities which are of legitimate relevance to the latter's capacity to govern: experience, leadership ability, and so on. . . . Why should a candidate's intelligence, administrative ability, etc., be any less a legitimate issue than where he stands on Medicare or aid to Israel?

That voters choose the candidate they find to have the greatest character, competence, or trustworthiness is quite reasonable, even if their candidate is not the one that is closest to the voters on policy issues.[13] Unfortunately, however, voters do not always have the necessary information to make good judgments about a candidate's character until after they are elected president.

The collective decisions voters make at election time contain elements of both stability and change. That most voting decisions are based on longstanding partisan loyalty adds an element of stability. Electoral shifts are normally only temporary because voters shifting toward the advantaged party or candidate do not change their identification in the process. Consequently they may surge in the opposition partisan direction in a subsequent election, or even do so when voting in another contest held on the same date. Yet it is also true that partisan loyalties continually evolve, in part due to the entry of new voters and the departure of old and in part due to partisan conversions (see chapters 4 and 5). In extreme, the change is sufficiently major to be labeled an electoral realignment. The most recent such realignment period, centered in the 1930s, produced a change from a considerable Republican advantage in national voting loyalties to a long-term Democratic edge in party identification that has persisted until recently. If another realignment is on the near horizon, it could restore the Republican Party to the predominant position it held a century years ago or restore the Democratic dominance of the latter twentieth century. Or it could change the focus of the issues that separate the two parties without producing a net change in the distribution of party loyalties. If any of these possibilities become true, the public will have arranged its partisan loyalties as a long-term electoral response to the decisive issues of the day.

NOTES

1. In Figure 9.1, the normal vote is constructed as the prediction of the House vote from regressing the vote on macrolevel party identification in quarter 3 of the election year and then smoothing the trendline via the LOWESS procedure.
2. See also Miller et al. (1976); Romero (1989).
3. Reasonable scholars have disagreed on the role of the ideology in voting behavior. Compare Luttbeg and Gant (1985), Tedin (1987), and Knight (1985).
4. Scholars disagree on the importance of racial sentiment in U.S. elections. Compare Carmines and Stimson (1980) and Abramowitz (1994).
5. On voter reaction to the economy, see Kiewiet (1983), Fiorina (1981), Markus (1988), Kinder et al. (1989), MacKuen et al. (1992), and Norpoth (1996).
6. Measuring candidate evaluations from the likes/dislikes responses has a long tradition (see Campbell et al. 1960). Some studies have measured candidate evaluations from "thermometer" ratings of the candidates. Such ratings measure more than candidate likeability and perceived leadership ability, and usually predict the vote so well that they may be considered surrogates for the vote decision. The result is the relatively empty prediction that people vote for the candidates they like best.
7. It has long been recognized that it is easy to predict voting decisions from known attitudes; for instance, see Campbell et al. (1954) and Kelley (1983). The best statistical procedure for predicting vote decisions from multiple attitudes is via a probit equation. Some readers may be interested in the probit equation predicting the vote from our three attitudinal predictors. We estimated the probit equation predicting 2000 presidential votes (Gore versus Bush) from the seven-point party identification scale, the twenty-one-point left-right scale, and the (in-theory) forty-one-point candidate affect scale. Using the McKelvay-Zavoina procedure for estimating a pseudo-R squared, the three variables together account for 75 percent of the variance in the latent dimension that accounts for vote decisions.
8. Projection, for example, can account for many of the instances of misperception shown in Table 9.2. For discussions of projection, see Conover and Feldman (1989) and Lodge et al. (1989).
9. On the linkages between macrolevels and microlevels of analysis as they pertain to aggregated vote decisions, see Wright (1989).
10. Figure 9.6 is based on Donald E. Stokes's (1966) "partisan components analysis," which is designed to estimate the relative effects of partisan attitudes on election results. Stokes applied the model to elections from 1952 through 1964. The procedure is based on a statistical analysis of SRC/NES respondents' reported likes and dislikes about parties and candidates. First the content of the likes and dislikes is divided into six components: (1) the Democratic candidate, (2) the Republican candidate, (3) government management, (4) domestic policy, (5) foreign policy, and (6) group benefits. The impact of each component on the election outcome is determined from a statistical analysis of how influential each component is in determining the vote and how one-sided the evaluations are for the particular component in the particular election.
11. Figure 9.6 does not extend beyond the 1992 election. In 1996, Republican respondents vented their frustration by verbalizing an exceptionally high number of negative comments about Clinton's character. This distorted the data, with Dole

leading Clinton in terms of net likes minus dislikes, overriding Clinton's perceived edge in leadership and competence. In 2000, the two major candidates were each viewed mildly positively in terms of the NES likes minus dislikes. For more on candidate evaluations as electoral predictors, see Erikson (2002).

12. There is statistical evidence that party platforms are good proxies for the ideology of presidential parties, with moderate platforms signifying more votes for a party (Erikson, MacKuen, and Stimson 2002), For more on presidential candidate ideology and presidential election outcomes, see MacKuen, Erikson, Stimson, and Knight (2003).

13. There is evidence that the most sophisticated voters are the most attentive and responsive to candidates' personal attributes; see Miller et al. (1986).

10 | The Public and Its Elected Leaders

As shown in the previous chapter, voters often use elections as a policy expression, as prescribed by the rational-activist model. Voters tend to reelect officeholders who show evidence of policy competence (e.g., presidents who produce economic prosperity or foreign policy success). Moreover, voters generally support candidates who are close to them in terms of their policy positions. By sorting candidates for office into winners and losers, voters do their part to achieve agreement between public preferences and public policy.

The degree of policy representation depends on the behavior not only of voters but also of politicians. The rational-activist model is one of five models of linkage between public opinion and policy that were introduced in chapter 1. In this chapter, we consider the four additional models by which public opinion translates into policy: the sharing model, the political parties model, the delegate model, and the interest groups model. To understand these models, our focus is on politicians rather than the public.

By the sharing model, representation is achieved because politicians are drawn from the same culture as their constituents. By the parties model, Republican and Democratic politicians diverge ideologically to provide the convenient cue of party affiliation, allowing voters to vote rationally using their habit of party identification. By the delegate model, politicians are sufficiently fearful of public opinion that they follow public opinion in their policies in advance of the next election. By the interest groups model, politicians respond to public opinion when they respond to articulated interest group opinion.

10-1 OPINION SHARING BETWEEN POLICYMAKERS AND THE PUBLIC

In this section, we consider political leaders as a class. We ask how different they are from the general public. If leaders (elected officials) and followers (the general public) are essentially alike in their interests and preferences, it matters less whether leaders' decisions follow from their own preferences or from trying to satisfy public opinion. In the extreme, public opinion and leader opinion could be the same thing.

The simplest form of linkage between public opinion and the policy decisions of political leaders is the simple sharing of common opinions by followers and leaders. Consider, for example, the result if we elected members of the House of Representatives by lottery. Just as a randomly selected sample of survey respondents is representative of the general population within a certain margin of error, so would an assembly of 435 randomly selected people acting as a House of Representatives be representative of the population. If such an assembly could act without being distracted by the demands of powerful interest groups or the actual rules of Congress that impede change, then—for better or worse—its decisions would reflect public opinion. In actuality, the Congress (and other legislatures) are less representative than a random sample, if for no other reason than that members are supposedly chosen for their superior capabilities rather than their typicality.

How then do members of Congress and other political leaders differ from the general population? To answer this question, we must find the traits that motivate some people but not others to pursue a political career and the traits that favor success in achieving this goal. When people who are active in politics—whether as a local party official or an elected legislator—are interviewed, they often report that a spur to their political career was a politically active family. The consensus, based on several studies, is that about 40 percent of the people who are presently politically active grew up in politically active homes. Thus, assuming only 10 percent of the public (at the most) are active in politics themselves, almost half of our political leaders come from the 10 percent of the nation's families that are most politically active (Prewitt 1970).

Intense political interest alone cannot push a person into a political leadership role. It helps to be recruited by others. To contest an election seriously, the would-be political leader must attract the base of support necessary to win. In some cases, the political leader is a self-starter who, because of his or her political interest and ambition, announces candidacy and then is able to accumulate support. In other cases, the future leader is selected by the local business or party elite for the task of getting elected.[1]

Because the wealthiest and best-educated people are most likely to be politically interested and articulate and have the visibility to be tapped for a leadership

TABLE 10.1 | **Occupations of Members of Congress (1993) Compared with the Public (1990) (in Percentages)**

Occupation	U.S. Senate	U.S. House	U.S. Labor Force
Farmer	6	4	1
Manager (business)	24	31	9
Teacher	11	15	5
Lawyer	58	42	1
Journalist	8	6	★
All others	4	5	84

Sources: Norman J. Ornstein, Thomas E. Mann, and Michael J. Malaben, eds. *Vital Statistics on Congress, 1993–1994* (Washington, DC: Congressional Quarterly Press, 1994); Statistical Abstract of the United States, 1992.

★Less than 0.5 percent. Senate and House percentages add to greater than 100 percent due to multiple listings. "All other" category does not include prior occupation in government or politics.

role, we are not surprised that these are the people who become some of our political leaders. Put simply, there is an upper-status bias to the political leadership opportunity structure. For example, as Table 10.1 shows, the occupations of the members of Congress are predominantly professional or managerial. In a society where only 18 percent of the workforce is engaged in such occupations, lawyers and businesspeople are particularly overrepresented in Congress. Lawyers and businesspeople are somewhat overrepresented in state legislatures as well. Additionally, greater percentages of legislators are white, male, Protestant, and middle-aged than in the general adult population.[2]

In part, the overrepresentation of the affluent and educated in the councils of government stems from the middle-class leadership structure of the two major political parties. Even the Democratic party—supposedly the more representative of the working class—draws its leaders from the middle class. By contrast, in many other democracies, the presence of a Socialist or Labor party draws working-class people into greater political activity. Although Socialist and Labor parties do not draw their leaders exclusively from the working class they represent, they do at least open the door for the political recruitment of blue-collar workers, a door that is rather closed in this country.

The disproportionate concentration of political leadership skills in the hands of the better educated and prosperous may make the class bias all but inevitable. For example, delegates to Democratic National Conventions are better educated and more affluent than the general population, even though representative on the basis of race, sex, and age. Even movements of economic protest draw their leaders from the most affluent strata within the protest group. For example, Lipset (1950, 166) finds this the pattern within agricultural protest movements: "The battle for higher prices and a better economic return for their labor has been conducted by the farmers who need it least."

The status bias to the leadership structure does not necessarily mean that the views of political leaders typify their class instead of that of the general public. For example, Democratic Convention delegates do not express the prevailing views of the economically comfortable. Still, a general consideration is that whatever their individual ideology, the generally affluent leaders might resist wealth-redistribution legislation that would work against their self-interest. For example, a study of the attitudes of national convention delegates (in 1956) found that one of the few issues on which delegates of both parties were clearly more conservative than the public was their resistance to making the rich pay a greater share of taxes (McClosky et al. 1960).

Of course, one could argue that virtually all political viewpoints found in the general population are also shared by some of the prosperous and better educated—and these might be our leaders. Those who run for office do not always represent the political views of their economic group. Thus, one can hope there is sufficient diversity of viewpoint among the candidates for office from which the people make their selections at the polls. And if not, there is still the possibility that electoral pressure can divert the behavior of political leaders from unrepresentative personal preferences.

We can try a direct approach to the question of whether political leaders and the general public share opinions by comparing the political attitudes of the two groups. In chapter 6 we already discussed one difference between public and leadership attitudes—leaders' greater support for civil liberties. For routine policy issues, however, only a few sets of data exist from which to assess the correspondence between the policy views of the public and its elected leaders.

One opportunity to assess the correspondence between public and leader opinion derives from CBS/*New York Times* polls that compare public and congressional responses to current political issues: in 1970 (by CBS) and in 1978 and 1982 (by CBS/*New York Times*). Examples for 1978 are shown in Table 10.2. For both the 1970 and 1982 surveys, the distributions of responses by the public sample and by U.S. House members generally differ by only a few percentage points.[3] Small differences between the views of the public and their elected officials were also found by Uslaner and Weber (1983) in their study of state legislators.

That the public and its elected leaders have similar opinions on a variety of issues may seem a surprise, given the differences of the two groups in income, education, and other background characteristics. The biases of leadership selection could have us expect that elected officials would share the opinions of the affluent and most educated rather than the opinions of the public as a whole. Instead, the apparent absence of bias in leadership opinions suggests that electoral politics works to weed out political candidates whose views are incongruent with public opinion.

10-2 POLITICAL PARTIES AND REPRESENTATION

So far we have compared politicians generally with the voting public generally. Averaged out, politicians might approximate a mirror image of the electorate.

TABLE 10.2 | Comparison of Public and Congressional Opinion on Selected Policy Issues, 1978 (in Percentages)

	Public	U.S. House Members
Defense: In favor of decreasing money for national defense	23	26
SALT: In favor of SALT II	67	74
Health Insurance: In favor of "National Health Insurance fully paid by government"	47	45
Tax cut: Opposed to a "large federal income tax cut"	53	51
Abortion: In favor of "government paying for abortions for the poor"	41	35

Source: Kathleen A. Frankovic and Laurily K. Epstein, "Congress and Its Constituency: The New Machine Politics" (paper delivered at American Political Science Association Meeting, Washington DC, Sept. 1979).

But this similarity can be misleading in that U.S. politicians come in two dominant and distinct flavors—as Democrats and as Republicans. In this section we look at this partisan distinction with an eye to determining the choice it affords voters.

According to the political parties model, party labels clarify the political choices available to the voters, allowing them to cast informed ballots with minimal search for information about candidates. Based on their histories of party behavior, Democratic politicians earn reputations as liberals and Republican politicians earn reputations as conservatives. These stereotypes then provide useful cues regarding what Democrats and Republicans will do once in office. This simplifies the task of the policy-oriented voter. Instead of monitoring each candidate's campaign statements and hoping they reflect what he or she would do if elected, the voter need only learn the differences between the parties and use party labels as a cue to rational voting.

As we have seen (chapter 3), ideological considerations compete with other factors (such as family history) as motivations for party choice. Increasingly, citizens are polarizing ideologically, with liberals as Democrats and conservatives as Republicans. This trend is present when comparing aggregated constituencies as well as individual citizens, with a growing tendency for local electorates to use ideology as their basis of partisan sorting. Figure 10.1 shows this ideological sorting among the states in the 2000 election. Based on exit polls, the most liberal states in terms of ideological identification also tended to be the most Democratic in terms of party identification.[4]

Just as individuals tend to vote according to their party identification, geographic constituencies tend to vote according to their net party identification. We can see this at the state level, as state electorates are strongly influenced by their partisan tendencies when they select their U.S. Senators. Table 10.3 shows

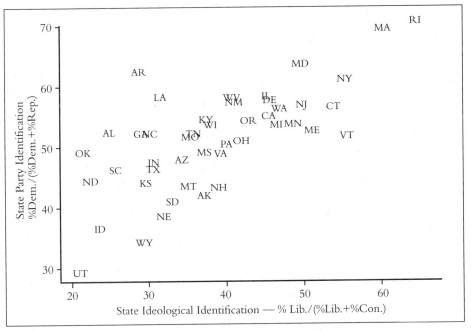

Figure 10.1   Partisanship and ideology of state electorates, 2000. *Source:* VNS Exit Polls.

TABLE 10.3 | **Partisanship of Senate Delegations by Partisanship of State Electorates**

Partisanship of State Senate Delegation, Post-2000 Election	Partisanship of State Electorate		
	Republican States (0–45% Dem., Macropartisanship)	Competitive States (45–55% Dem., Macropartisanship)	Democratic States (55–100% Dem., Macropartisanship)
Both Republicans	6	12	0
Split	2	8	4
Both Democrats	2	7	11

Note: Numbers in cells represent the number of states. Macropartisanship is the percentage of Democrats and Republicans in the state's 2000 VNS Exit Poll.

(with many prominent exceptions) that predominantly Republican states (in identification) elect mainly Republicans to the Senate while predominantly Democratic states elect mainly Democrats. Whether voters can achieve ideological representation by using party labels depends on the existence of actual differences between the programs of the two parties. Next we examine the extent to which Republican and Democratic leaders actually differ in their policy preferences, in the programs they offer to the voters, and in their behavior in office.

Ideology and Party Leaders

In chapter 3 we saw that ideology is a modest source of partisan division between ordinary Republican and Democratic party identifiers. Especially among those highly aware of party differences on issues, ordinary voters sort themselves ideologically, with liberals identifying as Democrats and conservatives as Republicans. Among political activists and politicians, ideology is an even stronger motivation force. When a strong ideology motivation spurs an individual to political activism, the individual usually develops an affinity for the ideologically appropriate party.[5]

For instance, in studies of delegates to the national conventions going back to 1956, each party's delegates are more ideologically extreme than the party rank and file. Republican delegates are to the right of Republicans in the electorate and Democratic delegates are to the left of Democrats in the electorate (McClosky, Hoffman, and O'Hara 1960; Miller and Jennings 1987). In terms of ideological identification, Democratic delegates tend to be liberal or moderate but rarely conservative; Republican delegates tend to be conservative or moderate but rarely liberal. Table 10.4 displays these patterns for delegates over five sets of national conventions.

Political parties obtain their political energy from their activists. But while the classic role of party leader is to balance the ideological preferences of the activists with the pragmatism necessary for winning elections, party activists may be more concerned with ideological correctness than with electoral victory. Increasingly, with the decline of traditional party organizations and the growing openness of party conventions brought by reforms of party rules beginning in the early 1970s, ideologues have increasingly dominated party leadership positions. There is an irony here. As the leadership structures of the political parties have become more internally democratic, the potential for greater policy choice between the parties is created. This increases the conflict between the parties' policies and the preferences of their less active rank-and-file supporters.

TABLE 10.4	Ideological Identification of National Convention Delegates, 1984–2000								
	1984		**1988**		**1992**		**1996**		**2000**	
Ideology	**Dem.**	**Rep.**	**Dem.**	**Rep.**	**Dem.**	**Rep.**	**Dem.**	**Rep.**	**Dem.**	**Rep.**
Liberal (%)	48	1	43	0	47	1	43	0	36	1
Moderate (%)	42	35	43	35	44	32	48	27	56	34
Conservative (%)	4	60	5	58	5	63	5	70	5	63

Source: Harold W. Stanley and Richard G. Niemi. *Vital Statistics of American Politics, 2003–2004.* (Washington, DC: Congressional Quarterly Press, 2003), 75.

Public Opinion Relative to the Public's Perceptions of the Parties

Here we examine party differences through the eyes of ordinary citizens as they perceive their personal positions in relation to the parties. Using the 2000 NES survey, we limit this presentation to survey respondents who recognize that the Democrats are to the left of the Republicans. Of this group, we ask how many perceive themselves to the left of both parties, how many see themselves to the right, and how many see themselves between the two parties ideologically.

We examine averages over three issues—liberalism-conservatism, domestic spending, and defense spending. On each issue, 2000 NES respondents were asked their own position, the Democrats' position, and the Republicans' position, all on the usual seven-point scale. Selecting only respondents who saw the Democrats to the left of the Republicans on all three issues, we ask whether the respondent saw his or her position as, on average, to the left of both parties, to the right of both parties, or in between. (Those who, according to our measure, perceive their average position as perfectly represented by one party— e.g., seeing the Republicans as just right but the Democrats as too liberal—are scored with those between the parties.)

Table 10.5 displays the relevant data. Overall, two-thirds of those who correctly order the parties ideologically see themselves as between the Democrats on their left and the Republicans on their right. The remainder are about evenly split between conservatives who see themselves even to the right of the Republican party and liberals who see themselves even to the left of the Democratic party.

Table 10.5 also shows perceptions of party positions broken down by party identification. The most interesting groups are the "strong Democrats" and

---

TABLE 10.5 | **Public Perceptions of Their Policy Positions Relative to the Two Major Parties**

Respondent's Perceived Position	Strong Dem.	Weak Dem.	Ind.	Weak Rep.	Strong Rep.	All Cases
Respondent left of both parties	43%	38%	11%	0%	0%	16%
Respondent in between both parties*	57	63	72	65	58	64
Respondent right of both parties	0	0	16	35	42	19
	100%	100%	100%	100%	100%	100%

Source: National Election Studies, 2000 election data. Based on respondent (voters only) perceptions of self and candidate positions on ideology, domestic spending, and defense spending. Includes only voters who saw the Democrats to the left of the Republicans on all three issues.

*Includes respondents who see themselves in the same location as one of the parties (15 percent).

"strong Republicans." A full 43 percent of the strong Democrats see themselves to the left of both parties. Similarly, 42 percent of the strong Republicans see themselves to the right of both parties. The two parties need to satisfy these polarized partisans, but they also need to woo the portion of the electorate—mainly weak partisans and Independents—in the middle of the ideological spectrum.

Each party's strong identifiers are typical of the party's primary electorate. Activists tend to dominate low-turnout party primaries, with an important segment urging the party in a more extreme ideological direction. But to the extent primary electorate chose extreme candidates over moderates, the party risks alienating voters in the center. Each party's more moderate candidates may have the greatest chance to become general election winners, but they face the problem first in securing the nomination from a hostile primary electorate.[6]

And what of that half of the relevant electorate who appear ideologically located between the two parties? These centrist voters seemingly face a distasteful choice of giving power either to a party that is too conservative or a party that is too liberal. However, these voters also have the opportunity to split their ticket, voting for a balance of Democrats and Republicans. The desire of moderates for an ideological balance of party power may help explain the frequent pattern of divided party control. Arguably, moderate voters should prefer the ideological balance of one party controlling the presidency and the other controlling Congress to unified control by either party (Fiorina 1992; Alesina and Rosenthal 1995).

The Relevance of Party Platforms

At national conventions every fourth year, each party devotes considerable time to spelling out the details of its platform in order to detail the party's official position on the issues of the day. Party platforms are often dismissed as mere ritualistic documentation because they are rarely read, quickly forgotten, and not officially binding on a party's candidates. Nevertheless, as research by Gerald Pomper with Susan Lederer (1980, chs. 7 and 8) shows, careful reading of party platforms provides clues to what the parties would do if they came to power.

Pomper examined the content of the Democratic and Republican platforms from 1944 to 1976. He found about half the platform statements to be relatively meaningless rhetoric ("The American Free Enterprise System is one of the greatest achievements of humankind") or statements about the issues that are too vague or broad to be meaningful ("The Anti-Trust Laws must be vigorously enforced"). About another quarter of the platform statements qualify as policy approval ("In the Nuclear Test Ban Treaty, we have written our commitment to limitations on the arms race"). Finally, about one-quarter are detailed policy statements like "The Security of the American Trade Unions must be strengthened by repealing 14B of the Taft-Hartley Act." Although people rarely read party platforms directly, platform statements reach voters indirectly "through interest groups, mass media, candidates' speeches, and incomplete popular perceptions" (Pomper 1980, 152).

Of particular relevance is whether parties keep their policy promises once in office. Pomper finds that about two-thirds of the winning presidential party's pledges become at least partially fulfilled during the next four years. Somewhat over half the pledges of the nonpresidential party do as well. When both parties offer the same pledge in their platforms, the pledge is fulfilled in some fashion about 80 percent of the time. Pomper (1980, 176) concludes, "We should take platforms seriously, because politicians take them seriously." A statistical analysis by Ian Budge and Richard Hofferbert (1990) reinforces Pomper's conclusion. They were able to connect changing federal expenditure patterns to changing priorities in party platforms, particularly the platform of the presidential party (see also McDonald et al. 1999).

Party Voting in Legislatures

Ideally, from the standpoint of the political parties model, the electorally dominant party not only would articulate a program that achieves voter approval but would be in a position to enact that program once in power. The dominant congressional party, for example, would be able to enact its preferred legislation, particularly if the president is of the same party and gives encouragement.

As is well known, events do not always work out this way in the American political system. About as often as not, the presidency and Congress are controlled by different parties, leading to the potential for gridlock or stalemate. Even when the president's party is in the congressional majority, the president still has difficulty pushing his proposals through Congress. For instance, President Clinton was unable to pass his health care legislation in 1993 and 1994, even though the Democrats held a healthy majority in both House and Senate.

This discussion may seem to suggest that party labels are not relevant in Congress. However, that is far from the truth. In fact, party affiliation is the single best predictor of roll-call voting in Congress. By almost all accounts, the degree of party polarization in Congress is increasing rather than decreasing (Aldrich 1996; Binder 1997; Coleman 1997; Sinclair 1997; Stonecash, Brewer, and Mariani 2002).

Figure 10.1 summarizes congressional party differences in terms of ideological voting scores on the Americans for Democratic Action (ADA) index in 2002. Among House members, almost all Republicans are more conservative than the least liberal Democrats. A similar but less severe pattern is found for U.S. senators. Know the Congress member's party affiliation, and you have a good idea of his or her ideological tendencies.

State legislatures show considerable variation in their degree of party polarization (Aldrich and Coleman-Battista 2002). At one extreme, Nebraska elects its legislators on a nonpartisan basis, with the result being a noticeable lack of ideological structure to roll-call votes (Wright and Schaffner 2002). At the other extreme, some state legislative parties behave as disciplined units, resulting in parties even more polarized than the U.S. Congress.

The source of the occasional discipline in state legislatures is a powerful presiding officer who can penalize members of his or her party for not supporting party positions, and sometimes it is the party caucus. When a legislative party operates according to the strong caucus system, members of the party democratically decide a party position on certain issues, which is sometimes binding on its members. The power of the governor also matters (Morehouse 1999).

In Congress, the source of growing party polarization is the subject of considerable debate among political scientists. Some say the visible increase in party differences reflects an increase in party discipline, as party leaders pressure members to support their position (Aldrich and Rohde 2001; Aldrich, Berger, and Rohde 2002; Cox and McCubbins 1993; Cox and McCubbins 2002; Campbell, Cox, and McCubbins 2002). Others say rather than the product of coercion, the polarization simply reflects the growing differences of opinion between Democratic and Republican activists (Krehbiel 1993, 1999, 2000). Resolving this debate empirically has been particularly challenging (Roberts and Smith 2003; McCarty, Poole, and Rosenthal 2001; Sinclair 2002; Snyder and Groseclose 2000; Krehbiel 2000). In any event, it is clear that the polarization of congressional parties provides voters with an ideological choice.

Party Labels as a Basis for Policy Choice

Although elected leaders from the Democratic and Republican parties differ ideologically, one might think this results simply because Democrats and Republicans represent distinct geographic constituencies rather than ideological competition within constituencies. What is required by the parties model is that prospective voters are provided a choice within specific constituencies. In this section, we examine the ideological choice provided by the Republican and Democratic parties at the constituency level. Our focus is on candidates in individual contests for the U.S. House of Representatives.

In U.S. House races, the electorate's choice is not between the typical congressional Democrat and the typical congressional Republican because (as we demonstrate) congressional candidates often adjust their issue stances according to the prevailing constituency views. A liberal district is generally given a choice between a relatively liberal Democrat and a relatively liberal Republican. Similarly, a conservative district is given a choice between Democrat and Republican candidates who are both relatively conservative for their party. We are interested in the extent to which candidates at the district level diverge and give the constituency voters a meaningful choice.

It is no understatement to say that almost always, when a district's congressional candidates differ on important issues, the Democrat is the more liberal than the Republican. Several studies have estimated the degree of candidate divergence from questionnaires administered to Republican and Democratic candidates in the same set of districts. For instance, a study of congressional candidates in 1982 found the Republican scoring as more conservative in 93 percent of the districts and ideological ties in 4 percent of the districts. Only in 3 percent was the Democrat to the right of the Republican (Erikson and Wright 1985). The in-constituency polarization has only increased since then. A similar study of districts in 1998 found the Republican to the right of the Democratic candidate in all 228 districts sampled (Erikson and Wright 2001), with no exceptions.[7] The expectation is that similar patterns would be found in most U.S. Senate elections (and for state legislature and most local offices).

A congressional voter has an easy decision rule for casting a partisan ballot: to help elect the most conservative candidate, vote Republican; to help elect the most liberal candidate, vote Democratic. When the public desires a more conservative or liberal Congress, it can simply elect more Republicans or Democrats accordingly. On one hand, changes in the party composition of Congress are often attributed to such factors as economic conditions, presidential coattails, and Watergates—not to changes in policy preferences by the public On the other hand, one can marshal statistical evidence that the over-time variation in the numbers of Republicans and Democrats in Congress is partially due to ideological shifts by the public (Erikson, MacKuen, and Stimson 2002). The mechanism of choice is available for the public to create a policy shift in Congress—and in state legislatures and other political arenas as well.

The Importance of Party Competition

The importance of parties is evident under circumstances when parties cease to play a major role—when elections are held on a truly nonpartisan basis, as in many American cities and sometimes for state offices. Reformers once saw nonpartisan elections as ideal because they weaken the role of corrupt political parties. But we know that nonpartisan elections make it more difficult for voters to get their preferred policies enacted and to hold leaders accountable for their actions (Cassel 1986).

When both major parties compete effectively for the electorate's favor, we would expect close elections. Sometimes, however, party competition breaks down and one party enjoys a monopoly. This has not happened at the national level since the Era of Good Feelings—which was around 1820. Often at the state and local levels, however, one party becomes so dominant as to win almost every election.

In theory, the effect of strong party competition should be to enhance representation. With election outcomes uncertain, each party has an added incentive to woo the marginal voter who otherwise would be ignored. The opposite result occurs under one-party dominance. The dominant party does not need to make policy appeals to a public whose loyalty (or apathy) they have already won.

V. O. Key (1949) argued that the lack of party competition in the American South allowed the once dominant Democratic party to ignore public opinion, with the result that the haves enacted public policy at the expense of the have-nots. There is, largely as a result of Key's position, a conviction among political scientists that parties would be more responsive to public opinion if competition among state political parties were to increase. The states have been moving more toward two-party systems, both in the South and nationwide. As the parties become more evenly matched in the contests for control of governorships and state legislatures, this can only be a positive step in terms of the political parties model.

Does Party Control Matter?

Readily following from our discussion, which party controls the levers of power can have important policy consequences. We have already seen that elected politicians often do turn party platform pledges into law. We can also see different policies under different types of party control. Liberal innovations in domestic policy, for example, are most frequent when Democrats control Congress and, especially, when the Democrats hold the White House (Browning 1986, Kiewiet and McCubbins 1985; Erikson, MacKuen, and Stimson 2002). Statistically speaking, unemployment (a major concern of the less affluent) is more likely to decline under Democratic presidents. And inflation (a major concern of the more affluent) is more likely to decline under Republican presidents (Hibbs 1987, ch. 7; Alesina and Rosenthal 1995). There is also statistical evidence that the income gap between the rich and the poor goes up under Republican presidents and down under Democratic presidents (Hibbs and Dennis 1988).

Of course there are important limits to the policy consequences of party control. The U.S. system of separation of powers and checks and balances slows the connection between policy proposals and policy enactment. For citizens with a radical perspective, the choices between the policies of the Democrats and Republicans can be viewed as merely slight variations on the status quo. If one's taste runs toward policies like government ownership of industry, legalization of drugs, or abandonment of the public school system, one will not be represented by either major party.

Actually, many see the major problem with today's parties as not the lack of choice but rather that they are too ideologically polarized. Faced with a choice between liberal Democrats and conservative Republicans, the moderate voter in the middle can achieve ideological satisfaction only by massive ticket-splitting. In theory, either party could gain votes by moving toward the center. But they do not do so, possibly because the parties' ideological reputations are so hardened that party leaders believe that voters will not respond to centrist gestures. Still, individual politicians sometimes move from the dominant ideological position of their party, moderating their policy positions in order to stay elected rather than pleasing their parties' ideological constituents. We turn to this aspect of democratic representation next.

10-3 LEADERSHIP RESPONSIVENESS TO PUBLIC OPINION

When in office, politicians face the choice of pursuing their personal policy agenda or following the dictates of the voters who elect them. In this section we ask whether politicians, even as partisan ideologues, respond to public opinion in a way that overrides their own policy taste. When they do respond to public opinion rather than personal taste, they play the role of the people's delegate or agent. This is the delegate model at work. By this model, politicians anticipate the next election, responding to public opinion in advance of the potential fury of the voters.

Officeholders are driven by two often conflicting motivations: to win elections and to make good policy (as they see it). How strongly they respond to public opinion depends both on the relative strengths of these two motivations and on how strongly they believe their reelection goals are affected by their behavior. For instance, suppose, counterfactually, that voters are incapable of responding to the policy choices candidates present. If voters ignore what politicians do, even electorally sensitive politicians are free to ignore the nominal policy preferences of the public when they make policy. On the other hand, suppose, again counterfactually, that voters are hypersensitive to candidate policy choices, always electing the candidate closest to their views. If voters care only about policy choices, even policy-centered politicians are compelled to follow the public's wishes because that is the only way to win elections.

In truth, citizen attention is highly variable—on average somewhere between no attention and full attention. Thus, the responses of politicians—with their mixed goals of election and policy—are also in between. They try to follow public opinion but are also guided by their personal policy preferences.

For the delegate model to work, the representative must have an incentive to choose the public's preference over his or her own. While this incentive may be the representative's belief that following public opinion is ordinarily the right thing to do, more likely it is the representative's fear that electoral defeat would be the consequence of ignoring public opinion. For reelection to properly motivate, the elected official must believe the public is watching. Also the official must also want to be reelected. Finally, for the model to work well, the representative must know what public opinion is, a task made easier by modern public opinion polling.

Political Ambition

The belief that their reelection chances hinge on how well they represent constituency opinion will not influence officeholders much unless they care about being reelected. When officeholders retire rather than seek reelection, the fear is that they shirk their responsibility to represent constituency opinion (Rothenberg and Sanders 2000). As Joseph Schlesinger (1966, 2) described the positive functions of political ambition, "no more irresponsible government is imaginable than one of high-minded men unconcerned for their political futures."

Politicians at the top of the political ladder usually try to continue in office as long as possible. For example, presidents normally want to stay in office for their constitutional allotment of two full terms. Even Truman and Johnson, who both opted for retirement in the spring of their reelection years, did so only after the results of the first presidential primaries indicated that even renomination by their party would have been a difficult hurdle.

Most governors (about 75 percent) also seek reelection when not constitutionally prohibited by term limits. Ambition also runs high for Congress members. When up for reelection, about 80 percent of senators and 90 percent of

House members try for another term (see Davidson and Oleszck 2002 for historical details.). Even when Congress members retire, they rarely leave political life; most House members who retire actually do so to seek the higher office of U.S. senator or state governor.

Preoccupation with reelection is a persistent theme in studies of congressional behavior. Douglas Arnold (1990) claims that staying elected is the dominant congressional motivation. Kingdon (1973) shows that representatives aim to please constituency interests even on routine legislation, while Fenno (1978) finds that representatives spend much of their time in their districts explaining their roll-call votes to constituents. Mayhew (1974) argues that the structural organization of the House of Representatives is best understood as a collective response to the members' need to stay elected, while Adler (2002) shows how the reelection concern has thwarted reform of the House committee system. Of course the desire to stay elected is not the sole congressional motivation. Parker (1992) reminds us that representatives focus on generating safe reelection prospects to free themselves in order to pursue their policy agendas.

Promoters of term limits for officeholders argue that the continuous preoccupation with staying elected detracts from the policymaking function. One concern is that elected officials may overrespond to the less enlightened aspects of public opinion. As V. O. Key (1961a, 490) observed, "Public men often act as if they thought the deciding margin in elections was cast by fools; moreover, by fools informed enough and alert enough to bring retribution to those who dare not demonstrate themselves equally foolish."

Interestingly, the inclination to hold onto office for several terms is a relatively recent phenomenon. In the nineteenth century, House and Senate members quite frequently returned to private life after a term or two (Price 1971). This is the pattern in many state legislatures even today, particularly in states offering low legislative pay (Squire 1988, 1992). With variation from state to state, perhaps one-fifth of state legislators retire before each election (Jewell and Breaux 1988; Montcrief 1999). Many retirements actually are to pursue alternative electoral opportunities.

Having strong policy goals does not free representatives from electoral concerns. Surely, many politicians are strongly motivated to advance their conception of the public interest. But this pursuit of accomplishments only feeds their ambition for further public service, which requires reelection. This reasoning suggests the hypothesis that the political leaders with the strongest policy motivations tend to feel the most electoral pressure to satisfy public opinion—at least on matters that concern them least.

Following Public Opinion

Ascertaining politicians' concern about public opinion is difficult. As V. O. Key lamented in 1961, "We have practically no systematic information about what goes on in the minds of public men as they ruminate about the weight to be given to public opinion in governmental decision" (Key 1961a, 490). If we take seriously the reported attitudes of politicians and the public when they are surveyed, it would seem that neither puts much credence in the delegate model. When asked, politicians are more likely to claim they act in their constituents' best interests as they see them rather than by slavishly following constituency preferences (Wahlke et al. 1962; Kuklinski and McCrone 1981; Friesema and Hedlund 1981). Similarly, citizens are more likely to claim they prefer their politicians to be of independent mind rather than asking them (the voters) what to do (Hedlund 1975).

Citizens and politicians alike claim to reject the notion that elected officials should follow the wishes of their constituents even if those wishes are contrary to their own. To be sure, many legislators would find it too humiliating to admit to being merely the voice of others. Indeed, most of us applaud the courage of the statesmanlike legislator who votes with his independent judgment rather than pander to the views of his constituency—particularly when we agree with that judgment.

Examining what elected representatives do rather than what they say produces strong circumstantial evidence that politicians follow district interests, at least in terms of broad ideological outline. Numerous studies have examined the statistical relationship between constituency opinion on one hand and legislative behavior on the other. For instance, Snyder (1996) was able to compare the votes cast in the California state legislature with constituency choices on several referenda issues. He found a strong statistical connection between constituency preferences and legislative behavior. For U.S. House districts, we have no direct measure of constituency opinion, although the constituency's vote for president is a serviceable indicator of district ideological preferences. For members of each party, district presidential voting correlates strongly with the ideological tendencies of the member's roll-call behavior; the more Democratic the district, the more liberal the member (Erikson and Wright 2001). Figure 10.3 shows this pattern for 2002 roll-call voting. Each party's most ideologically extreme members represent districts that voted one-sidedly for their party's candidate for president. Safe districts allow ideological voting, while competitive (moderate) districts require moderation of issue positions for electoral survival.[8]

In the U.S. Senate, we can measure constituency preferences directly from the liberal-conservative preferences in statewide surveys. State-level liberalism in surveys is strongly related to roll-call liberalism by the states' senators (Wright and Berkman 1986; Erikson 1990; Wood and Anderson 1998), even after controlling for the Senator's party. Figure 10.4 summarizes this pattern for 2002. For both Democrats and Republicans, the more liberal the state's opinion as measured by 2000 VNS exit polls, the more liberal is the senator's roll-call liberalism as measured by the ADA index of legislative liberalism. Thus, despite the general tendency for senators to be ideologically polarized by party, they moderate their views when faced with an ideologically adverse constituency.[9]

Electoral Timing

The alert reader will notice the circumstantial nature of our evidence of responsiveness to constituencies. While politicians' positions correlate with constituency

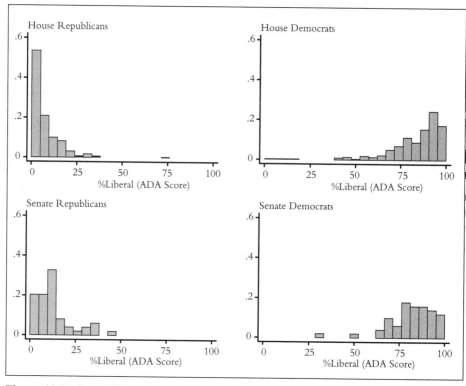

Figure 10.2 Party differences in roll-call liberalism, U.S. House of Representatives and Senate, 2002.

preferences (while holding party affiliation constant), the source could be either attentiveness (delegate model) or simply the sharing of interests by constituents and representatives (sharing model). The reason why each party's most conservative politicians represent conservative districts, for instance, could be that they are drawn from their constituencies and share their values rather than (or in addition to) a response to constituency concerns over their own preferences.

We would like a stronger test of responsiveness to constituency concerns. One test might be to see whether or not evidence of responsiveness increases with the approach of the next election. Another is whether or not politicians adapt ideologically when their constituency boundaries changes. Here we examine some of this evidence, from state legislators and the U.S. Congress.

In a study of California legislators, Kuklinski (1978) assessed representation by means of the correlation between constituency liberalism (as expressed in frequent referendum results) and the legislator's roll-call liberalism. He found that California assembly members in the lower house—who face reelection every two years—show a consistent pattern of responsiveness throughout the years examined. For California state senators, however, who face reelection only every four years, the pattern is more cyclical, more responsive in the two years before election than in the two years after election. These examples suggest representatives do respond to

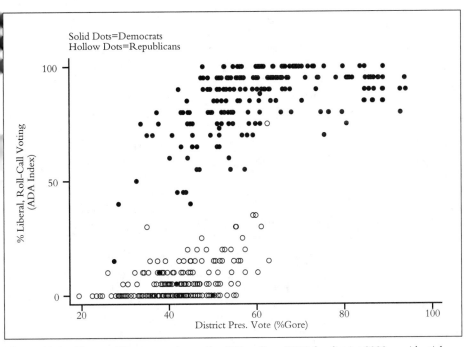

Figure 10.3   House of Representatives roll-call liberalism, 2002, by district 2000 presidential vote, by party of representative.

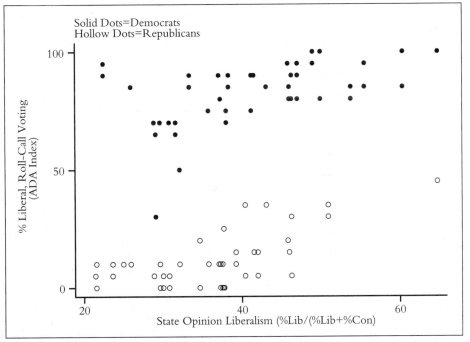

Figure 10.4   Senate roll-call liberalism, 2002, by state opinion (2000 VNS Exit Polls), by party of senator.

perceived electoral threats by seeking to better reflect their constituents' views as election time approaches.

The six-year senatorial term makes the U.S. Senate a particularly useful laboratory for watching elected leaders respond to public opinion. We might presume that senators act more constrained by opinion in their state late in their six-year term, as reelection time approaches, than early in the six-year cycle just after being elected. Democratic senators, whose personal beliefs are generally more liberal than those of their statewide constituencies, would act less liberal as their term progresses but then return to more liberal positions once reelected. Republican senators, whose personal beliefs generally are more conservative than those of their statewide constituencies, would act less conservative as their term progresses but then return to more conservative positions once reelected. In a study of Senate roll-call voting, Martin Thomas (1985) reports exactly these patterns. Both Democratic senators and Republican senators moderate their roll-call record as reelection time approaches. This is true, however, only for senators who seek reelection. Interestingly, Thomas shows that senators who do not run again moderate their views through the fifth year and then return to their original positions in the sixth year when the retirement decision has been made.

With their two-year term, U.S. House members must continually try to stay elected. Although we cannot watch their behavior change with the election cycle, an opportunity is sometimes present to watch them change when their constituency changes. U.S. House constituencies change every ten years following the U.S. Census, as district lines must be redrawn to reflect population changes. Amihai Glazer and Marc Robbins (1985) have statistically demonstrated that U.S. House members respond to these district changes in their roll-call voting. They measure changes in constituency opinion by comparing the past presidential voting of the new and the old district. By this measure, when the House member gets a more liberal district, the member usually becomes more liberal; when the member gets a more conservative district, the member usually becomes more conservative (see also Stratmann 2000).

Still one additional study found evidence of the delegate model at work at the aggregate level of national policymaking (Erikson, MacKuen, and Stimson 2002). Controlling for the presidential party and party composition of Congress, Congress enacts more liberal legislation when public opinion (lagged) is in a liberal mood. Similarly, policy conservatism follows from public conservatism.

Political Leaders as Educators

When we observe policy agreement between constituencies and their elected officials, it is natural to assume the causal mechanism is public opinion influencing the officials' position. Consider again the dilemma of public officials torn between their personal beliefs about good public policy and the contrary sentiment of public opinion. Their options are not limited to following public opinion or ignoring it altogether. A tempting alternative is to try to educate public opinion about their point of view. When this strategy works, the opinion-policy connection is instigated by the politicians rather than the public they represent. Just as public opinion can influence politicians, so too can politicians influence public opinion.

Politicians who can influence voters toward their point of view enjoy a win–win situation. They win on policy and electorally. Larry Jacobs and Robert Shapiro (2000) document this educating behavior among the contestants in the battle over national health care in the early Clinton administration. Rather than pandering to public opinion, both supporters and opponents of national health care drew their positions based on principal and then tried to influence the public. (The opponents won the battle.) More generally, when we observe Democrats and Republicans challenging each other with ideological rhetoric, they are not pandering to the median voter's point of view; they are trying to shift the median position in their direction. That politicians engage in this behavior in no way detracts from the importance of public opinion in the electoral process. They try to influence public opinion precisely because public opinion decides their electoral fates.

10-4 DO ELECTED OFFICIALS NEED TO FOLLOW PUBLIC OPINION?

We have seen that politicians apparently try to consider public opinion when making decisions—partly from fear of electoral retribution if they do not. Actually, one might suspect public officials do not need to weigh public opinion heavily in order to be reelected. Incumbent officeholders do not lose reelection bids at a rate that stimulates electoral anxiety. Furthermore, most people do not monitor their leaders' policy with sufficient attention to produce massive voter reactions. Could it be that elected officials have more freedom from public opinion than they realize?

Incumbency

Judging from their reelection rates, it may seem that elected politicians have little reason to fear the wrath of the voters. In the 1990s, 94 percent of U.S. House incumbents who sought reelection were returned to office. For U.S. senators, the reelection rate was only slightly lower (Davidson and Oleszck 2002). State legislators are also secure with reelection rates above 90 percent—but with important variations among states (Jewell and Breaux 1988).

There are five clear reasons incumbents almost always win reelection. First, many elections are partisan contests, decided along partisan lines. Consequently, elections tend to favor the locally dominant party. Where one party dominates the other, even an officeholder with a low personal standing can win repeated victories. District lines for legislative elections are typically carved in a way that creates one-party districts that are safe for incumbents. Statewide elections are far more competitive than district-level elections, which accounts for the greater electoral vulnerability of U.S. Senators and state governors.

Second, incumbents generally win because the status of incumbency gives them an advantage over their opponents. In U.S. House elections, incumbents gain 5 percent or more of the vote between their first victory and their first reelection attempt (Alford and Brady 1993). A spate of research on state legislative elections shows state legislators enjoy a similar incumbency advantage (Breaux and Jewell 1992; Holbrook and Tidmarch 1991; Cox and Morgenstern 1993; Carey, Niemi, and Powell 2000; Barry, Berkman, and Schneiderman 2000). The process that accounts for this incumbency advantage is not fully understood, but it seems House members and state legislators are able to exploit their office in terms of constituency service and easy publicity. Interestingly, the more visible U.S. senators and state governors do not seem to gain much of an advantage from incumbency status.

Third, incumbents generally win because they tend to obtain a strong, positive, personal vote due to their attractive candidate qualities. Candidates with strong personal appeal tend to win elections. Winners, therefore, tend to be strong candidates. And when winners seek reelection as incumbents, they generally continue to be strong candidates. In other words, winning creates incumbency status in addition to the other way around.

Fourth, incumbents gain votes by scaring off strong challenges. Potentially strong candidates tend not to run in elections they are likely to lose. Thus, potentially strong challengers avoid challenging strong incumbents, preferring to wait until the incumbent retires. In addition, the weaker candidates who do run against strong incumbents have few resources at their disposal, as potential supporters prefer not to concentrate their time and money on contests with little hope of success (Cox and Katz 1996; Jacobson and Kernell 1983).

A final reason why incumbents rarely lose is that anticipation of defeat make incumbents more likely to retire. Candidates are most likely to retire when their reelection prospects are at low ebb. The retirement of vulnerable incumbents in advance of potential voter wrath helps lower the observed rate of incumbent defeat. Far more incumbents would lose if they were forced to seek reelection rather than take their graceful exit by quitting.[10]

The electoral success of incumbents may signal both something wrong and something right about the status of representation. When elected officials are repeatedly returned to office because people vote for the dominant party or because people vote for the security of the familiar incumbent, incumbents can act unbound by constituency opinion. Under these circumstances, representation suffers. But there is also a positive side. Part of the reason for incumbent success is that candidates who do things to please voters are allowed to stay in office. Incumbents who represent their constituencies on policy issues are allowed to stay in office the longest.[11]

The Public's Attention to Policy Positions

To what extent do citizens react to the content of their leaders' policy decisions and policy proposals for the future? In the previous chapter we saw evidence of policy voting, particularly at the presidential level. But especially in subpresidential contests, the public's information is usually too low to allow the expectation of much policy voting. The best data in this regard concern people's awareness of the U.S. House of Representatives and their particular representative. Let us consider how visible House members' actions are to their constituents.

First, the local news media rarely give much coverage to the roll-call stands of members of Congress or to the substantive issues of congressional campaigns. Consequently, even if more people had the urge to follow the congressional politics of their district, they would have great difficulty in doing so (Huchings 2003)

Only slightly more than half the public can name their congressional representative. Similarly, at election time only about half claim to have read or heard anything about their representative in Washington or the opposing candidate. When interviewers probe to find out what respondents have read or heard about the incumbent congressional candidate, the answer is typically a vague reference such as "he (or she) is a good person," or "he (or she) knows the problems." In the National Election Studies, only about 15 percent express reactions to their U.S. House member in terms of positions taken on specific legislation (Jacobson 1987).

On even hotly debated congressional issues, few people know where their Congress member stands. Consider the following examples. Following Congress's passage of the Persian Gulf Use of Force Resolution in 1991 authorizing the first President Bush to conduct the first Gulf War, NES respondents were asked how their individual House member had voted on this contentious issue. Fifty-six percent correctly identified their member's position, while 30 percent got it wrong (Alvarez and Gronke 1996; Lapinski 2001).[12] In the biggest congressional vote of Clinton's presidency, Congress narrowly assented to Clinton's tax-raising, budget-balancing Budget Resolution of 1993. Following the vote, NES respondents were asked about their House member's vote. Sixty-three percent reported their member's vote correctly on this highly partisan issue, while 21 percent got it wrong (Lapinski 2001). Assuming as many were guessing the correct answer as gave the wrong answer, still less than half knew their Congress member's positions on these important votes. Part of the public's ignorance may have been due to lack of publicity, however. Representatives who publicized their votes were rewarded with greater recognition of their actions (Lapinski 2001).

Looking at these survey findings, one might well wonder whether the representatives need to pay attention to the views of their constituency when they weigh the alternatives of each legislative decision. As Warren Miller and Donald Stokes (1963, 54) put it, "Congressmen feel that their individual legislative actions may have considerable impact on the electorate, yet some simple facts about the representative's salience to his constituents imply that this could hardly be true."

Indeed, we may have a major political linkage between mass opinion and leader response that is generally overlooked—although the public is not watching, leaders sometimes do what they think the public wants because they mistakenly believe the public is paying attention! If this is true, then leaders' responsiveness to public opinion would quickly evaporate once somebody points out to them that surveys show the public to be rather indifferent to what they do. On the other hand, maybe the politicians do not exaggerate the importance of their record to their electoral fate as much as the polls seem to suggest. Let us explore the reasons officeholders must tread carefully when they consider violating public opinion.

First, the high reelection rate of incumbent officeholders does not actually provide much security because the officeholder may want to win not only the next election but also several thereafter. Consider the case of U.S. House members, who have a success rate of over 90 percent per reelection attempt. Most survive their next election, but in the long run about one-third eventually leave office via an electoral defeat (Erikson 1976c). Such odds on long-term electoral survival can give House members reason to pay special attention to constituency desires.

Second, the easiest way for citizens to become aware of their elected leader's record is for it to be exploited by an opponent as a stand against public opinion. Therefore, although name recognition generally wins votes, lack of public knowledge of a political leader's policy stands may sometimes actually be a sign of successful representation. Put another way, if members of Congress became more casual in their consideration of constituency views—for example, if representatives of liberal districts started acting like conservatives and vice versa—the polls might show much more evidence of constituency awareness, and on election day, more incumbents would be defeated. David Mayhew (1974, 37) explains it this way:

> When we say "Congressman Smith is unbeatable," we do not mean there is nothing he could do that would lose him his seat. Rather we mean, "Congressman Smith is unbeatable as long as he continues to do the things he is doing." If he stopped answering his mail, or stopped visiting his district, or began voting randomly on roll calls, or shifted his vote record eighty points on the ADA scale, he would bring on primary or November election troubles in a hurry.

Third, one should note that there does exist a sprinkling of informed voters who shift their political weight according to the policy views of the candidates. Even if these alert voters compose a tiny fraction of the total, their opinion leadership allows them to influence election outcomes to an extent beyond what their number would indicate. As information about the representative diffuses downward from relatively informed opinion leaders to the mass public, many voters may "get simple positive or negative cues about the Congressman which were provoked by his legislative actions but no longer have a recognizable policy content," as Miller and Stokes (1963, 55) suggest. By responding to such cues, a significant number of voters may act as if they are relatively informed about their representative's record. As a result, the collective electoral decisions in congressional contests may be more responsive to roll-call records than our knowledge about individual votes would indicate.

In the previous chapter, we saw the result of this process is visible in election returns. Members of Congress lose votes when they take ideologically extreme public positions. Normally such vote loss due to policy stands is not sufficient for defeat, as the representative is often protected by a modest incumbency advantage and a one-party district. But the few who do lose can often blame their own policy stands for their misfortune.

10-5 INTEREST GROUPS AND DEMOCRATIC REPRESENTATION

Public opinion is generally treated as a passive input for the consideration of elected officials, with politicians absorbing the costs of interpreting public preferences from polls and other indicators. But public opinion can take on an active voice when people try to gain attention by such actions as protesting, ranting on the Internet, and lobbying officials. Often people coordinate their activity so it becomes group activity. Then, politicians pay extra attention due to the power of numbers. At its best, this is the interest groups model at work.

Like the political parties model, the interest groups model allows for an intermediate agent (in this case, organized groups) between individuals and their government leaders. Group members need not engage in extensive activity themselves but can instead rely on their group's leaders and lobbyists to represent their interest. Members may be called on, however, to contribute to the group's strength by giving money, writing letters to officials, participating in demonstrations, or voting for the group's endorsed candidates. Elected leaders, according to the model, satisfy public opinion when they respond to (and anticipate) group pressures. To the extent the interest groups model is working, the influence of different interest groups reflects their membership and the intensity with which their views are held. When conflicting demands of different interest groups collide, the policy result is a compromise, with each side getting its way in proportion to the strength of its membership support.

Interest Groups Opinion as Public Opinion

By organizing as political interest groups, people take the initiative to get the attention of politicians. An argument can be made that organized interest groups facilitate the representation of public opinion. Policymakers want to be informed about public opinion so they can act without electoral surprises. Thus, they listen to spokespersons for the various groups with interests in the matter at hand (Herbst 1999). Without organized groups to facilitate their understanding of the varying interests of the public, politicians would be operating from ignorance. In the ideal case, the aggregation of group opinion represents public opinion.

Politically active interest groups include business groups (e.g., the National Association of Wholesale Distributors), labor unions (e.g., the United Auto

Workers), professional groups (e.g., the American Nurses Association), issue advocates (e.g., the National Rifle Association, the Sierra Club), identity groups (e.g., National Organization of Women, Mexican American Political Association) and ideological groups (e.g., Americans for Democratic Action, the American Conservative Union). This diversity masks the challenge that the various groups holding a political interest do not face equal costs of organizing or enjoy equal persuasive powers when they do. In fact, the startup costs for group action are considerable, so the advantage goes to the groups organized in advance (Olson 1968). Wealthy and educated people gain an advantage in influence via the group process, with studies repeatedly finding citizens at the high end of the socioeconomic ladder belonging to more political groups than those at the low end. (e.g., Verba and Nie 1972). The wealthy and educated gain a further advantage because officeholders tend to empathize more with higher-status citizens. For instance, elected officials are more likely to attend to the concerns of business leaders than to those of advocates for the homeless.

Implicit in any discussion of interest group success is the group's power to dispense or withhold rewards to elected officials. The most obvious source of reward or punishment is the group's vote on Election Day. Yet it is not always clear that group leaders speak for their members' interests nor whether their endorsements of candidates can influence voters (Lupia and McCubbins 1998).

Groups may lobby most effectively on issues outside the public spotlight. Generally, a group is successful if its goal would greatly benefit the group and cost little to others. Examples of such benefits include tax breaks, agricultural subsidies, oil import quotas, veterans' benefits, and land tariffs on commodities. Unfortunately, from the standpoint of the interest groups model, the beneficiaries of such policies are special interests that cannot claim to represent public opinion. Narrow but specialized interests have an advantage not only because they have a unity of purpose but also because the public is often not aware of their activities. Meanwhile, groups that depend on a large mass membership for support are often handicapped when their members become satisfied by public relations gestures and symbolic rewards (Edelman 1965).

Money, PACs, and the Electoral Process

Interest groups have additional political resources besides the power of the vote. For instance, they are often able to offer the government their technical expertise. Most important of all, interest groups dispense cash to finance politicians' campaigns. While most campaign contributions originate with individual citizens directly rather than groups, organized groups' Political Action Committees (PACs) play a special role in campaign financing by drawing money from their membership base, bundling it, and dispersing it to political candidates.

The role of PACs in campaign finance is widely regarded as giving too much power to well-financed groups at the expense of ordinary citizens. More is involved than simply the effect of money on election outcomes. The argument goes as follows. Contributors give to campaigns not as philanthropic generosity to the deserving class of righteous politicians but as policy investments. Otherwise, why would groups contribute so much to unopposed candidates or concentrate their contributions on electorally safe members of congressional committees that must vote on legislation relevant to the group? Although contributions are often given in gratitude for legislative support of the group's positions in the past rather than for explicit future favors, legislators can enhance their expectation of future group support if they support the group position in advance. Once they receive a PAC's support, individual legislators become even more receptive to the group's position. A legislator who votes against a PAC's interest can find its future contributions withdrawn or even given to an electoral opponent. Even when a PAC mistakenly backs the losing horse in an election, the PAC often recovers influence by funding the winner. In fact, PACs often spread their investment by contributing to both candidates in an election.

With reelection rates of over 90 percent, and with evidence showing that the money they spend in a campaign is rarely crucial to their reelection, we might ask why members of Congress could not boldly act independently of PAC influence. One argument is that politicians do not like to take electoral chances they can avoid. Certainly many politicians take PAC money without being influenced by it, and many others avoid all PAC money on principle. But there can be little doubt that PAC money buys access if not actual influence. Elected officials generally pay extra attention to the views of those who give them money.

Does PAC activity distort the political process in favor of groups with advantages in resources? Political scientists tend to be somewhat cautious in their conclusion because testing for statistical evidence of PAC influence is not easy. Scholars who have reviewed the evidence do see a tentative statistical pattern whereby Congress members give more weight to contributor opinion than their overall voting record, constituency preferences, and party affiliation would suggest.[13] However, one could argue that is exactly the pattern one would find if contributors gave to like-minded candidates, expecting nothing in return.

Although it stands to reason that people who give money to campaigns expect something in return (Snyder 1992), the statistical evidence suggests elected officials rarely take abrupt U-turns in policy in response to bursts of campaign cash (Wawro 2001). While corrupt deals undoubtedly occur behind closed doors, it is probably safe to say that with the mix of giving by business, labor, and ideological groups to campaigns, the net ideological balance of national policy making is not affected much by the influence of money (Ansolahebere, de Figueirido, and Snyder 2003).

Many informed observers doubt that significant reform of campaign financing would greatly diminish the overall role of interest groups in the policy process because organized groups would still possess the advantages of information, expertise, and direct monitoring of government officials—which the general public does not possess. The hoped-for change would be that a group's bankroll would play a smaller role in determining its degree of influence. When elected leaders respond to potential votes rather than potential cash, the different organized groups compete on a more level playing field.

Interest Groups: An Assessment

Because the positions voiced by influential organized groups do not necessarily correspond to even the most strongly held views within the general public, the actual group process seldom follows the prescription of the interest groups model. If group activity were the sole input into governmental decision, the result would be a distortion of public opinion. The problem is that the group process results in some opinions carrying more weight than others.

Although some people obtain more representation from group activity than others, this does not mean that interest groups' freedom to operate in the political arena works against the public interest. A fact of political life is that some people—particularly the wealthy, educated, articulate, and already politically powerful—are in the best position to advance their political preferences. This fact is only made clearer when we examine the role of interest groups in politics.

One could conduct a mental experiment of imagining a political world where all interest group access to government officials is somehow eliminated. While the "special interest" would lose access, so would the spokespersons for the general public. Rather than wishing the wholesale reduction in interest group influence, perhaps we should concentrate on ways to make the process of interest group access more equitable.

10-6 CONCLUSION

This chapter has explored sources beyond the direct mechanism of elections for additional linkages between public opinion and public policy. Four models were explored. The sharing model generates representation because politicians are drawn from the same community as their voters. The parties model generates representation because parties provide voters with an easy cue to cast rational ballots. The delegate model generates representation because elected leaders anticipate the need to please future voters. Finally, although it can lead to distortion, the interest groups model generates representation because the politicians' response to group interest can indirectly reflect the opinions of the general public.

A public that is not well informed gets its policy views represented by government, perhaps to a degree greater than it seems to deserve. In the next and final chapter, we assess the net influence of public opinion on policy in the United States, and we discuss possible ways to make the public's influence stronger.

Notes

1. In an early study of nonpartisan city councils, Kenneth Prewitt (1970) found many "lateral entrants" who were encouraged by friends and associates to run for office. In an early study of the partisan Connecticut legislature, James Barber (1965) identified many "reluctants"—serving not because of their raw ambition or political interest but because of the insistence of others.

2. In 2003, women constituted only 14 percent of both House and Senate member-ship. Also in 2003, 9 percent of House members were African American and 5 percent were Hispanic. Neither minority was represented in the Senate. Only 6 percent (in the House) and 2 percent (in the Senate) were under forty years of age. *Source:* Stanley and Niemi (2003, 207). On the social and economic charac-teristics of American legislators generally, see Thompson and Moncrief (1992), Bullock (1992), and Freeman and Lyons (1992).

3. Comparing opinions of the mass public with those of elites is difficult because the results of the comparison can depend on the issues that are chosen. In 1982, the CBS/*New York Times* survey included questions about school prayer and constitu-tional amendment to balance the budget. Elites appear more liberal on these issues because they are more aware of the complexities than the mass public, who treat questions about prayers and balanced budgets as referenda on God and the virtue of thrift, respectively. On the practical issues of what Congress should spend its money on, the 1982 mass and congressional samples were remarkably similar.

   In 1970, U.S. senators were also interviewed. Senators displayed slightly more liberal views than both the public and House members. For an analysis of the 1970 findings, see Backstrom (1977). For an analysis of the 1978 data, see Bishop and Frankovic (1981).

4. As recently as 1988 there had been virtually no statistical relationship between state-level ideology and state-level partisanship (Erikson 2001). Much—but not all—of the change in the states has been due to conservative Southern states con-verting to the Republican party.

5. On the partisan background of party activists, see Kweit (1986) and Nesbit (1988).

6. Although the image of primary elections as driven by the preferences of ideo-logues of the left (for Democrats) and right (Republicans) is a common one, support from survey analysis is elusive; see Norrander (1989).

7. For an earlier study showing in-district party differences on ideology, see Sullivan and O'Conner (1972).

8. The district vote for president is the vote in the old districts in force for 2000 rather than the new districts following the 2000 Census.

9. For further discussions of House-Senate differences in the representation process, see Lee and Oppenheimer (1998) and Gronke (2000).

10. An interesting example of early retirements helping ease the observed incumbent defeat rate was the aftermath of the House banking scandal of the early 1990s. See Banducci and Karp (1994), Jacobson and Dimmock (1994), Groseclose and Krehbiel (1994), and Alford et al. (1994).

11. For further discussion, see Erikson and Wright (2001a).

12. Voter knowledge of positions on the first Gulf War was equally slim for senators and representatives (Alvarez and Gronke 1996).

13. Consider two classic discussions of money and politics. Jacobson (1989, 141) con-cludes: "Still, at least some [Congress] members, on some issues (those drawing little public or district attention) seem to vote in a way that reflects prior PAC contributions independent of ideology, partisanship, or local interests." Sorauf (1988, 312) states it this way: "The results have been disappointingly mixed and ambiguous. Some studies find modest relationships and an independent effect of contributions but others do not—an outcome probably the result of the different methodologies and the different groups and votes in the various projects."

11 | Public Opinion and the Performance of Democracy

According to democratic theory, the health of a democracy depends on the existence of a politically informed and active citizenry. By carefully monitoring government affairs, citizens can develop informed opinions about policies that represent their interests. By working for and voting for candidates who represent their views, and by making their views known to elected leaders, citizens can collectively translate their policy preferences into government action. The resulting set of policies that governments enact represents a reasonable compromise between competing claims of equally powerful and informed citizens. This description is the democratic ideal. In this concluding chapter we assess the degree to which American democracy approaches the ideal and speculate about possible ways to achieve improvement.

11-1 ASSESSING THE IMPACT OF PUBLIC OPINION ON POLICY

We have discussed five models that have the potential to provide public policy consistent with what the public prefers. By voting for leaders who share their views, the public can fulfill the basic needs of the rational–activist model. If reliable voting cues are furnished by political parties, policy-oriented voters can fulfill the political parties model by choosing the party platform most compatible with their views. Aside from voting, people can influence policymakers by bringing the preferences of the group to which they belong to bear on officials, thus fulfilling the interest groups model. In addition, linkage between opinions and policy can be furnished by two models that do not demand public coercion of leaders. If policymakers try to follow public opinion and perceive that opinion accurately, the role-playing model is fulfilled. Finally, because leaders and followers share many political beliefs, the sharing model provides political linkage.

By itself, each of these sources of political linkage may provide only a small increase in the degree to which officials are responsive to the public. Their total effect may in fact be slight, as to show that public opinion can influence policy is not a demonstration that public opinion is followed all or even most of the time. Perhaps the evidence we need is some sort of counting of the frequency with which government policies are in accord with public opinion. A truly definitive study following this design would require information at the national, state, and local levels across a broad range of policies as to whether the process of political linkage results in public policy consistent with public opinion. We would want to be able to say which of the linkage models proves most viable, and on what issues. We would want to assess the consequences of linkage failure for the public's opinions about its government, for its participation in political affairs, and, ultimately, for political stability. Unfortunately, such a study does not exist.

Because presently available evidence of the frequency of political linkage is limited, conclusions based on it must be tentative—perhaps limited to the specific issues studied, the level of government considered, and the period involved. Moreover, congruence of majority opinion and government policy may not always be the best indicator of political linkage, as government decisions can be responses to the intense opinions of a minority rather than the preferences of the majority. Also, as we have seen, majority opinion on an issue fluctuates with the exact wording of a survey question. Keeping these cautions in mind, let us see what the evidence shows about the congruence of public opinion and government policy.

Evidence at the National Level

If acts of Congress were determined by the demands of public opinion, then Congress would act whenever public opinion built to majority support or higher behind a proposed program. Because polls do not regularly monitor opinions on specific proposals before Congress, we seldom know how much the public supports a policy before its enactment. However, polls can offer clues to how well Congress serves the broad policy guidelines preferred by the public.

Government policy on health care has been a major national issue for over half a century. The central event in the history of government health care was the passage of Medicare in 1965, extending free health care to senior citizens. Medicare is a good issue for examining the connection—or its lack—between opinion and policy. As early as 1935, a presidential commission proposed a plan for national health insurance that would have provided universal coverage. In 1945, President Truman endorsed such a plan. Twenty years later, Congress created Medicare, a comprehensive health insurance plan, but only for the elderly. Why was there such a delay? One reason is that although most people favored government assistance, they were not insistent. For example, consider the results of an NES poll in 1956 (when the health care issue was dormant) that asked people whether the government should "help people get doctors and health care at low cost" and also asked for an appraisal of government performance to date (too much, less than it should, about right, or "haven't heard yet what government is doing"). Although opinion was more than 2–1 in favor of government participation, only 30 percent said government was doing less than it should. The crystallized opposition—taking the position of both opposing government participation as well as saying the government either was doing about right or was going too far—made up only 15 percent of the sample (recomputed from Key 1961a, 269). Most people apparently did not have a coherent opinion one way or the other. Even when Medicare became a central issue in the 1960s, few were attentive. In a 1962 quiz of the public, only 57 percent of the respondents said they had heard of Medicare (then only a proposal) and had any understanding of it. In fact, only 7 percent knew the basic facts—that it would be financed by Social Security and limited to people receiving old-age insurance (Nadel 1972, 540). Only after Medicare became law in 1965 did most people become aware of its general provisions.

Perhaps if people had been politically mobilized by their views on medical care, Medicare or a program even more extensive would have been enacted much sooner. As things stood, the powerful American Medical Association was able to forestall satisfaction of a feeble-voiced public. In fact, neither Medicare nor its predecessors emerged from the House Ways and Means Committee in more than very diluted form until the 1964 Democratic landslide tipped the committee's balance in favor of such legislation (Marmor 1970; Jacobs 1993).

While the importance of public opinion in the enactment of Medicare remains ambiguous, we need to analyze more than a single issue. To develop a strong statistical argument that policy corresponds (or seems to follow) public opinion, we must find a consistent pattern of congruence over many issues. One form of congruence would be a pattern of policy changes usually following the direction of majority opinion. Even stronger evidence would be both opinion and policy changing in the same direction such that opinion change predicted a corresponding policy change.

Alan Monroe (1979, 1998) has examined opinion-policy congruence over the period from 1960 to 1974 and again from 1980 to 1993. For a variety of poll questions, Monroe ascertained whether or not the public preferred a specific change in national policy. For each issue, he then determined whether the public's preferred policy change eventually took place. His findings for the earlier period are shown in Table 11.1. On the seventy-four issues for which the public favored the status quo, the desired outcome of no change occurred 76 percent of the time. On the forty-eight issues on which the public preferred change, the desired outcome of designated change occurred 59 percent of the time. Evidently, the public is less likely to get its way when it prefers change than when it prefers the status quo. Of course, that the American political system tends to be status-quo-oriented has often been observed—that is, an intense minority (for example, opponents of gun control) can often block

TABLE 11.1 | **Congruence of Policy Preference Among the Mass Public and Policy Outcomes at the National Level**

	Preference	
Outcome	Status Quo	Change
Status Quo	76%	41%
Change	24	59
	100%	100%
	(n=74)	(n=148)

Source: Alan D. Monroe, "Consistency Between Public Preferences and National Policy Decisions," *American Politics Quarterly* 7 (Jan. 1979): 9. Copyright © 1979 by Sage Publications. Reprinted by permission of Sage Publications, Inc.

change. But in either case, the public's preference becomes policy more often than not. Over all cases—preferences for change and preferences for the status quo—Monroe finds policy corresponding to public opinion almost two-thirds of the time. For the later period (1980–1993), the rate of policy correspondence was somewhat lower for reasons that are not clear.

In a related study, Page and Shapiro (1983) examine over 300 instances of opinion change recorded by polls between 1935 and 1979. They find a healthy correspondence between the direction of the change in public preferences and the direction of change in public policy. In the 231 instances where opinion and policy both changed, they changed in the same direction 66 percent of the time. Page and Shapiro do not entirely rule out the possibility of some spurious relationship: Political elites could educate the public to like the policies they enact for their own interest. Support for the inference that opinion causes policy is strengthened, however, by the fact that their observed policy changes almost always followed the change in opinion rather than the other way around.

Recently, scholars have been exploring long-term relationships between opinion and national policy in search of statistical evidence of opinion influencing policy. Several positive results have been reported. The clearest evidence is for defense spending, with changes in defense spending seemingly following from shifts in public perceptions of need (Bartels 1991; Hartley and Russett 1992; Wlezien 1995b). Spending levels for domestic purposes also appear responsive to public preferences (Wlezien 1995a). Statistical evidence even suggests that Supreme Court decisions respond to shifts in public opinion (Mishler and Sheehan 1993; Flemming and Wood 1997).

Time-series evidence of an opinion-policy linkage at the national level can also be presented in terms of the electorate's ideological mood on the one hand and a composite of national policies on the other. As our measure of public opinion we use Stimson's "mood" indicator of public liberalism. Recall (chapter 4) that mood represents a composite of trends over several survey questions regarding national policy. As a measure of national policy, we count the number of major liberal laws minus the number of major conservative laws for each Congress, 1953–2002.[1] Figure 11.1 overlays public opinion (mood) and policy (laws) over the last half of the twentieth century, showing a seeming connection between public opinion and policy. When public opinion turns more liberal or conservative (and these movements of mood are small in magnitude), the index of national policy appears to follow. Although correlation does not prove causation, it would seem that the ideological tone of national policy draws its momentum from slight shifts in ideological taste on the part of the U.S. public (Erikson, MacKuen, and Stimson 2002).

Evidence at the State Level

At the state level, the opinion-policy linkage can be analyzed by seeing whether or not states where the public is most in favor of a given policy tend to be the states that enact that policy. Unfortunately, this kind of analysis is limited by the fact that polls rarely report reliable state-by-state breakdowns of opinion for comparison. Surprisingly, the best state-level opinion data are from polls conducted in 1930s, when national polls were based on much larger samples than today. One study examined three state-level issues for which there were available opinion data in 1936 (Erikson 1976a). On each of these issues—capital punishment, child labor regulation, and woman jurors—a strong correlation between state opinion and state policy was found. While these examples suggest an opinion-policy linkage, further analysis of this sort is hampered by the lack of available state opinion data.

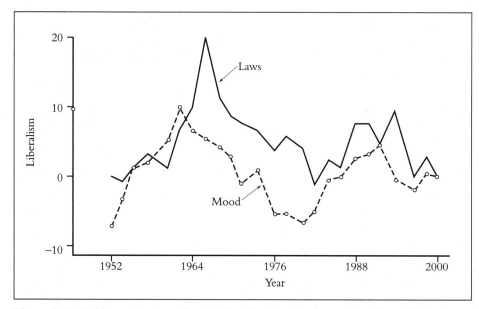

Figure 11.1   Public opinion (mood) and policy liberalism (laws) over time. *Source:* Updated from Erikson, MacKuen, and Stimson (2002, Figure 9.1).

For recent analysis of state policy, Erikson, Wright, and McIver (1994) pooled several CBS/*News York Times* surveys from the 1976–1988 period. Pooling of several surveys provided over 100,000 national respondents and large samples within states. Their measure of state opinion is based on the ideological self-identification (liberal, moderate, conservative) of the state samples. Their measure of state policy is a composite of eight policies with a liberal versus conservative content. They find a large correlation (+0.81) between the opinion measure and the policy measure.

This relationship is shown in Figure 11.2, where the ideological tendency of state public opinion and the ideological tendency of state policy is seen to almost always go together. The most liberal states enact the most liberal policies, and the most conservative states enact the most conservative policies. Although we cannot be totally secure about the causal direction, these data strongly suggest that public opinion matters when states make important policy decisions.

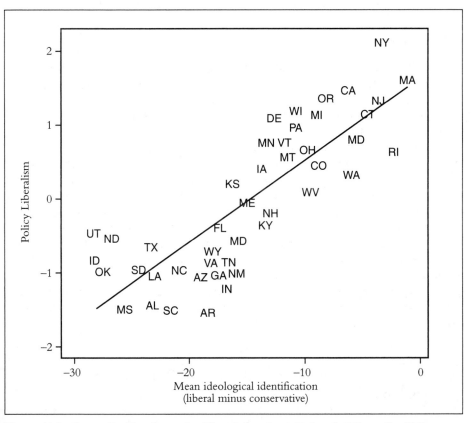

Figure 11.2   State policy liberalism and public opinion. *Source:* Robert S. Erikson, Gerald C. Wright, and John P. McIver, *Statehouse Democracy* (New York: Cambridge University Press, 1994).

Evidence at the Local Level

At the local level of government, we know very little about the relationship between public opinion and policy decisions. Apparently there are no studies that systematically attempt to determine whether or not existing differences among local policy choices are related to local political opinions. One study, however, examined the relationship between political participation levels and "policy congruence" for citizens and leaders in fifty-five American cities. *Policy congruence* is a measure of the extent to which citizens and elected officials agree on what are the most important local problems. A study by Sidney Verba and Norman Nie (1972) and a further analysis of the same data by Susan Hansen (1975) reveal that the higher the community's level of public participation—particularly its level of voting participation—the greater the congruence between mass and elite perceptions of community problems. Of further consequence are competitive elections. Hansen finds the combination of high voting turnout and close local elections produces the greatest citizen-leader congruence scores. Contrary evidence exists, however. Luttbeg (1999) finds in a study of thirty-seven Texas cities that leaders were the most anxious about satisfying public opinion in cities with the least competitive elections.

An Opinion-Policy Connection

Although the evidence is certainly incomplete, the few relevant studies that test for an opinion-policy linkage suggest that public opinion is far from inconsequential. At the national level we find that opinion and national policy are in agreement more often than not. At the state level we find that state opinion can be a good predictor of state policy. At the local level we find that high citizen participation is associated with citizen-leader agreement on important problems, although we have no data concerning solutions to those problems.

Such findings should not be surprising because, as we have seen, several linkages work to translate even feebly voiced public opinion into policy. This information, however, should not be cause for complacency about the current state of American democracy. Other forces besides public opinion shape government decisions—and we must keep in mind that public opinion is often uninformed, unenlightened, or simply wrong. For instance, public perceptions of the severity of the crime problem do not track well with the objective crime rate (Sharp 1999). On the positive side, the evidence that a rather inattentive public can sometimes influence policy suggests that a more attentive public would have even greater control over policy decisions.

11-2 INTERPRETING THE PUBLIC'S ROLE IN DEMOCRACY

As we have seen throughout this book, the public generally does not live up to its prescribed activist role. Moreover, while public opinion can often influence government policy, in reality it is not the sole determinant of policy outcomes. Why not? Public control of government decisions depends on both the extent to which people actually participate in politics and the equality of people's resources for effective participation. The first point is obvious: It seems logical that the more people participate in politics, the more they can influence government decisions. But some people can participate more effectively than others because they command a greater share of the necessary resources, such as money, information, articulateness, and access to decision makers. How inequitable one views the distribution of these political resources can determine one's view of how democratic the political system actually is. Some observers see effective political power concentrated in the hands of an elite that controls policy outcomes for its own interests. Others more optimistically see the inequality in the distribution of power limited basically to the different political skills that individuals have and their interest in using them.[2] Because this debate over the equality of the distribution of political power is not easily decided by scientific inquiry, we do not enter it directly here. But, taking into account that the tools of effective political participation are not equally distributed, how can we assess the less than active political role of the public? We discuss four plausible conclusions.

Public Apathy as Mass Political Incompetence

Perhaps the easiest view of the public's limited role in government affairs is that people are simply incapable of doing better. The frequency with which people fail to hold political opinions, the rarity of the liberal or conservative ideologue, and the difficulty in locating rational policy-oriented voters may all indicate that people generally lack the skills necessary to make sophisticated judgments about their political leaders and policies. Worse yet, the political views that people do hold may be intolerant, naive, or simply wrong. Viewed from this perspective, an increase in public participation would only make the situation worse because "bad" public opinion would drive "good" policymakers toward undesirable acts.

If the mass public is viewed as being inherently incapable of playing a useful role, then the remedy of trying to uplift public opinion becomes ineffective. Instead, one might have to rely on the proper training or careful recruitment of political leaders as a means of producing desired outcomes. If such desired outcomes include the preservation of the substance of democracy, then one must prescribe both a limited public role and the instillation of a heavy dose of democratic values among political elites. Thomas Dye and Harmon Ziegler (1987), who arrive at this position, call it the "irony of democracy."

Public Apathy as Rational Disengagement

Possibly the reason most people do not allow politics to intrude far into their lives is that to do so would be irrational. From a strict cost-benefit standpoint, one should not follow public affairs closely because the investment would get one nowhere. One person's vote is useless because it is fantasy to assume that a single vote can decide an election's outcome except in the most extraordinary circumstances. Even when an individual's economic interest is directly at stake in the political arena (which may be rare), organizing like-minded people for collective political pressure is irrational because the costs of organization outweigh the possible benefits one could expect (Olson 1968). The cynic might also suggest that increased public knowledge of governmental affairs would produce only greater political withdrawal, as people who learn about their leaders' corruption and unresponsiveness would feel even more helpless at the prospect of changing things.

If this logic is correct, then people who participate in politics usually are motivated by something other than tangible personal gains. Perhaps they "irrationally" participate in order to gratify a felt obligation or civic duty. If the major determinant of an individual's sense of obligation to participate is pre-adult political socialization, then a reformer might hope to increase public participation by improving the training of the next generation of citizens. Alternatively, one might hope to eliminate rational withdrawal from politics by somehow increasing the rewards of political participation.

Public Apathy as Elite Manipulation

One can also interpret the public's low participation in politics as the result of manipulation by leaders and their allies. When one observes political docility on the part of people who seemingly should have strong reasons for political protest, one can easily draw the conclusion that the individuals are being misled by elite propaganda. By this view, people are quiet and content because a ruling elite distracts them with bread and circuses.

One need not believe in a complex conspiracy in order to view political quiescence as the result of elite manipulation. Because most political events are remote from people's everyday lives, people willingly view these events through the interpretation of their leaders. Also, because people want to believe their political system is benign rather than corrupt or evil, they readily find reassurance from optimistic interpretations of the existing order and resist the voices that tell them otherwise (Edelman 1965).

If one sees people as unwilling to accept "truth" because they do not want to disturb their cherished beliefs, the obvious remedy would appear to be heavy doses of correct information. But how to make this remedy effective remains unclear.

Public Apathy as Public Contentment

Rather than viewing public apathy as a sign that the classical democratic model does not hold, one can interpret apathy as an indicator of public contentment. If people do not concern themselves with political matters, then they must not have any additional demands to make on their government. Conversely, when many people do participate in politics, it is a distressing signal either that government has ignored public needs or that conflicts between societal groups are no longer being successfully resolved by political leaders.

Actually, the view that public apathy means public satisfaction rests on the assumption that the public is rather politically sophisticated. It assumes that people are capable of articulating grievances, that they feel their expression of grievance would be effective, and that they are not easily led to ignore their interests. Only if these assumptions are made can one conclude that the lack of political participation indicates that people's needs are met by the proper working of a democratic system.

Evaluation

Although they contradict one another, each of these four possible explanations of the public's lack of political participation contains a grain of truth. For example, the public may not be capable of participation in all government decisions, particularly when the decision depends on proper evaluation of advanced technical knowledge. Equally obvious is that people can take only limited time from their personal affairs to participate in politics. Moreover, people may decide not to participate because they feel (perhaps mistakenly) they can trust their political leaders. Finally, people may retire from the political arena because they indeed have no grievances.

Simply holding them up to the light of scientific evidence cannot determine which of the explanations of low participation in politics is most valid, as individual observers will view the evidence through the filter of their own preconceptions and values. How observers view such matters as human nature, people's basic interest, and the benevolence of government can shape how strongly they conclude that political inactivity signifies incapability, rational withdrawal, manipulation, or contentment. Similarly, the extent to which observers see their own opinion in harmony with majority opinion might influence their views of whether public control of government should increase or decrease.

11-3 THE EXPANSION OF POLITICAL PARTICIPATION

Whether or not increased public political participation is desirable also depends on the type of political participation. Few would applaud increased mass participation that results in civil war or mass mobilization in support of an antidemocratic movement. But few would fear an increase in informed, democratic participation—particularly if we ignore possible disagreement over what *informed democratic participation* means. When there is little mass participation, the burden of responsibility falls on the political elites—both to ensure the continuation of the democratic rules and also to make policy decisions that are fair and equitable. But if one agrees that the purpose of democracy is to ensure political leaders are held accountable to the people, one can hardly applaud when people do not actively seek to protect their own interests. Are there ways to increase the number of active participants while at the same time ensuring this participation is rational and democratic?

Seemingly, part of the answer involves some way of creating a more politically informed public. The public can hardly be blamed for its political ignorance when it is given little information with which to make political judgments. One can readily endorse more thorough political reporting by news media and other efforts to induce a more informed public. Hopes should not be set too high, however, because information campaigns do not always reach the people most in need of them. Also, we must recognize the possible side effects produced by increased public knowledge, such as greater public cynicism or an intensification of conflicts among politically aroused mass groups.

However difficult the task of boosting information might be, we can readily imagine that a more informed public would be better able to serve its function in the American democracy. Furthermore, we can speculate about how different the opinions of a truly informed public would be from the actual public we know. Increasingly, political scientists are taking this matter seriously, asking in what ways an informed public would act differently and how a more informed public might be achieved. (Delli Carpini and Keeter 1996; Bartels 1996; Fishkin 1997; Lupia and McCubbins 1998; Althaus 1998; Gastil 2000; Gilens 2001; Luskin 2003).

Answering these questions is difficult. A particular challenge is that the public may not want to be thrust into the policymaking spotlight. Citizens see their job as keeping a watch over the rascal politicians at the helm rather than taking the helm themselves (Hibbing and Theiss-Morse 2002).

Apart from inducing the development of a more informed public, a related and equally daunting task is to induce more people to participate in politics. The most obvious way of doing so would be to legislate changes that lower the costs and burdens of participation. For instance, motor-voter legislation and other reforms reduce or eliminate the initial barriers to voter registration. If we register the unregistered, maybe they will vote and maybe they will become informed and cast informed votes. We await the evidence. In recent years, the voting rate (among eligible voters) threatened to fall to record lows, a disturbing phenomenon at a time when most of the entry costs for voter participation have been removed. Increasing numbers of Americans are *choosing* to be nonparticipants. Political scientists have failed to understand this trend and its underlying causes.

Perhaps the existing methods for translating public opinion into government policy are inaccurate relics of a technically primitive time when ballot-casting, face-to-face communication, and geographic representation were the only feasible conduits for public expression. New methods might be tried to encourage greater citizen participation, giving people greater opportunity to participate directly in local decisions, including perhaps more participatory democracy in nongovernmental groups such as the workplace, school, and religious organizations. Also, people could play a more direct role by deciding policy questions in referenda instead of letting their elected leaders decide them. Finally, it is now technologically feasible to allow people to vote in referenda via the Internet from the comfort of their home.

There is no question that greater citizen participation is a desired democratic value. But it is debatable whether additional opportunities to participate would lead to wiser government decisions than elected leaders currently make. While proposals for expanding participation deserve serious consideration, their practicability and desirability remain uncertain.

NOTES

1. Important laws are determined using the format of Mayhew (1991).
2. The debate is framed by two classic studies, now decades old: Mills (1956), claiming rule by a "power elite"; and Dahl (1961), arguing for the presence of pluralism.

The National
Election Study and
the General Social
Survey Questions

Two major national surveys, designed specifically for
academic analysis, are conducted on a regular basis. These are the National
Election Study (NES), done by the Center for Political Studies at the University of Michigan (conducted in even-number years), and the General Social
Survey (GSS), done by the National Opinion Research Center at the University of Chicago (usually conducted yearly). For academic purposes, these surveys are much more valuable than surveys done by commercial polling
organizations. One reason is that the interviews are done in person rather than
over the phone. Another is that the questionnaires are quite lengthy, usually
including hundreds of items administered over a period of more than one hour.
Also, many items are repeated over time, allowing for the analysis of changes.

Throughout this book, responses to opinion questions asked in either the
NES or GSS opinion surveys are examined. As their content usually appears in
abbreviated form, the complete wordings for the most frequently used questions in the book are presented below. Where appropriate, responses are labeled as [L] for liberal and [C] for conservative, according to how these terms
are applied to the response alternative within the text.

QUESTIONS FROM THE NATIONAL ELECTION STUDIES

1. Party Identification

Two questions are used to measure party identification. First, respondents are
asked:

> Generally speaking, do you usually think of yourself as a Republican, a Democrat, an Independent, or what?

This basic question provides the division between the three kinds of partisans. For the second question, partisans are probed regarding the strength of their partisanship, and Independents are probed to see whether they lean toward one of the major parties.

Republicans and Democrats are asked:

> Would you call yourself a strong Republican [Democrat] or not so strong Republican [Democrat]?

Independents are asked:

> Do you think of yourself as closer to the Republican Party or to the Democratic Party?

Independents who choose a party are called *Independent Leaners*. Many Independents respond that they lean toward neither party. They are often called *Pure Independents*.

The net result is a seven-point scale of partisanship.

1. Strong Democrat
2. Not so strong (or "weak") Democrat
3. Independent, leaning Democrat
4. Pure Independent
5. Independent, leaning Republican
6. Not so strong (or "weak") Republican
7. Strong Republican

Unless otherwise noted, we use the simpler three-way division: Democrats (1 and 2), Independents (3, 4, and 5), and Republicans (6 and 7).

2. Liberal/Conservative Ideology

People are asked to choose an ideological position on a seven-point scale. Respondents are first asked:

> We hear a lot of talk these days about liberals and conservatives. Here is a seven-point scale on which the political views that most people might hold are arranged from extremely liberal to extremely conservative.

Then they are asked:

> Where would you place yourself on this scale, or haven't you thought much about it?

1. Extremely liberal
2. Liberal
3. Slightly liberal
4. Moderate, middle-of-the-road
5. Slightly conservative
6. Conservative

7. Extremely conservative
8. Don't know
9. Haven't thought much about it

Where we show the basic division between self-identified liberals and conservatives, we combine responses 1, 2, and 3 as *liberal* and 5, 6, and 7 as *conservative*.

In recent years, the NES has used the following variation of the seven-point scale for most of its issue questions. Respondents are first presented with two extreme positions on the issue. Then they are asked to place themselves with regard to the issue on a scale ranging from 1 to 7. Shown the scale, respondents are asked: "Where would you place yourself on this scale, or haven't you thought much about it?" The scale position 1 generally represents the extreme liberal viewpoint and scale position 7 generally represents the extreme conservative viewpoint. For convenience, we often compress the scale, combining the responses 1, 2, and 3 as *liberal* responses and 5, 6, and 7 as *conservative* responses, with neutral "4" respondents and those who admit they "haven't thought much about it" combined as "non-opinion holders."

Following are the six 7-point issue scales used in our ten-item index of respondent liberalism-conservatism.

3. Government Services/Spending Scale

Some people think the government should provide fewer services, even in areas such as health and education, in order to reduce spending. . . . Other people feel it is important for the government to provide many more services even if it means an increase in spending. . . . Where would you place yourself on this scale? . . .

[C] Government should provide many fewer services, reduce spending a lot.
[L] Government should provide many more services, increase government spending a lot.
(On this one item, NES scores 1 to 7 as conservative to liberal. We reverse the polarity so that 1 represents the liberal and 7 the conservative end of the scale, consistent with the other items.)

4. Government Job and Standard of Living Scale

Some people feel the government in Washington should see to it that every person has a job and a good standard of living. Others think the government should just let each person get ahead on his own. . . . Where would you place yourself on this scale? . . .

[L] Government see to a job and a good standard of living
[C] Government let each person get ahead on own

5. National Health Insurance

There is much concern about the rapid rise in medical and hospital costs. Some people feel there should be a government insurance plan that would cover all medical and hospital expenses for everyone. . . . Others feel that all medical expenses should be paid by individuals and through private insurance plans like Blue Cross or other company plans. . . . Where would you place yourself on this scale? . . .

[L] Government insurance plan
[C] Private insurance plan

6. Aid to Blacks Scale

Some people feel that the government in Washington should make every effort to improve the social and economic positions of blacks. . . . Others feel that the government should not make any special effort to help blacks because they should help themselves. Where would you place yourself on this scale? . . .

[L] Government should help blacks
[C] Blacks should help themselves

7. Defense Spending Scale

Some people believe that we should spend much less for defense. . . . Others feel that spending should be greatly increased. . . . Where would you place yourself on this scale? . . .

[L] Greatly decrease defense spending
[C] Greatly increase defense spending

8. Environmental Protection

Some people think we need much tougher government regulations on business in order to protect the environment. . . . Others think that current regulations to protect the environment are already too much of a burden on business. . . . Where would you place yourself on this scale? . . .

[L] Tougher regulations needed.
[C] Regulations already too burdensome.

Items 3–8 are used as a part of our ten-item composite index of liberal–conservative policy positions from the 2000 NES Survey. For this composite scale, each component item is added as a -1 (liberal), +1 (conservative), or 0 (other or in between). The remaining four issues for the composite scale are the following four items from the 2000 NES Survey.

9. Gun Control

Do you think the federal government should make it more difficult for people to buy a gun than it is now, make it easier for people to buy a gun, or keep these rules about the same as they are now?

[L] More difficult
[C] Make it easier

10. Death Penalty

Do you favor or oppose the death penalty for persons convicted of murder?

[L] Favor
[C] Oppose

11. Laws Protecting Gays

Recently there has been a lot of talk about job discrimination. Do you favor or oppose laws to protect homosexuals against job discrimination?

[L] Favor
[C] Oppose

12. Abortion

There has been some discussion about abortion during recent years. Which of these opinions on this page best agree with your view?

1. By law, abortion should never be permitted.

2. The law should permit abortion only in case of rape, incest, or when the woman's life is in danger.

3. The law should permit abortion for reasons other than rape, incest, or danger to the woman's life, but only after the need for abortion has been clearly established.

4. By law, a woman should always be able to obtain an abortion as a matter of personal choice.

For purposes of ideological classification, responses 1 and 2 are coded as conservative, and responses 3 and 4 are coded as liberal.

13. Political Information Scale

For some items, the NES asked respondents to locate the positions of the major presidential candidates on the same scale. We used the candidate placements for items 2, 3, 7, 8, and 12 to form the political information scale used in chapters 3, 8, and 9. To construct this scale, every correct answer (Bush to the right of Gore) was scored as +1. Every incorrect answer (Gore to the right of Bush) was scored as -1. Every tied response was scored as zero. These scores were summed to create a composite knowledge score ranging from -5 (all incorrect) to +5 (all correct).

The -5 to +5 composite scores were grouped into three categories of high, medium, and low. High scores were perfect +5s. Low scores were +1 or less. For the lower scorers, the mean on the original -5 to +5 was zero, or in the guess range on candidate placement. All not scored at high or low were scored as medium on political knowledge.

QUESTIONS FROM THE GENERAL SOCIAL SURVEY

14. Abortion

Please tell me whether or not you think it should be possible for a pregnant woman to obtain a legal abortion. . . .

  a. If there is a strong chance of a serious defect in the baby?

  b. If she is married and does not want any more children?

  c. If the woman's own health is seriously endangered by the pregnancy?

  d. If the family has very low income and cannot afford any more children?

  e. If she became pregnant as a result of a rape?

  f. If she is not married and does not want to marry the man?

  g. If the woman wants it for any reason?

15. Political Tolerance

The GSS asks tolerance questions with a variety of groups as the target. The general form of the question, using atheists as the target group, is:

There are always some people whose ideas are considered bad or dangerous by other people. For instance, somebody who is against all churches and religion. . . .

  a. If such a person wanted to make a speech in your (city/town/community) against churches and religion, should he be allowed to speak or not?

  b. Should such a person be allowed to teach in a college or university, or not?

  c. If some people in your community suggested that a book he wrote against churches and religion should be taken out of your public library, would you favor removing this book, or not?

References

Aberbach, Joel, and Jack L. Walker. 1970. "Political Trust and Racial Ideology." *American Political Science Review* 63 (Dec.): 1199–1223.

Abramowitz, Alan I. 1994. "Issue Evolution Reconsidered: Racial Attitudes and Partisanship in the U.S. Electorate." *American Journal of Political Science* 38 (Feb.): 1–25.

———. 2000. "Bill and Al's Excellent Adventure. Forecasting the 1996 Presidential Election." In *Before the Vote: Forecasting American National Elections*, ed. James E. Campbell and James C. Garand. Thousand Oaks, CA: Sage.

Abramson, Paul R. 1983. *Political Attitudes in America*. San Francisco: Freeman.

Abramson, Paul R., and John H. Aldrich. 1982. "The Decline of Electoral Participation in America." *American Political Science Review* 76: 502–521.

Abravnel, Martin B., and Ronald J. Busch. 1975. "Political Competence, Political Trust, and the Action Orientation of University Students." *Journal of Politics* 37 (Feb.): 69–81.

Achen, Christopher. 1975. "Mass Political Attitudes and the Survey Response." *American Political Science Review* 69 (Dec.): 1218–1231.

Adelson, Joseph, and Robert P. O'Neil. 1966. "Growth of Political Ideas in Adolescence: The Sense of Community." *Journal of Personality and Social Psychology* 4 (July): 295–306.

Adler, Scott E. 2002. *Why Congressional Reforms Fail: Reelection and the House Committee System*. Chicago: University of Chicago Press.

Adorno, Theodore W., et al. 1950. *The Authoritarian Personality*. New York: Harper.

Aldrich, John H. 1996. *Why Parties? The Origin and Transformation of Party Politics in America*. Chicago: University of Chicago Press.

———. 2003. "Electoral Democracy during Politics as Usual—and Unusual." In *Electoral Democracy*, ed. George Rabinowitz and Michael B. MacKuen. Ann Arbor: University of Michigan Press.

Aldrich, John, Mark M. Berger, and David W. Rohde. 2002. "The Historic Variability in Conditional Party Government, 1877–1994." In *Party, Process, and Political Change in Congress*, ed. David W. Brady and Matthew D. McCubbins. Stanford, CA: Stanford University Press.

Aldrich, John, and James S. Coleman Battista. 2002. "Conditional Party Government in the States." *American Journal of Political Science* 46: 164–172.

Aldrich, John, and Richard Niemi. 1995. "The Sixth American Party System: Electoral Change, 1952–1992." In *Broken Contract?* ed. Stephen Craig. Boulder, CO: Westview Press.

Aldrich, John, and David W. Rohde. 2001. "The Logic of Conditional Party Government: Revisiting the Electoral Connection." In *Congress Reconsidered*, 7th ed., ed. Lawrence C. Dodd and Bruce I. Oppenheimer. Washington DC: Congressional Quarterly Press.

Alesina, Alberto, and Howard Rosenthal. 1995. *Partisan Politics, Divided Government, and the Economy*. New York: Cambridge University Press.

Alford, John R., and David W. Brady. 1993. "Personal and Partisan Advantage in U.S. Congressional Elections." In *Congress Reconsidered*, 5th ed., ed. Lawrence C. Dodd and Bruce I. Oppenheimer. Washington, DC: Congressional Quarterly Press.

Alford, John, Holly Teeters, Daniel Ward, and Rick Wilson. 1994. "Overdraft: The Political Cost of Congressional Malfeasance." *Journal of Politics* 56: 788–801.

Almond, Gabriel A. 1950. *The American People and Foreign Policy*. New York: Harcourt.

Almond, Gabriel A., and Sidney Verba. 1963. *The Civic Culture*. Boston: Little, Brown.

Altemeyer, Bob. 1981. *Right Wing Authoritarianism*. Winnipeg, ON.: University of Winnipeg Press.

———. 1988. *Enemies of Freedom: Understanding Right Wing Authoritarianism*. San Francisco: Jossey-Bass.

———. 1997. *The Authoritarian Spector*. Cambridge: Harvard University Press.

Alterman, Eric. 2003. *What Liberal Media?* New York: Basic Books.

Althaus, Scott L. 1998. "Information Effects in Collective Preferences." *American Political Science Review* 92 (Sept.): 545–558.

Alvarez, R. Michael, 1997. *Information and Elections*. Ann Arbor: University of Michigan Press.

Alvarez, Michael, and Paul Gronke. 1996. "Constituents and Legislators: Learning About the Persian Gulf Resolution." *Legislative Studies Quarterly* 21: 105–127.

Alwin, Duane F., Ronald L. Cohen, and Theodore M. Newcomb. 1991. *Political Attitudes Over the Life Span*. Madison: University of Wisconsin Press.

Andersen, Kristi. 1979. *The Creation of a Democratic Majority, 1928–1936*. Chicago: University of Chicago Press.

Anderson, Christopher, and Andrew LoTempio. 2002. "Winning, Losing, and Political Trust in America." *British Journal of Political Science* 32: 335–352.

Anderson, David D. 1981. *William Jennings Bryan*. Boston: Twayne.

Anderson, Lee, et al. 1990. *The Civics Report Card*. Princeton, NJ: National Assessment of Educational Progress, Educational Testing Service.

Ansolahebere, Stephen, John de Figueirido, and James Snyder. 2003. "Why Is There So Little Money in U.S. Politics?" *Journal of Economic Perspectives* 17 (Winter): 105–130.

Ansolabehere, Stephen, and Shanto Iyengar. 1995. *Going Negative*. New York: Free Press.

Arnold, Douglas. 1990. *The Logic of Congressional Action*. New Haven, CT: Yale University Press.

Arterton, F. Christopher. 1974. "The Impact of Watergate on Children's Attitudes Toward Authority." *Political Science Quarterly* 89 (June): 269–288.

Backstrom, Charles H. 1977. "Congress and the Public: How Representative Is One of the Other?" *American Politics Quarterly* 5 (Oct.): 411–36.

Bagdikian, Ben. 1997. *The Media Monopoly*, 5th ed. Boston: Beacon Press.

Banducci, Susan A., and Jeffrey A. Karp. 1994. "Electoral Consequences of Scandal and Reapportionment in the 1992 House Elections." *American Politics Quarterly* 22 (Jan.): 3–26.

Barber, James David. 1965. *The Lawmakers*. New Haven, CT: Yale University Press.

Barker, David C. 2002. *Rushed to Judgment: Talk Radio, Persuasion, and American Political Behavior*. New York: Columbia University Press.

Barreto, Matt, Rodolpho O. de la Garza, Jongho Lee, Jaesung Ryu, and Harry P. Pachon. 2002. "Latino Voter Mobilization in 2000: A Glimpse into Latino Policy and Voting Preferences." Report by Tomas Rivera Policy Institute, Claremont, CA.

Barry, William D., Michael B. Berkman, and Stuart Schneiderman. 2000. "Legislative Professionalism and Incumbent Reelection: The Development of Institutional Boundaries." *American Political Science Review* 94: 859–874.

Bartels, Larry. 1988. *Presidential Primaries and the Dynamics of Public Choice*. Princeton, NJ: Princeton University Press.

———. 1991. "Constituency Opinion and Congressional Policy Making: The Reagan Buildup." *American Political Science Review* 85 (June): 457–474.

———. 1993. "Messages Received: The Political Impact of Media Exposure." *American Political Science Review* 87 (Mar.): 267–286.

———. 1996. "Uninformed Voters: Information Effects in Presidential Elections." *American Journal of Political Science* 40: 194–230.

———. 2000. "Partisanship and Voting Behavior, 1952–1996." *American Journal of Political Science* 44: 35–51.

———. 2003. "Homer Gets a Tax Cut." Paper presented at the annual meeting of the American Political Science Association, Sept., Philadelphia.

Bartels, Larry, and C. Anthony Broh. 1989. "The Polls—A Review: The 1988 Presidential Primaries." *Public Opinion Quarterly* 53 (Winter): 563–568.

Baum, Mathew A. 2003. *Soft News Goes to War*. Princeton, NJ: Princeton University Press.

Baum, Mattew A., and Samuel Kernell. 1999. "Has Cable Ended the Golden Age of Presidential Television?" *American Political Science Review* 93 (March): 99–114.

Baumgartner, Frank R., and Bryan D. Jones. 1993. *Agendas and Instability in American Politics*. Chicago: University of Chicago Press.

Bawn, Kathleen. 1999. "Constructing 'US': Ideology, Coalition Politics, and False Consciousness." *American Journal of Political Science* 43: 303–34.

Beck, Paul Allen. 1974. "A Socialization Theory of Partisan Realignment." In *The Politics of Future Citizens*, ed. Richard G. Niemi. San Francisco: Jossey-Bass.

———. 1977. "The Role of Agents in Political Socialization." In *Handbook of Political Socialization*, ed. Stanley A. Renshon. New York: Free Press.

Beck, Paul Allen, and M. Kent Jennings. 1991. "Family Traditions, Political Periods, and the Development of Partisan Orientations." *Journal of Politics* 53 (Aug.): 742–63.

Behr, Roy, and Shanto Iyengar. 1985. "Television News, Real-World Cues, and Changes in the Public Agenda." *Public Opinion Quarterly* 49 (Spring): 38–57.

Bennett, Stephen. 1997. "Why Young Americans Hate Politics, and What We Should Do About It." *Politics and Political Science* 30 (Mar.): 47–52.

———. 1998. "Young American's Indifference to Media Coverage of Public Affairs." *Political Science and Politics* 31 (Sept.): 535–541.

Bennett, W. Lance. 1980. *Public Opinion in American Politics*. New York: Harcourt.

———. 1998. "The Uncivic Culture: Communication, Identity, and the Rise of Lifestyle Politics." *Political Science and Politics* 31 (Dec.): 741–762.

Bennett, Lance. 2003. *News: The Politics of Illusion*. New York: Longman.

Bereday, George Z. F., and Bonnie B. Stretch. 1963. "Political Education in the USA and USSR." *Comparative Education Review* 7 (June): 9–16.

Berelson, Bernard, Paul Lazarsfeld, and William McPhee. 1954. *Voting*. Chicago: University of Chicago Press.

Berger, Arthur A. 2003. *Media and Society*. New York: Rowan-Littlefield.

Berinsky, Adam J. 1999. "Two Faces of Public Opinion." *American Journal of Political Science* 43 (Oct.): 1209–1231.

———. 2002. "Silent Voices: Social Welfare Policy Opinions and Political Equality in America." *American Journal of Political Science* 46 (Apr.): 276–287.

Berkman, Ronald L., and Laura W. Kitch. 1986. *Politics in the Media Age*. New York: McGraw.

Berry, Jeffrey M. 1989. *The Interest Group Society*, 2nd ed. Glenview, IL: Scott.

Bettig, Ronald V., and Jeanne Lynn Hall. 2003. *Big Media, Big Money*. New York: Rowan-Littlefield.

Biemer, Paul, Ralph Folsom, Richard Dulka, Judith Lessler, Babu Shah, and Michael Weeks. 2003. "An Evaluation of Procedures and Operations Used by the Voter News Service for the 2000 Presidential Election." *Public Opinion Quarterly* 67 (Spring): 32–45.

Binder, Sarah A. 1997. *Minority Rights, Majority Rule*. New York: Cambridge University Press.

Bishop, George. 2002. "Illusion of Change." *Public Perspective* (May/June 2002): 38–43.

Bishop, George F., and Kathleen A. Frankovic. 1981. "Ideological Consensus and Constraint Among Party Leaders and Followers in the 1978 Election." *Micro-Politics* 3: 87–111.

Bishop, George F., Alfred J. Tuchfarber, and Robert W. Oldendick. 1978. "Change in the Structure of American Political Attitudes: The Nagging Question of Question Wording." *American Journal of Political Science* 22 (May): 250–269.

Bishop, George F., et al. 1980. "Pseudo-Opinions on Public Affairs." *Public Opinion Quarterly* 44 (Summer): 198–209.

Blumer, Herbert. 1948. "Public Opinion and Public Opinion Polling." *American Sociological Review* 13 (Oct.): 542–54.

Bogart, Leo. 1972. *Polls and the Awareness of Public Opinion*, 2nd ed. New Brunswick, NJ: Transaction.

———. 1998. "Politics, Polls, and Poltergeists." *Society* 35, no. 4 (May/June 1998).

Bond, Jon R., Richard Fleisher, and B. Dan Wood. 2003. The Marginal and Time-Varying Effect of Public Approval on Presidential Success in Congress." *Journal of Politics* 65: 92–110.

Box-Steffensmeir, Janet, Kathleen Knight, and Lee Sigelman. 1998. "The Interplay of Macroideology and Marcropartisanship: A Times Series Analysis." *Journal of Politics* 60: 131–149.

Boyer, Ernest, and Mary Jean Whitelaw. 1989. *The Condition of the Professoriate: Attitudes and Trends, 1989*. New York: Harper.

Bradburn, Norman, and Seymour Sudman. 1988. *Polls and Surveys*. San Francisco: Jossey-Bass.

Brady, Henry E., and Paul M. Sniderman. 1985. "Attitude Attribution: A Group Basis for Political Reasoning." *American Political Science Review* 79 (Dec.): 1061–1078.

Brady, Henry E., Sidney Verba, and Kay Lehman Scholzman. 1995. "Beyond SES: A Resource Model of Political Participation." *American Political Science Review* 89 (Mar.): 271–292.

Brandes, Lisa. 1992. "The Gender Gap and Attitudes Toward War." Paper presented at the annual meeting of the Midwest Political Science Association, Apr. 9–12, Chicago.

Breaux, David, and Malcolm Jewell. 1992. "Winning Big: The Incumbency Advantage in State Legislative Races." In *Changing Patterns in State Legislative Careers*, ed. Gary F. Moncrief and Joel A. Thompson. Ann Arbor: University of Michigan Press.

Brehm, John. 1993. *The Phantom Respondents*. Ann Arbor: University of Michigan Press.

Brians, Craig L., and Martin P. Wattenberg. 1996. "Campaign Issue Knowledge: Comparing Reception from TV Commercials, TV Shows, and Newspapers. *American Journal of Political Science* 40 (Feb.): 172–193.

Brody, Richard A. 1991. *Assessing the President*. Stanford, CA: Stanford University Press.

Brody, Richard A., and Lee Sigelman. 1983. "Presidential Popularity and Presidential Elections: An Update and Extension." *Public Opinion Quarterly* 47 (Fall): 325–28.

Browning, Robert X. 1986. *Politics and Social Welfare Policy in the United States*. Knoxville: University of Tennessee Press.

Bryce, James. 1900. *The American Commonwealth*. New York: Macmillan.

Buchanan, Bruce. 1991. *Electing a President*. Austin: University of Texas Press.

Budge, Ian, and Richard I. Hofferbert. 1990. "Mandates and Policy Outputs: U.S. Party Platforms and Federal Expenditures, 1950–1985." *American Political Science Review* 84 (Mar.): 248–261.

Bullock, Charles. 1992. "Minorities in State Legislatures." In *Changing Patterns of State Legislative Careers*, ed. Gary F. Moncrief and Joel A. Thompson. Ann Arbor: University of Michigan Press.

Burden, Barry C., and David C. Kimball. 2002. *Why Americans Split Their Tickets: Campaigns, Competition, and Divided Government.* Ann Arbor: University of Michigan Press.

Burnham, Walter Dean. 1970. *Critical Elections and the Mainsprings of American Politics.* New York: Norton.

Cain, Bruce, John Ferejohn, and Morris Fiorina. 1987. *The Personal Vote.* Cambridge, MA: Harvard University Press.

Caldicott, Helen. 1986. *Missile Envy: The Arms Race and Nuclear War.* New York: Bantam.

Campbell, Andrea C., Gary W. Cox, and Matthew D. McCubbins. 2002. "Agenda Power in the U.S. Senate, 1877–1986." In *Party, Process, and Political Change in Congress,* ed. David W. Brady and Matthew D. McCubbins. Stanford, CA: Stanford University Press.

Campbell, Angus. 1964. "Issues and Voters: Past and Present." *Journal of Politics* 26 (Nov.): 745–757.

Campbell, Angus, Philip E. Converse, Warren E. Miller, and Donald E. Stokes. 1960. *The American Voter.* New York: Wiley.

Campbell, Angus, Gerald Gurin, and Warren E. Miller. 1954. *The Voter Decides.* Evanston, IL: Row.

Campbell, James E. 1985. "Sources of the New Deal Realignment: The Contribution of Conversion and Mobilization to Partisan Change." *Western Political Quarterly* 38 (June): 357–376.

Canes–Wrone, Brandice, David W. Brady, and John F. Cogan. 2002. "Out of Step, Out of Office: Electoral Accountability and House Members' Voting." *American Political Science Review* 96: 127–140.

Canes–Wrone, Brandice, and Scott de Marchi. 2002. "Presidential Approval and Legislative Success." *Journal of Politics* 64: 491–509.

Cantril, Albert H. 1991. *The Opinion Connection.* Washington, DC: Brookings.

Cantril, Albert H., and Susan Davis Cantril. 1999. *Reading Mixed Signals: Ambivalence in American Public Opinion About Government.* Baltimore, MD: Johns Hopkins University Press.

Cantril, Hadley. 1951. *Public Opinion 1935–1946.* Princeton, NJ: Princeton University Press.

Cappella, Joseph, and Kathleen Jamieson. 1997. *Spiral of Cynicism: The Press and the Public Good.* New York: Oxford University Press.

Carey, John M., Richard G. Niemi, and Lynda W. Powell. 2000. "Incumbency and the Probability of Reelection in State Legislative Elections." *Journal of Politics* 62: 671–700.

Carmines, Edward G., John P. McIver, and James A. Stimson. 1987. "Unrealized Partisanship: A Theory of Dealignment." *Journal of Politics* 49 (June): 377–399.

Carmines, Edward G., and James A. Stimson. 1980. "The Two Faces of Issue Voting." *American Political Science Review* 74 (Jan.): 78–91.

———. 1989. *Issue Evolution: Race and the Transformation of American Politics.* Princeton, NJ: Princeton University Press.

Cassel, Carol A. 1986. "The Non-Partisan Ballot in the United States." In *Electoral Laws and Their Consequences,* ed. Bernard Grofman and Rend Lipjart. New York: Agathon.

Childs, Harwood. 1965. *Public Opinion: Nature, Formation and Role.* Princeton, NJ: Van Nostrand.

Chong, Dennis. 1993. "How People Think, Reason, and Feel about Civil Liberties." *American Journal of Political Science* 37 (Aug.): 867–899.

Clymer, Adam. 1993. "Opposition to Baird Grows As Senators Hear the People." *New York Times,* Jan. 22, sec. A3.

Cobb, Michael D., and James H. Kuklinski. 1997. "Changing Minds: Political Arguments and Political Persuasion." *American Journal of Political Science* 41 (Jan.): 88–121.

Cohen, Bernard. 1963. *The Press and Foreign Policy.* Princeton, NJ: Princeton University Press.

Coleman, John J. 1997. "The Decline and Resurgence of Congressional Party Conflict." *Journal of Politics* 59: 165–184.

Connell, Robert W. 1987. "Why the 'Political Socialization' Paradigm Failed and What Should Replace It." *International Political Science Review* 8 (July): 215–223.

Conover, Pamela, and Stanley Feldman. 1981. "The Origins and Meaning of Liberal and Conservative Self-Identifications." *American Journal of Political Science* 25 (Nov.): 617–645.

———. 1989. "Candidate Perceptions in an Ambiguous World: Campaigns, Cues, and Inference Processes." *American Journal of Political Science* 33 (Nov.): 912–941.

Converse, Jean. 1987. *Survey Research in the United States.* Berkeley: University of California Press.

Converse, Philip E. 1962. "Information Flow and the Stability of Partisan Attitudes." *Public Opinion Quarterly* 26 (Winter): 578–599.

———. 1964. "The Nature of Belief Systems in Mass Publics." In *Ideology and Discontent*, ed. David Apter. New York: Free Press.

———. 1966. "The Concept of the Normal Vote." In *Elections and the Political Order*, ed. Angus Campbell et al. New York: Wiley.

———. 1987. "Changing Conceptions of Public Opinion in the Political Process. *Public Opinion Quarterly* 51 (Spring): 12–24.

Converse, Philip E., Aage R. Clausen, and Warren E. Miller. 1965. "Electoral Myth and Reality: The 1964 Election." *American Political Science Review* 59 (June): 332–335.

Converse, Philip E., and Gregory B. Markus. 1979. "Plus ça change . . . : The New CPS Election Study Panel." *American Political Science Review* 73 (Mar.): 32–49.

Cook, Elizabeth Adell, Ted. G. Jelen, and Clyde Wilcox. 1992. *Between Two Absolutes.* Boulder, CO: Westview.

Cook, Fay Lomax, and Edith J. Barnett. 1992. *Support for the American Welfare State.* New York: Columbia University Press.

Cox, Gary, and Jonathan N. Katz. 1996. "Why Did the Incumbency Advantage in the U.S. House Grow?" *American Journal of Political Science* 43: 812–841.

Cox, Gary W., and Matthew D. McCubbins. 1993. *Legislative Leviathan: Party Government in the House.* Berkeley: University of California Press.

———. 2002. "Agenda Power in the U.S. House of Representatives, 1989–1999." In *Party, Process, and Political Change in Congress*, ed. David W. Brady and Matthew D. McCubbins. Stanford, CA: Stanford University Press.

Cox, Gary W., and Scott Morgenstern. 1993. "The Increased Advantage of Incumbency in the U.S. States." *Legislative Studies Quarterly* 18: 495–514.

Craig, Stephen G. 1993. *The Malevolent Leaders.* Boulder, CO: Westview.

Crespi, Irving. 1988. *Pre-Election Polling: Sources of Accuracy and Error.* New York: Russell Sage.

Dahl, Robert A. 1961. *Who Governs?* New Haven, CT: Yale University Press.

———. 1971. *Polyarchy.* New Haven, CT: Yale University Press.

———. 1982. *Democracy in the United States.* Chicago: Rand.

———. 1989. *Democracy and Its Critics.* New Haven, CT: Yale University Press.

Dalton, Russell. 1980. "Reassessing Parental Socialization: Indicator Unreliability Versus Generational Transfer." *American Political Science Review* 74 (June): 421–438.

Dalton, Russell J., Paul A. Beck, and Robert Huckfeldt. 1998. "Partisan Cues and the Media: Information Flows in the 1992 Presidential Election." *American Political Science Review* 92 (Mar.): 111–126.

Dautrich, Kenneth, and Jennifer Necci Deneen. 1996. "Media Bias: What Journalists and the Public Say About It." *Public Perspective* 7: 7–19.

Daves, Robert P. 2000. "Who Will Vote? Ascertaining the Likelihood to Vote and Modeling a Probable Electorate in Preelection Polls." In *Election Polls, the News Media and Democracy*, ed. Paul J. Lavrakas and Michael W. Traugott. Chatham, NJ: Chatham House.

Davidson, Roger H., and Walter J. Oleszck. 2002. *Congress and Its Members*, 8th ed. Washington, DC: Congressional Quarterly Press.

Davis, Darren W. 1997. "Nonrandom Measurement Error and Race of Interview Effects Among African-Americans." *Public Opinion Quarterly* 61 (Spring): 183–207.

Davis, Darren, and Brian Silver. 2003. "Civil Liberties Versus Security in the Context of the Terrorist Attacks on America." Paper presented at the annual meeting of the American Political Science Association, Aug. 27–Sept. 2.

———. 2004. "Civil Liberties Versus Security: Public Opinion in the Context of the Terrorist Attacks on America." *American Journal of Political Science* (Forthcoming).

Davis, Richard, and Diana Owen. 1999. *New Media and American Politics*. New York: Oxford University Press.

Davis, James A. 1992. "Changeable Weather in a Cooling Climate Atop the Liberal Plateau." *Public Opinion Quarterly* 56 (Fall): 261–295.

Dawson, Richard, Kenneth Prewitt, and Karen Dawson. 1977. *Political Socialization*, 2nd ed. Boston: Little, Brown.

Deane, Claudia. 2003. "About Washington Post Response Rates." www.washingtonpost.com/wp–srv/politics/poll response rate html.

Delli Carpini, Michael X. 1984. "Scooping the Voters? The Consequences of the Networks' Early Call of the 1980 Presidential Race." *Journal of Politics* 46 (Aug.): 866–885.

———. 1986. *Stability and Change in American Politics: The Coming of Age of the Generation of the 1960s*. New York: New York University Press.

Delli Carpini, Michael X., and Scott Keeter. 1996. *What Americans Know About Politics and Why It Matters*. New Haven, CT: Yale University Press.

Delli Carpini, Michael X., and Lee Sigelman. 1986. "Do Yuppies Matter? Competing Explanations of their Political Distinctiveness." *Public Opinion Quarterly* 50 (Winter): 502–518.

Dennis, Jack, and Carol Webster. 1975. "Children's Images of the President and Government in 1962 and 1974." *American Politics Quarterly* (Oct.): 211–238.

Deutscher, Irwin. 1973. *What We Say/What We Do*. Glenview, IL: Scott.

Dillman, Don A. 1978. *Mail and Telephone Surveys*. New York: Wiley.

Domke, David, David P. Fan, Michael Fibison, Dhavan V. Shah, Steven S. Smith, and Mark D. Watts. 1998. "Mass Media, Candidates and Issues, and Public Opinion in the 1996 Presidential Campaign." *Journalism and Mass Communications Quarterly* 74: 718–737.

Domke, David, Dhaven V. Shah, and Daniel Wackman. 1998. "Moral Referendums" Values, News Media, and the Process of Candidate Choice." *Political Communication* 15: 301–321.

Downs, Anthony. 1958. *An Economic Theory of Democracy*. New York: Harper.

Dreyer, Edward. 1971–1972. "Media Use and Electoral Choices: Some Political Consequences of Information Exposure." *Public Opinion Quarterly* 35 (Winter): 544–553.

Dry, Murray. 1996. "Review of National Standards for Civics and Government." *Political Science and Politics* 29 (Mar.): 49–52.

Duckitt, John. 1989. "Authoritarianism and Group Identification: A New View of an Old Construct." *Political Psychology* 10 (Feb.): 63–84.

Dye, Thomas R., and Harmon Ziegler. 1987. *The Irony of Democracy,* 7th ed. Belmont, CA: Wadsworth.

Easton, David. 1965. *A Systems Analysis of Political Life*. New York: Wiley.

Easton, David, and Jack Dennis. 1969. *Children and the Political System*. New York: McGraw.

Edelman, Murray. 1965. *The Symbolic Uses of Politics*. Urbana: University of Illinois Press.

Edlund, Lena, and Rohini Pande. 2002. "Why Have Women Become Left-Wing: The Politics of Gender and the Decline of Marriage." *Quarterly Journal of Economics* 117: 917–961.

Elms, Alan. 1972. *Social Psychology and Social Relevance*. Boston: Little, Brown.

Engelberg, Stephan. 1993. "A New Breed of Hired Hands Cultivates Grass-Roots Anger." *New York Times*, Mar. 27, sec. A1, 11.

Entmann, Robert M. 1989. "How the Media Affect What People Think: An Information Processing Approach." *Journal of Politics* 51 (May): 347–370.

Erikson, Robert S. 1971. "The Electoral Impact of Congressional Roll Call Voting." *American Political Science Review* 65 (Dec.): 1018–1032.

———. 2001. "The 2000 Election in Historical Perspective." *Political Science Quarterly* 116 (Spring): 29–52.

———. 1976a. "Is There Such a Thing as a Safe Seat?" *Polity* 8 (Summer): 613–632.

———. 1976b. "The Relationship Between Public Opinion and State Policy: A New Look at Some Forgotten Data." *American Journal of Political Science* 20 (Feb.): 25–36.

———. 1976c. "The Influence of Newspaper Endorsements in Presidential Elections: The Case of 1964." *American Journal of Political Science* 20 (May): 207–234.

———. 1979. "The SRC Panel Data and Mass Attitudes." *British Journal of Political Science* 9 (Jan.): 89–114.

———. 1988. "The Puzzle of Midterm Loss." *Journal of Politics* 50 (Nov.): 1011–1029.

———. 1989. "Economic Conditions and the Presidential Vote." *American Political Science Review* 83 (June): 567–573.

———. 1990. "Roll Calls, Reputations, and Representation in the U.S. Senate." *Legislative Studies Quarterly* 15: 623–642.

———. 1993. "Counting Likely Voters in Gallup's Tracking Poll." *Public Perspective* 4 (Mar./Apr.): 22–23.

———. 2002. "National Election Studies and Macro Analysis." *Electoral Studies* 21: 269–281.

Erikson, Robert S., Michael B. MacKuen, and James A. Stimson. 1998. "What Moves Macropartisanship? A Reply to Green, Palmquist, and Schickler." *American Political Science Review* 92: 901–912.

———. 2002. *The Macro Polity.* New York: Cambridge University Press.

Erikson, Robert S., and Kent L. Tedin. 1981. "The 1928–1936 Partisan Realignment: The Case for the Conversion Hypothesis." *American Political Science Review* 75 (Dec.): 951–962.

———. 1986. "Voter Conversion and the New Deal Realignment." *Western Political Quarterly* 39: 729–732.

Erikson, Robert S., and Christopher Wlezien. 1999. "Presidential Polls as a Time Series: The Case of 1996." *Public Opinion Quarterly* 63 (Summer): 163–178.

Erikson, Robert, and Gerald C. Wright. 1985. "Voters, Candidates, and Issues in Congressional Elections." In *Congress Reconsidered*, 3rd ed., ed. Lawrence C. Dodd and Bruce I. Oppenheimer. Washington, DC: Congressional Quarterly Press.

———. 2001a. "Voters, Candidates, and Issues in Congressional Elections." In *Congress Reconsidered*, 7th ed., ed. Lawrence C. Dodd and Bruce I. Oppenheimer. Washington, DC: Congressional Quarterly Press.

———. 2001b. "Representation of Constituency Ideology in Congress." In *Continuity and Change in Congressional Elections*, ed. David Brady and John Cogan (ch. 8). Stanford, CA: Stanford University Press.

Erikson, Robert S., Gerald C. Wright, and John P. McIver. 1994. *Statehouse Democracy: Public Opinion and Policy in the American States.* New York: Cambridge University Press.

Erskine, Hazel. 1962a. "The Polls: Race Relations." *Public Opinion Quarterly* 26 (Winter): 137–148.

———. 1962b. "The Polls: Attitudes." *Public Opinion Quarterly* 26 (Winter): 293.

———. 1975. "The Polls: Health Insurance." *Public Opinion Quarterly* 39 (Spring): 128–143.

Eskey, Kenneth. 1995. "American Youth Not Very Interested in Politics." *Houston Chronicle*, Jan. 9, 5A.

Farnsworth, Stephen J., and S. Robert Lichter (2003). *The Nightly News Nightmare.* New York: Rowan-Littlefield.

Farrand, Max. 1961. *The Records of the Federal Convention of 1787*, vol. 1. New Haven, CT: Yale University Press.

Fearon, James. 1999. "Electoral Accountability and the Control of Politicians. Selecting Good Types Versus Sanctioning Poor Performance." In *Democracy, Accountability, and Representation*, ed. Adam Przeworski, Susan C. Stokes, and Bernard Manin. Cambridge: Cambridge University Press.

Feldman, Kenneth, and Theodore M. Newcomb. 1969. *The Impact of College on Students*, vol. 2. San Francisco: Jossey-Bass.

Feldman, Stanley. 1989. "Reliability and Stability of Policy Positions: Evidence from a Five-Wave Panel." *Political Analysis* 1: 25–60.

———. 2003. "Enforcing Social Conformity: A Theory of Authoritarianism." *Political Psychology* 24: 41–74.

Feldman, Stanley, and Karen Stenner. 1997. "Perceived Threat and Authoritarianism." *Political Psychology* 18: 741–769.

Feldman, Stanley, and John Zaller. 1992. "The Political Culture of Ambivalence: Ideological Response to the Welfare State." *American Journal of Political Science* 36 (Feb.): 268–291.

Fenno, Richard F., Jr. 1978. *Home Style: House Members in Their Districts*. Boston: Little, Brown.

Ferejohn, John. 1999. "Accountability and Authority: Toward a Theory of Political Accountability. In *Democracy, Accountability, and Representation*, ed. Adam Przeworski, Susan C. Stokes, and Bernard Manin. Cambridge: Cambridge University Press.

Ferree, G. Donald. 1993. "Counting Likely Voters: A Reply to Erikson." *Public Perspective* 4 (Mar./Apr.): 22–23.

Finke, Roger, and Rodney Stark. 1994. *The Churching of America, 1776–1990*. New Brunswick, NJ: Rutgers University Press.

Finkel, Steven E., Edward N. Muller, and Karl-Dieter Opp. 1989. "Personal Influence, Collective Rationality, and Mass Political Action." *American Political Science Review* 83 (Sept.) 885–903.

Fiorina, Morris P. 1977. "An Outline for a Model of Party Choice." *American Journal of Political Science* 21 (Aug.): 601–625.

———. 1981. *Retrospective Voting in American National Elections*. New Haven, CT: Yale University Press.

———. 1992. *Divided Government*. New York: Macmillan.

Fischer, Claude S. 1975. "Toward a Subcultural Theory of Urbanism." *Social Forces* 53 (Mar.): 420–432.

Fischle, Mark. 2000. "Mass Response to the Lewinsky Scandal: Motivated Reasoning or Bayesian Updating?" *Political Psychology* 21: 135–159.

Fishkin, James S. 1997. *The Voice of the People: Public Opinion and Democracy*. New Haven, CT: Yale University Press.

Flanagan, Constance A., Jennifer M. Bowes, Britta Jonsson, Beno Csapo, and Elena Sheblanova. 1998. "Ties that Bind: Correlates of Adolescents' Civic Commitments in Seven Countries." *Journal of Social Issues* 54: 457–475.

Flanagan, Timothy J., and Dennis R. Longmire. 1996. *Americans View Crime and Justice: A National Public Opinion Survey*. Thousand Oaks, CA: Sage.

Flemming, Roy B., and B. Dan Wood. 1997. "The Public and the Supreme Court: Individual Justice Responsiveness to American Policy Moods." *American Journal of Political Science* 41: 468–498.

Franklin, Charles H., and John E. Jackson. 1983. "The Dynamics of Party Identification." *American Political Science Review* 77 (Dec.): 957–973.

Frankovic, Kathleen A. 1992. "The CBS News Call-In: 'Slip-ups in the Broadcast.'" *Public Perspective* 3 (Mar./Apr.): 19–21.

———. 2003. "News Organizations' Responses to the Mistakes of Election 2000: Why They Continue to Project Elections." *Public Opinion Quarterly* 67 (Spring): 19–31.

Free, Lloyd A., and Hadley Cantril. 1967. *The Political Beliefs of Americans.* New York: Simon and Schuster.

Freeman, Patricia, and William Lyons. 1992. "Female Legislators: Is There a New Type of Woman in Office?" In *Changing Patterns in State Legislative Careers,* ed. Gary F. Moncrief and Joel A. Thompson. Ann Arbor: University of Michigan Press.

Friesema, H. Paul, and Ronald D. Hedlund. 1981. "The Reality of Representational Roles." In *Public Opinion and Public Policy,* ed. Norman R. Luttbeg. Itasca, IL: Peacock.

Fritz, Sara, and Dwight Morris. 1992. *Handbook of Campaign Spending.* Washington, DC: Congressional Quarterly Press.

Gallup Organization. 2003. "Poll Analysis: Public Remains Skeptical of News Media." May 30, 2.

Gallup, George, and Saul Rae. 1940. *The Pulse of Democracy.* New York: Simon.

Gamble, Barbara. 1997. "Putting Civil Rights to a Popular Vote." *American Journal of Political Science* (Jan.): 245–269.

Gamson, William. 1968. *Power and Discontent.* Homewood, IL: Dorsey.

Garcia, F. Chris. 1973. *Political Socialization of Chicano Children.* New York: Praeger.

Gastil, John. 2000. *By Popular Demand: Revitalizing Representative Democracy Through Deliberative Elections.* Berkeley: University of California Press.

Gerber, George. 1998. "Who Is Shooting Whom? The Content and Analysis of Media Violence." In *Bang, Bang, Shoot Shoot: Essays in Guns and Popular Culture,* ed. Murray Pomerance and John Sakeris. Needham Heights, MA: Simon and Schuster.

Geer, John G. 1996. *From Tea Leaves to Opinion Polls.* New York: Columbia University Press.

Gibson, James L. 1986. "Pluralistic Intolerance in America." *American Politics Quarterly* 14 (Oct.): 267–293.

———. 1987. "Freedom and Tolerance in the United States." NORC (unpublished codebook).

———. 1988. "Political Intolerance and Political Repression During the McCarthy Red Scare." *American Political Science Review* 82 (June): 512–529.

———. 1992. "The Political Consequences of Intolerance: Cultural Conformity and Political Freedom." *American Political Science Review* 86 (June): 338–356.

———. 1996. "The Paradoxes of Political Tolerance in the Process of Democratization." *Politikon: South African Journal of Political Science* 23: 2–21.

Gibson, James L., and Richard D. Bingham. 1985. *Civil Liberties and the Nazis: The Skokie Free-Speech Controversy.* New York: Praeger.

Gibson, James L., and Kent L. Tedin. 1988. "The Etiology of Intolerance for Homosexual Politics." *Social Science Quarterly* 69 (Sept.): 587–604.

Gilens, Martin. 1999. *Why Americans Hate Welfare: Race, Media, and the Politics of Welfare Policy.* Chicago: University of Chicago Press.

———. 2001. "Political Ignorance and Collective Policy Preferences." *American Political Science Review* 95: 379–398.

Gilens, Martin, and Craig Hertzman. 2000. "Corporate Ownership of News Bias: Newspaper Coverage of the 1996 Telecommunications Act." *Journal of Politics* 62 (Aug.): 369–389.

Gilliam, Frank D., and Shanto Iyengar. 2000. "Prime Suspects: The Influence of Local Television on the Viewing Public." *American Journal of Political Science* 44 (July): 560–573.

Ginsberg, Benjamin. 1982. *The Consequences of Consent: Elections, Citizen Control and Popular Acquiescence.* Reading, MA: Addison-Wesley.

———. 1986. *The Captive Public.* New York: Basic.

Glazer, Amihai, and Marc Robbins. 1985. "Congressional Responsiveness to Constituency Change." *American Journal of Political Science* 29 (May): 259–273.

Goldberg, Barnard. 2001. *Bias in the News.* Washington, DC: Regnery.

Goldenberg, Edie N., and Michael W. Traugott. 1984. *Campaigning for Congress.* Washington, DC: Congressional Quarterly Press.

Goldstein, Amy, and Richard Morin. 2002. "Younger Voters' Disengagement Skews Politics." *Washington Post,* Oct. 20, A8.

Goldstein, Robert. 1978. *Political Repression in Modern America: From 1870 to the Present.* Cambridge, MA: Schenkman.

Goodman, Walter. 1994. "Tabloid Charge Rocks Network." *New York Times,* Feb. 13, sec. 2, p. 29.

Graber, Doris A. 1988. *Processing the News.* New York: Longman.

———. 1997. *Mass Media and American Politics.* Washington, DC: Congressional Quarterly Press.

Green, Donald, Bradley Palmquist, and Eric Schickler. 1998. "Macropartisanship: A Replication and Critique." *American Political Science Review* 92: 883–899.

———. 2002. *Partisan Hearts and Minds: Political Parties and the Social Identities of the Voters.* New Haven, CT: Yale University Press.

Greenberg, Edward. 1970. "Black Children and the Political System." *Public Opinion Quarterly* 34: 335–348.

Greenstein, Fred I. 1969. *Personality and Politics.* Chicago: Markham.

———. 1992. "Can Personality and Politics Be Studied Systematically?" *Political Psychology* 13 (Mar.): 105–128.

Groeling, Timothy, and Samuel Kernell. 1998. "Is Network News Coverage of the President Biased?" *Journal of Politics* 60: 1063–1087.

Gronke, Paul. 2000. *The Electorate, the Campaign, and the Office: A Unified Approach to Senate and House Elections.* Ann Arbor: Michigan University Press.

Gronke, Paul, Jeffrey Koch, and Matthew J. Wilson. 2003. "Follow the Leader? Presidential Approval, Presidential Support, and Representatives' Electoral Fortunes." *Journal of Politics* 65: 785–808.

Groseclose, Timothy, and Keith Krehbiel. 1994. "Golden Parachutes, Rubber Checks, and Strategic Retirements from the 102nd House." *American Journal of Political Science* 38: 75–99.

Groves, Robert, and Mick Couper. 1998. *Nonresponse in Household Surveys.* New York: John Wiley and Sons.

Hand, Learned. 1959. *The Spirit of Liberty. Papers and Addresses.* New York: Knopf.

Hansen, John Mark. 1998. "Individuals, Institutions, and Public Preferences over Public Finance." *American Political Science Review* 92 (Sept.): 513–531.

Hansen, Susan Blackwell. 1975. "Participation, Political Structure, and Concurrence." *American Political Science Review* 69 (Dec.): 1181–1191.

Harris, John F. 2001. "Presidency by Poll." *Washington Post,* National Weekly Edition, Jan. 8–14: 9.

Harris-Kojetin, Brian, and Clyde Tucker. 1999. "Exploring the Relation of Economic and Political Conditions with Refusal Rates to a Government Survey." *Journal of Official Statistics* 15 (June): 167–184.

Hartley, Thomas, and Bruce Russett. 1992. "Public Opinion and the Common Defense: Who Governs Military Spending in the United States?" *American Political Science Review* 86 (Dec.): 905–915.

Harvey, G. Ted. 1972. "Computer Simulation of Peer Group Influence on Adolescent Political Behavior." *American Journal of Political Science* 16 (Nov.): 588–621.

Harvey, O. J., and G. Beverly. 1961. "Some Personality Correlates of Concept Change Through Role Playing." *Journal of Abnormal and Social Psychology* 27 (Mar.): 125–130.

Harwood, John, and Cynthia Crossen. 2000. "Head Counting: Why Many Polls Put Different Spins on Presidential Race." *Wall Street Journal,* Sept. 29, A1.

Hawkins, Robert P., Suzanne Pingree, and Donald Roberts. 1975. "Watergate and Political Socialization." *American Politics Quarterly* 4 (Oct.): 406–436.

Hedges, Chris. 1999. "35% of High School Seniors Fail National Civics Test." *New York Times*, Nov. 12, 1999, sec. 1, p. 17.

Hedlund, Ronald D. 1975. "Perceptions of Decisional Referents in Legislative Decision-Making." *American Journal of Political Science* 19 (Aug.): 527–542.

Herbst, Susan. 1993. *Numbered Voices: How Public Opinion Has Shaped American Politics.* Chicago: University of Chicago Press.

———. 1998. *Reading Public Opinion: How Political Actors View the Democratic Process.* Chicago: University of Chicago Press.

Hero, Alfred O. n.d. "Public Reactions to Federal Policy: Some Comparative Trends." Unpublished paper.

Herrera, Richard. 1992. "The Understanding of Ideological Labels by Political Elites: A Research Note." *Western Political Quarterly* 45 (Dec.): 1021–1035.

Herson, Lawrence J. R., and C. Richard Hofstetter. 1975 "Tolerance, Consensus, and Democratic Creed." *Journal of Politics* 37 (Dec.): 1007–1032.

Hertsgaard, Mark. 1988. *On Bended Knee: The Press and the Reagan Presidency.* New York: Farrar.

Hess, Robert D., and Judith V. Torney. 1967. *The Development of Political Attitudes in Children.* Chicago: Aldine.

Hess, Stephen. 2000. "Poll Stories Are Often Wrong." The Hess Report on Campaign Coverage in Nightly Network News (Oct. 29). Brookings.

Hetherington, Mark J. 1996. "The Media's Role in Forming Voters' National Economic Evaluations in 1992." *American Journal of Political Science* 40 (May): 372–395.

———. 1998. "The Political Relevance of Political Trust." *American Political Science Review* 91 (Dec.): 791–808.

———. 1999. "The Effect of Political Trust on the Presidential Vote, 1968–1996." *American Political Science Review* 93 (June): 311–326.

———. 2001a. "Declining Trust and Shrinking Policy Agenda: Why Media Scholars Should Care?" In *Communication in U.S. Elections: New Agendas*, ed. Roderick P. Hart and Daron R. Shaw. Lanham, MD: Rowan-Littlefield.

———. 2001b. "Resurgent Mass Partisanship: The Role of Elite Polarization " *American Political Science Review* 95: 619–631.

Hibbing, John, and Elizabeth Theiss-Morse. 1998. "The Media's Role in Public Negativity Toward Congress: Distinguishing Emotional Reactions and Cognitive Evaluations." *American Journal of Political Science* 42 (May): 475–498.

———. 2002. *Stealth Democracy: Americans' Beliefs about How Government Should Work.* Cambridge: Cambridge University Press.

Hibbs, Douglas A., Jr. 1987. *The American Political Economy: Macroeconomics and Electoral Politics in the United States.* Cambridge, MA: Harvard University Press.

Hibbs, Douglas A., Jr., and Christopher Dennis. 1988. "Income Distribution in the United States." *American Political Science Review* 82 (June): 467–490.

Hilderbrand, Robert. 1981. *Power and the People: Executive Management of Public Opinion in Foreign Affairs.* Chapel Hill: University of North Carolina Press.

Hillygus, D. Sunshine, and Simon Jackman. 2003. "Voter Decision Making in Election 2000: Campaign Effects, Partisan Acitivation, and the Clinton Legacy," *American Journal of Political Science* 47: 583–596.

Hitchens, William A. 1992. "Voting in the Passive Voice." *Harper's* 284 (Apr.): 45–52.

Hite, Shere. 1987. *Women and Love: A Cultural Revolution in Progress.* New York: Knopf.

Holbrook, Thomas. 2000. "Reading the Political Tea Leaves: A Forecasting Model of Contemporary Presidential Elections." In *Before the Vote: Forecasting American National Elections*, ed. James E. Campbell and James C. Garand. Thousand Oaks, CA: Sage.

Holbrook, Thomas, and Charles Tidmarch. 1991. "Sophomore Surge in State Legislative Elections." *Legislative Studies Quarterly* 16: 49–64.

Holsti, Ole R. 1996. *Public Opinion and American Foreign Policy*. Ann Arbor: University of Michigan Press.

Hout, Michael, and Claude S. Fischer. 2002. "Americans with No Religion: Why Their Numbers are Growing." *American Sociological Review* 67 (Apr.): 165–190.

Hugick, Larry, and Guy Molyneux. 1993. "The Performance of the Gallup Tracking Poll: The Myth and the Reality." *Public Perspective* 4 (Jan./Feb.): 12–14.

Huntington, Samuel P. 1991. *The Third Wave: Democratization in the Late Twentieth Century*. Norman: University of Oklahoma Press.

Hurwitz, Jon, and Mark Peffley. 1987. "How Are Foreign Policy Attitudes Structured? A Hierarchical Model." *American Political Science Review* 81 (Dec.): 1099–1120.

Hutchings, Vincent L. 2003. *Public Opinion and Democratic Accountability*. Princeton, NJ: Princeton University Press.

Hyman, Herbert. 1959. *Political Socialization*. Glencoe, IL: Free Press.

Inglehart, Ronald. 1990. *Culture Shift*. Princeton, NJ: Princeton University Press.

———. 1997a. "Postmaterialist Values and the Erosion of Institutional Authority." In *Why People Don't Trust Government*, ed. Joseph S. Nye, Philip D. Zelikow, and David C. King. Cambridge, MA: Harvard University Press.

———. 1997b. *Modernization and Postmodernization*. Princeton, NJ: Princeton University Press.

Inkeles, Alex. 1961. "National Character and the Modern Political System." In *Psychological Anthropology: Approaches to Culture and Personality*, ed. Francis L. K. Hsu. Homewood, IL: Dorsey.

Iyengar, Shanto. 1991. *Is Anyone Responsible? How Television Frames Political News*. Chicago: University of Chicago Press.

Iyengar, Shanto, and Donald R. Kinder. 1987. *News That Matters*. Chicago: University of Chicago Press.

Iyengar, Shanto, Helmut Norpoth, and Kyu S. Hahn. 2004. "Consumer Demand for Election News: The Horserace Sells." *Journal of Politics* 66 (Feb.): 157–175.

Iyengar, Shanto, Mark D. Peters, and Donald R. Kinder. 1982. "Experimental Demonstrations of 'Not-So-Minimal' Consequences of Television News Programs." *American Political Science Review* 76 (Dec.): 848–858.

Jackman, Mary. 1978. "General and Applied Tolerance: Does Education Increase Commitment to Racial Integration?" *American Journal of Political Science* 22 (May): 302–324.

Jackman, Mary R., and Robert W. Jackman. 1983. *Class Awareness in the United States*. Berkeley: University of California Press.

Jackman, Mary, and Michael J. Mulha. 1984. "Education and Intergroup Attitudes: Moral Enlightenment, Superficial Democratic Commitment or Ideological Refinement." *American Sociological Review* 49 (Aug.): 751–769.

Jackman, Robert W. 1972. "Political Elites, Mass Publics, and Support for Democratic Principles." *Journal of Politics* 54 (Aug.): 753–773.

Jackman, Robert W., and Robert A. Miller. 1996. "A Renaissance of Political Culture?" *American Journal of Political Science* 40 (May): 632–659.

Jacob, Philip E. 1956. *Changing Values in College*. New Haven, CT: Hazen Foundation.

Jacobs, Lawrence R. 1993. *The Health of Nations: Public Opinions in the Making of American and British Health Policy*. Ithaca, NY: Cornell University Press.

Jacobs, Lawrence R., and Robert Y. Shapiro. 1993. "Polling and Opinion on Health Care Reform." *Public Perspective* 4 (May/June): 22–27.

———. 2000. *Politicians Don't Pander: Political Manipulation and the Loss of Democratic Responsiveness.* Chicago: University of Chicago Press.

Jacobson, Gary C. 1987. *The Politics of Congressional Elections,* 2nd ed. Boston: Little, Brown.

———. 1989. "Parties and PACs in Congressional Elections." In *Congress Reconsidered,* 4th ed., ed. Lawrence C. Dodd and Bruce I. Oppenheimer. Washington, DC: Congressional Quarterly Press.

Jacobson, Gary C., and Michael A. Dimmock. 1994. "Checking Out: The Effects of Bank Overdrafts on the 1992 House Elections." *American Journal of Political Science* 38: 601–624.

Jacobson, Gary C., and Samuel Kernell. 1983. *Strategy and Choice in Congressional Elections,* 2nd ed. New Haven, CT: Yale University Press.

Jacoby, William G. 1988. "The Impact of Party Identification on Issue Attitudes." *American Journal of Political Science* 32 (Aug.): 643–661.

———. 1991. "Ideological Identifications and Issue Attitudes." *American Journal of Political Science* 35 (Feb.): 178–205.

Jameison, Kathleen Hall, and Karlyn Coors Campbell. 2001. *The Interplay of Influence.* Belmont, CA: Wadsworth.

Jameison, Kathleen Hall, and Paul Waldman. 2003. *The Press Effect: Politicians, Journalists, and the Stories that Shape the Political World.* New York: Oxford University Press.

Jaros, Dean, Herbert Hirsch, and Frederick Fleron. 1968. "The Malevolent Leader: Political Socialization in an American Sub-Culture." *American Political Science Review* 62 (June): 564–575.

Jelen, Ted. G. 1992. "Political Christianity: A Contextual Analysis." *American Journal of Political Science* 36 (Aug.): 662–692.

———. 1993. "The Political Consequences of Religious Group Attitudes." *Journal of Politics* 55 (Feb.): 167–177.

Jennings, M. Kent. 1987. "Residuals of a Movement: The Aging of the American Protest Generation." *American Political Science Review* 81 (June): 365–381.

———. 1992. "Ideological Thinking Among Mass Publics and Political Elites." *Public Opinion Quarterly* 56 (Winter): 419–441.

Jennings, M. Kent, and Ellen Ann Andersen. 1996. "Support for Confrontational Tactics Among AIDS Activists: A Study of Intra–Movement Divisions." *American Journal of Political Science* 40 (May): 311–334.

Jennings, M. Kent, Lee H. Ehrman, and Richard G. Niemi. 1974. "Social Studies Teachers and Their Students." In *The Political Character of Adolescence,* eds. M. Kent Jennings and Richard G. Niemi. Princeton, NJ: Princeton University Press.

Jennings, M. Kent, and Gregory B. Markus. 1984. "Partisan Orientations Over the Long Haul: Results from the Three-Wave Political Socialization Panel Study." *American Political Science Review* 78 (Dec.): 1000–1018.

Jennings, M. Kent, and Richard G. Niemi. 1974. *The Political Character of Adolescence.* Princeton, NJ: Princeton University Press.

———. 1982. *Generations and Politics.* Princeton, NJ: Princeton University Press.

Jennings, M. Kent, and Laura Stoker. 1999. "The Persistence of the Past: The Class of 1965 Turns Fifty." Paper presented at the Midwest Political Science Convention, Apr. 1999.

Jensen, Richard. 1968. "American Election Analysis: A Case of History and Methodological Innovation and Diffusion." In *Politics and Social Science,* ed. Seymour Martin Lipset. New York: Oxford University Press.

Jewell, Malcolm E., and David Breaux. 1988. "The Effect of Incumbency on State Legislative Elections." *Legislative Studies Quarterly* 13 (Nov.): 495–514.

Johannes, John R., and John P. McAdams. 1981. "The Congressional Incumbency Effect: Is It Casework, Policy Compatibility, or Something Else? An Examination of the 1978 Election." *American Journal of Political Science* 25 (Aug.): 512–552.

Johnstone, David Cay. 1999. "Gap between Rich and Poor Found Substantially Wider." *New York Times*, Sept. 5, 1999, A14.

Joslyn, Mark R. 2003. "The Determinants and Consequences of Recall Error About Gulf War Preferences." *American Journal of Political Science* 47: 127–139.

Just, Marion, and Ann Crigler. 2000. "Leadership Image-Building: After Clinton and Watergate." *Political Psychology* 21: 179–188.

Kahn, Kim Fridkin, and Patrick J. Kenney. 1999. "Do Negative Campaigns Mobilize or Suppress Turnout? Clarifying the Relationship between Negativity and Participation." *American Political Science Review* 93: 877–889.

———. 2002. "The Slant of the News: How Editorial Endorsements Influence Campaign Coverage and Citizens' Views of Candidates." *American Political Science Review* 96 (June): 381–394.

Karp, Jeffrey A. 1995. "Support for Legislative Term Limits." *Public Opinion Quarterly* 59 (Fall): 373–391.

Katzenstein, Peter. 2000. "Confidence, Trust, International Relations, and the Lessons from Smaller Democracies." In *Disaffected Democracies*, ed. Susan Pharr and Robert Putnam. Princeton, NJ: Princeton University Press.

Kaufmann, Karen M., and John R. Petrocik. 1999. "The Changing Politics of Men: Understanding the Source of the Gender Gap." *American Journal of Political Science* 43 (July): 864–887.

Keene, Karlyn H. 1991. "Feminism Versus Women's Rights." *Public Perspective* 3 (Nov./Dec.): 3–4.

Keeter, Scott, Carolyn Miller, Andrew Kohut, Robert M. Groves, and Stanley Press. 2000. "Consequences of Reducing Nonresponse in a National Telephone Survey," *Public Opinion Quarterly* 64: 125–148.

Kelley, Stanley J., Jr. 1983. *Interpreting Elections*. Princeton, NJ: Princeton University Press.

Kellstedt, Paul M. 2000. "Media Framing and the Dynamics of Racial Preference Policy." *American Journal of Political Science* 44 (April): 245–260.

Kenski, Henry. 1988. "The Gender Factor in a Changing Electorate." In *The Politics of the Gender Gap*, ed. Carol M. Mueller. Beverly Hills, CA: Sage.

Kerlinger, Fred N. 1984. *Liberalism and Conservatism*. Hillsdale, NJ: Erlbaum.

Kernell, Samuel. 1978. "Explaining Presidential Popularity." *American Political Science Review* 72 (June): 506–523.

———. 1993. *Going Public: New Strategies for Presidential Leadership*. Washington, DC: Congressional Quarterly Press.

Kesler, Charles. 1979. "The Movement of Student Opinion." *National Review* 23 (Nov.): 1448.

Key, V. O., Jr. 1949. *Southern Politics in State and Nation*. New York: Knopf.

———. 1961a. "Public Opinion and the Decay of Democracy." *Virginia Quarterly Review* 37 (Autumn): 488–512.

———. 1961b. *Public Opinion and American Democracy*. New York: Knopf.

Kiewiet, D. Roderick. 1983. *Macroeconomics and Micropolitics*. Chicago: University of Chicago Press.

Kiewiet, D. Roderick, and Matthew D. McCubbins. 1985. "Congressional Appropriations and the Electoral Connection." *Journal of Politics* 47 (Spring): 59–82.

Kinder, Donald R., Gordon S. Adams, and Paul W. Gronke. 1989. "Economics and Politics in the 1984 American Presidential Elections." *American Journal of Political Science* 33 (May): 491–515.

Kinder, Donald R., and D. Roderick Kiewiet. 1979. "Economic Grievances and Political Behavior: The Role of Personal Discontents and Collective Judgments in Congressional Voting." *American Journal of Political Science* 23 (Aug.): 495–527.

———. 1981. "Sociotropic Politics." *British Journal of Political Science* 11 (Apr.): 129–161.

Kinder, Donald R., and Lynn M. Sanders. 1996. *Divided by Color*. Chicago: University of Chicago Press.

Kinder, Donald R., and Nicholas Winter. 2001. "Exploring the Racial Divide: Blacks, Whites and Opinions on National Policy." *American Journal of Political Science* 45: 439–452.

Kingdon, John W. 1973. *Congressmen's Voting Decisions*. New York: Harper.

Kirscht, John P., and Ronald C. Dillehay. 1967. *Dimensions of Authoritarianism: A Review of Research and Theory*. Lexington: University of Kentucky Press.

Knight, Kathleen. 1985. "Ideology in the 1980 Election: Political Sophistication Matters." *Journal of Politics* 47 (Aug.): 828–853.

Knoke, David, and Michael Hout. 1974. "Social and Demographic Factors in American Political Party Affiliations, 1952–1972." *American Sociological Review* 39 (Aug.): 700–713.

Koch, Jeffery W. 1998. "Political Rhetoric and Political Persuasion." *Public Opinion Quarterly* 62 (Summer): 209–229.

Kolbert, Elizabeth. 1993. "Did the Voting Experts Go Wrong?" *New York Times*, Nov. 4, sec. A.

Kornhouser, William. 1970. *The Politics of Mass Society*. Chicago: Markham.

Krehbiel, Keith. 1993. "Where's the Party?" *British Journal of Political Science* 23: 235–266.

———. 1999. "The Party Effect from A to Z and Beyond." *Journal of Politics* 61: 832–841.

———. 2000. "Party Discipline and the Measures of Partisanship." *American Journal of Political Science* 44: 212–227.

Krosnick, Jon A., and Laura Brannon. 1993. "The Impact of the Gulf War on the Ingredients of Presidential Evaluations: Multidimensional Effects of Political Involvement." *American Political Science Review* 87 (Dec.): 963–975.

Krosnick, Jon A., and Matthew K. Kerent. 1993. "Comparisons of Party Identification and Policy Preferences: The Impact of Survey Question Format." *American Journal of Political Science* 37 (Aug.): 941–964.

Krosnick, Jon A., and Donald Kinder. 1990. "Altering the Foundations of Support for the President Through Priming." *American Political Science Review* 84 (June): 497–512.

Kuklinski, James H. 1978. "Representatives and Elections: A Policy Analysis." *American Political Science Review* 72 (Mar.) 165–177.

Kuklinski, James H., Michael D. Cobb, and Martin Gilens. 1997. "Racial Attitudes in the New South." *Journal of Politics* 59 (May): 323–349.

Kuklinski, James H., and Donald J. McCrone. 1981. "Electoral Accountability as a Source of Policy Representation." In *Public Opinion and Public Policy*, ed. Norman R. Luttbeg. Itasca, IL: Peacock.

Kuklinski, James H., Paul J. Quirk, Jennifer Jerit, and Robert Rich. 2001. "The Political Environment of Citizen Competence." *American Journal of Political Science* 41 (Oct.): 410–429.

Kuklinski, James H., Paul J. Quirk, Jennifer Jerit, David Schwieder, and Robert F. Rich. 2000. "Misinformation and the Currency of Democratic Citizenship." *Journal of Politics* 45 (Aug.): 790–816.

Kuklinski, James H., Paul M. Sniderman, Kathleen Knight, Thomas Piazza, Philip E. Tetlock, Gordon R. Lawrence, and Barbara Mellers. 1997. "Racial Prejudice and Attitudes Toward Affirmative Action." *American Journal of Political Science* 41 (Apr.): 402–419.

Kweit, Mary Grisez. 1986. "Ideological Congruence of Party Switchers and Nonswitchers: The Case of Party Activists." *American Journal of Political Science* 30 (Feb.): 184–196.

Ladd, Everett Carl. 1970. *American Political Parties: Social Change and Political Response*. New York: Norton.

———. 1998a. *America's Social Capital: Change and Renewal in Civil Life.* New York: Free Press.

———. 1998b. "States and Regions in the U.S.: How Similar? Where Different?" *Public Perspective* 9 (June/July): 10–31.

———. 1989. *The American Polity.* New York: Norton.

Lane, Robert. 1962. *Political Ideology.* New York: Free Press.

Langer, Gary. 2002. "Trust in Government . . . " *Public Perspective* (July/Aug.): 7–10.

Langton, Kenneth P., and M. Kent Jennings. 1968. "Political Socialization and the High School Civics Curriculum in the United States." *American Political Science Review* 62 (Sept.): 852–877.

Lapinski, Daniel. 2001. "The Effect of Messages Communicated by Members of Congress: The Impact of Publicizing their Votes." *Legislative Studies Quarterly* 26: 81–100.

Larson, Stephanie G. 2001. "Poll Coverage of the 2000 Presidential Campaign on the Network News." Paper delivered at the annual meeting of the American Political Science Association, Sept., San Francisco.

Lasswell, Harold D. 1951. "Democratic Character." In *The Political Writings of Harold D. Lasswell.* Glencoe, IL: Free Press.

Laventhol, David. 2001. "Profit Pressures." *Columbia Journalism Review* (May/June): 19.

Lavrakas, Paul J. 1987. *Telephone Survey Methods.* Beverly Hills, CA: Sage.

———. 1993. *Telephone Survey Methods,* 2nd ed. Beverly Hills, CA: Sage.

Layman, Geoffrey C. 1997. "Religion and Political Behavior in the United States: The Impact of Beliefs, Affiliations, and Commitment from 1980 to 1994." *Public Opinion Quarterly* 61 (Summer): 261–287.

Lazarsfeld, Paul, Bernard Berelson, and Hazel Gaudet. 1948. *The People's Choice.* New York: Columbia University Press.

Lee, Frances E., and Bruce I. Oppenheimer. 1999. *Sizing Up the Senate: The Unequal Consequences of Equal Representation.* Chicago: University of Chicago Press.

Lee, Gahgheong ,and Joseph N. Cappella. 2001. "The Effects of Political Talk Radio on Political Attitude Formation: Exposure Versus Knowledge." *Political Communication* 18: 369–394.

Leege, David C., and Michael R. Welch. 1989. "Religious Roots of Political Orientations: Variations Among Catholic Parishioners." *Journal of Politics* 51 (Feb.): 137–164.

———. 1991. "Dual Reference Groups and Political Orientations: An Examination of Evangelically Oriented Catholics." *American Journal of Political Science* 35 (Feb.): 28–56.

Lewis, I. A. 1990. "Poll Wars and Poll Debacle in Nicaragua." *Public Perspective* 1: 6.

Lewis-Beck, Michael, and Tom Rice. 1982. "Presidential Popularity and the Presidential Vote." *Public Opinion Quarterly* 47 (Winter): 534–537.

Lewis-Beck, Michael, and Charles Tien. 2000. "The Future in Forecasting: Prospective Presidential Models." In *Before the Vote; Forecasting American National Elections,* ed. James E. Campbell and James C. Garand. Thousand Oaks, CA: Sage.

Light, Paul C., and Celinda Lake. 1985. "The Election: Candidates, Strategies, and Decision." In *The Elections of 1984,* ed. Michael Nelson. Washington, DC: Congressional Quarterly.

Lippmann, Walter. 1922. *Public Opinion.* New York: Harcourt.

———. 1925. *The Phantom Public.* New York: Harcourt.

Lipset, Seymour Martin. 1950. *Agrarian Socialism.* Berkeley: University of California Press.

———. 1959. "Some Social Requisites of Modern Democracy: Economic Development and Political Legitimacy." *American Political Science Review* 53 (Mar.): 69–105.

———. 1960. *Political Man.* Garden City, NY: Doubleday.

Lodge, Milton, Kathleen McGraw, and Patrick Stroh. 1989. "An Impression-Driven Model of Candidate Evaluation." *American Political Science Review* 83 (June): 399–419.

Lodge, Milton, Marco R. Steenbergen, and Shawn Brau. 1995. "The Responsive Voter: Candidate Information and the Dynamics of Candidate Evaluation." *American Political Science Review* 89 (June): 309–331.

Lodge, Milton, and Patrick Stroh. 1993. "Inside the Mental Voting Booth: An Impression-Driven Process." In *Explorations in Political Psychology*, ed. Shanto Iyengar and William J. McGuire. Durham, NC: Duke University Press.

Luker, Kristin. 1984. *Abortion and the Politics of Motherhood*. Berkeley: University of California Press.

Lupia, Arthur, and Mathew D. McCubbins. 1998. *The Democratic Dilemma: Can Citizens Learn What They Need to Know?* New York: Cambridge University Press.

Luskin, Robert C. 1987. "Measuring Political Sophistication." *American Journal of Political Science* 31 (Nov.): 856–899.

———. 2003. "The Heavenly Public: What Would a Fully Informed Citizenry Be Like?" In *Electoral Democracy*, ed. George Rabinowitz and Michael B. MacKuen. Ann Arbor: University of Michigan Press.

Luskin, Robert C., John P. McIver, and Edward G. Carmines. 1989. "Issues and the Transmission of Partisanships." *American Journal of Political Science* 33 (May): 440–458.

Luttbeg, Norman R. 1968. "Political Linkage in a Large Society." In *Public Opinion and Public Policy*, ed. Norman Luttbeg. Homewood, IL: Dorsey.

———. 1981. "Balance Theory as a Source of Perception of Where Political Parties Stand on the Issues." In *Public Opinion and Public Policy*, 3rd ed., ed. Norman R. Luttbeg. Itasca, IL: Peacock Press.

———. 1999. *The Grassroots of Democracy: A Comparative Study of Competition and Its Impact in the American Cities in the 1990s*. Lanham, MD: Lexington Books.

Luttbeg, Norman R., and Michael Gant. 1985. "The Failure of Liberal-Conservative Ideology as a Cognitive Structure." *Public Opinion Quarterly* 49 (Spring): 80–93.

Lyons, William, and John M. Scheb. 1992. "Ideology and Candidate Evaluation in the 1984 and 1988 Presidential Elections." *Journal of Politics* 54 (May): 573–586.

MacDougall, Curtis D. 1966. *Understanding Public Opinion*. Boston: Little, Brown.

MacKuen, Michael Bruce. 1981. "Social Communication and the Mass Policy Agenda." In *More Than News: Media Power in Public Affairs*, ed. Michael Bruce MacKuen and Steven Coombs. Beverly Hills, CA: Sage.

———. 1984. "Exposure to Information, Belief Integration, and Individual Responsiveness to Agenda Change." *American Political Science Review* 78 (June): 372–391.

MacKuen, Michael B., Robert S. Erikson, and James A. Stimson. 1989. "Macropartisanship." *American Political Science Review* 83 (Dec.): 1125–1142.

———. 1992. "Peasants or Bankers: The American Electorate and the U.S. Economy." *American Political Science Review* 86 (Sept.): 597–611.

Manin, Bernard, Adam Przeworski, and Susan C. Stokes. 1999. "Elections and Representation." In *Democracy, Accountability, and Representation*, ed. Adam Przeworski, Susan C. Stokes, and Bernard Manin. Cambridge: Cambridge University Press.

Mann, Sheilah. 1996. "Symposium: Political Scientists Examine Civic Standards." *Political Science and Politics* 29 (Mar.): 47–48.

———. 1999. "What the Survey of American College Freshman Tells Us about Their Interest in Politics and Political Science." *Political Science and Politics* 32 (June): 263–68.

Mann, Thomas E., and Norman J. Ornstein, eds. 1994. *Congress, the Press and the Public*. Washington, DC: Brookings.

Manza, Jeff, and Clem Brooks. 1999. *Social Cleavages and Political Change: Voter Alignments and U.S. Party Coalitions*. New York: Oxford University Press.

Mansbridge, Jane. 2003. "Rethinking Representation." *American Political Science Review* 97: 515–528.

Marcus, George E., and Michael B. MacKuen. 2001. "Emotions and Politics: The Dynamic Functions of Emotionality." In *Citizen and Politics: Perspectives from Political Psychology*, ed. James Kuklinski. Cambridge: Cambridge University Press.

Marcus, George E., John L. Sullivan, Elizabeth Theiss-Morse, and Sandra L. Wood. 1995. *With Malice Toward Some*. New York: Cambridge University Press.

Markus, Gregory B. 1979. "The Political Environment and the Dynamics of Public Attitudes." *American Journal of Political Science* 23 (May): 338–59.

———. 1982. "Political Attitudes in an Election Year: A Report on the 1980 NES Panel Study." *American Political Science Review* 76 (Sept.): 538–59.

———. 1988. "The Impact of Personal and National Economic Conditions on the Presidential Vote: A Pooled Cross - Sectional Analysis." *American Journal of Political Science* 32 (Feb.): 137–54.

Markus, Gregory B., and Philip E. Converse. 1979. "A Dynamic Simultaneous Equation Model of Public Choice." *American Political Science Review* 73 (Dec.): 1055–70.

Marmor, Theodore R. 1970. *The Politics of Medicare*. Chicago: Aldine.

Mayer, William G. 1992. *The Changing American Mind*. Ann Arbor: University of Michigan Press.

Mayhew, David R. 1974. *Congress: The Electoral Connection*. New Haven, CT: Yale University Press.

———. 1991. *Divided We Govern: Party Control, Lawmaking, and Investigations, 1946–1990*. New Haven, CT: Yale University Press.

———. 2002. *Electoral Realignments: A Critique of the American Genre*. New Haven, CT: Yale University Press.

McCarty, Keith T. Poole, and Howard Rosenthal. 2001. "The Hunt for Party Discipline in Congress." *American Political Science Review* 95: 673–688.

McChesney, Robert W. 2000. *Rich Media, Poor Democracy: Communications Politics in Dubious Times*. New York: New Press.

McCloskey, Herbert. 1964. "Consensus and Ideology in American Politics." *American Political Science Review* 58 (June).

McCloskey, Herbert, and Alida Brill. 1983. *Dimensions of Political Tolerance*. New York: Russell Sage.

McClosky, Herbert, Paul J. Hoffman, and Rosemary O'Hara. 1960. "Issue Conflict and Consensus Among Party Leaders and Followers." *American Political Science Review* 59 (June): 406–27.

McCombs, Maxwell E., and Donald L. Shaw. 1972. "The Agenda-Setting Function of the Mass Media." *Public Opinion Quarterly* 35 (Summer): 176–87.

McDonald, Michael D., Ian Budge, and Richard I. Hofferbert. 1999. "Party Mandate Theory and Time Series Analysis: A Theoretical and Methodological Response." *Electoral Studies* 18: 587–96.

McFarland, Sam G., Vladimir S. Ageyev, and Marina A. Abalakina. 1992. "Authoritarianism in the Former Soviet Union." *Journal of Personality and Social Psychology* 63 (Dec.): 1003–10.

McLean, Scott. 1999. "Land That I Love: Feelings Toward Country at Century's End." *Public Perspective* 10 (Apr./May): 21–25.

Media Monitor. 2000. "The Media at the Millennium." *Center for Media and Public Affairs* (July/Aug.): 3.

Meloen, J. D., G. van der Linden, and H. de Witte. 1996. "A Test of the Approaches of Adorno et al., Ledere, and Altemeyer of Authoritarianism in Belgian Flanders: A Research Note." *Political Psychology* 17: 643–656.

Mendelberg, Tali. 2001. *The Race Card: Campaign Strategy, Implicit Messages, and the Norm of Equality.* Princeton, NJ: Princeton University Press.

Mendelsohn, Matthew. 1996 "The Media and Interpersonal Communications: The Priming of Issues, Leaders, and Party Identification. *Journal of Politics* 58 (Feb.): 112–125.

Merelman, Richard. 1971. *Political Socialization and Educational Climates.* New York: Holt.

———. 1997. "Symbols and Substance in National Civics Standards." *Political Science and Politics* 29 (Mar.): 53–56.

Merkle, Daniel M., and Murray Edelman. 2000. "A Review of the 1996 Voter News Service Exit Polls from a Total Survey Error Perspective." In *Election Polls, the News Media and Democracy,* ed. Paul J. Lavrakas and Michael W. Traugott. Chatham, NJ: Chatham House.

Miedaian, Myriam. 1991. *Boys Will Be Boys: Breaking the Link Between Masculinity and Violence.* New York: Doubleday.

Milburn, Michael A., S. D. Conrad, and S. Carberry. 1995. "Childhood Punishment, Denial, and Political Attitudes." *Political Psychology* 16: 447–78.

Milgram, Stanley. 1969. *Obedience to Authority.* New York: Harper.

Miller, Arthur H. 1983. "Is Confidence Rebounding?" *Public Opinion* (June/July): 16–21.

———. 1988. "Gender and the Vote: 1984." In *The Politics of the Gender Gap: The Social Construction of Political Influence,* ed. Carol M. Mueller. Beverly Hills, CA: Sage.

Miller, Arthur H., and Stephen A. Borrelli. 1991. "Confidence in Government in the 1980s." *American Politics Quarterly* 19 (Apr.): 147–175.

Miller, Arthur H., Warren E. Miller, Alden S. Raine, and Thad A. Browne. 1976. "A Majority Party in Disarray: Policy Polarization in the 1972 Election." *American Political Science Review* 70 (Sept.): 753–778.

Miller, Arthur H., Eddie Goldenberg, and Lutz Ebring. 1979. "Type-Set Politics: Impact of Newspapers on Public Confidence." *American Political Science Review* 73: 67–84.

Miller, Arthur H., Martin P. Wattenberg, and Oksana Malanchuk. 1986. "Schematic Assessment of Presidential Candidates." *American Political Science Review* 80 (June): 522–540.

Miller, Arthur H., Christopher Wlezien, and Ann Hildreth. 1991. "A Reference Group Theory of Party Coalitions." *Journal of Politics* 53 (Nov.): 1134–1149.

Miller, Joanne M., and Jon A. Krosnick. 2000. "News Media Impact on the Ingredients of Presidential Evaluations: Politically Knowledgeable Citizens Are Guided by a Trusted Source." *American Journal of Political Science* 44 (Apr.): 301–315.

Miller, Warren E., and M. Kent Jennings. 1987. *Parties in Transition: A Longitudinal Study of Party Elites and Party Supporters.* New York: Russell Sage.

Miller, Warren E., and J. Merrill Shanks. 1996. *The New American Voter.* Cambridge, MA: Harvard University Press.

Miller, Warren E., and Donald W. Stokes. 1963. "Constituency Influence in Congress." *American Political Science Review* 57 (Mar.): 45–46.

Mills, C. Wright. 1956. *The Power Elite.* New York: Oxford University Press.

Mishler, William, and Reginald S. Sheehan. 1993. "The Supreme Court as a Countermajoritarian Institution? The Impact of Public Opinion on Supreme Court Decisions." *American Political Science Review* 87 (Mar.): 87–101.

Mitchell, Alison. 1998. "A New Form of Lobbying Puts Public Face on Private Interest." *New York Times,* Sept. 30, A1.

Monroe, Alan D. 1979. "Consistency Between Public Preferences and National Policy Decisions." *American Politics Quarterly* 7 (Jan.): 3–21.

———. 1998. "Public Opinion and Public Policy: 1980–93." *Public Opinion Quarterly* 62: 6–28.

Montaigne, Michel de. 1967. *The Complete Works of Montaigne.* Stanford, CA: Stanford University Press.

Moncrief, Gary. 1999. "Recruitment and Retention in U.S. Legislatures." *Legislative Studies Quarterly* 24: 173–208.

Moore, David W. 1992a. "The Sure Thing That Got Away." *New York Times*, Oct. 25, sec. A.

———. 1992b. *The SuperPollsters*. New York: Four Walls, Eight Windows.

Moore, Stanley W., James Lare, and Kenneth A. Wagner. 1985. *The Child's Political World*. New York: Praeger.

Morin, Richard. 1991. "The Outcome Is There in Black and White." *Washington Post*, weekly ed., Feb. 25–Mar. 3, p. 37.

———. 1992. "Surviving the Ups and Downs of Election '92." *Washington Post*, weekly ed., Nov. 9–15, p. 37.

Morehouse, Sarah McCally. 1998. *The Governor as Party Leader: Campaigning and Governing*. Ann Arbor: University of Michigan Press.

Mueller, John E. 1973. *War, Presidents, and Public Opinion*. New York: Wiley.

———. 1977. "Changes in American Attitudes Toward International Involvement." In *The Limits of Military Intervention*, ed. Ellen Stern. Beverly Hills, CA: Sage.

———. 1994. *Policy, Opinion, and the Gulf War*. Chicago: University of Chicago Press.

Murray, Charles. 1985. *Losing Ground*. New York: Basic.

Mutz, Diana. 1998. *Impersonal Influence: How Perceptions of Mass Collectives Affect Political Attitudes*. New York: Cambridge University Press.

Nadel, Mark V. 1972. "Public Policy and Public Opinion." In *American Democracy: Theory and Reality*, ed. Robert Weissberg and Mark V. Nadel. New York: Wiley.

Nelson, Thomas E., and Zoe M. Oxley. 1999. "Issue Framing Effects on Belief Importance and Opinions." *Journal of Politics* 61 (Nov.): 1040–1067.

Nelson, Thomas E., Rosalee A. Clawson, and Zoe M. Oxley. 1997. "Media Framing of Civil Liberties Conflict and Its Effect on Tolerance." *American Political Science Review* 91 (Sept.): 567–583.

Nesbit, Dorothy Davidson. 1988. "Partisan Changes Among Southern Activists." *Journal of Politics* 50 (May): 322–334.

Nie, Norman, and Kristi Anderson. 1974. "Mass Belief Systems Revisited: Political Change and Attitude Structure." *Journal of Politics* 36 (Aug.): 540–591.

Nie, Norman H., Jane Junn, and Kenneth Stehlik-Barry. 1998. *Education and Democratic Citizenship in America*. Chicago: University of Chicago Press.

Nie, Norman H., Sidney Verba, and John R. Petrocik. 1976. *The Changing American Voter*. Cambridge, MA: Harvard University Press.

Niemi, Richard G., Stephen C. Craig, and Franco Mattei. 1991. "Measuring Internal Political Efficacy in the 1988 National Election Study." *American Political Science Review* 85 (Dec.): 1407–1413.

Niemi, Richard G., and Jane Junn. 1998. *Civic Education: What Makes Students Learn*. New Haven, CT: Yale University Press.

Niemi, Richard G., John Mueller, and Tom W. Smith. 1989. *Trends in Public Opinion*. New York: Greenwood.

Norpoth, Helmut. 1996. "Politics and the Prospective Voter." *Journal of Politics* 58: 76–792.

Norrander, Barbara. 1989. "Ideological Representatives of Presidential Primary Voters." *American Journal of Political Science* 33 (Aug.): 570–87.

Norris, Pippa. 1988. "The Gender Gap: A Cross–National Trend?" In *The Politics of the Gender Gap*, ed. Carol M. Mueller. Beverly Hills, CA: Sage.

Nunn, Clyde Z., Harry J. Crockett, Jr., and J. Allen Williams, Jr. 1978. *Tolerance for Nonconformity*. San Francisco: Jossey-Bass.

Nye, Joseph S. 1997. "The Decline of Confidence in Government." In *Why People Don't Trust Government*, ed. Joseph S. Nye, Philip D. Zelikow, and David C. King. Cambridge, MA: Harvard University Press.

Nye, Joseph S., and Philip D. Zelikow. 1997. "Conclusion: Reflections, Conjectures, and Puzzles." In *Why People Don't Trust Government,* ed. Joseph S. Nye, Philip D. Zelikow, and David C. King. Cambridge, MA: Harvard University Press.

Nye, Joseph S., Philip D. Zelikow, and David King. 1997. *Why People Don't Trust Government.* Cambridge, MA: Harvard University Press.

O'Keefe, Garrett J. 1980. "Political Malaise and Reliance on Media." *Journalism Quarterly* 57: 122–128.

Olson, Mancur, Jr. 1968. *The Logic of Collective Action.* New York: Schocken.

Owen, Diana. 2000. "Popular Politics and the Clinton/Lewinsky Affair: The Implications of Leadership." *Political Psychology* 21: 161–177.

———. 2002. "Media Mayhem: Performance of the Press in Election 2000." In *Overtime*, ed. Larry Sabato. New York: Longman.

Owen, Diana, and Jack Dennis. 1999. "Kids and the Presidency: Assessing Clinton's Legacy." *Public Perspective* 10 (Apr./May): 41–44.

Page, Benjamin I., and Calvin Jones. 1979. "Reciprocal Effects of Policy Preferences, Party Loyalties, and the Vote." *American Political Science Review* 73 (Dec.): 1071–1089.

Page, Benjamin I., and Robert Y. Shapiro. 1983. "Effects of *Public Opinion* on Public Policy." *American Political Science Review* 77 (Mar.): 175–190.

———. 1989. "Foreign Policy and the Rational Public." *Journal of Conflict Resolution* 32 (June): 211–247.

———. 1992. *The Rational Public.* Chicago: University of Chicago Press.

Page, Benjamin I., Robert Y. Shapiro, and Glenn R. Dempsey. 1987. "What Moves Public Opinion?" *American Political Science Review* 81 (Mar.): 23–43.

Palmer, Paul A. 1936. "The Concept of *Public Opinion* in Political Theory." In *Essays in History and Political Thought*, ed. Carl F. Wittke. London: Oxford University Press.

Parker, Glen R. 1992. *Institutional Change, Discretion, and the Making of the Modern Congress.* Ann Arbor: University of Michigan Press.

Patterson, Thomas E. 1989. "The Press and Its Missed Assignment." In *The Election of 1988*, ed. Michael Nelson. Washington, DC: Congressional Quarterly Press.

———. 1994. *Out of Order.* New York: Vintage.

———. 1996. "Bad News, Period." *Political Science and Politics* 29 (Mar.): 17–20.

———. 2002. *The Vanishing Voter.* New York: Alfred A. Knopf.

Patterson, Thomas E., and Wolfgang Donsbach. 1996. "News Decisions: Journalists as Partisan Actors. *Political Communication* 13: 453–468.

Patterson, Thomas E., and Robert D. McClure. 1976. *The Unseeing Eye.* New York: Putnam.

Peterson, B. E., L. E. Duncan, and J. Pang. 2002. "Authoritarianism and Political Impoverishment: Deficits in Knowledge and Civic Disinterest." *Political Psychology* 23: 97–112.

Peterson, B. E., K. A. Smirles, and P. A. Wentworth. 1997. "Generativity and Authoritarianism: Implications for Personality, Political Involvement, and Parenting." *Journal of Personality and Social Psychology* 72: 1202–1216.

Petrocik, John R. 1989. "An Expected Party Vote: New Data for an Old Concept." *American Journal of Political Science* 33 (Feb.): 44–66.

Pettinico, George. 1996. "Civic Participation Alive and Well in Today's Environmental Movement." *Public Perspective* 31 (June/July): 27–30.

Pew Research Center for the People and the Press. 1999. "Too Much Money, Too Much Media, Say Voters." Sept. 15. http://people-press.org/reports/.

———. 2000. "Self-Censorship: How Often and Why: Journalists Avoiding the News." Apr. 30. http://people-press.org/reports/.

Phillips, Kevin. 1991. *The Politics of Rich and Poor.* New York: Harper.
———. 1993. *Boiling Point.* New York: Random.
———. 2002. *Wealth and Democracy.* New York: Broadway Books.
Pierce, Patrick A. 1993. "Political Sophistication and the Use of Candidate Traits in Candidate Evaluation." *Political Psychology* 14 (Mar.): 21–35.
Pomper, Gerald M., with Susan S. Lederman. 1980. *Elections in America: Control and Influence in Democratic Politics,* 2nd ed. New York: Longman.
Poole, Keith T., and Howard Rosenthal. 1997. *Congress: A Political-Economic History of Roll Call Voting.* Oxford: Oxford University Press.
Popkin, Samuel L. 1991. *The Reasoning Voter.* Chicago: University of Chicago Press.
Press, Charles, and Kenneth Verburn. 1988. *American Politicians and Journalists.* Boston: Scott.
Prewitt, Kenneth. 1970. *The Recruitment of Political Leaders: A Study of Citizen Politicians.* New York: Bobbs-Merrill.
Price, H. Douglas. 1971. "The Congressional Career—Then and Now." In *Congressional Behavior,* ed. Nelson W. Polsby. New York: Random.
Price, Vincent. 1992. *Public Opinion.* Newbury Park, CA: Sage.
Putnam, Robert. 1995a. "Bowling Alone: America's Declining Social Capital." *Journal of Democracy* 6: 65–78.
———. 1995b. "Tuning In, Tuning Out: The Strange Disappearance of Social Capital in America." *Political Science and Politics* 28: 664–83.
———. 2000. *Bowling Alone: The Collapse and Revival of American Community.* New York: Simon and Schuster.
Reichley, A. James. 1985. *Religion in American Public Life.* Washington, DC: Brookings.
Remmers, H. H., and Richard D. Franklin. 1963. "Sweet Land of Liberty." In *Anti-Democratic Attitudes in American Schools,* ed. H. H. Remmers. Evanston, IL: Northwestern University Press.
Roberts, Jason M., and Steven S. Smith. 2003. "Procedural Contexts, Party Strategy, and Conditional Party Voting in the U.S. House of Representatives, 1971–2000." *American Journal of Political Science* 47: 305–317.
Robinson, Claude. 1932. *Straw Votes: A Study of Political Predicting.* New York: Columbia University Press.
Robinson, John P., and Mark R. Levy. 1986. *The Main Source: Learning from Television News.* Beverly Hills, CA: Sage.
———. 1996. "News Media and the Informed Public: A 1990s Update." *Journal of Communications* 45: 129–37.
Robinson, Michael J. 1976. "Public Affairs Television and the Growth of Public Malaise: The Case of the 'The Selling of the Pentagon.'" *American Political Science Review* 70: 409–432.
Robinson, Michael, and Andrew Kohut. 1988. "Believability of the Press." *Public Opinion Quarterly* (Summer) 52: 174–189.
Rodgers, Harrell R., and Edward B. Lewis. 1975. "Student Attitudes Toward Mr. Nixon." *American Politics Quarterly* 4 (Oct.): 432–436.
Rogers, Lindsay. 1949. *The Pollsters.* New York: Knopf.
Rokeach, Milton. 1960. *The Open and Closed Mind.* New York: Basic.
Rokkan, Stein, and Angus Campbell. 1960. "Citizen Participation in Political Life: Norway and the United States of America." *International Social Science Journal* 12: 69–99.
Romero, David W. 1989. "The Changing American Voter Revisited: Candidate Evaluations in Presidential Elections, 1952 to 1984." *American Politics Quarterly* 17 (Oct.): 409–421.
Roper, Burns. 1980. "Reading the Signals in Today's Political Polls." *Public Opinion* (Feb./Mar.): 48.
Rose, A. M. 1964. "Alienation and Participation." *American Sociological Review* 27 (Dec.): 151–173.
Rosenberg, Milton J., et al. 1970. *Vietnam and the Silent Majority.* New York: Harper.

Rothenberg, Lawrence C., and Mitchell S. Sanders. 2000. "Severing the Electoral Connection: Shirking in the Contemporary Congress." *American Journal of Political Science* 44: 316–326.

Rotunda, Ronald D. 1986. *The Politics of Language: Liberalism as Word and Symbol.* Iowa City: University of Iowa Press.

Russett, Bruce, and Thomas W. Graham. 1989. "Public Opinion and National Security Policy: Relationships and Impacts." In *Handbook of War Studies,* ed. Manus J. Midlarsky. Boston: Unwin Hyman.

Sabato, Larry. 1993. *Feeding Frenzy: How Attack Journalism Has Transformed American Politics,* 2nd ed. New York: Free Press.

Sabato, Larry J., Mark Stencel, and S. Robert Lichter. 2000. *Peep Show: Media and Politics in an Age of Scandal.* Lanham, MD: Rowan-Littlefield.

Sabine, George. 1952. "The Two Democratic Traditions." *Philosophic Review* 61 (Aug.): 214–222.

Schlesinger, Joseph. 1966. *Ambition and Politics.* Chicago: Rand.

Schneider, William, and I. A. Lewis. 1985. "Views on the News." *Public Opinion* 8 (Aug./Sept.): 6–11, 58–59.

Scholz, John T., and Mark Lubell. 1998. "Trust and Taxpaying: Testing the Heuristic Approach to Collective Action." *American Journal of Political Science* 42 (Apr.): 398–417.

Schreiber, E. M. 1978. "Education and Change in American Opinions on a Woman for President." *Public Opinion Quarterly* 42 (Summer): 171–182.

Schuman, Howard, and Stanley Presser. 1996. *Questions and Answers in Attitude Surveys.* Thousand Oaks, CA: Sage.

Schuman, Howard, Charlotte Steeh, Lawrence Bobo, and Maria Krysan. 1997. *Racial Attitudes in America.* Cambridge, MA: Harvard University Press.

Schwartz, David. 1973. *Political Alienation and Political Behavior.* Chicago: Aldine.

Schwartz, Sandra K. 1975. "Preschoolers and Politics." In *New Directions in Political Socialization,* ed. David C. Schwartz and Sandra K. Schwartz. New York: Free Press.

Sears, David O., Jack Citrin. 1985. *Tax Revolt: Something for Nothing in California.* Cambridge: Harvard University Press.

Sears, David O., and Carolyn L. Funk. 1990. "Self-Interest in Americans' Political Opinions." In *Beyond Self-Interest,* ed. Jane J. Mansbridge. Chicago: University of Chicago Press.

———. 1999. "Evidence of the Long-Term Persistence of Adults' Political Predispositions." *Journal of Politics* 61 (Feb.): 1–28.

Sears, David O., Carl P. Hensler, and Leslie K. Speer. 1979. "Whites' Opposition to Busing: Self-Interest or Symbolic Politics?" *American Political Science Review* 73 (June): 369–384.

Sears, David O., and Donald R. Kinder. 1971. "Racial Tensions and Voting in Los Angeles." In *Los Angeles: Viability and Prospects for Metropolitan Leadership,* ed. W. Z. Hirsch. New York: Praeger.

Sears, David O., and Richard R. Lau. 1983. "Inducing Apparently Self-Interested Political Preferences." *American Journal of Political Science* 27 (May): 223–52.

Sears, David O., and Nicolas A. Valentino. 1997. "Politics Matters: Political Events as Catalysts for Preadult Socialization." *American Political Science Review* 91 (Mar.): 45–64.

Sears, David O., Colette Van Laar, Mary Carrillo, and Rick Kosterman. 1997. "Is It Really Racism?" *Public Opinion Quarterly* 61 (Spring): 16–53.

Sebert, Suzanne K., M. Kent Jennings, and Richard G. Niemi. 1974. "The Political Texture of Peer Groups." In *The Political Character of Adolescence,* ed. M. Kent Jennings and Richard G. Niemi. Princeton, NJ: Princeton University Press.

Shapiro, Robert Y., and Harpreet Mahajan. 1986. "Gender Differences in Policy Preferences: A Summary of Trends from the 1960s to the 1980s." *Public Opinion Quarterly* 50 (Spring): 47–55.

Sharp, Elaine B. 1999. *The Sometimes Connection: Public Opinion and Social Policy.* Albany: State University of New York Press.

Shaw, Greg M. 2003. "Trends: Abortion." *Public Opinion Quarterly* 67 (Fall): 407–429.

Shingles, Richard D. 1981. "Black Consciousness and Political Participation: The Missing Link." *American Political Science Review* 75 (Mar.): 76–91.

Sigel, Roberta S., and Marilyn Brookes. 1974. "Becoming Critical About Politics." In *The Politics of Future Citizens*, ed. Richard G. Niemi. San Francisco: Jossey-Bass.

Sigel, Roberta S., and Marilyn B. Hoskin. 1981. *The Political Involvement of Adolescents.* New Brunswick, NJ: Rutgers University Press.

Sigelman, Lee. 1981. "Question-Order Effects on Presidential Popularity." *Public Opinion Quarterly* 45 (Summer): 199–207.

Sigelman, Lee, and Susan Welch. 1991. *Black Americans' View of Racial Inequality: The Dream Deferred.* Cambridge: Cambridge University Press.

Silbiger, Sara S. 1977. "Peers and Political Socialization." *Youth and Society* 5 (Mar.): 169–178.

Simon, Rita J., and Jean M. Landis. 1989. "The Polls: Women's and Men's Attitudes About a Woman's Place and Role." *Public Opinion Quarterly* 53 (Summer): 271–276.

Sinclair, Barbara. 1997. *Unorthodox Lawmaking: New Legislative Processes in the U.S. Congress.* Washington, DC: Congressional Quarterly Press.

Sears, David O., and Nicolas A. Valentino. 1997. "Politics Matters: Political Events as Catalysts for Preadult Socialization." *American Political Science Review* 91 (Mar.): 45–64.

———. 2002. "Do Parties Matter?" In *Party, Process, and Political Change in Congress*, ed. David W. Brady and Matthew D. McCubbins. Stanford, CA: Stanford University Press.

Smith, Eric R.A.N., and Peverill Squire. 1990. "The Effects of Prestige Names in Question Wording." *Public Opinion Quarterly* 54 (Spring): 97–116.

Smith, M. B., J. S. Bruner, and R. W. White. 1956. *Opinions and Personality.* New York: Wiley.

Smith, Tom W. 1984. "Nonattitudes: A Review and Evaluation." In *Surveying Subjective Phenomena*, vol. 2, ed. Charles F. Turner and Elizabeth Martin. New York: Russell Sage.

———. 1985. "The Polls: America's Most Important Problem." *Public Opinion Quarterly* 54 (Winter): 479–507.

———. 1987. "That Which We Call Welfare by Any Other Name Would Smell Sweeter: An Analysis of the Impact of Question Wording on Response Patterns." *Public Opinion Quarterly* 51 (Spring): 75–83.

———.1990. "The First Straw? A Study of the Origins of Election Polls." *Public Opinion Quarterly* 54 (Spring): 21–36.

———. 1992. "Changing Racial Labels." *Public Opinion Quarterly* 56 (Winter): 496–514.

Smith, Tom W., and Paul Sheatsley. 1984. "American Attitudes Toward Race Relations." *Public Opinion* (Oct./Nov.): 14–15.

Sniderman, Paul M. 1975. *Personality and Democratic Politics.* Berkeley: University of California Press.

Sniderman, Paul M., and Edward G. Carmines. 1997. *Reaching Beyond Race.* Cambridge, MA: Harvard University Press.

Sniderman, Paul M., Joseph F. Fletcher, Peter H. Russell, and Philip E. Tetlock. 1996. *The Clash of Rights.* New Haven, CT: Yale University Press.

Sniderman, Paul M., and Thomas Piazza. 1993. *The Scar of Race.* Cambridge, MA: Harvard University Press.

Sniderman, Paul M., Philip E. Tetlock, James N. Glaser, Donald Philip Green, and Michael Hout. 1989. "Principled Tolerance and the American Mass Public." *British Journal of Political Science* 19 (Feb.): 25–45.

Snyder, James M. Jr. 1992. "Long-Term Investments in Politicians, or Give Early, Give Often." *Journal of Law and Economics* 35 (Apr.): 15–44.

———. 1996. "Constituency Preferences: California Ballot Propositions, 1974–1990." *Legislative Studies Quarterly* 21: 463–488.

Snyder, James M. Jr., and Tim Groseclose. 2000. "Estimating Party Influence in Congressional Roll Call Voting." *American Journal of Political Science* 44: 193–211.

Sobel, Richard. 1989. "The Polls—A Report: Public Opinion About United States Intervention in El Salvador and Nicaragua." *Public Opinion Quarterly* 53 (Spring): 114–128.

Somit, Albert, and S. A. Peterson. 1997. *Darwinism, Dominance and Democracy. The Biological Bases of Authoritarianism.* Westport, CT: Praeger.

Sorauf, Frank J. 1988. *Money in American Elections.* Boston: Scott.

Soss, Joe, Laura Langein, and Alan R. Metelko. 2003. "Why Do Americans Support the Death Penalty." *Journal of Politics* (May): 397–421.

Spitz, Elaine. 1984. *Majority Rule.* Chatham, NJ: Chatham House.

Squire, Peverill. 1988. "Why the 1937 *Literary Digest* Poll Failed." *Public Opinion Quarterly* 52 (Spring): 123–133.

———. 1992. "Changing State Legislative Careers." In *Changing Patterns in State Legislative Careers,* ed. Gary F. Moncrief and Joel A. Thompson. Ann Arbor: University of Michigan Press.

Stanley, Harold, and Richard Niemi. 2003. *Vital Statistics on American Politics 2003–2004.* Washington, DC: Congressional Quarterly Press.

Steeh, Charlotte, and Maria Krysan. 1996. "Trends: Affirmative Action and the Public, 1970–995." *Public Opinion Quarterly* 60 (Spring): 128–158.

Steeh, Charlotte, Nicole Kirgis, Brian Cannon, and Jeff DeWitt. 2001. "Are They Really As Bad As They Seem: Nonresponse Rates at the End of the Twentieth Century." *Journal of Official Statistics* 17: 227–247.

Stembler, Charles H. 1961. *Education and Attitude Change: The Effect of Schooling on Prejudice Against Minority Groups.* New York: Institute of Human Relations.

Stephens, William N., and C. Stephen Long. 1970. "Education and Political Behavior." In *Political Science Annual: An International Review,* vol. 2, ed. James A. Robinson. Indianapolis: Bobbs-Merrill.

Stimson, James A. 1975. "Belief Systems: Constraint, Complexity, and the 1972 Election." *American Journal of Political Science* 19 (Aug.): 393–417.

———. 1999. *Public Opinion in America: Moods, Cycles, and Swings,* 2nd. ed. Boulder, CO: Westview.

Stoker, Laura. 2001. "Citizen Value Judgments." In *Citizens and Politics,* ed. James H. Kuklinksi. New York: Cambridge University Press.

Stokes, Donald E. 1966. "Some Dynamic Elements of Contests for the Presidency." *American Political Science Review* 60 (Mar.): 19–28.

Stokes, Donald E., and Warren E. Miller. 1962. "Party Government and the Saliency of Congress." *Public Opinion Quarterly* 26 (Winter): 531–546.

Stonecash, Jeffrey M. 2000. *Class and Party in American Politics.* Boulder, CO: Westview.

Stonecash, Jeffrey M., Mark D. Brewer, and Mack D. Mariani. 2002. *Divergent Parties, Social Change, Realignment, and Party Polarization.* Boulder, CO: Westview Press.

Stouffer, Samuel A. 1949. *The American Soldier.* Princeton, NJ: Princeton University Press.

———. 1955. *Communism, Conformity, and Civil Liberties.* New York: Doubleday.

Stratmann, Thomas. 2000. "Congressional Voting over Congressional Careers: Shifting Careers and Changing Constraints." *American Political Science Review* 94: 665–676.

Sullivan, John L., and Robert E. O'Connor. 1972. "Electoral Choice and Popular Control of Public Policy: The Case of the 1966 House Elections." *American Political Science Review* 66 (Dec.): 1256–68.

Sullivan, John L., James E. Piereson, and George E. Marcus. 1978. "Ideological Constraint in the Mass Public: A Methodological Critique and Some New Findings." *American Journal of Political Science* 22 (May): 233–249.

———. 1982. *Political Tolerance and American Democracy.* Chicago: University of Chicago Press.

Sundquist, James L. 1973. *Dynamics of the Party System.* Washington, DC: Brookings.

Tarrow, Sidney. 1996. "Making Social Science Work Across Space and Time: A Critical Reflection on Robert Putnam's *Making Democracy Work.*" *American Political Science Review* 90 (June): 389–397.

Tedin, Kent L. 1974. "The Influence of Parents on the Political Attitudes of Adolescents." *American Political Science Review* 68 (Dec.): 1579–1592.

———. 1980. "Measuring Parent and Peer Influence on Adolescent Political Attitudes." *American Journal of Political Science* 24 (Feb.): 136–154.

———. 1987. "Political Ideology and the Vote." In *Research in Micro-Politics,* vol. 2, ed. Samuel Long. Greenwich, CT: JAI.

———. 1994a. "Mass Support for Competitive Elections in the Soviet Union." *Comparative Politics* 27 (Apr.): 241–71.

———. 1994b. "Self Interest, Symbolic Values, and the Financial Equalization of the Public Schools." *Journal of Politics* 56: (Aug.): 628–49.

Tedin, Kent L., Richard E. Matland and Gregory R. Weiher. 2001. "The Politics of Age and Race: Support and Opposition to a School Bond Referendum." *Journal of Politics* 63 (Feb.): 270–294.

Tedin, Kent L., and Oi–Kuan Fiona Yap. 1993. "The Gender Factor in Soviet Mass Politics: Survey Evidence from Greater Moscow." *Political Research Quarterly* 46 (Mar.): 179–211.

Tedin, Kent L., et al. 1977. "Social Background and Political Differences Between Pro- and Anti-ERA Activists." *American Politics Quarterly* 5 (July): 395–408.

Terman, Lewis M., and Melinda H. Oden. 1959. *Genetic Studies of Genius V: The Gifted Group at Midlife.* Stanford, CA: Stanford University Press.

Thomas, Martin. 1985. "Electoral Proximity and Senatorial Roll Call Voting." *American Journal of Political Science* 29 (Feb.): 96–111.

Thompson, Joel A., and Gary F. Moncrief. 1992. "Nativity, Mobility, and State Legislators." In *Changing Patterns in State Legislative Careers,* ed. Gary F. Moncrief and Joel A. Thompson. Ann Arbor: University of Michigan Press.

Tierney, John. 1992. "Journalists Reneging on Election Promises." *New York Times,* Jan. 31, sec. A.

Tocqueville, Alexis de. 1966. *Democracy in America,* eds. J. P. Mayer and Max Lerner. New York: Harper.

Torres, Aida, and Jacqueline Forrest. 1988. "Why Do Women Have Abortions?" *Family Planning Perspectives* 20: 169–76.

Traugott, Michael W. 1992. "The Impact of Media Polls on the Public." In *Media Polls in American Politics,* ed. Thomas E. Mann and Gary R. Orren. Washington, DC: Brookings.

Traugott, Michael W., and Mee-Eun Kang. 2000a. "Public Attention to Polls in an Election Year." In *Election Polls, the News Media, and Democracy,* ed. Paul J. Lavrakas and Michael W. Traugott. Chatham, NJ: Chatham House.

———. 2000b. "Push Polls as Negative Persuasive Strategies." In *Election Polls, the News Media, and Democracy,* ed. Paul J. Lavrakas and Michael W. Traugott. Chatham, NJ: Chatham House.

Tufte, Edward R. 1978. *Political Control of the Economy.* Princeton, NJ: Princeton University Press.

Turner, Charles, and Elizabeth Martin. 1984. *Surveying Subjective Phenomena*. New York: Russell Sage.

Uhlaner, Carole Jean, and F. Chris Garcia. 2002. "Latino Public Opinion." In *Understanding Public Opinion*, 2nd ed., ed. Barbara Norrander and Clyde Wilcox. Washington, DC: Congressional Quarterly Press.

Uslaner, Eric M. 2002. *The Moral Foundations of Trust*. New York: Cambridge University Press.

Uslaner, Eric M., and Ronald E. Weber. 1983. "Policy Congruence and American State Elites: Descriptive Representation Versus Electoral Accountability." *Journal of Politics* 45 (Feb.): 183–196.

Vallone, Robert, Less Ross, and Mark Lepper. 1985. "The Hostile Media Phenomenon: Bias Perception and Perceptions of Media Bias in Coverage of the Beirut Massacre." *Journal of Personality and Social Psychology* 49 (Sept.): 577–588.

Verba, Sidney, and Norman H. Nie. 1972. *Participation in America*. New York: Harper.

Verba, Sidney, Kay Lehman Schlozman, and Henry E. Brady. 1995. *Voice and Equality: Civic Voluntarism in American Democracy*. Cambridge, MA: Harvard University Press.

Wahlke, John C., et al. 1962. *The Legislative System*. New York: Wiley.

Wald, Kenneth D. 1997. *Religion and Politics in the United States*, 3rd ed. Washington, DC: Congressional Quarterly Press.

Wald, Kenneth D., Dennis E. Owen, and Samuel S. Hill. 1989. "Churches as Political Communities." *American Political Science Review* 82 (June): 532–548.

Wallis, Allen, and Harry Roberts. 1956. *Statistics*. Glencoe, IL: Free Press.

Warren, Mark. 1999. "Democratic Theory and Trust." In *Democracy and Trust*, ed. Mark Warren. London: Cambridge University Press.

Wattenberg, Martin P. 1998. *The Decline of American Political Parties*. Cambridge, MA: Harvard University Press.

———. 2002. *Where Have All the Voters Gone?* Cambridge, MA: Harvard University Press.

Wawro, Gregory. 2001. "A Panel Probit Analysis of Campaign Contributions and Roll Call Votes." *American Journal of Political Science* 45: 563–579.

Weatherford, Stephen. 1987. "How Does Government Performance Influence Political Support?" *Political Behavior* 9 (1): 5–27.

Weaver, David H., and G. Cleveland Wilhoit. 1996. *The American Journalist in the 1990s*. Mahwah, NJ: Erlbaum.

Weiner, Terry S. 1978. Homogeneity of Political Party Preference Between Spouses." *Journal of Politics* 40 (Feb.): 208–211.

Weisberg, Herbert. 1987. "The Demographics of New Voting Gap: Marital Differences in American Voting." *Public Opinion Quarterly* 51 (Fall): 335–343.

Weissberg, Robert. 1974. *Political Learning, Political Choice, and Democratic Citizenship*. Englewood Cliffs, NJ: Prentice Hall.

———. 1998. *Political Tolerance: Balancing Community and Diversity*. Thousand Oaks, CA: Sage.

West, Darrell M. 2001. *The Rise and Fall of the Media Establishment*. Bedford, MA: St. Martins Press.

Westholm, Anders. 1999. "The Perceptual Pathway: Tracing the Mechanisms of Political Value Transfer Across Generations." *Political Psychology* 20: 525–552.

Wetstein, Matthew E. 1993. "A LISREL Model of Public Opinion on Abortion." In *Understanding the New Politics of Abortion*, ed. Malcolm Goggin. Newbury Park, CA: Sage.

Williams, Christine B., and Daniel Richard Minns. 1986. "Agent Credibility and Receptivity Influences in Children's Political Learning." *Political Behavior* 8 (2): 175–200.

Williams, J. Allen, Jr., Clyde Z. Nunn, and Louis St. Peter. 1976. "Origins of Tolerance: Findings from a Replication of Stouffer's Communism, Conformity, and Civil Liberties." *Social Forces* 44 (Dec.): 394–408.

Wilson, Thomas C. 1985. "Urbanism and Tolerance: A Test of Some Hypotheses Drawn from Wirth and Stouffer." *American Sociological Review* 50: 117–123.

Wittkopf, Eugene R. 1990. *Faces of Internationalism: American Public Opinion and Foreign Policy.* Durham, NC: Duke University Press.

Wlezien, Christopher. 1995a. "Dynamic Representation: The Case of US Spending on Defense." *British Journal of Political Science* 26: 81–103.

———. 1995b. "The Public as Thermostat: The Dynamics of Public Preferences for Spending." *American Journal of Political Science* 39: 981–1000.

Wlezien, Christopher, and Robert S. Erikson. 2000. "Temporal Horizons and Presidential Election Forecasts." In *Before the Vote: Forecasting American National Elections*, ed. James E. Campbell and James C. Garand. Thousand Oaks, CA: Sage.

———. 2002. "The Time Line of Presidential Campaigns." *Journal of Politics* 64: 969–993.

Wood, B. Dan, and Angela Hinton Anderson. 1998. "The Dynamics of Senatorial Representation, 1952–1991." *Journal of Politics* 60: 705–736.

Wright, Gerald C., Jr. 1989. "Level-of-Analysis Effects on Explanations of Voting: The Case of U.S. Senate Elections." *British Journal of Political Science* 18 (July): 381–398.

Wright, Gerald C., Jr., and Michael Berkman. 1986. "Candidates and Policies in United States Senate Elections." *American Political Science Review* 80 (June): 567–588.

Wright, Gerald C., and Brian F. Schaffner. 2002. "The Influence of Party: Evidence from the State Legislatures." *American Political Science Review* 96: 367–380.

Wright, James D. 1976. *The Dissent of the Governed.* New York: Academic.

Wyer, Robert S., Jr., and Victor C. Ottati. 1993. "Political Information Processing." In *Explorations in Political Psychology*, ed. Shanto Iyengar and William J. McGuire. Durham, NC: Duke University Press.

Yang, Soon Joon, and Richard D. Alba. 1992. "Urbanism and Nontraditional Opinion: A Test of Fischer's Subcultural Theory." *Social Science Quarterly* 73 (Sept.): 596–609.

Zaller, John. 1992. *The Nature and Origins of Mass Opinion.* Cambridge: Cambridge University Press.

———. 1994. "Elite Leadership of Mass Opinion: New Evidence from the Gulf War." In *Taken by Storm: The Media, Public Opinion, and U.S. Foreign Policy in the Gulf War*, ed. W. Lance Bennett and David L. Paletz. Chicago: University of Chicago Press.

———. 1996. "The Myth of Massive Media Impact Revived: New Support for a Discredited Idea." In *Political Persuasion and Attitude Change*, ed. Diane C. Mutz, Paul M. Sniderman, and Richard A. Brody. Ann Arbor: University of Michigan Press.

———. 1997. "A Model of Communication Effects at the Outbreak of the Gulf War." In *Do the Media Govern? Politicians, Voters, and Reporters in America*, ed. Shanto Iyengar and Richard Reeves. Thousand Oaks, CA: Sage.

———. 1998. "Monica Lewinsky's Contribution to Political Science." *Political Science and Politics* 31: 182–189.

———. 2004. *A Theory of Media Politics.* Chicago: University of Chicago Press.

Zaller, John, and Stanley Feldman. 1992. "A Simple Theory of the Survey Response: Answering Questions and Revealing Preferences." *American Journal of Political Science* 36: 579–616.

Index